MW00445118

THE INSTITUTIONAL ETF TOOLBOX

The Bloomberg Financial Series provides both core reference knowledge and actionable information for financial professionals. The books are written by experts familiar with the work flows, challenges, and demands of investment professionals who trade the markets, manage money, and analyze investments in their capacity of growing and protecting wealth, hedging risk, and generating revenue.

Since 1996, Bloomberg Press has published books for financial professionals on investing, economics, and policy affecting investors. Titles are written by leading practitioners and authorities, and have been translated into more than 20 languages.

For a list of available titles, please visit our Web site at www.wiley.com/go/bloombergpress.

THE INSTITUTIONAL ETF TOOLBOX

How Institutions Can Understand and Utilize the Fast-Growing World of ETFs

Eric Balchunas

Cover image: 3d blue stock chart © Maxphotograph/iStockphoto;
Red toolbox © John Solie/iStockphoto; Digital font © lekkyjustdoit/iStockphoto;
Dark gray abstract background © Kritchanut/iStockphoto
Cover design: Wiley

Published by John Wiley & Sons, Inc., Hoboken, New Jersey.
Published simultaneously in Canada.

Library of Congress Cataloging-in-Publication Data:

ISBN 9781119093862 (Hardcover)
ISBN 9781119094104 (ePDF)
ISBN 9781119094241 (ePub)

Printed in the United States of America

10 9 8 7 6 5 4 3 2 1

For Trang, Gabriel, Elliott, and Mom and Dad.

Contents

Acknowledgments

I realize I'm not winning an Oscar here, but I feel some people need a shout-out. This book wouldn't have been written without both direct and indirect help from the following people.

In terms of direct help, I owe a huge thanks to Suzanne Woolley, my amazing editor at Bloomberg. She not only taught me a lot about writing, but also connected me to Stephen Isaacs of Bloomberg Press. If not for Suzanne's stamp of approval—and Stephen's guidance—this book would not exist. Second, I would like to thank Matt Kelly and Doug Kenney in Bloomberg Global Data. They have been supportive of me for years now—not only in this book project but also encouraging me to take opportunities necessary to turn my job into a career.

In terms of the book itself, Sara Prager and Ryan Kreger deserve the biggest thanks. They were the only two people (poor souls) who read the entire first draft, which was double the length it is now. This was crucial in figuring out what to chop out and what to expand on

I also got great feedback on sections of the book from my Bloomberg colleagues James Seyffart and Michael Baradas. I also have to thank our wonderful interns Madeleine Hart and Kayla Glenn, who did some serious data crunches for the book and elevated the formatting for the tables and figures.

Many people from the ETF industry helped me immensely. There are too many to list, but special thanks should go to Wes Gray, Daniel Gamba, Brendan Ahern, Kathryn Bernhardt, Mike Eschmann, Paris Smith, Stephen Bloom, Howard Kramer, and Robbie Ross. I interviewed over 60 people for this book and all of them were very helpful as well. While you may see two to three quotes from each person, they were drawn from an hour-plus interview. And what I didn't quote was highly useful background material that seeped into the overall content in some shape or form. So, big thanks to all of them.

I also have to give a special thanks to David Abner, who is a friend and a mentor within the industry. Dave has written two books on ETFs, which I've read multiple times. While this book is largely a different topic, his work and his attitude has influenced me and inspired me in subtle ways.

This book also would not exist if not for some folks in Bloomberg's media operation, namely, Catherine Cowdery of Bloomberg Radio, as well as the folks over at Bloomberg TV—namely, Ted Fine and Jonah Davis who first let me on the air to talk ETFs. Every Friday for five years now I've traveled up to New York City to do a weekly segment on ETFs for radio and TV. This consistent deadline was a huge motivating force for me; it sent me into every nook and cranny of the ETF world. All told, I've done over 500 segments, and all of the notes from those deep dives provided a solid resource for me in writing this book—especially in the "toolbox" half of the book.

Like any writer, I have influences. My biggest influences come from my favorite ETF trade publications, starting with Dave Nadig and Matt Hougan of ETF.com. When I was first developing myself as an analyst, their articles and podcasts were a major source of knowledge and inspiration. If ETF analysis has a cutting edge, it's those guys. I've also found enlightenment from fellow ETF analysts such as Todd Shriber, Victor Reklaitis, Chris Dieterich, Brendan Conway, Michael Rawson, Tom Lydon and Deborah Fuhr.

Every book I read, the author inevitably apologizes to his family for being so pre-occupied with writing their book. Now I know what they mean. It really does demand a lot of precious time. So to my wife and kids, thank you so much for all your support and patience during this book writing process. Daddy is as happy to be done writing it as you are!

Introduction: Institutions and ETFs

It is widely known that exchange-traded funds (ETFs) have democratized investing by giving the little guy (retail) the same access as the big guy (institutions). While that is very true, the less told story is that many institutions have also turned to ETFs for a wide variety of purposes. While retail investors and the advisors serving them largely see ETFs as a cheaper, more tax-efficient version of a mutual fund, many institutions see them as a versatile, liquid tool to help them deliver exposures within their portfolios.

This book explores how those institutions use ETFs as well as how they—or any investor—can use them better.

Institutions such as pension plans, foundations, endowments, hedge funds, insurance companies, asset managers, and foreign institutions are slowly increasing their usage of ETFs. "Slowly" is the key word here, though, because getting an institution to change its habits is a bit like turning around a battleship, as one endowment manager told me.

> *"My history with institutions is they are naturally skeptical and they are going to be slow to move. And they will probably leg in. Not too much different than what financial advisors did ten years ago."*
>
> James Ross, State Street Global Advisors

While ETFs tend to compete in terms of benefits when stacked up against the mutual funds used by retail investors and advisors, it is a different story for folks running pensions or endowments. ETFs are in competition with some of the cheapest and most efficient investment vehicles Wall Street has to offer, such as separately managed accounts, total return swaps, and futures contracts.

When an institution puts money to work, it isn't $200,000 or even $2 million; it can be $200 million or $2 billion. When you are putting that kind of money to work, the world opens up to you and gives you many more options at insanely cheap prices. In short, institutions get the royal treatment from asset managers and Wall Street banks via a broader array of investment vehicles.

"The goal of any investment vehicle or product is to get you to some type of investment strategy or purpose. Whether or not you have access to a conventional index fund, an institutional separate account, a futures contract or you have a swap desk you can trade with. At the end of the day, you care about what's my trade-off between the best possible tracking instrument at a cost that you find reasonable. The ETF is a new item in that discussion, but all of those things are on the table."

Jim Rowley, Vanguard

So while ETFs have earned a seat at the institutional product table, they are still the new kid on the block and are mostly used in small portions, for very specific needs. At this level, they are typically though not explicitly used more as tools to adjust the portfolio exposures or manage cash or stay liquid. We will explore all of these usages in full.

Many surveys have touted these usages and hyped up how institutions are adopting ETFs right and left. While usage is increasing, the actual percentage of institutions' assets that hold ETFs is still pretty minuscule, as seen in Table I.1. Using a collection of sources; I estimate generally that institutions are using ETFs for 1 percent of their assets on average. Of course, when you are talking about a combined $75 trillion or so in assets, that's nearly a trillion dollars and close to half of total ETF assets (advisors and retail make up the rest). And if that number inches up to even just 4 or 5 percent—which is not that that hard to imagine—that's trillions of new assets into ETFs.

TABLE I.1 Institutional Ownership (Estimated and Generalized) of ETFs

Institutions	Total Assets (billions)	ETF Assets (billions)	% of Their Assets in ETFs
Pensions	5,500	30	0.55%
Insurance companies (Gen Accts)	5,000	15	0.30%
Endowments	516	5	0.78%

Institutions	Total Assets (billions)	ETF Assets (billions)	% of Their Assets in ETFs
Asset managers	41,000	400	0.95%
Hedge funds	3,000	34	1.13%
Foreign institutions	20,000	200	1.00%

Sources: Pensions & Investments, NAIC, Bloomberg, Towers Watson, HFR, Sovereign Wealth Funds, Blackrock, Deutsche Bank

Historically speaking, institutions have used ETFs only in a limited fashion. Perhaps they bought some of the SPDR S&P 500 Trust (SPY) with some new cash to keep market exposure until they give it to an active manager. Many of them look at ETFs more as a retail product, in the same boat as an index mutual fund. How could some generic emerging markets ETF be better than the hot active manager they just hired who was picked after months of scrutiny by a consultant?

What's interesting about that is ETFs were originally designed specifically for big institutions in the early 1990s. And until around 2000, those were the *only* investors that used them. In fact, the first two major issuers—State Street and Barclays—were big institutional managers, and the ETF in some ways was a natural extension of what they were already doing. All that changed when Barclays launched iShares and saw the value of ETFs for retail investors and advisors.

"I think there has been a transition. Initially, it was institutional, and then the advisor market grabbed it. Then about five to six years ago the institutions really began to awaken to ETFs. We've come full circle."

Anthony Rochte, Fidelity Investments

Institutions have a lot at stake and a lot of pressure to deliver performance. This is why, as an outsider like myself, it was baffling to see how dedicated they still are to spending so much money on consultants, active managers, hedge funds, and so on.

It begs the question: why do institutions think they can outperform given the shaky track record and high costs of active management and hedge funds and private equity? Why not just make it easy and keep costs low and stay liquid by using an all-ETF portfolio like some asset managers and advisors now do? Have they ever used ETFs? Which ones and for what purpose? How do they choose them? When does an ETF not make sense? Do ETFs pose a threat to their very existence? These are some of the questions I asked many institutions directly as well as people in the ETF industry. I will share what I learned in the book.

Besides cost and a love of active management, another big reason institutions don't use ETFs is lack of understanding. In fact, in almost every institutional study and survey I reviewed, initial concerns around ETFs melted away as they learned more about the structure and got some hands-on experience with them.

But what is interesting is most institutions and their consultants apply such rigorous due diligence when picking an active manager, yet barely any when picking an ETF. That's a big mistake as the difference in returns between similar sounding ETFs can be just as wide as or wider than that of active managers

This brings me to the point of the book: to help an institution—or any investor—understand, utilize, and perform due diligence on the vast array of ETFs available to them. I will show examples of how other institutions were able to do this as well. We will also look at new perspectives on liquidity and trading that will unlock the full ETF toolbox.

One thing you will notice with institutional investors and their ETF usage is those who do use ETFs may be using inferior products and probably don't realize it. Sometimes the first ETF to come out in a category becomes the most liquid and everyone uses it, even though many new ones have come out that offer better exposures with fewer total costs. This is the ETF equivalent of using an iPhone 1. This book will help you feel comfortable going deeper into the toolbox in order to find the best ETF for you.

This toolbox is growing faster than anyone can keep up with. ETFs have evolved so much in only the last couple years. There are now over 1,800 ETFs for virtually every category of equities, fixed income, international, and alternatives with more flavors than Baskin-Robbins. Today, you can build a solid global allocation with using only ETFs for less than 0.10 percent. This was not possible 10 years ago as 98 percent of the ETFs were developed for market equity.

This product influx and innovation is why the ETF industry is like the tech sector of the financial world. There is definitely a Silicon Valley, gold rush vibe. But the pace of innovation and new products has outrun the education by a mile. And it has created more noise. This is why ETF due diligence is going to be very important going forward. This is why we work to make the best functions on Bloomberg. This is why we do ETF events all over the country. This is why I'm writing this book.

The tricky thing with ETFs is that they wrap up everything under the sun, including futures contracts, options, and swap agreements on top of stocks, bonds, or commodities. This is also one of the reasons it is so intellectually satisfying to be an ETF analyst. They take you to every nook and cranny of the financial markets and the world. You have to be a mile deep and a mile wide.

Now, as useful as ETFs can be, there can be some nasty surprises underneath some of them. Some ETFs hold pretty illiquid stuff, not to mention derivatives. Also, some ETFs are much more volatile than they look. Some ETFs have hidden fees or unusual tax treatment. I will share how to spot those things and how a "nasty surprise" rating system for ETFs may be useful.

This book is about tools, not theory. I'm not going to teach you about portfolio management techniques or how to do asset allocation or what will go up or down or what model works best. I'm not that guy. There are literally hundreds of books on investing written by more appropriate people than I.

I am an ETF analyst, or guru, or geek—whatever you want to call it. I have spent the past decade managing ETF data and developing new ETF functions on the Bloomberg terminal, as well as writing articles for Bloomberg.com and Bloomberg Intelligence. This is in addition to my weekly segments on Bloomberg Radio and TV. While I don't manage money or work at an ETF issuer, I've been eating, sleeping, and breathing ETFs for nearly a decade now. As such, I can offer an objective view and unique analysis.

I'm also not a fan of textbooks. I like reading books with a more conversational and informal tone. So that's how I wrote this book. Financial analysis and humanity are not mutually exclusive! So while this book is chock-full of substance for institutional investors to learn from, it is written in a language that both novice and expert investors can understand. At least that's my hope.

A few things before we start. First, there are simply too many ETFs to cover all of them in this book. That's probably a good thing, or else this would read like an encyclopedia instead of a book. I purposely tried to hone in on stories and case studies to make larger points that can be applied to other areas of the ETF landscape. I also did my best to highlight both the popular ones and the up-and-coming innovative ETFs. With that said, the ETFs covered in this book represent over 80 percent of the assets and trends.

I also use a lot of numbers in this book, such as assets, returns, fees, and trading figures. By the time you read this, some of those will have changed. It's like trying to hit a moving target. However, they won't change that much and the figures are key in showing relativity and providing case studies.

Now, because I'm not a money manager or an ETF issuer, I wanted to bring in outside voices to accompany my data analysis. This is why I conducted more than 50 interviews for this book with institutional fund managers, ETF issuers, ETF strategists, market makers, advisors, and others. Their quotes are peppered throughout the book to give it a documentary feel with me as the narrator. Also, every single quote in the book, unless otherwise stated, is from an interview I did specifically for the book. In other words, all the material is fresh and original and it has not been used anywhere else.

I also purposely didn't include their titles with their quotes in the name of brevity and informality. Suffice it to say though, I only interviewed people that I felt would help readers understand the topic better. You will see from the quality of their quotes that they know what they are talking about.

I spent a lot of time researching institution types, which was a bit like visiting different planets. You could spend years learning about them. For example, you could write an entire book on what is going on with state pensions right now, or how smaller endowments are faring with their alternative-heavy strategies. When you start asking questions and doing research, you end up seeing some loose threads here and there—more questions that pop up out of your original questions. I pulled some of these threads, but given that this is a book on ETFs, I left many of those threads alone in the name of brevity. However, a few of those threads could make for an interesting follow-up book!

And if researching each type of institution is like visiting a planet, getting information on what they invest in, and why, well, that's like solving a murder mystery. You have a tiny bit of data available from public filings, but it is largely sketchy and opaque. Let's just say researching this book taught me a lot about how little documents like 13F forms really tell you.

"Part of the challenge of all the reporting out there is it is incomplete. We all think if we look at what someone reports, we know what they are doing. But you really have no idea what they are doing."

Mark Yusko, Morgan Creek Capital Management

While surveys of institutional investors' usage are pretty good measures of how those institutions use ETFs, they are not really good measures of how *much* institutions are using ETFs or use specific examples or anecdotes. In addition, most of the surveys are sponsored by an issuer, so they tend to just focus on how ETF usage is increasing amongst certain institutions, but the fact is, wider adoption is still in the very early innings as noted in the asset figures above.

As a result, it took a lot of detective work, which involved researching a wide variety of sources, but mostly talking to people. One group of investors whose interviews I thought were especially useful was ETF strategists, which are asset managers who run all-ETF portfolios. I use them so much in the book is because they are master ETF users and their knowledge of the toolbox is unparalleled. I thought some of their insight and hard-won experience using ETFs would be beneficial to all investors.

The book includes all of this in an arrangement that I thought was natural to the topic. Just like an old-school vinyl album has two sides, with several songs on each side, this book will be laid out in a similar fashion, with two distinct sections and several chapters within each section.

The first section will be a dive into the "ETF phenomenon." We will look at the advantages that make ETFs so popular. We will then look at their growth, not just assets, but in volume and product count. Then, we will learn about ETF mechanics via the story of how the first ETF was invented, followed by an examination of the myriad ways different institutions are using ETFs. The section will end with a thorough look at how to vet and select ETFs including a look at trading. All this will arm you for Section Two.

Section Two is a tour through the "ETF toolbox" with me as your tour guide. We will look at each asset class including equities, fixed income, and alternatives. We will spend some extra time in hot areas such as smart beta, currency hedging, China, gold, and liquid alts. The book will end with some parting thoughts from me as well as some resources for additional and ongoing education.

Now that we got that out of the way, let's get started!

SECTION I

The ETF Phenomenon

CHAPTER 1

Why Are ETFs So Popular?

They say that as a customer you can only get two of these three things: fast/good/cheap. If it's fast and good, it isn't cheap. If it is good and cheap, it isn't fast. And if it's cheap and fast, well, it probably isn't that good.

Turns out, I have found two things that prove this wrong: Vietnamese restaurants and exchange-traded funds (ETFs). Those are two times when fast, good, and cheap all tend to exist in wonderful harmony.

How this can happen requires a bit of background into what an ETF is.

Essentially, an ETF is the marriage of an index fund (passively managed with low-costs and diversification) with the trading features of a stock (intraday trading, price transparency). That is how most people know them. And that is true on a base level. But that is only half the story. Thanks to the ingenious way ETF shares are created and redeemed—something we will explore in Chapter 3—an ETF has additional qualities that make it rise above the blunt definition of "a fund that trades." I tend to agree with some in the industry who have called ETFs a "disruptive technology."

As an analyst who has covered everything from mutual funds to hedge funds to closed-end funds, I have been amazed at the sheer number of advantages that ETFs offer up. They take many evolutionary steps forward and as such are fast becoming the investment vehicle for the twenty-first century.

The best way to support this lofty description is to just dive into the advantages. These are the things that make them fast, good, and cheap. This isn't to say they are perfect. And there are many things you need to watch out for—which we will go over throughout the book—but they—like other great technologies—offer up several benefits in one shot that can make life easier.

Low Cost

ETFs are cheap. The asset-weighted average fee is 0.30 percent, which is less than half the cost as the asset-weighted average active mutual fund fee of 0.66 percent. And when you look at the top 20 largest ETFs—where a lot of the institutional money gravitates—the average fee is 0.19 percent, as seen in Table 1.1.

And the good news is costs keep coming down. Some call it a fee war, but I call it "fee innovation." After all, it is a technological marvel that issuers can offer these products at such low costs. At this point you can get a deep and diverse all-ETF portfolio for a blended fee of about 0.08 percent.

TABLE 1.1 Fees for the Top 20 Largest ETFs

Ticker	Name	Total Assets ($million)	Expense Ratio
SPY US	SPDR S&P 500 ETF Trust	177,863.06	0.09%
IVV US	iShares Core S&P 500 ETF	68,940.23	0.07%
EFA US	iShares MSCI EAFE ETF	60,793.88	0.33%
VTI US	Vanguard Total Stock Mkt ETF	57,159.11	0.05%
VWO US	Vanguard FTSE Emerging Market	47,665.84	0.15%
QQQ US	Powershares QQQ Trust Series	41,528.99	0.20%
VOO US	Vanguard S&P 500 ETF	32,408.59	0.05%
IWM US	iShares Russell 2000 ETF	26,256.59	0.20%
IWF US	iShares Russell 1000 Growth	30,289.73	0.20%
EEM US	iShares MSCI Emerging Market	25,560.05	0.67%
VEA US	Vanguard FTSE Developed ETF	27,824.86	0.09%
IJH US	iShares Core S&P Midcap ETF	25,896.63	0.12%
BND US	Vanguard Total Bond Market	26,988.95	0.08%
GLD US	SPDR Gold Shares	23,627.12	0.40%
IWD US	iShares Russell 1000 Value E	25,520.39	0.20%
VNQ US	Vanguard REIT ETF	23,728.75	0.12%
AGG US	iShares Core U.S. Aggregate	25,500.20	0.08%
LQD US	iShares iBoxx Investment Grade	21,667.93	0.15%
VIG US	Vanguard Dividend Apprec ETF	19,797.96	0.10%
HEDJ US	Wisdomtree Europe Hedged Equity	21,814.08	0.58%

Source: Bloomberg

When the Schwab U.S. Broad Market ETF (SCHB) cut its expense ratio in 2013 from 0.06 percent to 0.04 percent, it took cheap to a whole other level. Since then, it cut it to 0.03 percent along with the iShares Core S&P Total U.S. Stock Market ETF (ITOT) SCHB and ITOT hold over 2,000 large-, mid- and small-cap stocks, that comes out to about 700 stocks per basis point in fees. SCHB and ITOT are leading what many are calling a "race to the bottom." Some of the leaders in this race to the bottom can be seen in Table 1.2.

And the reason I listed this as the first advantage is that investment costs are one of the most important variables you can control. Performance is fickle, but costs keep coming every day, rain or shine.

When it comes to the fee war, low-cost king Vanguard in particular should be given most of the credit. When they enter a category with a new ETF, it is like Wal-Mart coming to town. They cause a gnashing of teeth from the other issuers, who typically respond by lowering their fees as well. This "Vanguard Effect" is evidenced in the fact that in categories where there is no Vanguard ETF, such as micro-caps or junk bonds, the cheapest ETF is 3 to 6 times more expensive than categories Vanguard has an ETF in. In other words, the fee war is more about the fear of Vanguard than anything else. In the end, though, the investor is the ultimate winner in all of this.

TABLE 1.2 A Race to the Bottom in ETF Fees

Name	Expense Ratio
Schwab U.S. Broad Market ETF	0.03%
iShares Core S&P Total U.S. Stock Market	0.03%
Schwab U.S. Large-Cap ETF	0.03%
Vanguard Total Stock Market	0.05%
Vanguard S&P 500 ETF	0.05%
iShares Core S&P 500 ETF	0.07%
Schwab U.S. Dividend Equity ETF	0.07%
Schwab U.S. Large-Cap Growth	0.07%
Schwab U.S. Mid-Cap ETF	0.07%
Schwab U.S. Large-Cap Value	0.07%
Schwab U.S. REIT ETF	0.07%

Source: Bloomberg

For investors used to buying pricey mutual funds, ETFs' low cost is godsend. But for massive institutions with loads of money, ETFs can actually be expensive compared to passive separately managed accounts (SMAs). They can get an SMA that gives them index exposure for next to nothing and have it custom-made for their needs. It is the equivalent of getting a tailored suit for $10.

"If I'm a large institution, I can go direct to a service provider and say, 'I'm going to dump $10 billion on you and you're going to give me [S&P 500 exposure] for one basis point.' People are going to whine and complain, but guess what happens? The manager is going to say, 'Yes, sir, we're going to do it for one basis point.'"

Wesley Gray, Alpha Architect

And for many large institutions, every basis point translates into a lot of money. In the case above, let's say the institution paid one basis point for the SMA instead of 0.03 percent for SCHB or ITOT, the cheapest broad-market ETFs in the world. Those two basis points equal $2 million a year. That amount could be several fireman pensions that are now funded. This is why the very largest institutions negotiate over every basis point, and even dirt-cheap ETFs lose if fees are the only criteria.

Like mutual funds, SMAs get more expensive the less you can pony up. So it isn't a black-and-white issue, but certainly at the larger institutional fund levels, they can be a cheaper option.

However, cost isn't the only consideration for an institution, and that brings us to our next advantage.

Liquidity

Liquidity may not be the most attractive feature of ETFs for retail investors, but for institutions it is beloved. ETFs trade throughout the day like stocks. If an asset manager wants to buy mainland China at 2:13 P.M., they could punch up the Deutsche X-trackers Harvest CSI 300 China A-Shares ETF (ASHR) and put in an order and own it within seconds. They could then sell it a minute later or year later.

This is much more expedient than using a mutual fund or hedge fund or owning the aforementioned SMA. None of those things can be gotten into and out of so quickly and easily. That's why the liquidity advantage is really about freedom—something institutions don't have a ton of. With ETFs you can buy and sell whenever you want without having to ask anyone's permission. Institutions in particular value this trait because much of their existence is slow moving and waiting for boards to approve things and dealing with redemption schedules of managers and the like.

> *"It's less paperwork. There are no gates. It's just easy to do business with ETFs because they are exchange traded."*
>
> Matt Goulet, Fidelity Investments

Since the financial crisis of 2008, institutions have been aware of the importance of liquidity in a portfolio. When it comes to liquidity, ETFs are now right up there with stocks. In fact, on any given day, ETFs will typically make up half of the top 10 most traded equities as shown in Table 1.3.

> *"Liquidity and precision are definitely the big benefits of ETFs."*
>
> John Linder, Pension Consulting Alliance

A nice residual benefit of all this liquidity is that some ETFs end up costing less to trade than the basket of holdings they track. Some examples of this can be seen in Table 1.4. For instance, the Vanguard FTSE Emerging Markets ETF (VWO) has a spread of 0.21 percent, while VWO has a spread of 0.03 percent.

TABLE 1.3 Top 10 Most Traded Equities as of June 30, 2015

Ticker	Name	Volume (in $million)
SPY US	SPDR S&P 500 ETF Trust	21,181.54
AAPL US	Apple Inc	5,964.08
IWM US	iShares Russell 2000 ETF	3,976.85
QQQ US	Powershares QQQ Trust Series	2,854.02
EEM US	iShares MSCI Emerging Market	1,767.23
MSFT US	Microsoft Corp	1,442.14
NFLX US	Netflix Inc	1,435.62
GILD US	Gilead Sciences Inc	1,382.10
TLT US	iShares 20+ Year Treasury Bond ETF	1,305.30

Source: Bloomberg

TABLE 1.4 ETF Spreads versus Their Underlying Basket

ETF	ETF Bid/Ask %	Basket Bid/Ask %	Difference %
SPDR S&P 500 ETF Trust (SPY)	0.00	0.03	0.02
Vanguard FTSE Emerging Markets ETF (VWO)	0.02	0.21	0.20
iShares MSCI EAFE ETF (EFA)	0.02	0.07	0.06
iShares Russell 2000 ETF (IWM)	0.01	0.23	0.22
SPDR Barclays HY Bond ETF (JNK)	0.03	0.45	0.44
iShares iBoxx Invst Grd Corp Bond ETF (LQD)	0.01	0.49	0.49

Source: Bloomberg

You can also see that the iShares iBoxx Investment Grade Corporate Bond ETF (HYG) trades for significantly less cost than its basket. And yes, SPY trades so much that the spread is 0.004 percent, which rounds down to 0.00 percent, slightly less than the 0.03 for the Standard & Poor's (S&P) 500 stocks. We'll look at SPY's freakishly high trading volume throughout the book.

This concept is referred to as "price improvement" and is one of the rare cases where you don't have to pay more for convenience, but rather less. While this applies to only the most traded ETFs out there, it isn't something lost on investors.

> *"I can go do a swap on a basket of securities. I can create my own custom basket. I can buy the index myself. But for us it comes down to does the ETF make more sense than going out and spending the physical capital. Usually, it does."*
>
> Jim Dunn, Verger Capital Management

However, it should be noted that you can also get hurt trading ETFs if you aren't careful or rack up some unwanted trading costs. We will dive deeper into ETF liquidity and trading in Chapter 5.

Tax Efficiency

While there are few minor exceptions, ETFs overall have a near-perfect record of not issuing capital gains taxes that can plague mutual funds and hedge funds. Obviously, this advantage means zilch for an institution that is tax exempt. But

TABLE 1.5 Asset-Weighted 5-Year Average Capital Gains Ending 2011

Type	Active MF	Passive MF	ETF
Large-Cap Blend	1.92%	0.16%	0.00%
Large-Cap Value	2.01%	0.08%	0.00%
Large-Cap Growth	1.65%	0.04%	0.00%
Mid-Cap Blend	4.26%	0.13%	0.00%
Small-Cap Blend	3.54%	1.31%	0.00%
Foreign Large Blend	2.50%	0.32%	0.00%
Emerging Market	6.46%	0.02%	0.01%

Source: Morningstar, Inc.

as you go beyond tax-exempt institutions, it matters and is certainly, by anyone's standards, a nice residual benefit of the ETF and worth an explanation.

When there are large redemptions in a mutual fund, the manager must go and sell some stocks in the fund in order to cash out the big investor. Selling those stocks for a gain can trigger a tax event for the fund, which affects all of the existing investors. In other words, the good soldiers who stayed in the fund have to foot the tax bill of the people leaving. Alternatively, the fund manager could keep cash on the side for redemptions, but then they have cash drag on returns.

In contrast, when someone sells their shares of an ETF in the open market for a gain, that is on them and it does nothing to affect investors in the ETF. This is due to the way ETFs shares are created and destroyed using an "in-kind" method which we will learn about in Chapter 3.

The bottom line is ETFs shift the tax burden onto the seller, not the existing shareholders. This makes ETFs even more tax efficient than traditional index funds, as seen in Table 1.5.

Transparency

Transparency is a value that many people hold dear in all aspects of life. We like transparency in our government (even though it is rare), our relationships, our community, and our business. So it is not a shocker that it is a valued trait of ETFs. ETFs are considered transparent because almost all of them report their holdings every day. This is an advantage that is best contrasted to mutual funds, which only report holdings quarterly and with a 60-day delay, and hedge funds, which never report the holdings of their funds.

Knowing what is in your ETF can come in handy in monitoring overlap with other investments. If a stock has some kind of major event, you can check quickly and know how exposed you are to it. In an actively managed fund you just don't know.

For example, if Elon Musk suddenly quits Tesla today, you could quickly figure out how much Tesla you are exposed to across your ETFs and make any necessary adjustments. With mutual funds, you'd be looking at data that were four to six months old, so you'd be in the dark, having no idea exactly how bad the situation was for you.

Figure 1.1 shows us the ETFs and mutual funds that have the biggest weighting to Tesla as of 6/16/2015. You can see that all of the ETFs have holding dates as of the day before, while the mutual funds are months old, and you don't know if they've beefed up or unwound that Tesla position.

There is one caveat to ETFs' daily transparency and that is Vanguard. Vanguard only releases their ETF holdings monthly with a 15-day lag. Across

FIGURE 1.1 ETFs Show Their Holdings Every Day

	Portfolio Name	Ticker	Mkt Val	% Portfolio↑	% Out	File Dt
1.	Market Vectors Global Alternative Energy	GEX US	11.67MLN	12.519	0.04	06/15/15
2.	PRUDENTIAL JENNISON MARKET NEUTRAL FUND	PJNAX US	313,868.8	11.797	0.00	01/31/15
3.	FIRST TRUST NASDAQ CLEAN EDGE U.S. LIQUID...	QCLN US	8.3MLN	9.389	0.03	06/15/15
4.	BARON RETIREMENT INCOME FUND	BFGFX US	20.76MLN	7.713	0.06	03/31/15
5.	BARON PARTNERS FUND	BPTRX US	208.82MLN	6.704	0.65	03/31/15
6.	RIDGEWORTH AGGRESSIVE GROWTH STOCK FUND	SAGAX US	3.01MLN	6.449	0.01	03/31/15
7.	ARK Industrial Innovation ETF	ARKQ US	773,787.84	5.959	0.00	06/15/15
8.	FIDELITY SELECT AUTOMOTIVE	FSAVX US	7.67MLN	5.918	0.02	04/30/15
9.	T ROWE PRICE GLOBAL TECHNOLOGY FUND	PRGTX US	127.34MLN	5.092	0.40	03/31/15
10.	GLOBAL X LITHIUM ETF	LIT US	2.47MLN	5.000	0.01	06/15/15
11.	FIRST TRUST NASDAQ GLOBAL AUTO INDEX FUND	CARZ US	1.7MLN	4.968	0.01	06/15/15
12.	ARK Innovation ETF	ARKK US	374,111.36	4.964	0.00	06/15/15
13.	ALLIANZGI TECHNOLOGY FUND	DRGTX US	60.02MLN	4.471	0.19	04/30/15
14.	WESTCORE SELECT FUND	WTSLX US	3.72MLN	4.465	0.01	04/30/15
15.	RYDEX VA TRANSPORTATION FUND	VRTRANV US	406,763.84	3.270	0.00	05/31/15
16.	RYDEX TRANSPORTATION FUND	RYPIX US	1.35MLN	3.264	0.00	05/31/15
17.	TRANSAMERICA VAN KAMPEN MID CAP GROWTH...	TRVKMGV US	36.75MLN	3.145	0.11	03/31/15
18.	TRANSAMERICA GROWTH OPPORTUNITIES	ITCBX US	33.38MLN	3.073	0.10	03/31/15
19.	SHELTON GREEN ALPHA FUND	NEXTX US	911,232	3.058	0.00	04/30/15
20.	AZL VK MIDCAP GROWTH		18.87MLN	3.043	0.06	03/31/15
21.	MORGAN STANLEY INST FD TRST- MID CAP GR...	MPEGX US	268.32MLN	3.039	0.84	03/31/15
22.	TRANSAMERICA LEGG MASON PARTNERS ALL CA...	TRLMACV US	10.38MLN	3.015	0.03	03/31/15
23.	MORGAN STANLEY UNIVERSAL EQUITY GROWTH	UEGIX US	8.45MLN	3.011	0.03	03/31/15
24.	MORGAN STANLEY CAPITAL OPPORTUNITIES TR...	CPOAX US	15.35MLN	2.998	0.05	03/31/15

Source: Bloomberg

only Vanguard's ETF roster the ETF exists as a share class of Vanguard's index mutual funds, and as such they don't want those funds to be victims of front-running by disclosing holdings daily like other ETF providers do.[1] Many of the early issuers chose to voluntarily disclose daily holdings for competitive reasons, but not because they are required. Still, the stand alone, transparent ETF structure is a consistent improvement relative to other types of funds.

Diversification

Whether it is small caps, China, or biotech, there are just areas where even a large institutional investor simply won't have an opinion or research on single security names. They may not have the resources to study the area or have chosen not to make a single security bet. ETFs offer an alternative to this by offering exposure to an entire market or country or sector.

"I'm a stock picker, but I use ETFs for things I don't know about."

Larry Seibert, 780 Riverside Drive, LLC

Let's say you are interested in getting exposure to health care. There are hundreds and hundreds of stocks to choose from. Which one do you pick? Many people will opt to use an ETF, which puts your eggs in many baskets. In this way, ETFs let you be more of an economist and less of a stock analyst.

Another important aspect of diversification is dampening volatility. Investing in a group of securities protects you from single-company blow-ups.

Let's look at an example using the Guggenheim Solar Energy Index ETF (TAN). In October 2014, a sapphire glass company named GT Advanced Technologies Inc. (GTAT) declared bankruptcy after Apple decided not to use their glass in the screen of the iPhone 6.[2] The stock quickly dropped 90 percent—a nightmare scenario for GTAT's stock holders. Imagine if you were bullish solar energy but had only bought GTAT.

Meanwhile, TAN barely noticed it. GTAT was a 3.2 percent weighting, so its contribution to total return (CTR) for TAN on the year was 0.72 percent, as seen in Figure 1.2. Not desirable, but pretty minor considering the stock blew up. ETFs help investors play their themes without the stock selection process undoing the thematic or allocation work up front.

GTAT was also immediately thrown out of the index because it broke the index rules by declaring bankruptcy. This example also exhibits an

ETF's regeneration process—a benefit that doesn't get brought up too often. Because ETFs track indexes and because those indexes have rules, if a company slips up and breaks the rules, it is going to be kicked out of the index and replaced with a new one.

Not every company burns out; some fade away and before long they are replaced. This Darwinistic process helps your ETF stay in playing shape and evolve with the times. And you don't have to lift a finger—it's all done as part of the normal periodic reconstitutions and rebalances and of the index. Figure 1.2 shows the weekly holdings of TAN during October 2014. In the case of GTAT, it was quickly booted out of the index within days of its bankruptcy.

FIGURE 1.2 TAN's Holdings Each Week during October 2014

Name	Avg % Wgt	CTR	Tot Rtn
GUGGENHEIM SOLAR ENERGY INDE...	100.00	-1.39	-1.39
5N PLUS INC	1.50	0.12	-5.04
ABENGOA YIELD PLC	0.65	-0.68	-26.77
ADVANCED ENERGY INDUSTRIES	3.16	0.12	3.67
CANADIAN SOLAR INC	4.32	-0.18	-18.88
CHINA SINGYES SOLAR TECH	3.08	1.30	39.62
COMTEC SOLAR SYSTEMS GROUP	1.16	-0.45	-29.45
DAQO NEW ENERGY CORP-ADR	1.48	-0.30	-27.44
ENPHASE ENERGY INC	1.31	0.92	125.39
FIRST SOLAR INC	7.84	-2.70	-18.38
GCL-POLY ENERGY HOLDINGS LTD	6.58	-2.68	-25.00
GT ADVANCED TECHNOLOGIES INC	4.13	-0.72	-87.39
HANERGY THIN FILM POWER GROU	6.69	10.15	265.25
HANWHA Q CELLS CO LTD - ADR	1.07	-0.82	-60.29
JA SOLAR HOLDINGS CO LTD-ADR	2.61	-0.10	-10.74
JINKOSOLAR HOLDING CO-ADR	3.44	-0.88	-32.73
MEYER BURGER TECHNOLOGY AG	3.94	-1.52	-45.60
REC SILICON ASA	3.83	-0.45	-40.86
REC SOLAR ASA	3.35	0.28	-1.49
RENESOLA LTD-ADR	2.11	-1.04	-59.13
SHUNFENG INTERNATIONAL CLEAN	4.02	0.04	-11.31
SMA SOLAR TECHNOLOGY AG	2.89	-0.25	-41.52
SOLARCITY CORP	6.79	-0.32	-5.88

Source: Bloomberg

"ETFs reduce the risk of a WorldCom or an Enron. You have so many risks using just one stock. How do you know there is not fraud risk or an accounting error or a bad product? There's no way we can do that level of due diligence to figure out if that's occurring. The ETF is rebalancing. It's taking out the losers and putting in the winners. We don't have to do that."

Sharon Snow, Metropolitan Capital Strategies

Bankruptcies and frauds aside, diversification also dampens day-to-day volatility as well. For example, TAN holds 32 companies involved in solar energy business. Most are newer, younger, and smaller companies. The average standard deviation for each of the 32 stocks is 63 percent. Meanwhile, the ETF's standard deviation is about half that, at 38 percent. That is still about triple the standard deviation of the S&P 500 index, but it is just much less volatile than the stocks it holds. This is because the stocks neutralize each other somewhat inside the fund. This is a story you will see across many ETFs.

It must be noted that there is a flip side to diversification, and that is single stock investing can pay off *big* when a stock surges. Single stock selection lets you feel every basis point of a positive return. Using an example from TAN's holdings, if you were lucky enough to pick SolarCity Corporation (SCTY), you would have been up 246 percent in the past two years, compared to the diversified TAN, which was up (only) 87 percent.

For those who put in the research and time and think they can pick the right stock (at the right time) and outsmart the army of analysts out there, the ETF probably doesn't make any sense. But in cases where you don't put in the time and research or don't want to take on single-security risk, the diversification of ETFs is a huge benefit. This is also why ETFs are not just drawing their assets from other investment vehicles like mutual funds, but also from single security investors.

Easy Asset Allocation

Everyone will tell you that getting your asset allocation is much more important than picking the right securities. The narrower you go in your investment decisions, the less impactful those decisions become. And when it comes to doing asset allocation, ETFs are like hitting the easy button.

"We'll get broad exposure using ETFs. It's a really easy, cheap way to accomplish what we are trying to accomplish, which is to own risk factors or asset classes, and it is the smart way to do it."

Josh Brown, Ritholtz Wealth Management

ETFs are both broad and precise. They have packaged up virtually every single asset class, strategy, region, country, and even derivative that you can think of. Any investor—both institutional and retail—can now immediately get exposure to everything from real estate companies to short-term high-yield bonds to corn futures to China A-shares.

"What ETFs allow is a more focused or segmented approach than in the old days."

Mark Yusko, Morgan Creek Capital Management

While asset allocation is typically associated with long-term buy-and-hold investors, it is also employed by managers with shorter horizons as well. You've heard of stock pickers. Now there are ETF pickers—except they are called ETF strategists.

"There are many people who pick stocks. If you walk down the streets of Boston, I would expect that 9 out of 10 investment managers you bump into pick securities. Yet at the asset class level, there are fewer people who compare assets. But the macro environments across the globe are not in sync, whether it is the economic cycle, credit cycle, or business cycle. So that creates opportunity to generate alpha through asset selection. ETFs are a perfect vehicle for that."

Linda Zhang, Windhaven Investment Management

This also touches on one of the most fascinating aspect of ETFs, which is how they are at once a replacement for a mutual fund, hedge fund, or an SMA as well as a tool for a mutual fund, hedge fund, or SMA. That makes them a two-headed monster. It's also why institutional exposure to ETFs can come from direct usage and/or indirect usage via external managers.

"What makes ETFs really different is that in addition to being a funds solution, they are actually a single security or exposure solution. That means they can be used as a substitute for an SMA or mutual fund, or they can be used as part of the SMA or mutual fund. And that's what makes them unique.

Matthew Tucker, Blackrock

Standardization

We like it when things are standardized. Whether it is USB ports or gas pumps, it is easier when it works the same way regardless of other variables. When it comes to investing, ETFs have standardized every asset class so that they trade like equities. Investors love the fairness and price transparency of equity investing on a stock exchange. ETFs have simply equity-ized every type of investment.

For example, bonds don't have a common exchange. They trade over the counter (off exchange) in relatively opaque markets, whereas bond ETFs trade like stocks. Some other assets that have been standardized by ETFs include physical gold, oil futures, swap agreements, currencies, and hedge fund strategies. All of these things and more can now be bought and sold on a stock exchange just like shares of General Electric. This has standardized investing, and even more importantly, it has created another venue where investors can buy or sell the ETF's underlying exposures

While this standardization is mostly hailed as a breakthrough in convenience, it has also brought with it a few concerns. Just like *Jurassic Park,* when you try and bring ancient beasts into the modern world, you have to be careful. A popular example is junk bond ETFs. Those bonds are pretty illiquid while the ETFs that hold them can be very liquid. This creates a bona fide "liquidity mismatch" and is one of the issues we will look at more in Chapter 9.

This standardization of the financial markets has also challenged embedded taxonomies and structures all over the financial world. Nowhere is this symbolized more than on the Bloomberg terminal keyboard, which is divided by yellow keys for government bonds, corporate bonds, mortgage bonds, money markets, municipal bonds, preferred, equities, commodities, indexes, and currencies, as shown in Table 1.6. Each asset class has different functions,

TABLE 1.6 The Yellow Keys on the Bloomberg Terminal

LAW	F1	Global law and regulation, litigation, legal analysis, news, etc.
GOVT	F2	Securities issued by national governments and securities by quasi-governmental agencies
CORP	F3	Corporate bonds
MTGE	F4	Mortgage market instruments
M-MKT	F5	Money market securities
MUNI	F6	U.S. municipal bonds
PFD	F7	Preferred securities
EQUITY	F8	Common stocks, American depositary receipts (ADRs), mutual funds, rights, options, warrants
CMDTY	F9	Commodities and associated futures and options
INDEX	F10	Equity indices and economic indices
CRNCY	F11	Foreign currencies
CLIENT	F12	Portfolio and risk management

Source: Bloomberg

traits, and the like. Meanwhile, the ETF covers all the yellow keys. They are at once everywhere but nowhere.

This chameleon nature of ETFs is also making it difficult for companies and desks on Wall Street to figure out where to put them. The ETF desk could be part of equities or fixed income or even derivatives. Some are starting ETF-specific desks. The entire financial system is trying to figure out how to adapt to the "disruptive technology" that is ETFs.

Democratic

ETFs are democratic in two ways. First, they have democratized investing by providing retail access to many asset classes, countries, and strategies.

ETFs have also democratized things by providing this access at the same cost. For the first time ever in the history of investing, big institutional investors and small retail investors are using the same investment products and paying the same expense ratios. Unlike mutual funds and SMAs, which have a fee system equivalent to a regressive tax—the less money you can invest, the more you get charged—ETFs are like a flat tax. So my Aunt Joyce investing $1,000 in an ETF gets charged the same annual expense ratio as would Yale University's endowment or a hedge fund investing $100 million.

In this way, you could argue that ETFs are like the Sam's Club of funds. Just as Sam's Club offers wholesale prices on everything, similarly ETFs are priced about the same as the institutional class of a mutual fund. This fairness provides a philosophical undercurrent that is totally in tune with the times and something that has made them a big hit with millennials who generally like fairness and transparency while distrusting anything Wall Street.

While democratization is heartwarming and great for the little guy, how does this benefit institutions? The benefit to institutions is simple: more liquidity. That's ultimately their favorite thing about ETFs. With retail and advisors using ETFs alongside institutions, they both benefit the increase in liquidity because it brings the bid/ask spread down and makes it cheaper to trade. This advantage is unique to ETFs relative to SMAs and mutual funds—the more users of the ETF, the better the user experience, be it a retail of institutional one.

No Emotion

Making an investment strategy is easy. Sticking to it is hard. This is because things change. Portfolio managers can get swept away in trends, groupthink, and fear and emotion. An ETF is immune to all that, and this is an advantage. This is a trait the ETF shares with index funds.

An ETF is programmed to do nothing but track the index. They are like those spider robots from *Minority Report* that mindlessly fulfill their duty. ETF portfolio managers follow the rules dictated by the index to deliver index-like results. The holdings and allocations inside the ETF are generally outside the control of subjective, emotional, vulnerable humans. The ETF isn't reading the *Financial Times* or watching CNBC. It doesn't even have a Twitter account. It just does its best to follow the index returns by adhering to the index rules. Ironically, this robotic, *passive* functionality is highly useful to someone who is *actively* managing money.

This advantage relies on the indexes having solid rules that they stick to. For the most part, indexes simply do not change their rules even when the pressure builds up because of some hot trend.

> *"If we have some rule and we change it overnight, we have riots on our hands. There are situations that naturally happen in the capital markets, which put those rules under pressure, but they are relatively rare. People like what we do to be stable and reliable, and we can't just change the rules on them at the drop of a hat."*
>
> C. D. Baer Pettit, MSCI

Passive Investing

Lack of emotion is related to the overall move to passive investing. More and more people are losing faith in a manager's ability to pick winning securities. And why shouldn't they—it is very difficult to beat the market.

This dips into a concept known as efficient market hypothesis, which is that at any given time the market has already priced in all the available data, and thus it is nearly impossible to know more than the market. This is not a hard concept to fathom when you consider all the manpower dedicated to analyzing securities. For example, Amazon alone

FIGURE 1.3 Total Analyst Recommendations for Large U.S. Stocks

	Ticker		Short Name	Tot Analyst Rec:D-1
1)	AAPL	US	APPLE INC	56
2)	FB	US	FACEBOOK INC-A	52
3)	BABA	US	ALIBABA GRP-ADR	51
4)	CRM	US	SALESFORCE.COM	50
5)	GOOGL	US	GOOGLE INC-A	49
6)	INTC	US	INTEL CORP	49
7)	EBAY	US	EBAY INC	49
8)	VMW	US	VMWARE INC-CL A	49
9)	AMZN	US	AMAZON.COM INC	48
10)	CSCO	US	CISCO SYSTEMS	46
11)	ORCL	US	ORACLE CORP	46
12)	EMC	US	EMC CORP/MA	45
13)	SLB	US	SCHLUMBERGER LTD	45
14)	MA	US	MASTERCARD INC-A	45
15)	MSFT	US	MICROSOFT CORP	44
16)	V	US	VISA INC-CLASS A	43
17)	PXD	US	PIONEER NATURAL	43
18)	NFLX	US	NETFLIX INC	43
19)	BAC	US	BANK OF AMERICA	42
20)	EOG	US	EOG RESOURCES	42

Source: Bloomberg

has 40+ analysts covering it. These are people that do nothing but look at Amazon and the industry it operates in. Many U.S. stocks have 40+ analysts, as shown in Figure 1.3.

The broad analyst coverage makes it difficult to gain any kind of an edge. Other areas such as fixed income and emerging markets may have less coverage and may present more opportunity for a stock picker. And that's why in those areas—plus fixed income—you will find institutions tend to go active, while going passive with U.S. equities.

Just look at the top 5 funds in the world (including ETFs) as shown in Table 1.7, and you will see that literally all of them are passive stock index funds.

Index investing gets associated with Average Joes using their 401(k) plans. But some of the most successful people in the financial industry who know the most about Wall Street are index investors when it comes to their own personal money. I call them "celebrity indexers." They include Jack Lew, Janet Yellen, Michael Lewis, and Ben Stein. We know this from what they've said in interviews or their financial disclosure documents. Heck, even Bernie Madoff endorsed index investing from his jail cell as the least likely way to get ripped off.

TABLE 1.7 The Top 5 Largest Funds in the World

Ticker	Name	Total Asset ($million)
VTSMX US	Vanguard Tot Stk Mkt-Inv	353,736.625
VINIX US	Vanguard Inst Index-Inst	198,316.672
SPY US	SPDR S&P 500 ETF Trust	182,275.703
VFINX US	Vanguard 500 Index Fund-Inv	180,535.922
VGTSX US	Vanguard Tot Int St Idx-Inv	162,158.187

Source: Bloomberg

But perhaps, the most famous fan of indexing is Warren Buffett. Here's what Buffett said in a recent letter to shareholders about what he would invest in right now:

> What I advise here is essentially identical to certain instructions I've laid out in my will. My advice to the trustee could not be more simple. Put 10% of the cash in short-term government bonds and 90% in a very low-cost S&P 500 index fund. I believe the trust's long-term results from this policy will be superior to those attained by most investors—whether pension funds, institutions, individuals—who employ high fee managers."[3]

Buffett specifically points to pensions and other institutions. Given who is saying this, you have to wonder why institutions don't just follow the Oracle of Omaha and use the Vanguard S&P 500 ETF (VOO) and the iShares 1–3 Year Treasury Bond ETF (SHY), two very liquid ETFs with a blended fee of 0.06 percent a year. Not to mention a 10-year annualized return of 7.5 percent, right in line with the bogey most institutions are trying—but typically fail—to hit. I will be referring to this mini-portfolio as the "Buffett Special" throughout the book.

Flexibility

Flexibility is huge to institutions. This is what the book is about. See, there are many ways ETFs can be used beside a long-term investment. This book covers about a dozen of those usages. You can go long or short with an ETF. You can use them as portfolio adjustment mechanisms. You can do tax-loss harvesting with them. You can use them as placeholders or lend them out to generate income or use options with them. The list goes on.

"We use ETFs in a lot of different ways here. And flexibility is really the nice thing."
Michael Brakebill, Tennessee Consolidated Retirement System

ETFs also allow investors to access both beta (market return) and alpha (excess return). On one hand, ETFs can be used to grab as much beta as they can for those who simply want to own the market(s). Sort of like the aforementioned Buffett Special portfolio. This is a worthy pursuit for sure, especially for buy-and-hold investors.

But for those investors looking to find alpha, or excess return above the market, ETFs are useful for that, too. Alpha can be generated in two main ways using passive ETFs. First is by organizing your ETFs in such a way that you overweight or underweight different sectors, countries, or factors that you think will outperform. Many have called this "alpha through beta." This is what ETF strategists have built a $100 billion industry doing.

The other way is through buying an ETF that is designed to try and generate alpha on its own, either through different weighting schemes—frequently called "smart beta"—and/or actively managed ETFs. We will discuss in great detail in Chapter 7.

Anonymity

As an ETF analyst, I'm always asked, "Where did the flows come from?" or "Who did that big trade?" My answer is always the same: "I don't know."

No one knows. Even the issuers don't know. There's an anonymity and privacy to ETF investing. Anonymity—and freedom—are advantages that I never really noticed until I spent some time chatting with institutions. These advantages were brought up time and time again in discussions with institutions themselves and the ETF issuers.

While ETFs are bought and sold all the time, it is unknown who is doing the buying and selling. This is a beneficial feature to larger institutions—especially ones doing active management—because it keeps their moves on the down low. Even massive block trades that send billions into an ETF in one shot are anonymous.

"With an ETF, no one knows exactly what you are doing and you can hide behind the ETF without having to show your hand."
Ben Fulton, Elkhorn Capital Group

FIGURE 1.4 The Largest Trades for HEDJ from March 19, 2015, to June 19, 2015

HEDJ US Equity 98) Time Ranges 99) Actions Page 1/2 VWAP
08:49 03/19/15 Price Filter Calculation Bloomberg Definition
17:12 06/19/15 Vol Filter Amount @ Part%

Calculation	VWAP	VWAP Volume	Value Traded	Trades	Avg Size	Std Dev
Bloomberg	65.6826	352,961,172	23.183BLN	1,209,3€	292	1.600188
Custom	65.6826	352,961,172	23.183BLN	1,209,3€	292	1.600188

1) Summary 2) Top Trades (AQR) 3) Price Chart (VAP) 4) Price Table (TSM)

Trades with the Largest Impact Spread / Price Ratio .000159

Date	Time	Volume	Price	Exch	Date	Time	Volume	Price	Exch
04/01	16:05:18	2,374,075	66.71	D	04/20	09:36:47	524,000	66.79 ↑	D
03/31	14:01:58	1,568,431	66.195	D	03/23	14:31:57	511,065	66.46 ↑	D
05/11	09:46:58	1,493,900	65.41 ↑	D	06/10	16:06:26	500,000	64.0867	D
04/01	12:21:13	1,152,307	66.41 ↑	D	04/17	10:11:12	471,579	66.44 ↑	D
06/10	09:48:07	1,000,000	63.43 ↑	D	03/19	09:30:00	448,777	65.95	P
04/14	16:00:00	876,656	68.17	P	04/10	14:12:46	430,000	68.48	D
04/30	15:46:25	854,000	64.16 ↑	D	03/24	09:55:55	400,680	66.48	D
04/20	11:53:40	818,381	66.80 ↑	D	05/12	13:02:30	393,269	64.81 ↑	D
06/10	10:13:43	800,000	63.49 ↑	D	04/30	16:11:58	386,000	64.26	D
04/29	11:06:04	777,108	65.15	D	04/17	14:39:03	373,400	66.15	D
05/11	10:33:28	750,000	65.55 ↑	D	05/05	11:36:22	371,581	63.85	D
04/29	11:21:18	622,484	65.00	D	05/18	10:21:05	320,000	64.76 ↑	D
05/08	15:37:47	595,306	65.69 ↑	D	04/17	16:39:17	316,000	66.21	D
04/16	12:33:28	534,480	67.602	D	05/19	10:47:16	300,000	66.46	D

Source: Bloomberg

Figure 1.4 shows a list of the largest trades in the WisdomTree Europe Hedged Equity ETF (HEDJ) during a three-month stretch. You can see that five of the trades are over one million shares, yet it is unknown who did them. We know the when, the where, and even the how (exchange order versus creation). But we don't know the who, and we also don't know the why. And that's just how institutional investors like it.

Price Discovery

If you want to know what the market really thinks about something, just look at where the ETF is trading. This real-time information can be useful both in normal market environments and on days of intense market stress. ETFs are the tip of the spear in terms of trying to figure out how a market is valuing something. They rival the futures market in this aspect.

For example, many international ETFs trade while the markets they track are closed. Suppose news in the United States of new Russian sanctions comes out at 2 P.M. EST. Russian ETFs will trade immediately on that news and inform investors as to what the underlying Russian stocks are worth and where they may open. This also applies to less liquid areas of fixed income as well.

"ETFs in many ways offer opportunities in price discovery in fixed income. Very much the same way when you trade Japan or Germany equity ETFs. When those markets close, that doesn't mean there isn't a value or people stop thinking about the situation."

Linda Zhang, Windhaven Investment Management

Day-to-day, ETFs are slowly starting to replace indexes as the proxies for different markets as well. And why not? Unlike an index, you can actually *invest* in the ETF.

Beyond the day-to-day, there have been some extreme examples where the ETF served as a discovery tool in market-moving events when markets were closed or incredibly stressed.

One example is after the terrorist attacks of 9/11 and SPY. All trading of stock and bonds was halted from 9/11 through 9/17. When trading opened at 9:30 A.M. on 9/17, SPY began trading immediately and effectively, even though some of the stocks in the S&P 500 had not yet begun trading. Because of this, investors were able to use SPY as a price discovery vehicle and make implied valuations on those stocks that not yet begun trading.

Another example is when Egypt's stock market closed for two months between January and March 2011 due to violent protests in the country. The Market Vectors Egypt ETF (EGPT) continued to trade and serve as a guide as to where the market was trading. Many used the ETF to trade Egypt as volume on the ETF more than tripled during the time—all the while, investors holding individual Egyptian stocks were locked up entirely. They had no venue to unload or acquire those shares. Not surprisingly, the ETF deviated from the net asset value (NAV) and traded at a premium (price goes above its NAV) because the underlying stocks had no updated prices to feed into the NAV calculation. Additionally, creations and redemptions could not be done due to the stock market being closed, as shown in Figure 1.5. We will explore creations and redemptions more in Chapter 3 and premiums in Chapter 5.

The most recent example was in Greece, where the stock market closed for a few weeks in July as the country was in a debt crisis. Meanwhile, the

FIGURE 1.5 EGPT's Price and NAV Graph with Flows at Bottom

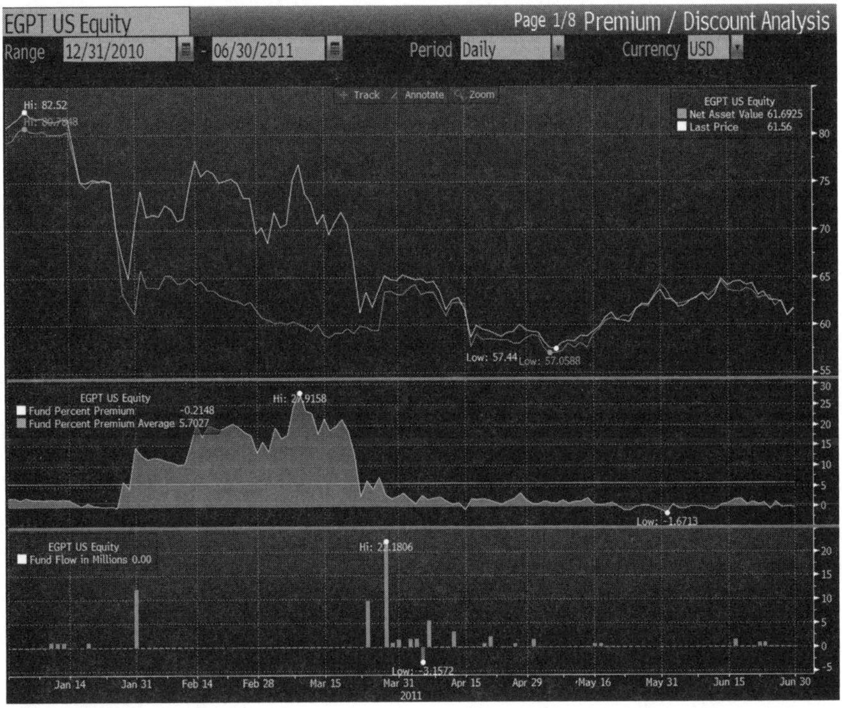

Source: Bloomberg

Global X FTSE Greece 20 ETF (GREK) continued to trade about triple its average volume. When it finally came down, it was very close to what the stocks were priced at when they opened.

The idea that you can invest in, trade or simply monitor an ETF even though the markets the ETF tracks are experiencing issues, can be helpful in terms of pricing and portfolio management.

Fiduciary Vehicles

ETFs have to be approved by the Securities and Exchange Commission (SEC) and most, like mutual funds, are regulated funds under the Investment Company Act of 1940. This means they have to have an independent board of directors and that the manager of the ETFs has a fiduciary obligation to act in the best interest of the fund holders. This is in contrast to other institutional vehicles such as swaps, futures, and other bank-issued vehicles including structured products.

This can be very important to some institutions that have mandates that forbid them from using the aforementioned derivatives.

"It is always nice when you have a pretty prospectus wrapped around an idea. It has all the disclosures and has gone through a vetting process [with the SEC]. There is good governance around the product. It is a nice, neatly wrapped package that can give asset managers a nice turnkey way of getting exposure."

Ben Fulton, Elkhorn Capital Group

One quick note, though: Not every ETF is registered under the 1940 Act, and some aren't even "funds" at all. However, those products only have about 4 percent of the assets. We will further examine the specific differences in structures in Chapter 5.

Battle Proven

ETFs have been around for over 23 years now and have lived through numerous traumatic market events, including the Internet bubble bursting, the attacks on 9/11, the 2008 financial crisis, the flash crash, the taper tantrum, and countless market spasms. Their assets continued to grow after these events.

ETFs' durability through these market sell-offs, dislocations, natural disasters, human errors, closures, and trading suspensions is part of the reason even conservative institutions feel more comfortable using them. Over the next few decades, there will be new and trying events that shake the markets and subsequently ETFs, but their design has shown they can handle the pressure and the stress.

Convenience

Last, but definitely not least, is convenience. You could argue that all of the preceding advantages in this chapter really speak to convenience, and people love convenience.

To understand just how powerful convenience is, consider that ETFs give away their secret sauce every single day when they post their holdings and their weightings on a variety of public web sites. If the ETF was not convenient, investors could bypass the ETF, save the management fee, and recreate the ETF themselves. But then they would have to deal with the operational duties of tracking an index, such as rebalances, dividends, spin-offs, warrants, and capital gains. Those are a few of the many instances like tax loss harvesting or securities lending where the portfolio manager at an ETF shop adds value.

Most people would rather just click a button and be done with it. Although it probably helps that ETFs have proven their value above and beyond their commonly minimal expense ratios.

The convenience factor is not lost on Tom Dorsey, founder of Dorsey Wright, whose indices are used in many ETFs. He likes to quote Harvard Professor Theodore Levitt, who said, "People don't want to buy a quarter-inch drill, they want to buy a quarter-inch hole!"

> *"We have been hiding in the open for 28 years. Every day we tell our clients exactly what we do. But people want the hole, not the drill."*
>
> Tom Dorsey, Dorsey Wright

Notes

1. Burton, Jonathan, "Why Is Vanguard Secretive on Stock ETFs?" *Wall Street Journal,* March 8, 2015; www.wsj.com/articles/why-vanguard-is-secretive-about-its-stock-etfs-1425870188.
2. O'Donnell, Carl, "Apple Supplier GT Advanced Technologies' Stock Dives 90% after Bankruptcy Filing." *Forbes,* October 6, 2014; www.forbes.com/sites/carlodonnell/2014/10/06/apple-supplier-gt-advanced-technologies-stock-dives-90-after-bankruptcy-filing/.
3. Sam Ro, "Warren Buffett Has Some Incredibly Specific Advice for Where the Average Investor Should Invest." *Business Insider,* March 2014; www.businessinsider.com/warren-buffett-recommends-sp-500-index-2014-3.

CHAPTER 2

ETF Growth

When you put that many benefits into one investment vehicle chances are you are going to get some users. But exchange-traded funds (ETFs) have far surpassed what most people had expected for them. Many thought they would remain a niche product, like closed-end funds, used by a small audience of traders. But, instead, they have been commercialized and are used by all types of investors around the world today

These investors use ETFs for all kinds of purposes. And that has led to ETFs taking assets away from mutual funds, single securities, futures, swaps, and separately managed accounts (SMAs).

Asset Growth

U.S. ETF assets are now at $2.1 trillion in the United States and $3 trillion globally as of this writing The asset compound annual growth rate of ETFs over the past 15 years is just over 25 percent.[1] And while it took U.S. ETFs 18 years to get to $1 trillion in assets, it took only four years to get to $2 trillion.

While they pale in comparison to the $15.9 trillion of assets in U.S. mutual funds, they are growing faster than just about anything in the financial world. In fact, to compare ETFs' year-over-year asset growth, you really have to look at another popular technology.

The chart in Figure 2.1 is courtesy of my friend and fellow ETF analyst Sebastian Mercado of Deutsche Bank. It shows the growth in worldwide Internet users and U.S. ETF assets, which have a 97 percent correlation!

FIGURE 2.1 Twenty-First-Century Disruptive Forces: The Internet and ETFs

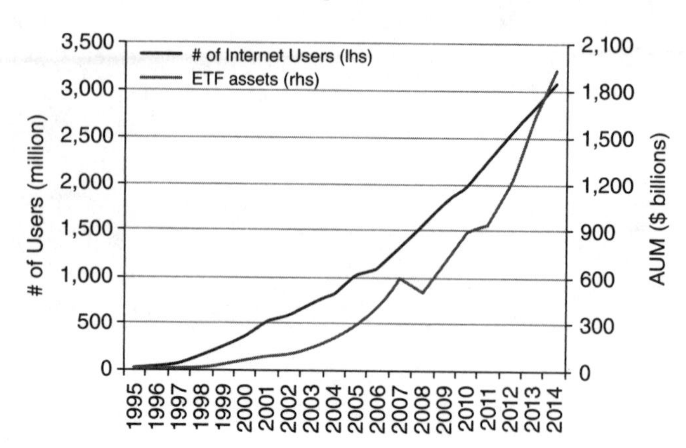

Sources: Deutsche Bank, Bloomberg Finance LP, International Communications Union

Do I think ETFs are as big or important as the Internet? Not quite. But a case could be made that ETFs are doing to the investment world what digital music did to the music world.

As the digitization of music challenged the business model for music, ETFs are bringing change to the entire financial system. Whether we are talking about a big buy-side fund manager or a sell-side bank, they are all looking at charts like Mercado's and trying to figure out a way to work this new technology into their business.

A case in point is the fact that there are now over 60 ETF issuers in the United States alone. Just five years ago, there were half as many. And some of these newbies include powerhouses like Goldman Sachs, JPMorgan, and Fidelity, not to mention other powerhouses looking to come in, such as Prudential, Nuveen, and American Funds. This could lead to large chunks of new assets.

"You have to talk about the number of ETF sponsors about to enter the marketplace. That's 50 new asset managers looking to launch ETFs, and what will they bring in terms of their internal assets? Look at Prudential, for example; they have $1 trillion under management. They are about to come into the ETF space. But what they are going to do, nobody knows."

Reggie Browne, Cantor Fitzgerald

In 2014 and 2015, ETFs took in a total of nearly $500 billion. They led all investment vehicles in flows, followed by index funds, which took in about $300 billion, and then hedge funds, which took in about $150 billion.[2]

Meanwhile, actively managed mutual funds lost about $200 billion, according to the Investment Company Institute.

ETFs are part of a broader trend toward passive investments. While institutions for the most part still believe in active management, for retail investors and advisors, index investing is sweeping the nation. And why not—this money moving into low-cost passive vehicles is like a huge transfer of wealth from Wall Street back to investors. I estimate that Vanguard alone saves investors about $15 billion each year in fees and another few billion in turnover costs. If Wall Street is big oil, the index fund is the electric car.

The move into index funds helped lift ETF assets along with it. After all, the ETF is an index fund at heart.

"Largely speaking, ETFs are just another way to get indexing. They are overwhelmingly 40 Act funds. They are predicated upon a philosophy based on indexing. Ninety-four percent of the DNA is the same as a conventional index fund, yet they look like a shiny new toy."

Jim Rowley, Vanguard

What makes all the ETF growth especially impressive is that ETFs do not offer brokers any commissions, loads, or kickbacks. This is why people say they are bought and not sold. The lack of commissions means fewer middlemen getting paid. This is why ETFs haven't grown even faster.

"ETFs are really disintermediating the financial industry."

Daniel Gamba, Blackrock

This is why I say that ETFs got their $2.1 trillion in assets the hard way. All the money that goes into ETFs is after tax and picky. No one is getting paid to sell them, and they aren't in 401(k) plans. It is purely a grassroots movement, where constituents are telling their advisors and institutions they want them. And I have even heard of some institutions telling their consultants they want them.

ETF Assets in Perspective

However, despite all this growth, ETFs really don't have that much in assets, relatively speaking. As mentioned earlier, mutual funds have about $16 trillion, separately managed accounts (SMAs) have $3.4 trillion,[3] and hedge funds have $3 trillion.[4] Hell, U.S. ETFs have fewer assets than Vanguard alone.

TABLE 2.1 ETFs' Percentage Ownership of the Asset Classes They Track

Asset Class	Total Market Cap	ETF Assets	% ETF Ownership
U.S. Equities	$25 trillion	$1.2 trillion	4.80%
U.S. Bonds	$39 trillion	$350 billion	0.89%
Gold	$7.5 trillion	$35 billion	0.47%

Sources: Bloomberg, World Gold Council, SIFMA

So while their growth and their growth potential are huge, assets today aren't as big as people think. This is why ETFs are not quite the tail wagging the dog when it comes to increasing correlations to the stocks and bonds or gold they hold. While there has been a slight uptick in correlations in certain scenarios for a few of the smaller sector ETFs holding some very illiquid stocks,[5] for the most part ETFs do not own that much of their underlying holdings to have any real impact, as shown in Table 2.1. Consider fixed income, for example, a market that is worth $39 trillion. Fixed-income ETFs have $350 billion in assets making them less than 1 percent owners of U.S. bonds.

So while these products are growing in both assets and numbers, they really only make up a small fraction of the actual markets they operate in.

Trading Growth

While ETFs may *own* less than people think, they *trade* more than people think. Some of the statistics here can be astonishing. ETFs trade about $70 billion worth of shares each day, which translates to $18.2 trillion a year. That's more than the U.S. gross domestic product (GDP), which is $17.4 trillion—although, sadly, less than our $18.5 trillion in debt.

That $70 billion/day accounts for 25 to 30 percent of the dollar volume of all equities trading in the United States, as seen in Figure 2.2, according to the New York Stock Exchange.

If those numbers don't impress you, it may help to look at specific examples. Many ETFs trade as just as much—or more—as some popular blue-chip stocks that everyone knows and loves. Table 2.2 shows a matrix of a mix of ETFs and a stock that trades about the same amount each day.

The incredible volume on the U.S. exchanges is why many exchanges across the world have rushed to get on the ETF bandwagon. ETFs are now

FIGURE 2.2 ETFs vs Stocks Percent Volume on Exchange

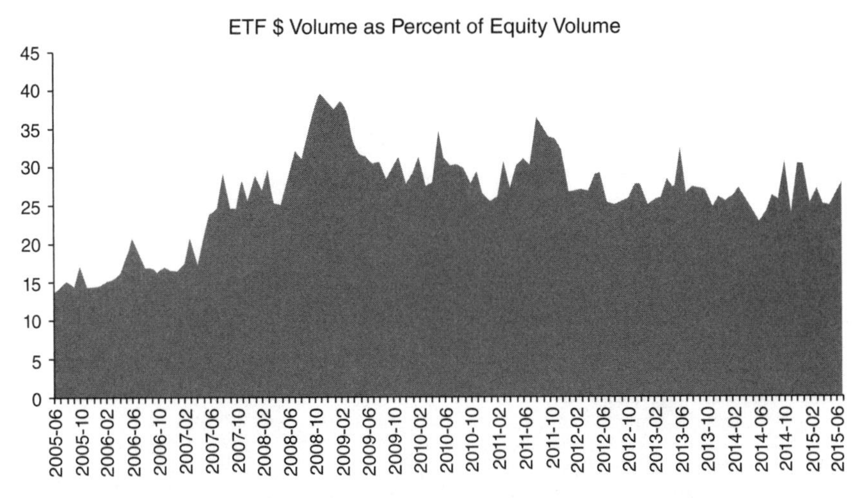

Source: New York Stock Exchange

traded on over 60 exchanges worldwide. Some of the most recent exchanges to add homegrown ETF listings include Iceland, Ghana, and Iran.

But at the end of the day, nothing compares to the liquidity in the United States. While U.S. ETFs make up 26 percent of the number of products in the world and 70 percent of the assets, they are responsible for 86 percent of the world's reported ETF exchange dollar volume, as shown in Figure 2.3.

TABLE 2.2 ETFs' Dollar Volume and the Stock Equivalent

ETF	Avg $ Vol/Day	Stock Equivalent
SPDR S&P 500 ETF (SPY)	$22 billion	Apple, Inc.
iShares MSCI Emerging Markets ETF (EEM)	$2 billion	Microsoft
iShares China Large Cap ETF (FXI)	$1 billion	Citigroup
Energy Select Sector SPDR (XLE)	$850 million	Google
VelocityShares Inverse Short-Term VIX (XIV)	$600 million	Disney
SPDR Gold Shares (GLD)	$600 million	Merck
Market Vectors Gold Miners ETF (GDX)	$500 million	Wal-Mart
Direxion Daily Small Cap Bull 3x Shares (TNA)	$400 million	eBay
United States Oil Fund (USO)	$350 million	Starbucks
SPDR High Yield Bond ETF (JNK)	$340 million	Hewlett-Packard

Source: Bloomberg

FIGURE 2.3 Breakdown of Dollar Volume of ETFs by Country

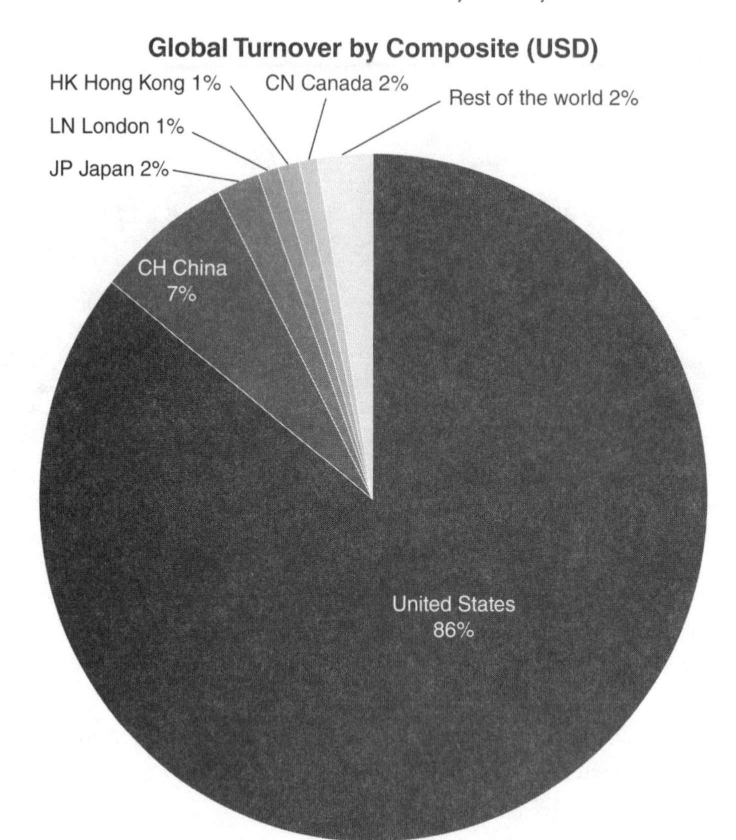

Sources: Bloomberg, New York Stock Exchange

The disproportion of volume in the United States isn't just because U.S. investors are out of their minds when it comes to trading. Well, maybe there's a little truth to that. But a chunk of that 86 percent is actually foreign institutions. Blackrock said that roughly 20 percent of their ETF ownership is non-U.S. investors. So it is not a stretch to assume that a decent amount of U.S. trading volume is actually foreign investors.

Nowhere is this more pronounced than in Latin America, where pension funds own approximately $50 billion of U.S. ETFs while locally domiciled Latin American ETFs have only a couple of billion in assets. But why would a foreign institution invest in U.S. ETFs when there are local ETFs in their home countries they could use? One word: *liquidity.*

"All these institutions care about is liquidity."

Daniel Gamba, Blackrock

At the end of the day, whether it is a Middle East sovereign wealth fund or a Japan pension, large institutions are just drawn to the most liquid products. Trading volume is such a big deal to institutions, and it is a theme we will hit on many times in this book.

Of course, all this trading and subsequent liquidity has a dark side and speaks to John Bogle's famous quote that "an ETF is like handing an arsonist a match."[6] Let's take one minute to explore the ongoing debate between the father of the index fund versus ETF advocates.

"Trading has always been a big part of our market, but not always this much. When I came into the business, the turnover on the Big Board was 25 percent a year. Even before the ETF started, it was probably up to 150 percent. It is now 250 percent. The average turnover for an ETF is 400 percent a year. And SPDR is 3,000 percent. And here you are talking to a guy who thinks 3 percent turnover is pushing the envelope."

John Bogle, Vanguard

Forgetting the irony for a second that Vanguard is the second-largest ETF company in the world, Bogle has a point. Using the weighted-average bid-ask spread of 0.05 percent, which is the market maker's cut, ETFs bring in an estimated $9 billion in revenue for those firms. This is actually more than the estimated $6 billion that ETF issuers make each year based on an average weighted expense ratio of 0.30 percent. This is where index mutual funds may be a bigger threat to Wall Street than ETFs since they aren't traded.

But as to whether ETFs are to blame for an increase in trading, that's a bit of a chicken-or-the-egg debate. But certainly there is no debating that people who like trading probably love ETFs and are contributing heavily to the volume.

"I think the temptation to trade—whether there are ETFs in the world or not—is going to be there. There are people that are always going to want to twiddle the knobs. It doesn't really matter if you provide the product, they will find it. They will find currencies. They'll find futures. They'll find a sports book. I don't think (ETFs) are going to force a certain type of behavior on people. I think the people that are traditionally passive will remain passive and the people that are traditionally more aggressive will act in a more aggressive way."

Josh Brown, Ritholtz Wealth Management

But some argue that it doesn't matter that the ETFs trade a lot. Those who are trading do no harm to the people who don't. Many buy-and-hold investors are sitting tight in the ETF happy as a clam while the trading crowd is creating the majority of the turnover. Hedge funds may buy and sell the SPDR S&P 500 Trust (SPY) within 10 minutes, but that does nothing to affect my Aunt Joyce's 10-year investment in the fund.

"The structure was meant to take the cost of trading out of the fund. And that's the thing that, with all due respect to Jack Bogle, he's never gotten."

James Ross, State Street Global Advisors

Despite the hyper-trading activity, you can always just buy and hold an ETF. You don't have to sell it. Maybe ETFs are matches, but not everyone is an arsonist. I guess this is a bit like the "guns don't kill people, people kill people" mantra, but it is a good point. And judging from some of the holding periods of ETFs there are plenty of investors—even institutions—who are able to use ETFs for long-term investing.

Finally, all that trading—perhaps ironically—is *good* for long-term buy-and-hold investors because it lowers round-trip costs by bringing down spreads. So I suppose like many other things in life, it is at once a devil and an angel.

Product Growth

I can't think of a better word than *explosion* when it comes to the number of new ETFs that have come out in the past five years. As shown in Figure 2.4, there have been over 1,000 ETFs launched this decade so far (since 12/31/2009) during a span of about 1,400 business days. In other words, a new ETF comes out nearly every day! And that's just in the United States.

This explosion of growth and products has made it harder for new ETFs to be successful. And the bar for what is a success has been lowered.

"Back in the day when we launched the first products, anything that didn't trade 30,000 shares was a massive disaster. These days, if you launch and trade 8,000 shares, that's really good."

Bruno del Ama, Global X

FIGURE 2.4 New ETF Launches by Year, as of June 30, 2015

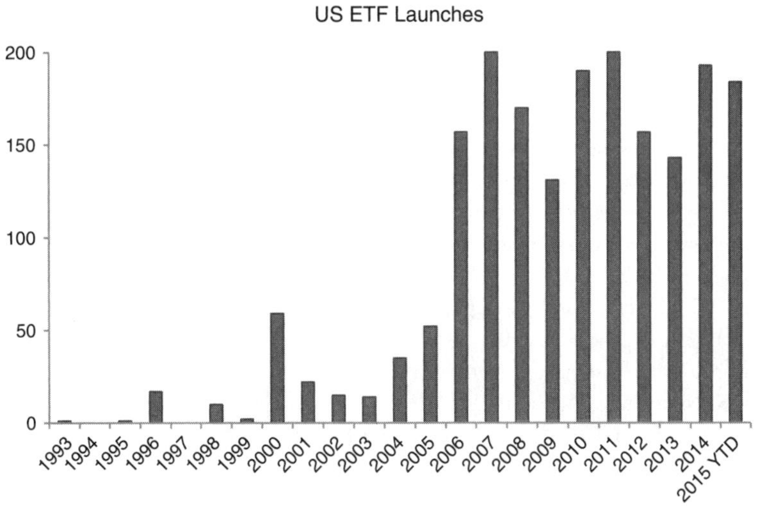

US ETF Launches

Source: Bloomberg

To put all this product proliferation in perspective consider that there have been more new launches this decade so far than the last two decades combined. Moreover, there are over 1,200 ETFs currently in registration with the SEC, according to ETF.com. Let that sink in for a minute.

Bogle can't fathom how there are 1,400 indexes tracked by some 1,800 ETFs. When I interviewed him for this book, he showed me a table of hundreds of ETFs and was mystified at the sheer number of ETFs. *"What's going on here? It doesn't make any sense."*

What makes all this product proliferation that much more noteworthy is that many of the new products coming out are getting more and more complex. Nearly half of the new launches in 2014 were something other than a plain vanilla market cap–weighted equity ETF.

I don't think anyone would argue that product proliferation is far outpacing the education needed to use these products. I spend a lot of my time educating clients and colleagues on ETFs and how to do due diligence on them. This is also a big reason why I'm writing this book.

Now that we've seen the ETF phenomenon in all its modern-day glory, in the next chapter we will go back in time and look at how the first ETF was designed in order to deconstruct how these things tick.

Notes

1. Mercado, Sebastian, "Deutsche Bank: Special ETF Research—A Stock Picker's Guide to ETFs," June 5, 2015.
2. Press Release, "Hedge Funds Conclude 2014 with Inflows as Investors Position for Volatility." Hedge Fund Research (HFR), January 20, 2015; www.hedgefundresearch.com/pdf/pr_20150120.pdf.
3. Press Release, "Managed Solutions Assets Rise 26% in 2013 to $3.4 Trillion." Money Management Institute, March 10, 2014; www.mminst.org/press-room/press-releases/managed-solutions-assets-rise-26-2013-34-trillion.
4. Press Release, "Capital Inflows Drive Hedge Fund Assets towards Milestone in 2Q." Hedge Fund Research (HFR), July 20, 2015; www.hedgefundresearch.com/?fuse=products-irglo.
5. Boroujerdi, Robert, and Katherine Fogertey, "ETFs: The Rise of the Machines." Goldman Sachs, April 10, 2015.
6. Ferri, Rick, "ETFs May Be Bogle's Best Friend." *Forbes*, September 30, 2013.

CHAPTER 3

ETF Mechanics

In the 1980s classic movie *Back to the Future*, an old scientist named "Doc" builds a time machine out of a DeLorean. The key to the automobile-turned-time machine is something called the flux capacitor. It's "what makes time travel possible," he says. Exchange-traded funds (ETFs) have their own flux capacitor, and it is called the creation/redemption process—a biblical-sounding name that is at the heart of why ETFs work so well for many different kinds of investors and in all kinds of market environments.

While it is not totally necessary for an investor to understand the creation/redemption process in order to use the products successfully, it will help you feel more confidence and trust in these products if you know how they tick.

Learning ETF "mechanics" can also help investors understand why ETFs have lasted this long through a variety of market events. It will also explain how hedge funds and pensions and retail investors can all play in the same ETF sandbox without causing a problem for each other.

In terms of presenting this information, I have found in the classes I teach on ETFs at Bloomberg, whenever I tell the story of the invention of the ETF, I'm told that it makes understanding ETF mechanics much easier. So we are going to do it here.

To write this chapter, I went on a bit of a pilgrimage to meet and interview as many people as I could who were there in the early days. I wanted to fill in any gaps in my own knowledge and include their voices as well, since they were there and I wasn't. It was a great experience and I'm very grateful to those people who spoke with me.

So here is the abridged version of the story of how the first ETF, the SPDR S&P 500 Trust (SPY), came into existence and eventually became the most traded security in the world three times over.

The Story of the ETF

Let me take you back to early 1988. Magic Johnson and the Lakers were dominating basketball, George Michael's *Faith* was the number one song, and Michael Dukakis was on the verge of winning the Democratic presidential primary.

Oh, and the stock market had just crashed a few months earlier. On October 19, 1987 (Black Monday), the Dow lost 508 points, or 22 percent.

Meanwhile, a man named Nathan (Nate) Most was working as senior vice president for new product development at the American Stock Exchange (AMEX). The AMEX was struggling. It had slipped to third place in equity trading among exchanges after the New York Stock Exchange (NYSE) and Nasdaq and was having difficulties attracting business.[1]

Most and his young colleague Steven Bloom, a PhD in economics brought in from Harvard, were trying to increase the exchange's business by attracting more trading from the institutional community, which it had very little connection with anymore. In fact, the AMEX had been the exchange of choice for just a handful of the companies in the S&P 500.

"We were not really first in anything. So we thought, if we can't list Volkswagens anymore, why don't we create our own Ferraris?"

Dr. Steven Bloom, Eisenhower School, National Defense University

---

The AMEX's voracious desire to increase trading business collided with the release of a post-mortem paper by the SEC on what went wrong in the 1987 crash. The thick and detailed report was called "The October 1987 Market Break" and was circulated in February 1988.[2]

Buried in the phone book-sized report, the SEC put forward the idea that if there had been a market basket instrument that traded like a share of stock on the day of the crash, it is quite possible that the market would not have unwound to the extent that it did. The logic goes that if there had been a layer of liquidity in something like a market basket, it could have helped to alleviate the individual volatility that was being caused by the computerized selling required by portfolio insurance hedges. This put all the selling pressure on the stocks themselves.

This SEC was wanted something to help buffer the stock market in New York from the futures market in Chicago. Their idea for how this would work was sketched out in Chapter 3 on page 18 in the report, as shown in Figure 3.1.

FIGURE 3.1 SEC Lays out Idea for Market Basket Instrument in a 1988 Paper

We suggest that an alternative approach be examined. Presently, program trades must be broken up and distributed around the stock floor with the resulting substantial transaction costs and effects discussed above. The creation, however, of one or more posts where the actual market baskets could be traded might alter the dynamics of program trading. The availability of basket trading on the NYSE would, in effect, restore program trades to more traditional block trading techniques. The basket specialists would be able to identify the nature of each trade and we are hopeful that this would encourage block positioners to again become active in providing capital to position the program blocks. While arbitrage would continue to flow directly to the individual stocks to maintain their pricing efficiency, other institutional trades could be focused on the basket posts where the specialist and trading crowd could provide an additional layer of liquidity to the system and cushion somewhat the individual stocks from the intra-day volatility caused by program activity. 48/

The feasibility and design of basket trading would require substantial analysis. To be useful, it would require an extremely well-capitalized specialist, perhaps affiliated with a major block positioning firm, and perhaps additional supplementary market makers. While the product would require physical settlement of the basket, this would not appear to impose greater burdens than exist in settling program trades today. A requirement that any participant have the capability to settle the trade through automated book-entry delivery of the securities, however, may be appropriate. In addition, the design and need for more than one basket raises difficult questions. There are already a number of futures and options now trading based on a wide variety of indexes. Moreover, many educational institutions are prohibited from purchasing certain stocks that logically might be included in any basket because of social and political policies. While these issues are substantial, we believe the concept of basket trading warrants consideration. 49/

Source: Securities and Exchange Commission

Even though it is rough, it does provide a pretty complete vision, specifically calling for well-capitalized specialists and supplementary market makers who would trade baskets of stocks that required physical delivery. This little paragraph tucked away in a thick government agency report written by lawyers was the inception moment for what would eventually become the multi-trillion-dollar ETF industry.

So yeah, basically the U.S. government had a hand in inventing the ETF.

"When the staff and the Commission had analyzed what had happened, the theory presented was that it would be possible to create baskets of key stocks available for sale. Those baskets would then be able to be sold without causing the whole market to collapse. That particular premise was in the report, but was there only as a suggestion."

David S. Ruder, SEC Chairman, 1987–1989

In addition to the design sketch, the SEC also said that such a product would get fast approval. This really got the AMEX's attention. They began work immediately.

"We read that report and saw the SEC would give expedited approval to a market basket instrument. That's what caused us to start to think of every way possible to create this. We were essentially reverse engineering what the SEC called for in their report."

Dr. Steven Bloom, Eisenhower School, National Defense University

Nate Most was in his late 70s at this point and had a rich background of experience to draw upon at that time. He had studied physics at UCLA, worked as an engineer in World War II, and was executive vice president of Pacific Vegetable Oil and president of the Pacific Commodities Exchange before arriving at the AMEX in 1977.[3]

"Nate was an incredibly practical person. He thought we need to increase tape revenue, so we need a trading vehicle. So what is it that people like to buy that isn't currently traded?"

Kathleen Moriarty, Kaye Scholer LLP

Most and Bloom's first idea was a basic one: to see if index funds—as they existed—could be traded.

Most took this idea of trading mutual funds to John Bogle of Vanguard in what is now a legendary meeting. After all, these two guys are the Edison and Franklin of investment vehicles, and together their two designs account for the majority of all new inflows nowadays.

"Nate Most walked into my office when I was running this place. Nicest guy. He came in and said he wanted us to partner. He wanted to use our S&P 500 Index fund for his [ETF]. First, I said his idea had three flaws. Here they are. But second, even if you fix them, I'm just not interested. The idea of trading all day long in real time is just anathema to me. So we left friends, and by the time he got off the train in New York, he fixed the three errors and then goes up to State Street and sells it. Guess how much regret I have about that decision, and guess how many people I talked to before making it? Zero and zero."

John Bogle, Vanguard

Bogle didn't recall the exact flaws when I met with him but he definitely recalled the main reason for his rejection. He didn't like the idea of investors coming in and out of his fund because it would substantially increase operating costs. This feedback/rejection from Bogle was used constructively by

Most. He told MarketWatch that the meeting with Bogle got him "thinking about a product where you don't go in and out of the fund."[4]

Most and Bloom needed *something else* involved so that a fund could be traded all day without actually driving up costs in the fund. Something that would keep the "exchange trading" and the fund's operation separate.

They found inspiration from Most's time working with warehouse receipts as a commodities trader and president of Pacific Commodities Exchange. Many commodities, such as grains, cotton, coffee, or palm oil, can be stored in warehouses, which issue receipts, which can then be traded among people or used to finance. That is where Most's imagination came into play.

"You store a commodity and you get a warehouse receipt. You can sell it, do a lot of things with it. Because you don't want to be moving merchandise back and forth all the time, so you keep it in place and you simply transfer the warehouse receipt."[5]

Nate Most

Most and Bloom wondered why that couldn't be applied to a basket of equities. Instead of palm oil, you could have a basket of stocks handed in to a custodian (the warehouse) in return for ETF shares (the receipts) that could then be broken up and sold on the exchange. On the flip side, you can also buy up enough ETF shares on the exchange and hand them in for the basket of stocks back. This "in-kind" trade would allow for the creating and redeeming of shares while not affecting shareholders in the fund. People could trade their receipts till the cows come home while not disturbing the securities in the warehouse.

That right there is the creation redemption process in a nutshell. That is the flux capacitor.

This idea of commodities-warehouse receipts being applied to the SEC's basket trading idea is how the ETF was born. It is what makes an ETF more than a "fund that trades" and more than a typical derivative product. It would serve the expedient needs that a futures contract serves but do it with the safety of a mutual fund. This creation/redemption process is what many other residual benefits of the ETF spring from that we will learn throughout the book.

"The in-kind creation/redemption process was to deal with Bogle's concerns and to deal with the transactional drag."

Kathleen Moriarty, Kaye Scholer LLP

The Creation/Redemption Process

Most and Bloom needed a warehouse to put the securities in, so they ultimately teamed up with State Street as a trustee and custody agent. Someone had to take the creation and redemption orders. And the securities would be the S&P 500, an index chosen because it was the most widely followed index by institutional investors. It would be set up as a Unit Investment Trust (UIT) under the Investment Company Act of 1940. UITs did not require a board of directors or a portfolio manager.

> *"The reason we made the first ETF a UIT was because Nate said, 'Why should we pay for a board of directors and four meetings a year? We're not managing this. It's an index fund. All we need to do is follow the S&P.'"*
>
> Kathleen Moriarty, Kaye Scholer LLP

That made sense then, but after a few years, the norm became to launch ETFs as open-end management companies—also under the 1940 Act—instead of UITs. The reason for the shift away from the UIT structure was because open-end investment companies can be managed. Not actively managed per se, but you can do more things in an open-end investment company such as engage in securities lending and use derivatives.

The SEC took its sweet time to approve it—four years to be exact. The long delay was due to the SEC's regulatory process for this new and unusual product. The fact that it was registered under the 1940 Act meant the heaviest scrutiny. While the ETF was born out of the 1987 stock market crash, the 1940 Act was born out of the 1929 stock market crash as a way regulate investment companies that offer their securities to the public. As we discussed earlier, the 1940 Act means the SEC is signing off on it.

> *"Getting through the SEC is why it took us five years to bring the product out. The product was actually developed within a year. We had (the ETF) developed by early 1989. It took us four years just working on the legal."*
>
> Dr. Steven Bloom, Eisenhower School, National Defense University

The thing is ETFs were a whole new animal. They weren't just a tiny variation on a mutual fund. The exchange-trading aspect of ETFs combined with the creation/redemption process really required an entirely new ecosystem—one that would depend on Wall Street banks.

"In order to create all 500 stocks you'd have a portfolio basket that was worth about $1 million. The average person was never going to come in and out for a million. So we need to deal with companies who were dealing with DTC or NSCC, so people who were broker-dealers. It had to be someone hooked up to the system."

Kathleen Moriarity, Kaye Scholer LLP

This "someone hooked up to the system" is the authorized participant (AP). APs are the "well-capitalized market specialists" the SEC called for. They are large self-clearing broker/dealers designated by the ETF issuer to do creations and redemptions and interact with the ETF issuer in what is called the "primary market."

Each ETF has a list of designated APs that are allowed to do creations and redemptions such as Citibank, Credit Suisse, Goldman Sachs, and Merrill Lynch. This is why it doesn't matter who is invested in the ETF. It could be a hedge fund or my Aunt Joyce—all of the actual shares being created and destroyed are done by the AP.

While APs serve a crucial role in the ETF ecosystem, their role is really more of a back office function. The real action is with the market makers who deal with actual investors and the APs. This was all part of the SEC's idea, which called for "additional supplementary market makers" to help with liquidity. Figure 3.2 shows this ETF ecosystem in a diagram form.

A market maker is a broker-dealer firm that stands between buyers and sellers in order to ease the process of trading the security in the secondary

FIGURE 3.2 The Crucial Role of the ETF Ecosystem

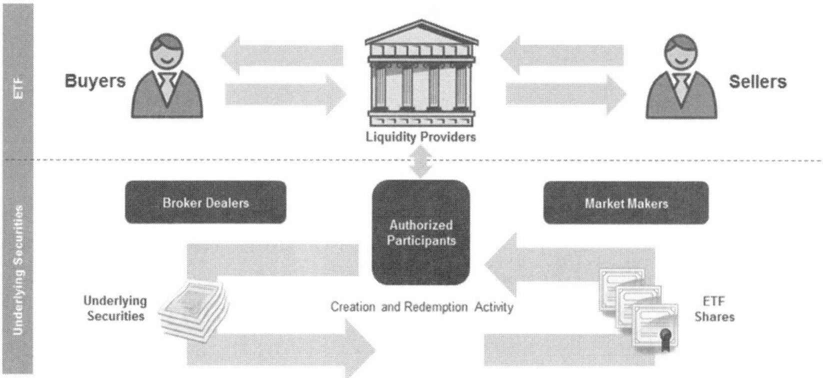

Source: Blackrock

markets. They are motivated by the tiny bit of money they make on each trade. A market maker will take on a trade no matter what side you are on. They make money from the bid-ask spread, or the difference between what you can buy and sell an ETF for. In short, they are the oil running through the ETF engine. Some of the largest market makers include KCG, Cantor Fitzgerald, and Jane Street.

Many ETFs will designate a lead market maker (LMM) for each of their ETFs. These are firms that have signed up to guarantee quotes for that particular ETF in exchange for incentives from the exchange. This is especially useful for smaller, newer ETFs and/or ones that are extra complicated.

Both APs and market makers will arbitrage the price of the ETF and its underlying basket—a natural process that keeps the price of the ETF close to its net asset value. We will analyze this more in Chapter 5.

This whole system is why ETFs are not a "derivative" despite the occasional label in the media. Not that derivatives are necessarily a bad thing either. The most important difference is that the ETF is fully asset backed with zero counterparty risk—the opposite of most derivatives. Even if the ETF issuer goes out of business, the investors still have ownership of their assets sitting in the custodian. Having that element of safety in the design was a key component to the design and definitely worth the long wait with the SEC.

"The concept behind this was to have something that would trade like a fully funded futures contract on an exchange and would have assets behind it so that in times of stress there was something there. The view from Nate Most's standpoint was that portfolio insurance was something that failed in the crash of '87."

James Ross, State Street Global Advisors

AMEX Wasn't Alone

Now, just as Steve Jobs and Steve Wozniak weren't the only guys working on a personal computer in the late 1970s, Most and his crew weren't the only people thinking about trading baskets of stocks.

In fact, Canada was actually out with the first ETF technically—called Toronto Index Participation Shares (TIPS). It came out in 1990—before AMEX's product. TIPS tracked the Toronto Stock Exchange 35 Index.

Nate Most and Steve Bloom showed the Toronto team—in the name of exchange relations—what they had built while they were waiting for regulatory approval, according to Bloom. The folks who helped launch TIPS say they were influenced by more than just SPY, but TIPS did have the same design as SPY. Toronto didn't have the same regulatory molasses that the U.S. team was stuck in. Getting through regulation was really fast for them, according to Peter Haynes, who worked at the Toronto Stock Exchange at the time.

"The idea was hatched in the U.S., but was launched in Canada first. I don't think we should feel bad that we were able to get it through regulatory approval and bring it to market first."

Peter Haynes, TD Securities

Thus, technically they had the first ETF out. This is why they are recognized for it by some inside the ETF industry. But to the broader world, SPY gets all the glory. There are a few understandable reasons for this. First, TIPS didn't even come close to achieving the stratospheric success of SPY. Second, TIPS also had a very unusual "modified basket-weighting" index that wasn't as widely appreciated as market-cap weighting.

Perhaps even more important, though, is that TIPS doesn't exist today. Back in 1999, it was folded into the iShares S&P/TSX 60 Index (XIU CN) and turned into a market cap–weighted index. History might have been more acknowledging if TIPS actually still existed today in the same form in which it launched, but it doesn't and is now relegated to a footnote in history.

In and around the time between 1988 and 1992, there was something in the air, with many variations of index-trackers listing on different U.S. exchanges as well. The Philadelphia Stock Exchange led it all off with their Cash Index Participation contracts (CIPs), the AMEX had Equity Index Participations (EIPs), the Chicago Board Options Exchange (CBOE) had Value of Index Participations (VIPs), and the NYSE had Exchange Stock Portfolios (ESPs).

It would be an extra five pages to go through all of their tales, but suffice it to say all of these failed to gain traction for different reasons, be it legal problems, design weaknesses, or simply not exciting investors. In the end, none of them had the structural brilliance, durability, residual advantages, and public acceptance of Most's design. Joseph Rizzello, who worked on CIPs at the Philadelphia Stock Exchange during this time says that AMEX should not be given all the credit, but acknowledges that Most and his team ended up with the best design.

"There is no question that we had the right idea, but the better design came later."

Joseph Rizzello, NewSquare Capital

Finally Ready for Launch

After years of painstaking regulatory issues, this unique new product was finally approved by the SEC and ready for launch in January 1993—a full four years after the idea was formed. The entire culture had changed since they started working on it. Bill Clinton was president, Michael Jordan was winning championships, and Nirvana had taken over the music world.

After a few iterations, they would settle on naming it the Standard & Poor's Depositary Receipts (SPDRs) and it would have the ticker "SPY."

SPY launched on January 22, 1993, with an expense ratio of 0.20 percent—more than double the 0.095 percent it costs today. This was done to match the expense ratio of the Vanguard S&P 500 Index Trust, which had billions in assets at that point. If they were going to appeal to institutional investors, they couldn't be any more expensive than what was otherwise available to them. In some ways, SPY matching Vanguard kicked off a fee war that is still going on today.

There was a lot of fanfare for the launch of SPY, a nine-foot inflatable spider dangling from the ceiling of the AMEX circa a Halloween dance. They were originally going to go even further and try and hire Spiderman to walk down the side of the building. But that idea died along the way, unfortunately. They did also have hats galore—a very popular item on a trading floor.

SPY traded over 1 million shares the first day of trading. Everyone was happy about the initial success of their labor of love; however, a decent chunk of the trading that first day was market makers and specialists trading it back and forth creating volume, according to Ross, who took the call for the first-ever creation.

Then after the novelty—and the specialists trading—was gone, it started to trade less and less … and less. SPY's trading trickled down to the point where it traded 28,000 shares on June 1, 1993, as shown in Figure 3.3. To put that into perspective, even obscure ETFs such as the First Trust Global Wind Energy Fund (FAN) average more volume than that.

"Nobody knew what to do with it."

Kathleen Moriarty, Kaye Scholer LLP

FIGURE 3.3 SPY's Daily Volume January–June 1993

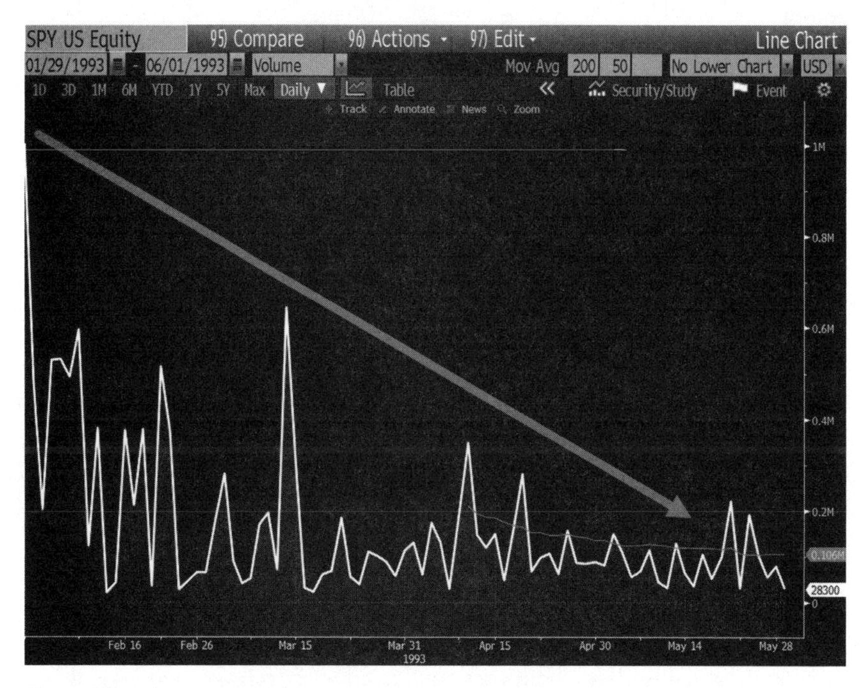

Source: Bloomberg

One of the biggest hurdles was that nobody was compensated to sell it. To this day, the lack of kickbacks offered by the ETF to brokers is at once a tailwind and a headwind to their growth. Cost-conscious investors love the fact that it doesn't take their money to pay a broker to sell it to them. Not surprisingly, brokers hated it for the same reason.

SPY did eventually catch on the way other successful products eventually catch on: pounding the pavement with guerrilla marketing by people who truly believed in its potential. One such guy was Gary Eisenreich, who worked as a specialist at Spear, Leeds & Kellogg. Gary was the first big market maker in SPY.

"I'm a horrible salesman. I really am. But I'm very good when it comes to a cause. And I looked at SPDRs as a thing I could sell my grandmother. I didn't mind doing it. I believed in the product. There were total naysayers. I had friends on the train who would say, 'Gary what are you doing? You are wasting your time.' I would say, 'No, I think this is a product that works for everyone.'"

Gary Eisenreich, Fairfield Advisors

One early bright spot came when Daiwa Securities Group had put $90 million into the trust increasing assets by 50 percent to $278 million.[6] This showed that the ETF could handle big orders. But still, SPY managed to get to only $461 million by the end of year one and then it lost assets in year two to finish 1994 with $419 million. Many people thought it would just sort of live as a $400 million fund forever. If this happened, it is likely that the ETF industry as we know it would not be.

Another early bright spot was via super-wealthy investor who liked that you could buy options on the ETF as a way to insure the position.

"A wealthy, wealthy Seattle investor's broker would come in and buy puts and then he would buy SPDRs at 100,000 shares at a clip. He would buy SPDRs so he had the upside and then for only two percent he could protect with puts. So probably one of those early spikes in volume is from this."

Gary Eisenreich, Fairfield Advisors

Institutions in particular found it useful as a way to equitize cash and as a way to get cheap, liquid exposure to the market in a vehicle that you didn't have to roll like a futures contracts. And unlike a separately managed account, you could get in and out whenever you pleased with freedom and expediency. Plus, you could lend the ETF out to pick up some extra return. This appealed to the "maverick" institutions at the time, such as California's largest pension funds, insurance companies, and asset managers, all of whom showed up in early 13-F filings for SPY.[7]

There was also the residual benefit of ETFs being tax efficient. Since the creation and redemption involves exchanging a basket of securities for shares of the ETF and vice versa. No money is actually exchanging hands. When no money is exchanging hands, there is no taxable event. The ETF portfolio manager is able to use the creation and redemption baskets they post each day as a way to wash out any built-up capital gains that would otherwise be distributed to shareholders.

According to Moriarty, the tax efficiency wasn't realized right away. It was just a happy accident that benefited anyone investing using a taxable account.

> We had been told by the tax [lawyers working on the project] that an unintended, but wonderful, consequence of the in-kind [creation] process was tax benefits. That was not part of the plan. That happened as a wonderful side effect.

You may be wondering why the IRS wouldn't change this and make the creation redemption process taxable. According to Moriarty, they couldn't because they had a section in the tax code that specifically stated it wasn't taxable. They would have to change the tax code.

As institutions began to discover many of the ETF's benefits, they started using it again and again and again. By the end of year two, it had $500 million in assets. Aided by the mid-'90s bull market, it started doubling in assets every year as shown in Figure 3.4. The rest, as they say, is history.

Today, SPY is the most traded security in the world by far. It trades on average $25 billion worth of shares each day, or $6 trillion a year. That's three times as much as Apple, the second-most-traded security in the world. Moreover, SPY trades more than the top 10 most-traded stocks *combined.* It also accounts for a large portion of the equity options market with open interest equaling about $400 billion.

SPY is also the largest ETF, with $175 billion in assets. It is used by everyone from hedge funds to endowments to retail investors. It spawned a $3 trillion global industry that now includes over 6,500 ETFs for every asset class and then some.

FIGURE 3.4 SPY's Yearly Assets 1993–2014

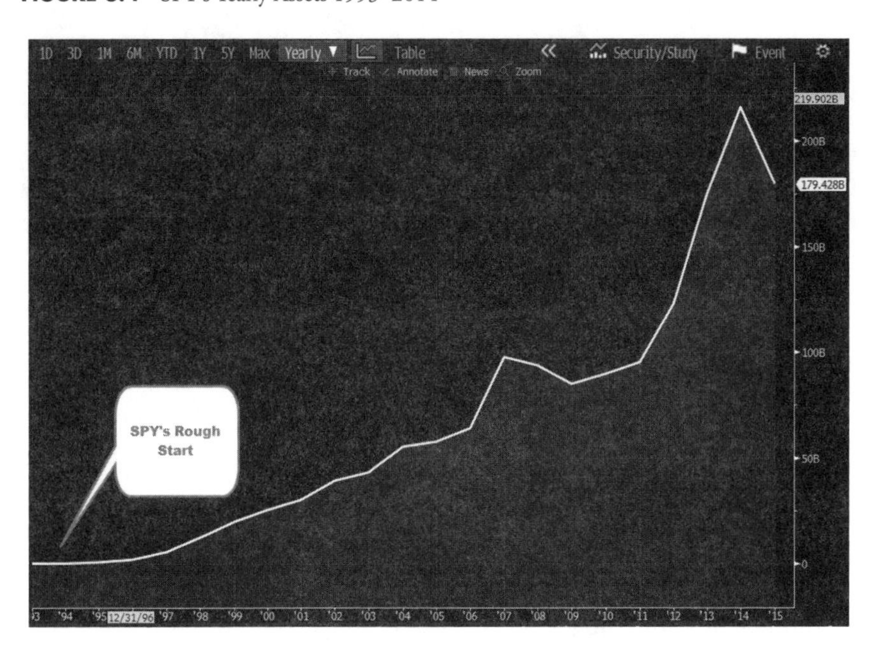

Source: Bloomberg

Suffice it to say the SEC didn't really plan on all this happening—that's for sure—especially the expansion of ETFs into other asset classes like fixed income and commodities. The original intent of the SEC paper was just a stock basket instrument.

"I don't think we envisioned at the time we wrote the report that use of baskets would be widespread. I think we saw the baskets as a way to provide relief to the volatility problems that we were facing. Additionally, the kind of baskets we were talking about were not baskets containing non-stocks."

David S. Ruder, SEC Chairman 1987–1989

Part of the eventual explosion of growth of ETFs came from sticky retail money. It showed that ETFs were not just volume generators but could be asset gatherers. In fact, the adoption by advisors and retail investors was so successful that many institutions now view ETFs as a retail vehicle. But the fact is they were originally built for institutions to trade.

"Really, the focus in the early days was how to get people trading it, not how to get people investing it in. I think that was the transition that we saw that happen later."

James Ross, State Street Global Advisors

Nate Most eventually retired from the AMEX in 1996. He didn't stop there though. He went to Barclays and served as the first chairman of the iShares board.[8] He died in 2004 at the age of 90. While he didn't see just how crazy massive ETFs would get, he did see their early success and innovative launches for ETFs tracking international equities, bonds, and gold.

"It is clear to me that the ETF design is only beginning its trading and investment penetration. Its design has made it a multipurpose instrument for many an investor's needs."[9]

Nate Most

Eventually, even Vanguard came to launch ETFs, albeit not until 2001 after Bogle was neither CEO nor chairman. Since then, Vanguard has grown ETF assets at what can only be described as ludicrous speed to become the second-largest brand after iShares. Despite Bogle's misgivings, he was well aware of just how brilliant and robust the structure was.

"(Nate) Most and I used to kid around with each other afterward. He basically understood my point of view. But I just didn't want to do it. And there are probably people around here who would tell you that the biggest mistake we ever made was Bogle's stupidity. But why don't I feel that way about myself?"

John Bogle, Vanguard

Everyone I spoke to—including Bogle—who was there from these early days knew the product was good and had a solid shot at becoming successful. But they all admitted that the mega-success that ETFs have seen has exceeded all of their expectations.

"It started out as a product and it became an industry."

Dr. Steven Bloom, Eisenhower School, National Defense University

---

Notes

1. Wiandt, Jim, "Nate Most, Exchange-Traded Fund Inventor, Dies at Age 90." ETF.com, December 8, 2004; www.etf.com/sections/features/281.html?qt-etf_related_articles=1.
2. "The October 1987 Market Break," February 1988; www.sechistorical.org/museum/papers/1980/page-12.php.
3. Bayot, Jennifer, "Nathan Most Is Dead at 90; Investment Fund Innovator." New York Times, December 10, 2004; www.nytimes.com/2004/12/10/obituaries/10most.html?_r=0.
4. Spence, John, "ETF Inventor Most Dies at 90." MarketWatch, December 7, 2004; www.marketwatch.com/story/etf-inventor-nate-most-dies-at-90.
5. Wiandt, 2004.
6. "SPDR S&P 500 ETF: The Idea that Spawned an Industry." SPDR University; www.spdrs.com.sg/education/files/SPY%20Spawned%20Industry-SG-public.pdf.
7. Ibid.
8. Spence, 2004.
9. Wiandt, 2004.

CHAPTER 4

Institutional Usages

Since those early days of SPY, institutional investors have found all kinds of creative uses for exchange-traded funds (ETFs) over the years. While many advisors and retail investors love ETFs as a cheaper alternative to mutual funds, pensions, endowments, insurance companies, asset managers, and even hedge funds use ETFs as liquid tools for portfolio management. Long-term investing is just one of a plethora of uses.

Following is a list of common usages of ETFs by institutions that we will discuss briefly in this chapter:

1. Cash equitization
2. Manager transitions
3. Portfolio rebalancing
4. Portfolio completion
5. Liquidity sleeves
6. Shorting/Hedging
7. Long and lend
8. Tactical moves
9. In-kind creation/redemptions
10. Bespoke ETFs
11. Tax-loss harvesting
12. Long-term allocation
13. Personal usage

There are arguably even more usages and maybe ways to combine some of these usages. But these are the ones that came up time and again, not just in the various surveys but in the interviews I conducted with different institutions. Most of these usages are short- and medium-term, with institutions using the ETF for its liquidity and precision. And given the $18 trillion that ETFs traded during the past year, we know people are using them *very* actively.

"The majority of investors using ETFs are doing active management. Only about 30 percent of ETF investors look at these as passive funds, who are just there long term. Those are the minority. Most of the users are active users, not passive users."

Daniel Gamba, Blackrock

When it comes to ETF usage for institutions, such as pensions and endowments, it can happen directly or indirectly. The largest institutional funds are most likely to have resources and personnel to manage their money internally. As such, they may directly use ETFs as part of their own active management. They can also own ETFs indirectly via the external active managers they hire. Generally speaking, the smaller the institution is, the more likely it is to outsource the management of the fund to a consultant and/or external manager(s).

"If you have $100 billion and you manage $20 billion in-house and $80 billion is managed externally, you most likely now have some level of ETF exposure in the internally managed portion in addition to the ETF exposure from the external managers using ETFs as well."

Robert Trumbull, State Street Global Advisors

Either way, the common thread between using ETFs internally or via external management is as tools. It is an active usage. This usage usually starts with short-term cash management, and like a gateway drug, it can grow from there into other purposes such as portfolio rebalancing, liquidity overlays, tactical bets, and occasionally even a long-term allocation.

"The good news is for the industry, given the size of the ETFs and liquidity and the number, there are more places in the large pension funds for them than there would have been a decade ago."

Dave Underwood, Arizona State Retirement System

Cash Equitization

In cash equitization, institutional investors receive cash or sell an investment and quickly invest it in an ETF to keep the fund invested in the market and help eliminate cash drag and a performance shortfall to their benchmark. This is also called *interim beta.*

For example, many institutions may put a temporary chunk of cash in one of the Standard & Poor's (S&P) 500 ETFs while they think of something better to do with it or wait until they can deploy it to one of their managers. This usage of ETFs has been going on since the early days of ETFs.

"Some institutions saw the first ETFs as an easy way to equitize cash, even though they weren't sold for that purpose. It was just that some people early on figured out that ETFs were an easier way to park my money and keep liquid. It was really early adopters and mavericks who were the first to figure this out."

Kathleen Moriarty, Kaye Scholer LLP

Even the very largest institutions, such as pensions and endowments who can get their core passive exposure in a separately managed account (SMA) for cheaper than the ETF may still use ETFs for this purpose. The reason for that is that the ETF is so liquid and expedient. No contracts or requests for proposals (RFPs) needed. They can get the exposure they need quickly, cheaply, and anonymously and with the peace of mind that they can get out just as quickly, cheaply, and anonymously. This was a big benefit according to Ben Carlson, who has had experience managing a large endowment fund.

"If we need to rebalance, or get cash back from a manager, or get a big contribution into the fund, we immediately put it into ETFs. It could be SPY, but it could also be the iShares Russell 3000 ETF (IWV) or the Vanguard Emerging Markets ETF (VWO). And if we're looking at a European manager, we will look at one of the European ETFs."

Ben Carlson, Ritholtz Wealth Management

Before ETFs, an institution might use the futures market to equitize cash. But institutions are finding that ETFs can also be used, and so now there is a growing battle between ETFs and futures. Both have their pros and cons.

Futures can be cheaper in some cases, especially with shorter holding periods. But the thing with futures is that they expire. And you don't want that to happen, so you have to continually buy and sell (roll) them to keep the position going. This takes work and the ability to trade futures.

It also creates the potential for rolling costs if you are holding for a long period of time. While S&P 500 Index futures are nowhere near the roll costs in, say, oil or VIX futures, even minor rolling costs that can add up at times, as seen in Figure 4.1.

Some research has shown that these roll costs have gone up in the past few years as a result of new regulations that have required banks to take less risk.

In 2014, Anand Omprakash of BNP Paribas wrote about the situation in a note to clients:

> ... uncertainty surrounding future banking regulations has the potential to reignite volatility in future futures rolls. To avoid potentially elevated futures costs (and cost volatility), our analysis finds that investors not seeking levered exposure may consider ETFs as a suitable alternative to maintain a long position in the underlying S&P 500 index.[1]

FIGURE 4.1 Varying Costs of Rolling S&P 500 Futures

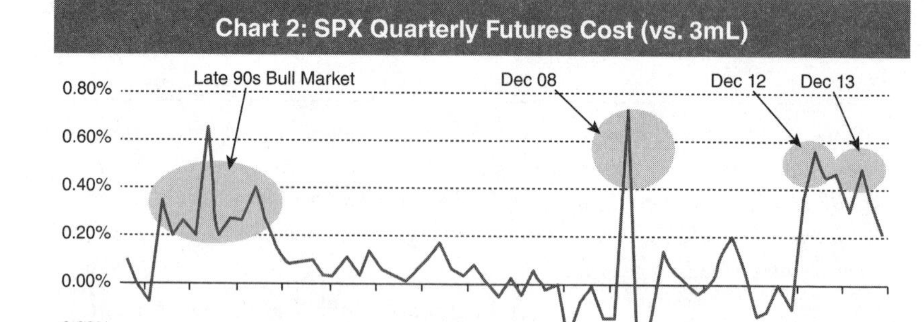

Source: BNP

This opportunity to beat futures at their own game isn't lost on ETF issuers. Similar to the way you may see marketing documents aimed at retail investors comparing the cost of an ETF versus a mutual fund; institutional salespeople at the ETF issuers have documents that compare the cost of the ETF to the cost of a futures position.

Blackrock has a regular report called the "Delta-One Landscape" in which they break out the individual costs associated with a synthetic position in futures versus the physical position in an ETF for several of their ETFs for a one-year holding period. They look at the trading commission, spread, impact costs, roll costs or yields, management fee, and taxes to determine which is more efficient. It is all added up like a balance sheet to determine the relative cost differences. Figure 4.2 is straight from the report and shows how Blackrock compares futures versus an ETF.

The other aspect to futures is that they are derivatives that come with counterparty risk, while ETFs are fully funded 1940 Act vehicles. And many pensions and endowments may not be able to use derivatives or simply want to avoid them if possible.

"It's a lot of work to buy futures. You need margin and they expire quarterly so you have to manage that risk. Many fund managers prefer to avoid that."

Mohit Bajaj, WallachBeth Capital

A final possible advantage ETFs have over futures is they simply allow for greater customization than futures. For the manager of a technology-focused mutual fund, they may want to use a tech ETF rather than an S&P 500 futures contract to equitize cash. Likewise, a high-yield manager may use a high-yield ETF. In other words, cash equitization is getting more precise as ETFs in these different categories get more liquid.

It must be noted, though, that this doesn't apply to every ETF. Only the most liquid ETF need apply for the job. This is why maybe 50 ETFs at most can be used for this purpose, the rest are not liquid enough. This is why Sebastian Mercado at Deutsche Bank dubs the most liquid ETFs "pseudo futures." Here is his description of these ultra-liquid ETFs in his report:

> Many times these ETFs they also trade at a cheaper level than their underlying basket, and offer large amounts of liquidity which can make them attractive for market making activities as well. Secondary and short liquidity (ease to borrow), and fund size tend to be more relevant characteristics at the moment of selecting these types of ETFs. There usually are no more than one pseudo futures ETF per asset class.[2]

FIGURE 4.2 How an Institution Would Compare Mid-Cap Futures versus an ETF

$100 Million Long Exposure		S&P MidCap 400	iShares Core S&P Mid-Cap ETF
All cost are round trip and in bps		EMD	IJH
Costs	Cost/Revenue Item	Future	ETF
Entry & Exit Trade	Commission	0.3	2.7
	Impact & Spread	38.5	14.9
	Total	**38.8**	**17.6**
Holding Period	Futures Roll Commissions	1.2	--
	Richness/ (Cheapness)	19.5	--
	ETF Management Fee	--	12.0
	Basket Lending Revenue	--	(4.5)
	Foreign Tax Advantage	--	--
	Total	**20.8**	**7.5**
Total Cost		**59.6**	**25.1**
Funding Assumptions		Future	ETF
	Base Funding Rate	22.0	--
	ETF Breakeven Required Cash Return	**56.5**	
Liquidity & Lending		Future	ETF
	ETF Lending Revenue (bps)		(4.3)
	20-Day ADV ($)	$3,235,696,720	$139,510,030
	Basket 20-Day ADV ($)		$18,354,149,575

Source: Blackrock

This is a case when all due diligence will get thrown out and the institution will just pick the one with the most volume. End of story. The good news is that as volume has grown, more and more asset classes now sport pseudo futures ETFs usable for cash equitization. Five years down the line, it is possible that we will see asset classes with multiple ETFs with this mega-liquidity to pick from. Just looking at the top 50 most traded ETFs—all of which trade over $200 million/day approximately—in Table 4.1, you can see many different asset classes and strategies covered.

TABLE 4.1 Top 50 Most Traded ETFs

Ticker	Name	Avg 30-Day Vol (in $million)
SPY US	SPDR S&P 500 ETF Trust	22909.21
IWM US	iShares Russell 2000 ETF	3700.77
QQQ US	Powershares QQQ Trust Series	2709.13
EEM US	iShares MSCI Emerging Market	1792.29
EFA US	iShares MSCI EAFE ETF	1210.94
TLT US	iShares 20+ Year Treasury BO	1184.77
VXX US	iPath S&P 500 VIX S/T FU ETN	978.69
FXI US	iShares China Large-Cap ETF	925.70
DIA US	SPDR DJIA Trust	839.21
XLE US	Energy Select Sector SPDR	826.92
XLF US	Financial Select Sector SPDR	805.23
IYR US	iShares US Real Estate ETF	672.68
IVV US	iShares Core S&P 500 ETF	668.13
XIV US	VelocityShares Inv VIX SH-TM	644.52
HYG US	iShares iBoxx High Yield Cor	600.35
IBB US	iShares Nasdaq Biotechnology	583.90
XLV US	Health Care Select Sector	554.00
GDX US	Market Vectors Gold Miners	527.83
GLD US	SPDR Gold Shares	521.31
XLU US	Utilities Select Sector SPDR	496.39
UVXY US	ProShares Ultra VIX ST Futur	496.11
VWO US	Vanguard FTSE Emerging Market	469.69
EWZ US	iShares MSCI Brazil Capped E	450.49
MDY US	SPDR S&P Midcap 400 ETF Trst	444.67

(*Continued*)

TABLE 4.1 (*Continued*)

Ticker	Name	Avg 30-Day Vol (in $million)
XLI US	Industrial Select Sect SPDR	433.17
TNA US	Direxion Dly Sm Cap Bull 3X	398.09
XLY US	Consumer Discretionary Selt	389.91
LQD US	iShares iBoxx Investment Gra	364.94
XLP US	Consumer Staples SPDR	339.57
VNQ US	Vanguard REIT ETF	335.26
USO US	United States Oil Fund LP	324.92
JNK US	SPDR Barclays High Yield Bd	324.79
XLK US	Technology Select Sect SPDR	320.98
UCO US	ProShares Ultra Bloomberg CR	312.32
EWJ US	iShares MSCI Japan ETF	311.99
HEDJ US	WisdomTree Europe Hedged Equ	303.46
TQQQ US	ProShares Ultrapro QQQ	303.25
VTI US	Vanguard Total Stock Mkt ETF	289.82
VOO US	Vanguard S&P 500 ETF	286.89
DXJ US	WisdomTree Japan Hedged Eq	282.71
EZU US	iShares MSCI Eurozone ETF	280.87
XBI US	SPDR S&P Biotech ETF	275.06
XOP US	SPDR S&P Oil & Gas Exp & PR	274.78
SSO US	ProShares Ultra S&P 500	267.06
VGK US	Vanguard FTSE Europe ETF	253.37
AGG US	iShares Core U.S. Aggregate	217.14
KRE US	SPDR S&P Regional Banking	203.51
IJH US	iShares Core S&P Midcap ETF	200.86
TBT US	ProShares ultrashort 20+Y TR	191.15

Source: Bloomberg

Manager Transitions

Many institutions use ETFs as a temporary holding place in between external managers. ETFs keep the portfolio exposed while they search for a new active manager. These beauty parades can take a while, and so sometimes the holding period in a transition can end up looking a lot like a long-term allocation.

They typically pick an ETF that is similar in exposure to their manager. Similar to cash equitization, this is a cost-effective way of keeping assets invested during times of change. Nearly every single pension and endowment I spoke with was enthusiastic about ETFs being used for this purpose. Manager transitions is one of the few times even the consultants tend to recommend an ETF.

"We have had situations where we were bringing a new manager on board and we would let them use those (ETFs) as a transition tool. Say you hire an international manager and they start doing this portfolio transition. But instead of them transitioning from a base of cash where they are investing directly, basically, if they have an ETF, they are already kind of hedged, so they can slowly work into their stuff. That's something we've done as well."

Michael Brakebill, Tennessee Consolidated Retirement System

The ETFs allow for a more seamless integration of an outside manager than going from cash, which can be a drag on the portfolio and cause tracking error with a benchmark. Conventional index funds are typically reluctant to be used for this purpose due to the huge movements in and out of the fund, which can add transactions costs.[3] That isn't an issue for the ETF. Like a revolving door, they welcome—and thrive off of—the traffic.

When selecting the ETF to use, most institutions balance the need for liquidity with the exposure that is closest to the asset allocation call they are making.

"ETFs play a role when you are doing cross asset allocations—moving to another asset class in order or hedge it. One can do this with futures in some cases. But you can also do it with ETFs in order to have the exposure, and then parse that exposure out to individual managers that you're selecting as you can fund those. They are important tools to do such things."

Dave Underwood, Arizona State Retirement System

One of the most high-profile cases of a manager transition was when Bill Gross abruptly left Pimco in September 2014. Many institutional investors who had been with him for years and even decades pretty quickly moved billions upon billions out of the fund and created what one market maker called "The Pimco Derby." Many of these investors used ETFs to buy themselves time while they went through the due diligence process of finding a new manager.

We know this because a couple of fixed-income ETFs hauled in over $7 billion the week after Gross left, much more than they had ever taken in in that short a period of time. Again, there is no way to pinpoint exactly where the cash came from, but given no traumatic events in the bond market that month and the types of ETFs that brought in the cash, it isn't a stretch to say most or all of it was refugees from the Pimco Total Return Fund.

Most of that money went into three fixed-income ETFs. The iShares 1–3 Year Treasury Bond ETF (SHY) took in almost $2 billion of that cash. SHY is a popular parking spot to store cash. This is one way to transition your money. Hold it in cash until you find a new manager.

About $3 billion it went into the iShares Core U.S. Aggregate Bond ETF (AGG) and the Vanguard Total Bond Market ETF (BND), which are more true replacements for Gross since they hold a variety of bonds just like his mutual fund did. Of course, they don't have Gross's active management prowess, but they more or less fill the void while you wait for Gross to settle at Janus or look for a new bond manager.

Money kept pouring into AGG and BND, and by the end of the year both of them had taken in more than $15 billion, making them big winners in the Pimco Derby. AGG took in $7.5 billion, as shown in Figure 4.3, while BND took in $7.8 billion—both of which blew away the cash intake compared to other years in their existence.

As expected, some of that money came right back out in early 2015. If you look at the volume and flows in AGG in early 2015, you can see some very

FIGURE 4.3 AGG's Yearly Flows Since Inception

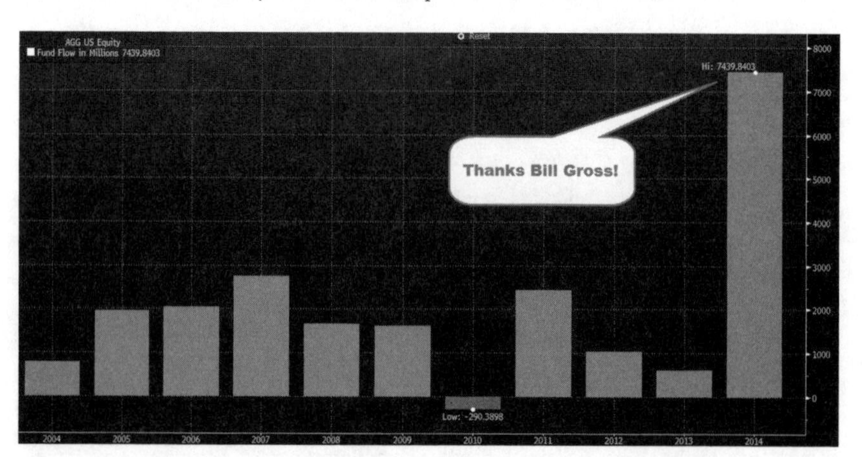

Source: Bloomberg

large sell orders, in particular on one day in January and another in March, where it saw volume in excess of $5 billion in one day (50 times the average). Most likely, those were institutions ending their stay at the Hotel AGG.

Portfolio Rebalancing

Like the knobs on a stereo that allow you to keep the sound of the music exactly as you like it, ETFs allow institutions to keep their portfolio allocations just as they like them in a rebalance. This is ETFs serving the role as an adjustment mechanism.

It is not hard to imagine one area of the portfolio lacking when there is a rebalance. An ETF can be used quickly to fill in the gap or reduce an underweight, either temporarily or permanently, to get the sound exactly as you want it.

"We look at our underlying managers' holdings and take a look at the risk in the portfolio and then use ETFs to overlay where we want to take less or more risk, depending on what our underlying managers are doing."

Jim Dunn, Verger Capital Management

Institutions like using ETFs for this purpose because first and foremost they are liquid and precise. The external managers they have money with don't allow for easy adjustments of your investments. With liquid ETFs now available for basic and specific asset classes, a manager can adjust the knobs and tune things as finely and quickly. They may do this outside of their managers, or they may even work with their managers to do it.

"We did a series of trades where we wanted to get back into international developed markets. It was really easy for us to go out and buy a bunch of ETFs immediately. And then we can even notify our managers to start purchasing and the wind down the ETFs. We have done things like that historically."

Michael Brakebill, Tennessee Consolidated Retirement System

Portfolio Completion

ETFs are also used by institutions as gap fillers to complete a portfolio or round out exposure. ETFs allow for institutions to access areas they don't have the time or resources to research thoroughly. If portfolio rebalancing makes ETFs like knobs on a stereo, portfolio completion makes ETFs like the last few missing pieces to a jigsaw puzzle.

"(ETFs) are an augmentation tool. We might have a systematic (smart-beta) portfolio or a truly active manager. Or a combination of both. And in between them, as a completion product or completion role, might be an ETF."

Dave Underwood, Arizona State Retirement System

Some institutions have completion funds. Completion funds do nothing but hold these missing pieces and/or tweak exposures to rebalance the portfolio back to where it needs to be. For example, an institution may build a primary portfolio with a value manager, a growth manager, a large-cap manager, a small-cap manager, some hedge funds, and some private equity funds. But after all that, there could be some categories they just don't have a manager for or resources to devote to.

"We want to have an asset allocation that meets the model that we have drawn up. And we will fill in the holes with ETFs. One example is gold."

Jim Dunn, Verger Capital Management

Frontier markets is also case of where an institution may use an ETF to complete an allocation. In one example, an insurance company wanted to add a little frontier exposure to its emerging-markets exposure. Frontier markets are not easy to access and can be illiquid.

Looking at the current holdings for the iShares MSCI Frontier 100 ETF (FM), many institutions have slowly increased their position over the past year of FM. One example is New York Life Investment Management LLC, which has increased its ownership of FM over the last four quarters, as shown in Figure 4.4.

Liquidity Sleeves

Institutions may also hold some ETFs in different asset classes as a way to keep themselves liquid and flexible. Like portfolio rebalancing, this gives an institution more control and options when it comes to managing the portfolio and meeting their operational cash needs.

FIGURE 4.4 New York Life Group's Historical Ownership of FM

Holder Name	2014 Q3	2014 Q4	2015 Q1	2015 Q2	Position
1. ENVESTNET ASSET MANAGEMENT	452,395	71,091	732,660	732,660	732,660
2. MORGAN STANLEY	1.2MLN	807,184	677,514	677,514	677,514
3. BANK OF AMERICA CORPORATION	597,244	732,991	427,746	427,746	427,746
4. JANE STREET GROUP LLC	134,185	0	366,511	366,511	366,511
5. ROCK CREEK GROUP LP	565,754	565,754	331,374	331,374	331,374
6. CABOT WEALTH MANAGEMENT INC	177,608	193,121	329,605	329,605	329,605
7. ADVANCE DEVELOPING MARKETS TRUST	--	321,029.3	321,029.3	321,029.3	321,029
8. WELLS FARGO & COMPANY	274,577	307,939	296,123	296,123	296,123
9. NEW YORK LIFE GROUP	180,492	246,244	254,345	254,345	254,345
10. STONEHEARTH CAPITAL MANAGEMENT L	--	192,853	251,207	251,207	251,207
11. BURT WEALTH ADVISORS	--	110,376	238,138	238,138	238,138
12. BROUWER & JANACHOWSKI LLC	6,358	225,371	228,851	228,851	228,851
13. EXANE DERIVATIVES	--	130,629	212,705	212,705	212,705
14. CREDIT SUISSE AG	126,345	173,063	195,896	195,896	195,896
15. UBS	712,060	129,513	193,409	193,409	193,409
16. ROYAL BANK OF CANADA	858,316	174,148	164,594	164,594	164,594
17. LPL FINANCIAL CORP	95,539	40,770	156,491	156,491	156,491

Source: Bloomberg

> *"If for some reason you need to raise cash, or need intraday liquidity, or are beholden to short-term trading restrictions, you can use an ETF to stay liquid."*
>
> Jim Rowley, Vanguard

Many institutions invest in illiquid investments such as private equity or real estate. While ETFs can't compete with the exposure offered by private investments, private investments can't compete with the liquidity offered by ETFs. By using an ETF here and there in the portfolio, an institution can quickly get cash, if necessary, or adjust things.

This is easier than dealing with an external manager. An institution could call up the manager and ask to add to an account. But that could take time to implement. Also, if the move is short term, it may be uncomfortable to call back up to get your money back. ETFs can help diffuse the relationship component between an institution and their managers.

> *"ETFs allow an institution to quickly reduce exposure to an area without having to fire a manager. There is also some 'manager hedging' going on here, as well as you can react more quickly where it is a little harder to do that with just using a manager. And I think the world moves a lot faster than it used to."*
>
> Ben Fulton, Elkhorn Capital Group

Asset managers may also employ ETFs to provide liquidity. Instead of keeping cash, they can keep the money in an ETF to keep them exposed to the market, while at the same time using it to cash in and out investors so as to not disturb their stock or bond holdings.

"I had one manager describe [using ETFs] to me as building a moat around his portfolio. He said, 'Look, I am in the business of building a high-yield portfolio. I am an individual credit expert. I got out and found all the best individual bonds, and I put them in my portfolios. The last thing I want to do is to have to sell those securities if I have withdrawals.' So he allocates 95 percent of the fund's capital to buying these individual bonds that he has handpicked and researched, and he puts 5 percent in a high-yield ETF. And he views the high-yield ETF as building a moat around his individual names."

Matt Tucker, Blackrock

The need for liquidity for an institution is huge. This is why they tend to pick the biggest, most liquid ETFs. After all, that is what they can't really get anywhere else.

"We prioritize ETFs by liquidity. After 2008, the lesson that a lot of endowments learned, including us when I was at Duke, is that we undervalued how important having liquidity is in your portfolio."

Anders Hall, Vanderbilt University Office of Investments

Shorting/Hedging

Institutions also use ETFs to hedge market risk—or bet against something—by shorting an ETF. We know this because approximately $170 billion worth of ETFs is currently shorted, according to short interest data from Bloomberg. The majority of this shorting comes from hedge funds. While hedge funds have a mere $34 billion in long ETF positions, they have $116 billion in short ETF positions.[4]

Many of them use ETFs to hedge out their market exposure and isolate the risk premia they are looking to capture. For example, a hedge fund will go long a stock while shorting out the sector ETF the stock belongs to, thereby eliminating market risk. Unlike the media's portrayal, hedge funds are not all looking to shoot the lights out, but rather employ complex strategies that aim for noncorrelated, risk-adjusted returns. The ETF helps them get their hedge on, which is half the battle.

I found the Goldman Sachs *Hedge Fund Monitor* to be the best report that looks at hedge funds' ETF usage. The Goldman report also found that ETFs represented only 2.3 percent of hedge funds' long equity positions, but accounted for 27 percent of their short equity positions. That is extraordinary. You can see in Table 4.2 in the far right column how all but two ETFs are net short.

TABLE 4.2 Hedge Funds' ETF Ownership

ETF Name	Ticker	Long ($million)	Short ($million)	Net ($million)
Vanguard FTSE Emerging Markets	VWO	5,057	263	4,794
SPDR Gold Trust	GLD	1,986	1,349	638
iShares MSCI Emerging Markets	EEM	3,322	3,419	(97)
iShares China Large-Cap	FXI	669	1,154	(485)
iShares MSCI Brazil Capped	EWZ	557	1,109	(552)
SPDR S&P Retail	XRT	239	1,157	(918)
Consumer Discretionary Select Sector SPDR	XLY	178	1,115	(937)
iPath S&P 500 VIX Short-Term Futures ETN	VXX	—	1,227	(1,227)
iShares MSCI EAFE	EFA	371	1,623	(1,251)
iShares iBoxx USD High Yield Corp Bond	HYG	210	1,478	(1,268)
SPDR S&P Midcap 400 ETF Trust	MDY	104	1,475	(1,370)
SPDR S&P Biotech	XBI	18	1,413	(1,395)
SPDR Dow Jones Industrial Average ETF Trust	DIA	60	1,523	(1,464)
SPDR S&P Oil & Gas Exploration & Production	XOP	—	1,486	(1,486)
iShares Nasdaq Biotechnology	IBB	86	1,587	(1,502)
Industrial Select Sector SPDR	XLI	127	1,734	(1,607)
iShares 20+ Year Treasury Bond ETF	TLT	394	2,046	(1,651)
Financial Select Sector SPDR	XLF	712	2,372	(1,660)
Health Care Select Sector SPDR	XLV	118	2,042	(1,924)
Utilities Select Sector SPDR	XLU	54	2,072	(2,018)
Energy Select Sector SPDR	XLE	559	4,226	(3,667)
PowerShares QQQ Trust Series	QQQ	—	3,989	(3,989)
iShares U.S. Real Estate ETF	IYR	257	4,452	(4,194)
iShares Russell 2000 ETF	IWM	533	9,503	(8,969)
SPDR S&P 500 ETF Trust	SPY	11,981	39,985	(28,003)

Source: Goldman Sachs

Another thing that jumps out from the top holdings—that probably isn't too surprising—is that they obviously love the most liquid ETFs and put them above all else. This isn't unusual. The level of short interest in ETFs is highly correlated with their volume.

"If you are going short, you are looking for liquidity."

James Ross, State Street Global Advisors

When you short an ETF, it is just like a stock where you have to borrow the security while posting collateral and a small fee. However, with ETFs you can also have a market maker create new ETF shares for you on the spot through the creation/redemption process, and then you just sell them ("create to lend"). Which route to take will depend on many of the cost variables.

Most ETFs have a very small portion of their shares shorted. For example, the iShares MSCI EAFE ETF (EFA) has 3 percent of its shares shorted, while the iShares MSCI Emerging Markets ETF (EEM) has 12 percent of its shares shorted. No big deal. Nothing to see here. However, there are some ETFs that are shorted beyond the norm.

A classic example of a heavily shorted ETF is the SPDR S&P Retail ETF (XRT), which seems to consistently have more than 200 percent of its shares shorted. XRT currently has 252 percent of its shares shorted as shown in Figure 4.5, along with the other most shorted ETFs. The reason XRT is so shorted is that it holds a lot of small retail stocks that tend to be hard to borrow. And because it equal-weights the holdings, those small stocks are very correlated to the ETF. So the hedge fund or whoever can use the ETF as a cheaper way to short an individual stock.

FIGURE 4.5 ETFs Ranked by Highest Percentage of Shares Shorted

Selected Criteria — 1) Modify Screening Criteria
Exchange: United States

1748 matching funds

11) Key Metrics | 12) Cost | 13) Performance | 14) Flow | 15) Liquidity | 16) Allocations | 17) Regulatory Structure

Name	Today Vol	30D Vol	Implied Liquidity	Bid Ask Spread	Short Interest%↑	Open Interest
Median	13.29k	19.86k	2.72M	.05	.79	997.50
100) Market Vectors Semiconductor E	3.63M	3.33M	5.80M	.02	325.15	184.79k
101) SPDR S&P Retail ETF	848.43k	1.85M	966.46k	.02	251.97	59.91k
102) SPDR S&P Oil & Gas Exploration	7.32M	6.11M	2.26M	.01	130.92	711.35k
103) CurrencyShares Japanese Yen Tr	35.77k	171.76k	--	.01	118.86	111.14k
104) SPDR S&P Biotech ETF	632.42k	1.11M	533.41k	.04	115.05	164.47k
105) iShares US Real Estate ETF	7.69M	9.27M	9.71M	.01	112.03	565.47k
106) CurrencyShares Euro Trust	449.08k	894.97k	--	.01	100.73	686.45k
107) iPATH S&P 500 VIX Short-Term F	81.60M	49.01M	--	.01	87.87	2.84M
108) iPATH S&P 500 VIX Mid-Term Fut	514.51k	545.87k	--	.01	85.87	6.29k
109) Direxion Daily Real Estate Bea	48.69k	64.43k	--	.04	77.50	1.19k

Source: Bloomberg

Now, obviously, 252 percent shorted seems impossible but it is just people lending out shares more than once. This is fine because at any point in time new shares of XRT can be created using the creation/redemption process. This gives investors a release valve that can be tapped at any moment to cover all the shorts.

Investors also have the option of going long to go short by using an inverse ETF in order to achieve the same goal. These ETFs allow investors to get short quickly without having to worry about borrowing the security. Although the downside is you have to watch out for some of the issues related to the daily resetting of inverse and leveraged ETFs, which we will cover in Chapter 11.

"Institutions see a lot of advantages to getting leveraged and short exposure though geared ETFs. In some cases you will have institutions that have charters that were put together a hundred years ago before modern portfolio techniques came to be. And they don't have the ability to hedge themselves when they need to, so this gives them the ability to employ some more modern portfolio techniques."

Michael Sapir, ProShares

Mark Yusko, a former endowment manager at the University of North Carolina, had an example of using leveraged ETFs to make an expedient rebalance of his portfolio.

Back in 2007, he made the call that housing was looking troubling, and so he went out to get short subprime and allocated money to a bunch of different managers including John Paulson. But even with that exposure, he felt they had too much financial exposure in their long/short equity fund of funds. So, they went out and bought the UltraShort Financials ProShares (SKF), a 2× leveraged short ETF, to not only reduce their exposure to financials but to get net short to financials in the portfolio. It wasn't a huge bet, but it was not something they could have easily done before.

"In order to do this before ETFs, you would have had to redeem from the manager who was long financials, which is a 90-day process at a minimum. Then you had to go find someone who was short financials, and there weren't many of those. But with the ETF, it was quite easy. We have done a number of things like that over a number of years."

Mark Yusko, Morgan Creek Capital Management

Long and Lend

We just discussed how an institution can short ETFs. In order to do that, someone needs to lend it to you so you can sell it. That someone could also be an institutional investor. Lending out ETF shares can generate an extra return stream for an institution. ETFs can be lent out by the custodian bank or even the ETF issuer for the client. Or new shares can be created for the sole purpose of being lent out.

> *"You can lend the ETF out as part of your securities lending program. It's not big money but its incremental return to the plan. So you are getting the return, but you are also getting the additional return on that ETF simply by virtue of the revenue stream from the lending."*
>
> Dave Underwood, Arizona State Retirement System

The additional revenue stream is also what can sometimes help an ETF overcome the cost differential with an SMA.

> *"You can take an ETF and embed a lending income into it where the cost difference between having an ETF and a big separately managed account are pretty darn close."*
>
> Michael Brakebill, Tennessee Consolidated Retirement System

Of course, in order to do a long and lend, an institution needs to want to be in that asset class or sector *and* the borrowing rate has to be high enough for it to be worth it. The "borrow market" is as antiquated as the bond market, but when those rates creep up an alert institution may go in and exploit the opportunity.

> *"There's some large pension funds that will swap their whole S&P 500 separate account when the lend is there and flip it back out if they can make a basis point or two. It's a lot of money when you can make an extra basis point, so they are going to do it."*
>
> James Ross, State Street Global Advisors

Table 4.3 shows some examples of annual borrow rates as of April 2015 for ETFs as compiled by Deutsche Bank.[5] Keep in mind these are market dependent and client dependent. There are just too many variables to really keep aggregate data on them, not to mention that most people won't let you use their borrow cost sheets for publication. These numbers may be more than you could get, but it gives you a ballpark, proportional idea.

TABLE 4.3 Some of the Larger ETFs and Their Respective Borrowing Costs per Year

Ticker	Focus	Index/Sub Focus	Apr. D Avg. Borrow Rate
SPY	US Large Cap	S&P 500	0.40%
QQQ	US Large Cap	Nasdaq 100	0.40%
DIA	US Large Cap	DJ Industrials	0.40%
MDY	US Mid Cap	S&P 400	0.83%
IWM	US Small Cap	Russell 2000	1.16%
IBB	US Sector	Biotech & Pharma	1.90%
XLY	US Sector	Cons. Discretionary	0.48%
XLP	US Sector	Cons. Staples	0.72%
XLE	US Sector	Energy	0.51%
OIH	US Sector	Energy Equip. & Services	1.40%
XOP	US Sector	Energy Exp. & Prod.	2.53%
EEM	EM	MSCI Emerging Markets	0.46%
EWZ	Brazil	MSCI Brazil	1.10%
FXI	China	FTSE China 50	1.08%
EWW	Mexico	MSCI Mexico	0.51%
RSX	Russia	Market Vectors Russia	0.53%
EWT	Taiwan	MSCI Taiwan	0.69%

Source: Deutsche Bank

One example of an ETF that is used a lot in this capacity is iShares Russell 2000 ETF (IWM), which typically fetches a decent fee—almost 1 percent of gross lending yield based on a three-year average—on the borrow market. As shown in Figure 4.6, some of heavy hitters have stockpiles of IWM. Many of these firms may be lending out shares. Also, if you look at the bottom of the screen, it shows that the shares reported in 13Fs account for 125 percent of IWM's shares outstanding. You rarely see a number that high. This is further evidence that IWM is being lent out—possibly multiple times—and subsequently getting double counted in some of the filings.

"If you look at these institutions and they hold a product for four quarters or eight quarters, they are probably doing some kind of lending underneath. And it is probably some difficult to access asset class like small caps or emerging markets."

Matt Goulet, Fidelity Investments

FIGURE 4.6 Holder of IWM Ranked by Size of Position

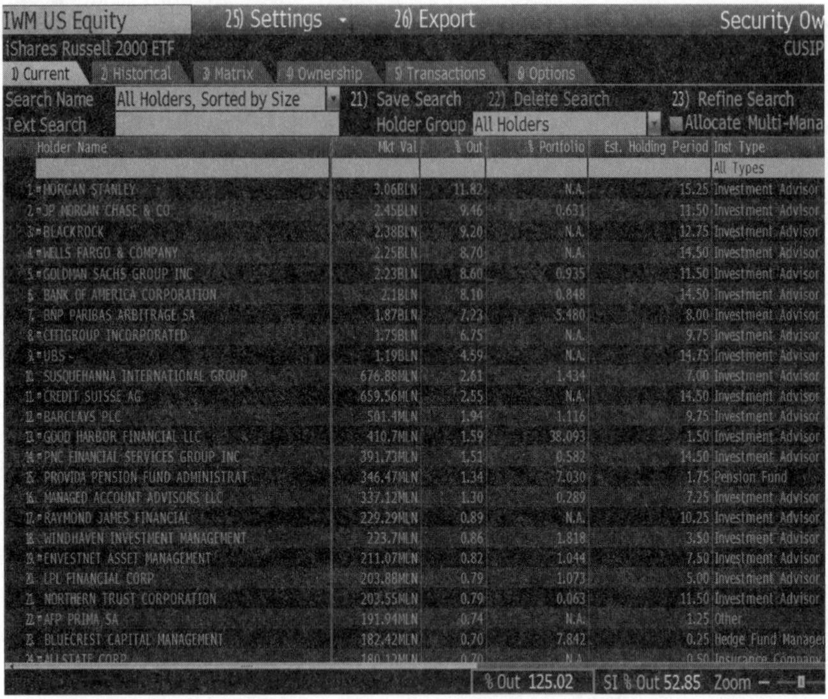

IWM US Equity | 25) Settings | 26) Export | Security Ow

iShares Russell 2000 ETF | CUSIP

1) Current | 2) Historical | 3) Matrix | 4) Ownership | 5) Transactions | 6) Options

Search Name: All Holders, Sorted by Size | 21) Save Search | 22) Delete Search | 23) Refine Search

Text Search | Holder Group: All Holders | Allocate Multi-Mana

Holder Name	Mkt Val	% Out	% Portfolio	Est. Holding Period	Inst Type
					All Types
1. MORGAN STANLEY	3.06BLN	11.82	N.A.	15.25	Investment Advisor
2. JP MORGAN CHASE & CO	2.45BLN	9.46	0.631	11.50	Investment Advisor
3. BLACKROCK	2.38BLN	9.20	N.A.	12.75	Investment Advisor
4. WELLS FARGO & COMPANY	2.25BLN	8.70	N.A.	14.50	Investment Advisor
5. GOLDMAN SACHS GROUP INC	2.23BLN	8.60	0.935	11.50	Investment Advisor
6. BANK OF AMERICA CORPORATION	2.1BLN	8.10	0.848	14.50	Investment Advisor
7. BNP PARIBAS ARBITRAGE SA	1.87BLN	7.23	5.480	8.00	Investment Advisor
8. CITIGROUP INCORPORATED	1.75BLN	6.75	N.A.	9.75	Investment Advisor
9. UBS	1.19BLN	4.59	N.A.	14.75	Investment Advisor
10. SUSQUEHANNA INTERNATIONAL GROUP	676.88MLN	2.61	1.434	7.00	Investment Advisor
11. CREDIT SUISSE AG	659.56MLN	2.55	N.A.	14.50	Investment Advisor
12. BARCLAYS PLC	501.4MLN	1.94	1.116	9.75	Investment Advisor
13. GOOD HARBOR FINANCIAL LLC	410.7MLN	1.59	38.093	1.50	Investment Advisor
14. PNC FINANCIAL SERVICES GROUP INC	391.73MLN	1.51	0.582	14.50	Investment Advisor
15. PROVIDA PENSION FUND ADMINISTRAT	346.47MLN	1.34	7.030	1.75	Pension Fund
16. MANAGED ACCOUNT ADVISORS LLC	337.12MLN	1.30	0.289	7.25	Investment Advisor
17. RAYMOND JAMES FINANCIAL	229.29MLN	0.89	N.A.	10.25	Investment Advisor
18. WINDHAVEN INVESTMENT MANAGEMENT	223.7MLN	0.86	1.818	3.50	Investment Advisor
19. ENVESTNET ASSET MANAGEMENT	211.07MLN	0.82	1.044	7.50	Investment Advisor
20. LPL FINANCIAL CORP	203.88MLN	0.79	1.073	5.00	Investment Advisor
21. NORTHERN TRUST CORPORATION	203.55MLN	0.79	0.063	11.50	Investment Advisor
22. AFP PRIMA SA	191.94MLN	0.74	N.A.	1.25	Other
23. BLUECREST CAPITAL MANAGEMENT	182.42MLN	0.70	7.842	0.25	Hedge Fund Manager
24. ALLSTATE CORP	180.12MLN	0.70	N.A.	0.50	Insurance Company

% Out 125.02 | SI % Out 52.85 | Zoom

Source: Bloomberg

Tactical Moves

ETFs can be used for very short-term moves. Trends change and institutions like to adapt to those trends, so when they rebalance they can use an ETF to conveniently slide into a new area. If something gets super-hot that an institution didn't see coming, such as senior loans or China A-shares, they can always jump in and out with an ETF. We know there are lots of tactical moves going on, judging from the volume that ETFs see.

"Hedge funds tend to use our ETFs as a tactical play to get in and out of segments that are difficult for them to access directly. Greece is a good example. GREK has seen a lot hedge fund trading."

Bruno del Ama, Global X

One type of institutional investor that tends to use ETFs tactically is ETF strategists. They make model ETFs portfolio that are both strategic and tactical. These ETF strategists have about $86 billion in assets, according to Morningstar. These firms put together portfolios of ETFs that are mostly available as separate accounts. The largest ones are Windhaven Investment Management, F-Squared Investments, and Riverfront Investment Group, according to Morningstar. They are used by both advisors and institutions.

Like master ETF chefs, they whip up different concoctions of ETFs and then sell them to advisors and even other institutions that may not have the resources or in-house management to do it themselves. And while the term *ETF strategist* seems to have stuck, most of them don't like to be called that.

"There has been confusion as to what Windhaven and other ETF strategists are. We are an asset manager. Period. We are an asset manager that happens to use ETFs to implement our views."

Linda Zhang, Windhaven Investment Management

I've also heard them called ETF "assemblers." Regardless of the moniker, they are unique in that they are active managers who use ETFs instead of stocks and bonds. They have Jedi-esque knowledge of ETFs. You can throw any ETF category at them and they'll tell you their detailed opinion, as they have sniffed through nearly every part of the ETF toolbox. They have great stories on why they picked certain ETFs and not others. Unlike the vast majority of institutions, they are not simply picking the most traded ETF.

Just look at the holdings of Windhaven, as shown in Figure 4.7. Not only do they show you nearly all of their total assets, but 100 percent of it is in ETFs. Unlike pensions and endowments, which tease you with their 13F by showing only the tip of the tip of the tip of the iceberg, strategists typically show you everything in the 13F because ETFs are considered equities, and that is what they hold. I sorted their holdings in Figure 4.7 alphabetically by ticker so you could get a taste of the breadth of products used.

The ETF is a godsend to these types of entrepreneurial asset managers. They can then access pretty much anything they need with ETFs. They don't need to rely on a big bank or asset manager.

"The fact that the toolbox has evolved has helped sell ETFs, especially for small institutions who leave bigger firms. Now they can invest in anything they want. They have many more tools to create their own practice."

Daniel Gamba, Blackrock

FIGURE 4.7 Windhaven's 13F Filing as of 3/31/2015

Port WINDHAVEN INVE vs Default (None) by Security Type in USD

Name	Ticker	Wgt	Mkt Val
WINDHAVEN INVESTMENT MANAGEMENT INC		100.00	13,476,762,541
ETFs		100.00	13,476,762,541
EGSHARES BEYOND BRICS ETF	BBRC US	0.61	81,614,799
VANGUARD TOTAL BOND MARKET	BND US	7.93	1,068,903,677
VANGUARD TOTAL INTL BOND ETF	BNDX US	0.61	82,851,785
SPDR BARCLAYS INTL TREASURY	BWX US	0.00	423,320
ISHARES COMMOD SELECT STRAT	COMT US	1.98	266,489,477
POWERSHARES DB COMMODITY IND	DBC US	0.02	2,937,838
WISDOMTREE JAPAN HEDGED EQ	DXJ US	3.51	472,942,801
EGSHARES EM CONSUMER ETF	ECON US	1.22	164,670,425
ISHARES MSCI EAFE MINIMUM VO	EFAV US	0.35	46,710,446
ISHARES JP MORGAN USD EMERGI	EMB US	0.81	109,798,997
GLOBAL X NEXT EMERGING & FRO	EMFM US	0.69	92,739,796
WISDOMTREE INDIA EARNINGS	EPI US	1.24	166,738,887
ISHARES MSCI GERMANY ETF	EWG US	3.17	427,447,409
ISHARES MSCI HONG KONG ETF	EWH US	3.37	453,565,645
ISHARES MSCI JAPAN ETF	EWJ US	3.57	480,741,668
ISHARES MSCI UNITED KINGDOM	EWU US	0.02	2,484,112
SPDR GOLD SHARES	GLD US	0.11	15,412,151
ISHA HEDGED MSCI GERMANY	HEWG US	3.27	440,650,886
PIMCO 0-5 YEAR H/Y CORP BOND	HYS US	1.09	146,544,089

Source: Bloomberg

These entrepreneurial, tactical-oriented companies like Windhaven and Riverfront have influenced larger asset managers as well, who are now serving up similar all-ETF portfolios that investors can use as well. Even Vanguard bundles ETFs into portfolios.

> *"Some of the global asset managers are really just building businesses off of using ETFs for their tactical asset allocation portfolios. It's not just strategists; Fidelity has these asset allocation funds, we do, a bunch of folks do. ETFs have become a larger part of those portfolios."*
>
> James Ross, State Street Global Advisors

In-Kind Creation/Redemption

Institutions can also use ETFs as a way to get rid of, or purchase, a lot of securities in one shot. The most common direction is to hand over a bunch of individual names and get back a few ETFs as way to decrease line items in a portfolio.

In one case that was told to me, a $15 billion institutional fund was using many different managers. It turned over all the collective holdings to an asset manager to dissect. They found that they had 6,000 securities that basically amounted to nothing more than the MSCI ACWI Index, plus one or two factor tilts to quality and momentum. They were paying a lot of fees to get what they could have gotten in three or four liquid ETFs for about 0.15 percent.

This kind of awakening during a portfolio screening was a common phenomenon, according to many of the asset managers I spoke with.

"How did they get all of these disjointed pieces? Because at some point in time they may have been thinking we have a core basket of large-cap stocks, then we got into the separate account craze. Maybe we have some structured products. Then we dabbled in ETFs. Then you say, 'So why do we have all these things?' We are having the discussion that more products does not mean more diversification."

Jim Rowley, Vanguard

Institutions can also go the opposite direction and use the ETF to get their hands on individual securities without having to go into the open market.

An institution can buy little chunks of the ETF and eventually build up a sizable position and then in one shot redeem all of the ETF shares for the underlying securities using the creation/redemption process. A purposeful redemption makes the most sense in a market where the ETF is very liquid but the underlying securities are not as liquid, but it could be used wherever, so long as the ETF does in-kind redemptions, which most do.

"If we wanted immediate exposure to an asset class—be it equity or fixed income—we could buy the ETF and then take the physicals (underlying basket) out the backside and disassemble our participation."

Dave Underwood, Arizona State Retirement System

Doing this is less expensive in some cases than going out and buying all of the underlying securities one by one. And because the ETF posts the creation and redemptions baskets every day, you know exactly what they hold.

FIGURE 4.8 JNK's Daily Flows in 2012

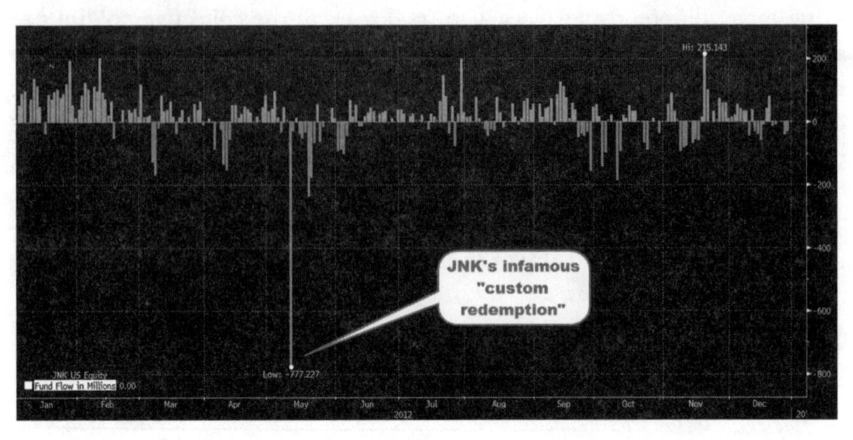

Source: Bloomberg

"The transparency allows for people to now look and decide what they can distill, either for accumulation or exposure. In an active product, you just can't do it."

Ben Fulton, Elkhorn Capital Group

The most famous case of this was a $777 million redemption out of the SPDR Barclays High Yield Bond ETF (JNK). To this day, it is still the largest one-day outflow from the ETF two times over. See Figure 4.8.

An institution had slowly taken up a large position in JNK and then worked with State Street to get delivery of nearly $1 billion worth of junk bonds in one shot. Remember, State Street has all the bonds sitting with the custodian. It is on-demand access. We don't know whether they wanted the bonds or this was part of some arbitrage, but the institution essentially "got ahead" of the illiquid bonds by using the ETF as a bond dealer.

The deal turned heads. It seemed so random because it happened on an otherwise normal week for bonds. So it was completely unconnected to any other market moves or investor sentiment.

It also caused a bit of concern in the media as to whether retail owners of the ETF may be hurt by big trades like this. But it turned out to not really affect the ETF in any way. This practice happens across other bond ETFs and other asset classes all the time, albeit in less dramatic fashion.[6]

"We are seeing a lot more usage of ETFs by institutions as a way to either get bonds or as a way to remove bonds or sell bonds in the market. We are seeing a lot more transactions where, for example, a pension plan might do a large-scale in-kind [creation] of securities into ETFs as a way of consolidating their book and removing line items. At the same time, we are seeing investors go the other direction, where they want to acquire fixed-income securities, and they may find that it's actually more efficient for them from a cost-of-time perspective to buy an ETF and then in-kind redeem and take delivery of those securities."

Matt Tucker, Blackrock

Bespoke ETFs

Another option for institutions—and a growing trend—is to simply have an ETF custom-made for them. These "bespoke" ETFs are typically an idea hatched by an institution that is made into a reality by an ETF issuer.[7] Like an anchor tenant in a building, the institutional client seeds the ETF with over $100 million, so the ETF is instantly profitable for the issuer. The institution gets easy access to their idea plus the possibility of liquidity. It is the definition of a win-win.

Let's look at a few high-profile examples.

United Nations

The United Nations Joint Staff Pension Fund, which has $53 billion in assets, provided initial seeding to two low-carbon ETFs from both State Street and Blackrock. This was the statement from the UN:

> The United Nations Joint Staff Pension Fund ("UNJSPF") welcomes the introduction of two "low carbon" Exchange Traded Funds (ETFs). The UNJSPF provided initial funding for these two ETFs along with BlackRock and State Street Global Advisors, the creators of CRBN and LOWC, respectively.[8]

Both ETFs are low-carbon versions of the MSCI ACWI Index. This is in contrast to, say, solar energy or clean energy ETFs that typically hold volatile upstart companies in a very specific industry. Those can't be used as a core allocation, but these can. These ETFs basically decarbonize your entire plain vanilla world exposure in one shot.

The UN isn't alone in its need to reduce the emissions within its portfolio. Many institutions I spoke with said they wanted to do the same because their constituents were asking.

Arizona State Retirement System

The Arizona State Retirement System, which includes the State of Arizona, three universities, and other organizations, helped create and seed four factor-based ETFs with iShares ETFs using MSCI indices:

iShares MSCI USA Momentum Factor ETF (MTUM)
iShares MSCI USA Size Factor ETF (SIZE)
iShares MSCI USA Value Factor ETF (VLUE)
iShares MSCI USA Quality Factor ETF (QUAL)

The idea came from their need to create an overlay program that would allow for them to adjust the factor-risk exposure of the entire portfolio more easily. They were looking for ways to adjust risk factors in the total portfolio without having to reallocate assets. The ETFs would allow them to adjust their risk factors to desired levels with just a few trades using these ETFs.[9]

They spoke with Blackrock about it, who then spoke with their other institutional clients and found broad interest. iShares then built the ETFs. To this day, Arizona is still one of the largest holders of each factor ETF as seen in Figure 4.9.

What is interesting about this is how the ETFs become a way to plug holes that arise from differences between their passive and active allocations. So, while they trust the active managers, they are also trying to track a benchmark.

FIGURE 4.9 Arizona's 13F from December 31, 2014

Name	Ticker	% Out	% Portfolio	Market Value↑
1. APPLE INC	AAPL US	.028	2.141	181.717M
2. EXXON MOBIL CORP	XOM US	.040	1.834	155.615M
3. MICROSOFT CORP	MSFT US	.039	1.746	148.160M
4. ISH USA MOMENTUM	MTUM US	28.394	1.617	137.209M
5. ISHARES USA QUAL	QUAL US	18.823	1.601	135.923M
6. ISH USA VAL FCTR	VLUE US	25.879	1.580	134.099M
7. ISH USA SIZE FAC	SIZE US	61.908	1.553	131.846M
8. JOHNSON&JOHNSON	JNJ US	.043	1.500	127.315M
9. PROCTER & GAMBLE	PG US	.045	1.304	110.687M
10. CHEVRON CORP	CVX US	.044	1.087	92.296M

Source: Bloomberg

"It's really looking for every place that you can where you might be leaking off relative performance—either through the active managers or the allocation bets. If we could perfectly allocate and keep the portfolio balanced perfectly to the index, we probably wouldn't have to do any factor adjustments. But that's just not possible."

Dave Underwood, Arizona State Retirement System

Fisher Investments

There are examples of bespoke exchange-traded notes (ETNs) as well. In fact, the bespoke ETNs' billions in seed capital makes the ETF side look like child's play. Fisher Asset Management LLC, owned by billionaire chief executive officer Ken Fisher, has worked with different banks to construct ETNs so that it would fill specific investment needs for the firm's clients. They ended up seeding nine ETNs thus far with just over $4 billion.

The Fisher "family" of ETNs includes the Barclays ETN+ Enhanced Global High Yield ETN (FIGY), the DB FI Enhanced Global High Yield Exchange Traded Notes (FIEG), the Barclays ETN+ FI Enhanced Europe 50 ETN (FEEU), the Credit Suisse FI Enhanced Europe 50 ETN (FIEU) and the UBS AG FI Enhanced Big Cap Growth ETN (FBG). You can see from Figure 4.10 that 4 out of the top 12 largest ETNs are Fisher-made.

FIGURE 4.10 ETNs Sorted by Assets Highlighting Four Fisher-Created ETNs

208 funds

Ticker	Name	Fund Type		Tot Asset (M)
1) AMJ US	JPMORGAN ALERIAN MLP INDEX	Exchange Traded Notes		4,919.080
2) MLPI US	ETRACS ALERIAN INFRASTRUCTUR	Exchange Traded Notes		2,329.531
3) FIGY US	FI ENHANCED GLOBAL HIGH YLD	Exchange Traded Notes	✔	1,389.371
4) DJP US	IPATH BLOOMBERG COMMODITY IN	Exchange Traded Notes		1,349.415
5) VXX US	IPATH S&P 500 VIX S/T FU ETN	Exchange Traded Notes		1,151.214
6) OIL US	IPATH S&P GSCI CRUDE OIL TR	Exchange Traded Notes		1,008.939
7) UWTI US	VELOCITYSHARES 3X LONG CRUDE	Exchange Traded Notes		953.538
8) FEEU US	FI ENHANCED EUROPE 50 ETN	Exchange Traded Notes	✔	928.599
9) FBGX US	FI ENHANCED LARGE CAP GROWTH	Exchange Traded Notes	✔	777.109
10) MLPN US	X-LINKS CUSHING MLP INFRASTR	Exchange Traded Notes		695.388
11) IMLP US	IPATH S&P MLP ETN	Exchange Traded Notes		674.048
12) XIV US	VELOCITYSHARES INV VIX SH-TM	Exchange Traded Notes		603.372
13) FLGE US	FI LARGE CAP GROWTH ENHANCED	Exchange Traded Notes	✔	585.214
14) UGAZ US	VELOCITYSHARES 3X LONG NATUR	Exchange Traded Notes		561.226
15) RJI US	ELEMENTS ROGERS TOTAL RETURN	Exchange Traded Notes		548.666
16) VQT US	BARCLAYS ETN+ DYN VEQTOR	Exchange Traded Notes		544.467
17) TRND US	RBS US L/C TRENDPILOT ETN	Exchange Traded Notes		478.200
18) ATMP US	BARCLAYS ETN+ SELECT MLP ETN	Exchange Traded Notes		396.018
19) AMU US	ETRACS ALERIAN MLP ETN	Exchange Traded Notes		375.737
20) INP US	IPATH MSCI INDIA INDEX ETN	Exchange Traded Notes		351.154

They like the ETN structure because it allows for flows in and out easily and is listed on an exchange, so their advisory network can accommodate inflows and outflows.[10] Fisher used different banks to spread the credit risk around and presumably save costs. In addition, they also may have been drawn to the tax benefits of ETNs. As we will discuss in Chapter 5, ETFs that hold derivatives get taxed differently, whereas an ETN with the same strategy is taxed just like shares of Microsoft stock because it doesn't actually hold anything.

"The ETN enables an institutional customer to invest in a complex investment strategy that is packaged in single security like shares of IBM. It allows them to do this in a convenient way, doesn't require an ISDA [for a swap], and will show up on statements right away. Plus they are able to go out and put five or six banks in competition to get the best price for their clients [when making bespoke ETNs]."

Chris Yeagley, UBS

Edelman Financial

Edelman Financial teamed up with iShares and Morningstar to launch the iShares Exponential Technologies ETF (XT), which is an intriguing multi-sector theme ETF that tracks stocks that have developing or are leveraging promising technologies. So it isn't quite a tech-sector play, either. This new thematic concept for Edelman made the most sense in an ETF wrapper.

"We were trying to solve a specific problem for our firm and our firm's clients. Our clients are generally mass affluent. And there are lots of them. We have 27,000 clients. So we needed a vehicle that provided liquidity, very low investment costs, and low account minimum. And there's no vehicle I know of that can match an ETF in those criteria."

Ric Edelman, Edelman Financial

Thanks to Edelman's seed capital, XT was one of the largest ETF launches of all time, with $520 million, although far less than the Fisher ETNs. This chunk of change makes XT instantly profitable for iShares, while Edelman now has a liquid publicly listed product for their clients to use.

Riverfront

While a handful of ETFs were literally custom-made like the ones above, the idea of having institutional or advisor interest prior to launching an ETF is a huge for an issuer. It is something they are compelled to do more and more as the field for ETFs grows increasingly crowded. And in some cases, the best ideas can come from these conversations about what ETFs an institutional investor would like to see.

A great example of this is a company called Riverfront. You may as well call them the "ETF Whisperer" because they have contributed some of the best ideas—and capital—to ETF issuers over the years. Riverfront's ideas are either directly or partially behind ETFs such as WisdomTree Japan Hedged Equity Fund (DXJ), PowerShares Senior Loan Portfolio (BKLN), PowerShares S&P 500 Low Volatility Portfolio (SPLV), and Global X MLP & Energy Infrastructure ETF (MLPX), which collectively have over $33 billion in assets.

In the case of DXJ, Riverfront wasn't the one to suggest currency hedging. But they did suggest a screen for more export-oriented companies that would profit from a weakened currency. At the time, DXJ used a dividend screen, which leaned toward utilities, telecom, and financials. Riverfront thought if Japan ever engaged in U.S.-style quantitative easing, they'd rather be in sectors like industrials and consumer stocks. A filter for exporters would do this.

"We were talking to Jeremy Schwartz (WisdomTree) and we put this idea out to them. We said, you know what would be awesome is if it had this export tilt. We explained the investment rationale, and a couple of months later he came back to town very excited and he had done all this work and went into Bloomberg and went in co by co and said, 'This is actually a really interesting concept.'"

Adam Grossman, Riverfront Investment Group

In the case of MLPX, Riverfront wasn't happy using the MLP ETN or ETF (a dilemma we will discuss in Chapter 6) so they approached Global X about a "third way."

"Riverfront wanted more exposure to MLPs [master limited partnerships] but didn't want the tax issue with the MLP ETFs. They wanted to work on a better structure that gave them exposure to MLPs. So we developed this product that is approximately 75 percent general partners and less than 25 percent MLPs. We worked together on the research and development of it. They seeded and they continued to allocate to it."

Bruno del Ama, Global X

Basically, if you are an ETF issuer, you should be friends with Riverfront—these guys have some seriously good ideas.

"A lot of us are active managers who have come into the strategist space. We have a macro view but we also have a series of people who do bottom-up implementation. So you have a natural gift for going in and looking at the underlying and building themes from the bottom up. So when you combine the intelligence here with the idea that we put our capital behind it, it can make sense. It's just planting seeds with the ETF provider."

Adam Grossman, Riverfront Investment Group

Tax-Loss Harvesting

One of the most popular uses of ETFs is tax-loss harvesting. This simply refers to jumping out of a losing position—either short or long term—in your portfolio and into an ETF with similar exposure. By doing this you keep your exposure, while utilizing the loss to offset gains.

Of course, none of this matters at all if an institution is tax exempt. But for taxable institutions or certain asset pools, it is a popular usage. Asset managers in particular like to use ETFs to do tax-loss harvesting since they are trying to avoid their own capital gains distributions.

ETFs are used a lot for this because they come in such variety that you can go into one that is close in exposure, but not too close. This way you don't violate the wash-sale rule. While many do simply swap out for an ETF with the same index, the general rule of thumb is you should not swap out of ETFs tracking the same index.[11] So you can't sell SPY and jump into IVV. However, you could sell SPY and jump into a number of different large-cap, or broad-market ETFs. There are literally dozens of ETFs with over 95 percent correlation to SPY.

Tax-loss harvesting can also be used with individual stocks. For example, say a mutual fund is sitting on a loss in Schlumberger stock. They may run a correlation screen on ETFs that have high correlations to the stock. In Figure 4.11 we can see that both iShares U.S. Oil Equipment & Services ETF (IEZ) and Market Vectors Oil Service ETF (OIH) would do the best job, which is not a shocker considering they both have over a 20 percent allocation to Schlumberger. Also noteworthy is that the Energy Select Sector SPDR Fund (XLE) is probably what most institutions would reach for, but in the end it is only the fifth-highest correlation.

FIGURE 4.11 The Most Correlated ETFs to Schlumberger Limited

12/31/2013 - 12/31/2014

<Filter>

Security	SLB ↑
11) IEZ	0.891
12) OIH	0.881
13) PXJ	0.841
14) XES	0.821
15) XLE	0.820
16) VDE	0.817
17) IGE	0.811
18) IYE	0.810
19) IXC	0.803
20) FXN	0.791

Source: Bloomberg

Long-Term Allocation

Long-term allocation is this far down the list on purpose. That is because, frankly, most institutions are not using ETFs like this. They may end up with a long-term allocation, but it may not have been their initial reason for buying the ETF.

Again, this goes back to the fact that large institutions can get any core, long-term passive exposure via an SMA for cheaper than the ETF costs. It is hard to believe from a retail point of view that you can get a better deal than 0.05 percent. But you can—if you have billions in assets, the world is your oyster.

"Our index fund cost is half a basis point."

Bob Maynard, Public Employee Retirement System of Idaho

And the SMA isn't just cheaper; it is also customizable exactly to an institution's liking. It is also not porous like a publicly traded ETF with investors coming in and out. An SMA lives in a vacuum. The SMA is like having a pool in your backyard, while the ETF is like the public pool down the street.

"A large institutional investor like us can get U.S. stock exposure for one or two basis points and have the securities lending on top of that. So if you want to get competitive for institutional business, that's the kind of numbers you need to talk about."

Vijoy Chattergy, Hawaii Employees' Retirement System

So the question is: can an ETFs ever win in a fight versus an SMA and see more long-term allocations from institutions? It depends. Even for the massive institutions that get the royal treatment from asset managers, the ETF does have a few tricks up its sleeve that can help it overcome the cost differential in certain instances.

"A huge, huge institution may be able to get an S&P 500 position for 0.02 percent or less and the asset manager will also handle the tracking. But this is much less flexible than an ETF because if you want to sell, you will have to call someone who may try and talk you out of it. ETFs give the institution freedom and also privacy."

Daniel Gamba, Blackrock

For those larger institutions that are internally managed, an ETF can give greater flexibility. You don't have to loop any third parties in or go through a contract process or set up an account.

"One of the things about the separately managed accounts is you can have gates on timing. And also you have to notify and have someone sell it. With ETFs we don't have to do it, we just tell our trading desk to buy or sell it and they do it instantly and so that's really nice."

Michael Brakebill, Tennessee Consolidated Retirement System

While the ETF's value proposition as a long-term passive vehicle for a massive pension fund can be debated, all sides agree on the fact that when you get to the small-level institutions where they aren't getting treated like royalty, the ETF could be the lowest-cost, most benefit-rich option. The only problem with that is that smaller institutions tend to outsource to a consultant.

Generally speaking, consultants aren't very motivated to recommend ETFs. Why would they? Their business has been built around active manager databases that they worked years refining. How would they show value if they don't spend time picking out and finding the next star manager? Then when a manager doesn't perform, they can fire those bad managers and hire new managers.

"I think the traditional institutional consulting community historically has been a little bit asleep at the wheel on [ETFs]. I think some of it also is the consideration of the erosion of their investment base of knowledge on individual active managers. But they seem still a little bit behind the curve in using these and therefore advocating them."

Dave Underwood, Arizona State Retirement System

Many of the people I spoke with also pointed out that consultants can add a layer of protection to the pension fund manager if the portfolio returns aren't up to par. In other words, they can be a scapegoat to point the finger and/or fire if the portfolio's returns aren't up to par. It is like outsourcing blame.

> *"The great thing about using ETFs is you can put all these pieces together. You can build what you want and execute at a very low cost. But on the flip side, the buck stops with you. There is nobody to fire. If you build a portfolio of all index products and put on your small-cap value tilt, there's no active manager (or consultant) to fire if it doesn't work out."*
>
> Jim Rowley, Vanguard

However, despite these headwinds for ETFs as buy-and-hold tools, there there has been some evidence to the contrary in both surveys and holdings data. On Bloomberg, we now have a new field that tells you the holding period of an institution. Some are in fact holding ETFs for long periods of time. One example is EAFE ETF (EFA). This is an ETF that institutions use

FIGURE 4.12 Holding Periods of Pensions, Endowments, and Insurance Companies of EFA

Holder Name	Mkt Val	% Portfolio	% Out	Est. Holding	Inst Type
					[Select Multiple]
1. UNITED SERVICES AUTOMOBILE ASSOC	902.47MLN	N.A.	1.47	9.00	Insurance Company
2. AMERIPRISE FIN GRP	792.12MLN	N.A.	1.29	13.75	Insurance Company
3. NORTHWESTERN MUTUAL	292.43MLN	N.A.	0.48	7.75	Insurance Company
4. NEW JERSEY DIVISION OF INVESTMEN	243.12MLN	0.935	0.40	4.25	Pension Fund
5. DOCTORS CO AN INTERINSURANCE EXC [M..	120.66MLN	N.A.	0.20	1.50	Insurance Company
6. RAYTHEON COMPANY EMPLOYEE BENEFI	85.72MLN	12.401	0.14	0.75	Pension Fund
7. NEW JERSEY MANUFACTURERS INSURAN	54.38MLN	N.A.	0.09	8.75	Insurance Company
8. YALE UNIVERSITY	54.09MLN	77.144	0.09	8.00	Endowment
9. SENTRY LIFE INSURANCE COMPANY	50.95MLN	N.A.	0.08	12.75	Insurance Company
10. BCBS OF MICHIGAN GROUP	42.08MLN	N.A.	0.07	1.25	Insurance Company
11. SWISS RE LTD	37.62MLN	3.291	0.06	1.00	Insurance Company
12. METROPOLITAN LIFE INSURANCE CO	37.28MLN	0.270	0.06	13.75	Insurance Company
13. IBM RETIREMENT FUND	34.99MLN	0.648	0.06	1.00	Pension Fund
14. MANULIFE FINANCIAL CORP	32.39MLN	N.A.	0.05	13.25	Insurance Company
15. AUTO CLUB INSURANCE ASSOCIATION [M...	30.08MLN	N.A.	0.05	0.75	Insurance Company
16. PRUDENTIAL OF AMERICA GROUP	29.18MLN	N.A.	0.05	11.50	Insurance Company
17. GUARDIAN LIFE GROUP	20.89MLN	N.A.	0.03	2.00	Insurance Company
18. WESTFIELD GROUP	19.64MLN	N.A.	0.03	8.50	Insurance Company
19. HOSPITAL SERVICE ASSN OF NE PA [Multi...	19.19MLN	N.A.	0.03	10.50	Insurance Company
20. WESTERN & SOUTHERN LIFE INSURANC [M...	17.42MLN	N.A.	0.03	6.75	Insurance Company
21. KEMPER CORPORATION	15.61MLN	4.812	0.03	3.75	Insurance Company
22. COMMONWEALTH OF PENNSYLVANIA PUB	15.38MLN	0.271	0.03	5.50	Pension Fund
23. OMERS ADMINISTRATION CORP	13.14MLN	0.486	0.02	6.50	Pension Fund

Source: Bloomberg

a lot. Figure 4.12 shows the largest pension, endowment, and insurance company holders of EFA, with most of them holding it for multiple years. Again, is this a long-term allocation or a liquidity sleeve or portfolio rebalance that just lasted a while? Maybe it doesn't matter.

One fascinating case of long-term allocation is Bridgewater Associates, the world's largest hedge fund. They hold a whopping $3 billion worth of EEM and $4.6 billion worth of VWO as well. These two ETFs—plus SPY—make up 87 percent of their 13F filing, as shown in Figure 4.13. However, their 13F filing makes up less than 5 percent of their total assets. No one knows exactly what is happening, but given that they have held both EEM and VWO for over half a decade, it is most likely a basic long-term allocation, probably connected to one of their funds strategies.

Many folks told me that institutions may start off with a more short-term usage as their motivation but that it turns into long-term allocation. There could be situations where some of these positions were bought as placeholders but ended up happy with the returns of the ETF and stopped looking for a manager.

Another scenario for institutions holding an ETF long term is simply that they don't have any research dedicated to a certain area. For example, maybe they simply don't know much about mid-cap stocks so just "plug and play" with something like the SPDR S&P MidCap 400 ETF Trust (MDY), which tracks 400 mid-caps. Then they could play with the large- and small-cap areas where they have research to make individual security beta and/or an

FIGURE 4.13 Bridgewater's ETF-Heavy 13F Filing as of March 31, 2015

Port BRIDGEWATER AS vs Default (None) by Security Type in USD

Name	Ticker	Wgt	Mkt Val
BRIDGEWATER ASSOCIATES LP		100.00	12,799,252,690
Common Stocks		11.98	1,533,725,978
ETFs		87.15	11,154,781,152
VANGUARD FTSE EMERGING MARKE	VWO US	35.94	4,599,827,597
SPDR S&P 500 ETF TRUST	SPY US	26.58	3,401,646,135
ISHARES MSCI EMERGING MARKET	EEM US	23.85	3,052,856,072
ISHARES IBOXX INVESTMENT GRA	LQD US	0.50	63,948,098
ISHARES CORE S&P 500 ETF	IVV US	0.29	36,503,250
REITs		0.19	24,224,862
Depository Receipts		0.66	83,879,695

Source: Bloomberg

active manager they like. This is portfolio completion turning into long-term allocation.

"You can make yourself market weight. And at a minimum you now know that with one purchase you have risk-controlled that stratified sample of your risk matrix until either you want to overweight the sector or get fundamental analysts that can make individual picks for you."

Jim Rowley, Vanguard

But what about if an institution stopped stopped what they were doing and just used ETFs for all their needs? That's what more and more advisors and retail investors are doing. Could we see institutions slash their overhead and gut their infrastructure and go low-cost ETF all around? Maybe using the "Buffett Special" of 90 percent VOO and 10 percent SHY? After all, it has a 10-year annualized return of 7.5 percent, which is slightly more than the average endowment 10-year return of 7.1 percent[12] and a good deal more than the 6.6 percent 10-year return of pension funds.[13] That Buffett sure knows what he's talking about, huh?

Or even going more diverse with four to five core ETFs and then four to five more for satellite positions or income generators and be done with it. Could this be a model for more institutions going forward? Only time will tell.

"I personally think that would make sense for a lot of them. I think changing the structure of institutional funds is kind of like turning the battleship. This goes back to what David Swensen said that you can't really get caught up in the middle of half-assing an alternative program. You have to be all in. And a lot of places don't have the bandwidth to be able to handle the due diligence, the tracking, and the risk reporting of an active portfolio. So, yeah, [an all-ETF portfolio] would probably be a good idea for many. It's just getting them to admit it's a good idea. It would take time, probably longer than common sense would dictate."

Ben Carlson, Ritholtz Wealth Management

Personal Usage

Long-term usage brings us to personal usage. I found in my own research and interviews that many of the people who run institutional money use ETFs in their personal accounts. This is how many of them get introduced to ETFs.

ETF industry veteran Anthony Rochte recalled doing ETF luncheons, and many times afterwards he'd have an institutional fund manager come up to him and ask him to come to his office for follow-up. They were interested for two reasons. One was to use them as a placeholder after they fired one manager while they looked for another. But the other reason was that they were interested to use them for their personal account.

Another ETF issuer noted to me that he would hear the same things from institutional managers using ETFs in their personal account. He would ask them why they like ETFs for their personal account, and they'd tell him that they liked that ETFs track an index and are low-cost and liquid. He would then try to point out that those same things apply to his work portfolio, too.

So why would they do one thing for their personal accounts, yet another for their institutional funds? When researching this book I heard many different reasons for this. For one, there could be an element of self-preservation. There could be some fear that picking a couple of ETFs may make their job obsolete. Another was that institutions have access to better managers than retail investors and the negotiating power to lower fees.

"It's a distinction I would make that as a retail investor myself, I don't think I can access the types of managers that Duke or Vanderbilt can access. I stick it all with Vanguard. The low fees and low tracking error are very attractive to me."

Anders Hall, Vanderbilt University Office of Investments

When I met with John Bogle to talk about this book, I brought up to him how the people who know the most about Wall Street and investing seemed to lean towards using index funds and ETFs over active management. He expanded on this notion that when it comes down to someone's personal money, the smarter they are the more likely they are to index.

"Look at all the directors of our mutual fund competitors. You know what they own when they buy their kids' college plan? They're going to Vanguard. Look at a security salesman at Merrill Lynch and his uncle comes in and doesn't know what to do. He says "Buy Vanguard" because it keeps him from looking like an idiot."

John Bogle, Vanguard

Will that personal usage ever translate into institutional fund usage? Again, if an institution thinks they have access to the best managers that are not available to retail investors and those managers outperform, then probably not. I have a feeling this debate will persist in the coming years, though.

Notes

1. Omprakash, Anand, "Accessing Efficient Beta: ETFs vs. Futures." BNP Paribas, October 2014.
2. Mercado, Sebastian, "Deutsche Bank: Special ETF Research—A Stock Picker's Guide to ETFs," June 2015.
3. Sauter, Gus, "Investment Opportunities Abound with Exchange-Traded Funds." *Institutional Investor Journals,* 2001 no. 1 (2001): 16–22.
4. Snider, Ben, "Hedge Fund Trend Monitor." Goldman Sachs, August 2014.
5. Mercado, 2015.
6. Conway, Brendan, "That Big Junk-Bond Trade: Not So Unusual After All." *Barron's,* May 22, 2012; blogs.barrons.com/focusonfunds/2012/05/22/that-big-junk-bond-trade-not-so-unusual-after-all/.
7. Conway, Brendan, "New Trend: The 'Bespoke' ETF." *Barron's,* January 17, 2014; www.bing.com/search?q=New+Trend%3A+The+%E2%80%98Bespoke%E2%80%99&src=IE-TopResult&FORM=IETR02.
8. Dieterich, Chris, "United Nations Helped Fund Two 'Low Carbon' ETFs." *Barron's,* December 11, 2014; blogs.barrons.com/focusonfunds/2014/12/11/united-nations-helped-fund-two-low-carbon-etfs/.
9. Bell, Heather, "Why Arizona Teamed Up with iShares on 4 ETFs." ETF.com, July 17, 2013; www.etf.com/sections/features/19311-why-arizona-teamed-up-with-ishares-on-4-etfs.html?nopaging=1.
10. Dugan, Kevin, "Fisher Asset Holds $1.4 Billion of ETNs in Second Notes Foray." Bloomberg, August 8, 2013; www.bloomberg.com/news/articles/2013-08-08/fisher-asset-holds-1-4-billion-of-etns-in-second-notes-foray.
11. Nadig, Dave, "ETFs Made Easy: Tax Loss Harvesting." ETF.com, December 23, 2014; www.etf.com/sections/blog/24110-etfs-made-easy-tax-loss-harvesting.html.
12. "Building on 11.7% Gain in FY2013, Educational Endowments' Investment Returns Averaged 15.5% in FY2014." National Association of College and University Business Officers (NACUBO), Press Release, January 29, 2015; www.nacubo.org/About_NACUBO/Press_Room/2014_NACUBO-Commonfund_Study_of_Endowments_(Final_Data).html.
13. Braum, Martin, "U.S. Public Pensions Return 6.8% in 2014 for Six Years of Gains." Bloomberg, February 9, 2015; www.bloomberg.com/news/articles/2015-02-09/u-s-public-pensions-return-6-8-in-2014-for-six-years-of-gains.

CHAPTER 5

ETF Due Diligence

Now that we know how exchange-traded funds (ETFs) work and why and how institutions use them, it is time to talk about how they could use them better. As we know, most of them just pick the most traded ETF in a category and are done with it. This chapter will show why it doesn't need to be like that and how to vet and trade ETFs properly. This chapter is like eating your vegetables. It is the transition between your background in ETFs and actually meeting the ETFs in Section two.

Choosing an ETF is like shopping for a pair of shoes. Just as there is no right or wrong shoe at the shoe store, there is no "right" or "wrong" ETF. It depends on what your needs are and what your style is. That's why there is no magic bullet number or star rating that proves one ETF is better than another for every type investor in every type of scenario. There are several ETFs that would be horrible long-term investments for my mom, but they are perfect products for a hedge fund doing a short-term trade.

This is why ETF due diligence is both an art and a science. The process is going to be driven by the immediate and long-term goals and preferences of the investors. While exposure should be the most important consideration, beyond that it will depend. For example, liquidity may trump cost for a pension looking to do a manager transition or to rebalance the portfolio, while index weighting may trump liquidity for an asset manager making a strategic allocation. That's why it is important to know what your goal is before picking an ETF.

"You really just want to start with a clear idea of what you want to accomplish in a fund, then go looking for the tools to do that. Don't start with the tool."

Dave Underwood, Arizona State Retirement System

As mentioned earlier, when an institution picks an ETF, it almost always just uses the most traded ETF in the category—end of story. This is in stark contrast to how much time and energy they will spend on due diligence on managers or single securities. Why wouldn't you apply the same rigorous process to ETFs? After all, the difference in returns amongst similar ETFs can be just as wide, if not wider, as the difference between managers.

"Institutions are going to need to develop expertise on due diligence on ETFs in the same way you used to do it on individual securities and managers."

Daniel Gamba, Blackrock

I've been doing nothing but comparing ETFs for nearly a decade now and I can tell you that, just like snowflakes, no two ETFs are exactly the same. And there is no perfect ETF. If you line up three or four ETFs in the same category, you will find both big differences and/or small differences. Every one of them has a couple of pros and a couple of cons relative to their peers.

"My view is that people don't do enough due diligence. People will see ETFs with the same name and then just go with the cheapest or most liquid option without digging into the specifics and without understanding the trading complexities."

Justin Sibears, Newfound Research LLC

To help deal with this, I've developed a checklist for evaluating ETFs that is made up of a few simple categories:

1. Exposure
2. Cost
3. Liquidity
4. Risk
5. Regulatory structure

This checklist is not only very similar to the checklist that ETF strategists use, it is also the foundation for an analytical tool I helped design—and use a lot for my research—for the Bloomberg terminal called ETF<GO>, as shown in Figure 5.1. Each tab in the middle of the screen is a different category of due diligence with many fields that support it.

Beyond going through this checklist, this chapter will also pivot into different areas while doing some myth-busting in order to educate. So roll with it, but know everything eventually links back to one of those five things.

FIGURE 5.1 ETF<GO>

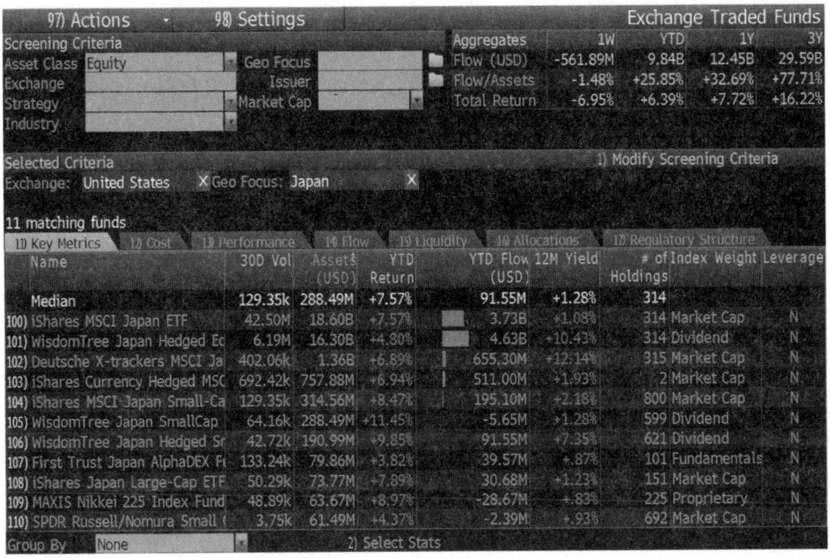

97) Actions 98) Settings Exchange Traded Funds

Screening Criteria

Asset Class Equity | Geo Focus
Exchange | Issuer
Strategy | Market Cap
Industry

Aggregates	1W	YTD	1Y	3Y
Flow (USD)	-561.89M	9.84B	12.45B	29.59B
Flow/Assets	-1.48%	+25.85%	+32.69%	+77.71%
Total Return	-6.95%	+6.39%	+7.72%	+16.22%

Selected Criteria 1) Modify Screening Criteria

Exchange: United States X Geo Focus: Japan X

11 matching funds

11) Key Metrics 12) Cost 13) Performance 14) Flow 15) Liquidity 16) Allocations 17) Regulatory Structure

Name	30D Vol	Assets (USD)	YTD Return	YTD Flow (USD)	12M Yield	# of Holdings	Index Weight	Leverage
Median	129.35k	288.49M	+7.57%	91.55M	+1.28%	314		
100) iShares MSCI Japan ETF	42.50M	18.60B	+7.57%	3.73B	+1.08%	314	Market Cap	N
101) WisdomTree Japan Hedged Ec	6.19M	16.30B	+4.80%	4.63B	+10.43%	314	Dividend	N
102) Deutsche X-trackers MSCI Ja	402.06k	1.36B	+6.89%	655.30M	+12.14%	315	Market Cap	N
103) iShares Currency Hedged MSC	692.42k	757.88M	+6.94%	511.00M	+1.93%	2	Market Cap	N
104) iShares MSCI Japan Small-Ca	129.35k	314.56M	+8.47%	195.10M	+2.18%	800	Market Cap	N
105) WisdomTree Japan SmallCap	64.16k	288.49M	+11.45%	-5.65M	+1.28%	599	Dividend	N
106) WisdomTree Japan Hedged Sr	42.72k	190.99M	+9.85%	91.55M	+7.35%	621	Dividend	N
107) First Trust Japan AlphaDEX Fu	133.24k	79.86M	+3.82%	39.57M	+.87%	101	Fundamentals	N
108) iShares Japan Large-Cap ETF	50.29k	73.77M	+7.89%	30.68M	+1.23%	151	Market Cap	N
109) MAXIS Nikkei 225 Index Fund	48.89k	63.67M	+8.97%	-28.67M	+.83%	225	Proprietary	N
110) SPDR Russell/Nomura Small (	3.75k	61.49M	+4.37%	-2.39M	+.93%	692	Market Cap	N

Group By None 2) Select Stats

Source: Bloomberg

While performance is a tab on ETF<GO>, it is not part of my checklist. I realize that performance is what it is all about, but really is just a by-product of other aspects of the ETF and market forces beyond your control. That's one of the biggest mistakes investors consistently make—choosing an investment based solely on past performance.

> *"People always buy what they wish they wish they would have bought and sell what they are about to need."*
>
> Mark Yusko, Morgan Creek Capital Management

Now that all of that is out of the way, let's take a look at the different categories for comparing ETFs.

Exposure

It may be obvious, but it has to be said anyway: you have to know what is *in* the ETF. The exposure is far and away the most important thing. What does it hold, and how does it hold it? How is the index constructed? How does it weight the stocks? What are the fundamentals? After all, this is what you are buying. This determines the performance. This is the engine of the car.

The Holdings

Let's start with looking at the securities in the ETF. Find out what stocks are in there. For example, when you look at something like the Market Vectors Oil Service ETF (OIH) and look at the top holdings, it is clear: you better really love Schlumberger Ltd and Halliburton, because they make up a third of your holdings, as we can see in Table 5.1.

It is a good idea to look at not only the actual stocks or bonds in the portfolio but also the allocation breakdowns by sector, country, and market cap size, or by credit quality and maturity for bond ETFs. If you get into the habit of doing this, you will avoid being surprised. Getting surprised on your birthday is fun; getting surprised because of an investment product is not.

This is why if I had to come up with a "golden rule" for ETF due diligence, it would be "Thou shalt not pick an ETF based on the name alone." Yes, sometimes the name and the holdings are pretty well matched, but there are many cases where there's more going on inside the ETF than the name lets on.

For example, did you know that the Global X Social Media ETF (SOCL) has nearly a third of its holdings in the emerging markets? Or that the iShares Large Cap China ETF (FXI) has nearly 50 percent of its assets in the financial sector? Or that the SPDR S&P Emerging Middle East & Africa ETF (GAF) has 76 percent of its holdings in South Africa? Or that the PowerShares DB

TABLE 5.1 Top 10 Holdings of OIH as of June 30, 2015

Top 10 Fund Hlds (MHD)	Net Fund
Schlumberger Ltd	20.154%
Halliburton Co	12.495%
Baker Hughes Inc	7.836%
Cameron International	5.239%
National Oilwell Varco Inc	5.172%
Helmerich & Payne Inc	4.572%
Weatherford International	4.401%
FMC Technologies Inc	4.028%
Tenaris SA	3.783%
Dresser-Rand Group Inc	3.693%

Source: Bloomberg

Gold Fund (DGL) doesn't hold actual gold, but rather gold futures? Or that the PowerShares Water Resources Portfolio (PHO) has only 16 percent of its holdings in actual water utility companies?

Not that any of those ETFs is bad per se; it's just that their names don't tell you enough. And this can have a major effect on performance and user experience. An extreme example of this is the case of the two frontier-market ETFs back in 2014. They have nearly identical names: iShares MSCI Frontier 100 ETF (FM) and the Guggenheim Frontier Markets ETF (FRN).

That's where the similarities end, as FM had a 70 percent allocation to Middle Eastern countries, while FRN had a 75 percent allocation to South American countries. The difference was simply because FM invested in local shares, while FRN used American depositary receipts (ADRs). This allocation difference created a performance gap that you could drive a Mack truck through. Since FM launched in September 2012, through the end of 2014 it returned 38 percent, while FRN lost 22 percent, as seen in Figure 5.2. If

FIGURE 5.2 Total Return of Two Frontier-Market ETFs, September 11, 2012, to December 31, 2014

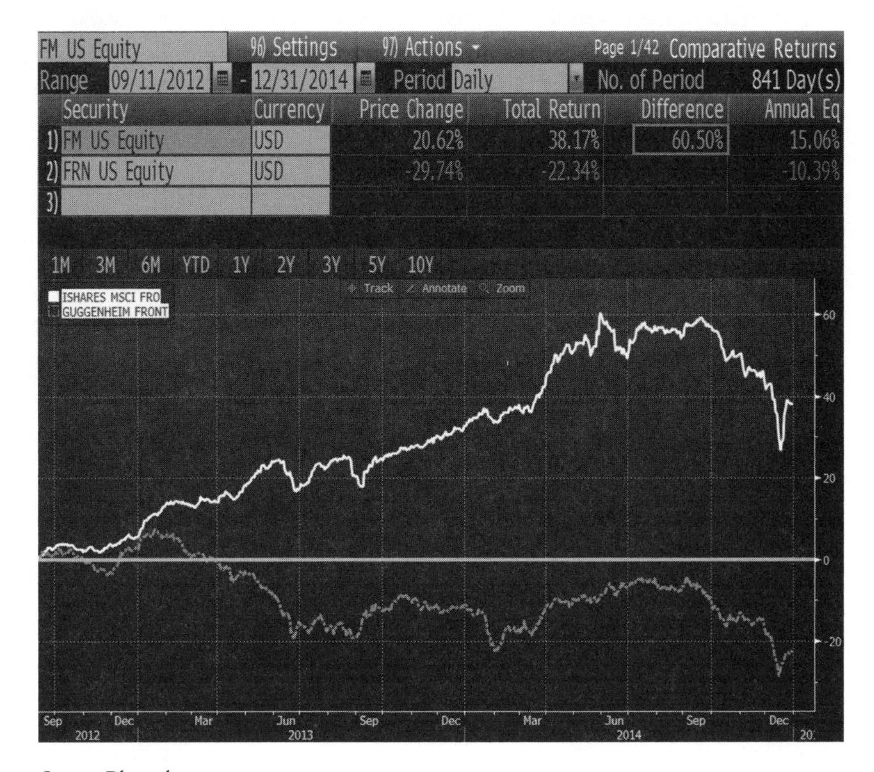

Source: Bloomberg

a 60 percent performance differential doesn't scare investors into lifting the hood and looking at what an ETF holds, nothing will.

To even further complicate this, Guggenheim revised FRN's index methodology in April 2015, and now it looks a lot more like FM. This move resulted in the ETF slashing its South America weighting from 75 percent down to 20 percent, while their Middle East exposure jumped from 19 percent to 46 percent. Since the change toward a more FM-like look, FRN's performance has been virtually the same since the change.

The point here is that even if you think you know the ETF and looked under the hood last time, do it again just to be sure. The holdings and allocations always tell the truth.

Index Weighting Methodology

The underlying positions in the ETF all need to be given a weighting. This can vary greatly. Most of the big, popular ETFs that institutions use are market cap weighted, which is weighting companies based on their size. However, many ETFs track indexes that don't weight their holdings using market cap.

Frequently called "smart beta," these ETFs will use dividends, fundamentals, or factors such as momentum or volatility to weight the holdings. There are over 20 different weighting methodologies and counting. In any large group of ETFs, there will always be a handful of smart-beta options, as shown in Figure 5.3. We will deep dive into smart beta later in the book.

A great example of how impactful the index weighting methodology can be is the SPDR Oil & Gas Exploration & Production ETF (XOP), which

FIGURE 5.3 Index Weighting Methodology

Name	30D Vol	Assets (USD)	YTD Return	YTD Flow (USD)	12M Yield	# of Holdings	Index Weight	Leverage
137) Vanguard FTSE Pacific ETF	423.41k	3.33B	+11.59%	452.90M	+2.41%	840	Market Cap	N
138) iShares MSCI United Kingdom	3.14M	3.61B	+7.99%	442.30M	+7.03%	111	Market Cap	N
139) Schwab Fundamental U.S. La	239.27k	696.53M	+2.33%	431.00M	+1.64%	621	Fundamentals	N
140) Schwab Fundamental Interna	219.02k	656.31M	+8.92%	421.20M	+1.69%	824	Fundamentals	N
141) Alerian MLP ETF	4.05M	8.79B	-4.86%	377.20M	+7.21%	23	Market Cap	N
142) iShares U.S. Energy ETF	1.00M	1.52B	-1.41%	373.40M	+2.46%	93	Market Cap	N
143) Vanguard Total World Stock I	348.02k	4.40B	+6.95%	357.90M	+2.26%	7115	Market Cap	N
144) ProShares UltraShort S&P50C	8.13M	1.32B	-9.75%	351.80M	--	--	Market Cap	Y
145) Schwab Emerging Markets Eq	392.99k	1.52B	+5.56%	345.00M	+2.71%	726	Market Cap	N
146) WisdomTree International He	108.08k	365.99M	+13.72%	341.60M	+4.62%	237	Dividend	N
147) iShares MSCI EAFE Value ETF	225.82k	3.05B	+9.21%	320.60M	+4.46%	491	Market Cap	N
148) iShares U.S. Healthcare ETF	165.61k	2.45B	+13.39%	318.30M	+.92%	105	Market Cap	N

Source: Bloomberg

FIGURE 5.4 XOP's Equal Weighting Gives It Extra Volatility

XOP US Equity 98) Report Page 1/5 Description

1) Profile 2) Performance 3) Holdings 4) Allocations 5) Organizational

SPDR S&P OIL & GAS EXP & PR Objective Energy

SPDR S&P Oil & Gas Exploration & Production ETF is an exchange-traded fund incorporated in the USA. The Fund's objective is to replicate as closely as possible the S&P Oil & Gas Exploration & Production Select Industry Index, an equal-weighted index. [FIGI BBG000BGB482]

6) Current Data (COMP)		Bloomberg Classification		Appropriations	
1 yr Tot Ret vs Index		Fund Type	ETF	Leverage	No
SPSIOPTR Index -38.1346		Asset Class	Equity	Actively Managed	No
XOP US Equity -37.9455		Industry	Energy	Swap Based	No
		Market Cap	Broad Market	Derivatives Based	No
		Strategy	Blend	Currency Hedged	No
		Geo. Focu...	U.S.	Replication Strategy	Full
				Securities Lending	Yes
7) Price (GP)	USD 49.09	Trading Data		Characteristics	
8) NAV 06/23/15	USD 49.13	Bid Ask Spread	0.720	Und. Index	11) SPSIOPTR
INAV	USD 48.97	30D Avg Volume	6.1M	Index Weight	Equal
Fund Percent Premium	0.020%	10) Implied Liquidity	2.1M	Px Track. Error	.899
52 Wk H 06/24/14	USD 83.49	Market Cap	USD 1.70B	NAV Track. Error	.110
52 Wk L 01/14/15	USD 41.63	Shares Out	34.7M	Inception Date	06/22/06
9) Options(OMON)	Yes	Total Assets	USD 1.70B	Expense Ratio	.350%

Source: Bloomberg

tracks a subsector of the energy sector. As shown in Figure 5.4, XOP equal weights all of the stocks, which include mid and small caps. By giving equal exposure to smaller companies, you introduce additional volatility, above and beyond an already volatile industry. So investors should brace for a very bumpy ride with XOP, which is currently at three times the volatility of the Standard & Poor's (S&P) 500 index.

> *"What's interesting is some ETFs that might not seem small cap, at least by their name, tend to have some pretty strong small-cap characteristics."*
>
> Justin Sibears, Newfound Research LLC

Related to the weighting methodology is the index selection criteria. Mostly, this is related to the weighting methodology, but sometimes it isn't and you should watch out for it. One popular example of this is the Vanguard Dividend Appreciation ETF (VIG), which screens for companies that have increased their annual dividends for 10 or more consecutive years. So the selection is very specific, but it market cap weights them. Investors should be aware of the selection and weighting methodologies and the biases within them.

Index Replication Strategy

An ETF has two main ways it can replicate the returns of the index. It can "fully" replicate the index's returns by holding all the securities that are in the index, or it can "optimize" by holding a representative sample of securities in the index's return. Some ETFs in Europe do synthetic replication using swaps, but in the United States the main dilemma is whether to pick full or optimized replication. Which one is better? Again, it depends.

"We favor full replication for sure. With optimization, now you are introducing the risk that the ETF portfolio manager is going to get it right. And there's a chance that they can't."

Gary Stringer, Stringer Asset Management

While it may seem like investors would automatically prefer full replication, it actually depends on the investor and asset classes involved. Some asset classes—such as fixed income and emerging markets—are not as liquid as others, and ETFs may optimize so that the holdings are more liquid and they can track better. Neither way necessarily leads to better or worse performance. It is more nuanced and depends on many factors.

"Full replication gives you more precision and it may give you tighter tracking. But sometimes we find an optimized ETF might be preferable in a particular asset class if there are liquidity concerns like fixed income or emerging markets. There are trade-offs to each."

Linda Zhang, Windhaven Investment Management

Fundamentals

It can be useful to look at the portfolio statistics related to an ETF. Essentially this calculating stats on the ETF as if it we a single security. For equity ETFs this means looking at the weighted averages for fundamentals such as price-to-earnings or price-to-book. For fixed-income ETFs it could mean looking at the duration or credit quality. While portfolio stats can be a little tricky in certain cases, for the most part they can help in the vetting process.

A good example is comparing the average price-to-earnings ratio (P/E) for two of the most popular China ETFs: the Deutsche X-trackers Harvest CSI 300 China A-Shares ETF (ASHR) and the iShares China Large-Cap ETF (FXI).

They are both China ETFs by name. They both track large caps. But one has a P/E of 20, while the other is 11. By looking at the fundamentals, you would have stopped to do more research and found that the reason is that ASHR tracks large-cap A-shares listed in Mainland China and FXI tracks large-cap H-shares listed in Hong Kong—two totally different worlds. Figure 5.5 also shows just how wide the dispersion of P/E ratios is among popular China ETFs.

Of course, using average P/E alone to make a decision is unwise. Just because you see that the Global X Nigeria ETF (NGE) has a P/E of 7 doesn't

FIGURE 5.5 Some Serious Dispersion of P/E Ratios among China ETFs

<Search name or ticker> 97) Output 98) Actions 99) View Fund Screening

20 funds

Ticker	Name	Fund Geographical Focus	Avg Price/Earnings
1) KWEB US	KRANESHARES CSI CHINA INTERN	China	127.003
2) ASHS US	DEUTSCHE X-TRACKERS HARVEST	China	68.958
3) CNXT US	MARKET VECTORS CHINA AMC SME	China	62.819
4) PGJ US	POWERSHARES GLD DRG CHINA	China	50.468
5) CQQQ US	GUGGENHEIM CHINA TECHNOLOGY	China	30.220
6) CHIQ US	GLOBAL X CHINA CONSUMER ETF	China	26.429
7) ECNS US	ISHARES MSCI CHINA SMALL-CAP	China	22.999
8) ASHR US	DEUTSCHE X-TRACKERS HARVEST	China	20.272
9) CHAU US	DIREXION DAILY CSI 300 CHINA	China	20.156
10) PEK US	MARKET VECTORS CHINAAMC A-SH	China	19.969
11) HAO US	GUGGENHEIM CHINA SMALL CAP E	China	19.803
12) GXC US	SPDR S&P CHINA ETF	China	13.326
13) YAO US	GUGGENHEIM CHINA ALL-CAP ETF	China	12.955
14) AFTY US	CSOP FTSE CHINA A50 ETF	China	12.048
15) MCHI US	ISHARES MSCI CHINA ETF	China	11.734
16) FXI US	ISHARES CHINA LARGE-CAP ETF	China	10.582
17) YINN US	DIREXION DAILY FTSE CHINA BU	China	10.464
18) CHIX US	GLOBAL X CHINA FINANCIALS	China	8.052

Source: Bloomberg

mean it is necessarily a bargain and that the SPDR S&P 500 Trust (SPY) with a P/E of 20 is expensive. Still, it is important information when vetting the ETF.

You can also go beyond the P/E ratio to look at things like the price-to-book ratio, free cash flows, debt-to-equity, operating margin dividend yield, and market cap. The sky is the limit really. Figure 5.6 shows average fundamentals for the ETF at the top as well as the individual constituents below.

Where average P/E can be tricky and should be approached with extra caution is in high-flying growth-y areas like biotech or social media, where some companies may not be making a profit yet, so they can produce a negative P/E. That can mess up the math. There can also be differences in a bond ETF's duration or yield. Different sources have different calculations, and it greatly impacts the numbers you will see.

In defense of the data vendors of the world, even though we may represent different ways of doing it, we are consistent across all ETFs. The same cannot be said about ETF issuer fact sheets or web sites. The problem there is that each ETF issuer may have different methods of calculating stats such as P/E or duration. This makes it sketchy to compare ETFs from different issuers. You may not agree with Bloomberg or another data service's method, but at least you know what it is and that it is being applied to all ETFs apples to apples.

Cost

What is the total cost of an ETF? It depends. There are so many variables and they change from investor to investor. Some costs are the same for all investors, such as the expense ratio and tracking error, but other costs, such as trading costs and taxes, can totally depend. This section will include a look at all fixed as well as variable costs.

Expense Ratio

The most important cost that comes with an ETF is the expense ratio. This is the annual fee that gets taken out of the assets of the ETF. But it doesn't get taken out once a year; it gets taken out a tiny bit each day. I like to use the metaphor of a termite. Just as a termite lives inside of a wall, nibbling away at the wood every day, an expense ratio lives inside of your total return, nibbling away at basis points. As such, the lower the expense ratio, the smaller the termite. It's that simple.

FIGURE 5.6 Fundamental Breakdown of the Holdings of SPY

Name	Ticker	Wgt	P/E	P/B	Free CF	Debt/Equity	Op Margin	Div Yld	Market Ca
SPDR S&P 500 ETF TRUST (SP...		100.00	19.89	2.84	8,165	113.08	13.30	1.99	20,285,385
APPLE INC	AAPL US	3.88	15.70	5.67	64,518	34.01	30.15	1.52	731,824
MICROSOFT CORP	MSFT US	1.97	17.88	4.13	26,285	35.36	28.17	2.64	371,392
EXXON MOBIL CORP	XOM US	1.89	12.89	2.08	5,543	19.14	8.39	3.29	355,687
GENERAL ELECTRIC CO	GE US	1.47	18.48	2.56	15,462	239.16	6.44	3.30	277,592
JOHNSON & JOHNSON	JNJ US	1.47	16.82	4.08	13,793	27.97	28.10	2.86	276,694
WELLS FARGO & CO	WFC US	1.44	14.15	1.79	20,044	156.47	37.89	2.46	298,087
JPMORGAN CHASE & CO	JPM US	1.37	11.32	1.21	36,805	325.33	29.64	2.29	258,848
BERKSHIRE HATHAWAY INC-CL B	BRK/B US	1.37	20.70	1.44	17,207	34.70	16.49		348,236
PROCTER & GAMBLE CO/THE	PG US	1.15	20.08	3.51	11,423	52.62	16.73	3.25	216,470
PFIZER INC	PFE US	1.13	19.10	3.16	13,488	53.40	26.10	3.13	212,440
VERIZON COMMUNICATIONS INC	VZ US	1.03	13.55	20.86	16,955	1,214.13	15.91	4.56	194,829
CHEVRON CORP	CVX US	1.00	10.88	1.21	-9,088	21.78	8.49	4.28	188,217
AT&T INC	T US	0.99	14.75	2.16	9,946	111.51	8.24	5.18	186,481
BANK OF AMERICA CORP	BAC US	0.98	12.73	0.82	-1,749	241.18	13.13	1.13	185,572
FACEBOOK INC-A	FB US	0.98	85.32	6.58	3,902	0.50	35.93		246,788
GILEAD SCIENCES INC	GILD US	0.95	13.84	10.51	16,433	72.03	64.01	0.35	179,601
WALT DISNEY CO/THE	DIS US	0.95	24.51	4.22	6,957	32.49	23.93	1.01	194,126
CITIGROUP INC	C US	0.92	10.94	0.86	34,425	270.81	17.07	0.14	174,129
AMAZON.COM INC	AMZN US	0.90		19.11	3,161	75.94	0.31		207,689
MERCK & CO. INC	MRK US	0.89	30.22	3.50	6,468	63.30	12.51	3.03	166,773
GOOGLE INC-CL A	GOOGL US	0.86	27.70	3.54	13,061	4.83	24.81		376,034

Source: Bloomberg

The longer your planned holding period, the more important the expense ratio becomes in your cost analysis since it is ongoing and relentless. And unlike a termite, you can't kill it.

That said, simply choosing the ETF with the lowest expense ratio isn't necessarily a good strategy. Just because an ETF is cheap doesn't make it the best one for you. Think about the example with the frontier-market ETFs. If you had picked FRN simply because it was cheaper, the small amount saved in fees would be totally decimated by its 60 percent underperformance of FM.

However, if there are similar ETFs giving similar exposures, expense ratio should be a big factor. A great example of the power of the expense ratio comes from the world's largest hedge fund, Bridgewater Associates. As we learned in the preceding chapter, they are the largest holder of the iShares MSCI Emerging Markets ETF (EEM), with $3.3 billion worth of shares, as shown in Figure 5.7.

EEM charges 0.67 percent in fees, about four times more than what's charged for several other emerging-market ETFs with solid liquidity. If Bridgewater switched to the iShares Core MSCI Emerging Markets ETF (IEMG), which charges 0.18 percent, they'd save about $15 million each year

FIGURE 5.7 Largest Holders of EEM as of June 30, 2015

EEM US Equity 25) Settings 26) Export Security Ownership
iShares MSCI Emerging Markets CUSIP 46428723
1) Current 2) Historical 3) Matrix 4) Ownership 5) Transactions 6) Options
Search Name All Holders, Sorted by Size 21) Save Search 22) Delete Search 23) Refine Search
Text Search Holder Group All Holders Allocate Multi-Managed

Holder Name	Ticker	Mkt Val	% Portfolio	% Out	Est. Holding F	Inst Type	% Chg Pos	Latest Chg
						All Types		
1. BRIDGEWATER ASSOCIATES LP	20273Z US	3.15BLN	24.000	10.33	5.25	Hedge Fund Manager	-2.28	-1,793,103
2. BANK OF AMERICA CORPORATION	BAC US	1.41BLN	0.547	4.64	11.25	Investment Advisor	-17.48	-7,304,363
3. BLACKROCK		1.35BLN	N.A.	4.43	10.00	Investment Advisor	17.87	7,167,104
4. WELLS FARGO & COMPANY		1.35BLN	N.A.	4.42	11.75	Investment Advisor	113.67	17,469,587
5. NEW JERSEY DIVISION OF INVESTMEN	2738283Z US	992.2MLN	3.789	3.26	5.50	Pension Fund	-8.09	-2,130,400
6. GOLDMAN SACHS GROUP INC	GS US	827.04MLN	0.335	2.72	11.25	Investment Advisor	-6.41	-1,381,512
7. ONTARIO TEACHERS PENSION PLAN BO	1885Z CN	713.85MLN	5.138	2.34	4.00	Pension Fund	-32.80	-8,500,000
8. FMR LLC		670.79MLN	N.A.	2.20	10.50	Investment Advisor	152.98	9,893,559
9. MORGAN STANLEY		611.45MLN	N.A.	2.01	12.00	Investment Advisor	-47.66	-13,580,041
10. RETIREMENT SYSTEMS OF ALABAMA/TH	8167983Z US	502.61MLN	2.653	1.65	2.25	Investment Advisor	0.00	0
11. MIZUHO FINANCIAL GROUP INC		407.62MLN	N.A.	1.34	2.50	Bank	1.22	119,426
12. PNC FINANCIAL SERVICES GROUP INC	PNC US	399.06MLN	0.553	1.31	11.50	Investment Advisor	0.70	67,185
13. UBS		387.79MLN	N.A.	1.27	11.25	Investment Advisor	20.62	1,616,774
14. US BANCORP	USB US	357.85MLN	1.346	1.17	8.25	Investment Advisor	2.91	261,816
15. BANK OF NEW YORK MELLON CORP	BK US	331.48MLN	0.086	1.09	9.50	Investment Advisor	-14.61	-1,382,877
16. BNP PARIBAS		323.68MLN	N.A.	1.06	9.00	Investment Advisor	172.92	5,001,986
17. LINCOLN NATIONAL CORP	LNC US	288.81MLN	22.866	0.95	1.00	Insurance Company	12.93	806,480
18. APG ALL PENSIONS GROUP	1245675D NA	282.32MLN	0.571	0.93	2.50	Investment Advisor	54.01	-8,085,000
19. JP MORGAN CHASE & CO	JPM US	258.6MLN	0.061	0.85	11.00	Investment Advisor	4.68	281,848
20. BP INVESTMENT MANAGEMENT	1299706Z US	253.47MLN	7.906	0.83	1.50	Investment Advisor	-70.00	-14,424,850
21. CITIGROUP INCORPORATED		246.25MLN	N.A.	0.81	9.50	Investment Advisor	-32.86	-2,939,199
22. GRANTHAM MAYO VAN OTTERLOO & CO	31986Z US	216.01MLN	0.631	0.71	2.25	Investment Advisor	-29.02	-2,154,386
23. AMERIPRISE FIN GRP		200.77MLN	N.A.	0.66	9.50	Insurance Company	-19.14	-1,159,122

Source: Bloomberg

just on the expense ratio. And since they have held EEM for over five years, we are talking about $70 million. Bridgewater could hire one or perhaps even two new portfolio managers for that kind of money.

The higher fees in EEM also make it harder for the ETF to track its index, as seen in Figure 5.8. In 2014, EEM lagged its benchmark by 0.64 percent, while IEMG lagged its index by only 0.25 percent. It's no accident that the amount they lagged is roughly the same as their respective expense ratios.

Tracking Error

When an ETF lags its index this is also considered a cost. After all, an ETF's point in life is to mimic the performance of an index. How well the ETF tracks is paramount to an institution since every basis point can mean millions. That is what tracking error is all about.

FIGURE 5.8 EEM's Tracking Difference for 2014

Source: Bloomberg

"Among all those due diligence variables, overwhelmingly it comes down to the extent to which you can replicate the index."

Jim Rowley, Vanguard

This is also the one factor that is far greater to institutions than maybe even the issuers realize, according to a recent survey by Ernst & Young. Figure 5.9 shows the disconnect between the issuer and the investors when it comes to the importance of tracking error.

"As a CIO, I can control two things: risk and fees. I can't control return. So what is the tracking error against the beta we are trying to get access to?"

Jim Dunn, Verger Capital Management

So how do you measure an ETF's ability to track its index? There are two ways to skin this cat: tracking error and tracking difference.

Tracking error is the average standard deviation from the daily excess return of the ETF versus its index. In plain English, it is how consistent or inconsistent the ETF at matching the daily returns of the index. We calculate this on Bloomberg and display it on every ETF's description page. Tracking error is more valuable for short-term holding periods because it uses daily returns.

Tracking difference, however, is simply the difference between the ETF's return and the index return over a given time period. It is expressed as an absolute number. It gets confusing because most people will call this tracking error when really they mean tracking difference.

FIGURE 5.9 ETF Issuers Underestimate Tracking

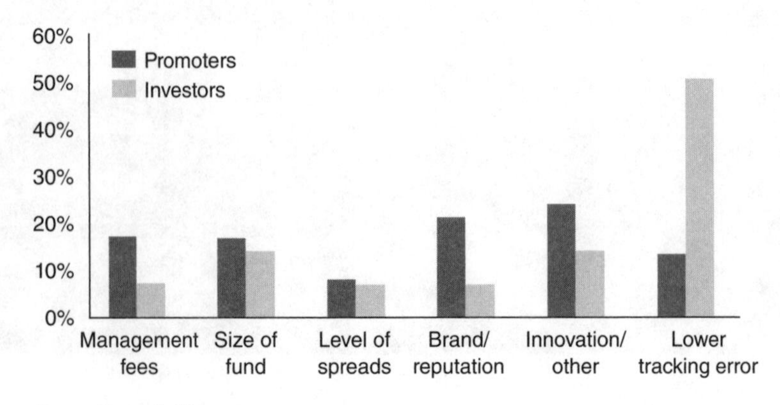

Source: Ernst & Young

The good news is that tracking difference—the more popular measure—is much easier to understand and more logical really. ETF.com has a great way of looking at tracking difference, which is to look at the ETF's return against the index using the median of 250 observations of historical one-year returns.[1]

In theory, the median one-year tracking difference for an ETF should be roughly equal to the expense ratio since that is taken out of the NAV of the ETF. And mostly this is what happens, as is the case with IEMG and EEM. In some cases, it misses by more due to illiquid underlying holdings or poor management. On the flip side, an ETF can also track better than its expense ratio. This is the ideal situation.

An example of better than expected tracking is the Vanguard Total Stock Market ETF (VTI) which charges 0.05 percent but sometimes averages just 0.02 percent tracking difference and over some stretches has no difference whatsoever, as shown in Figure 5.10. How can this be?

Tracking can be reduced beyond the expense ratio in two ways by the ETF issuer.

FIGURE 5.10 VTI's Tracking Difference Is Less than Its Expense Ratio

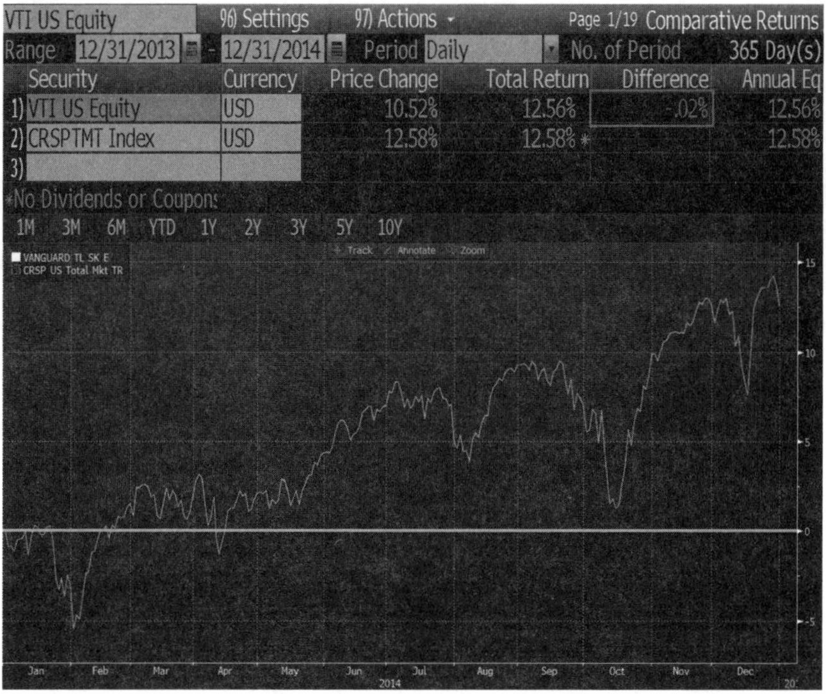

VTI US Equity 96) Settings 97) Actions Page 1/19 Comparative Returns

Range 12/31/2013 - 12/31/2014 Period Daily No. of Period 365 Day(s)

	Security	Currency	Price Change	Total Return	Difference	Annual Eq
1)	VTI US Equity	USD	10.52%	12.56%	-.02%	12.56%
2)	CRSPTMT Index	USD	12.58%	12.58% *		12.58%
3)						

*No Dividends or Coupons

1M 3M 6M YTD 1Y 2Y 3Y 5Y 10Y

VANGUARD TL SK E
CRSP US Total Mkt TR

Jan Feb Mar Apr May Jun Jul Aug Sep Oct Nov Dec
2014

Source: Bloomberg

One way to lower tracking difference is by securities lending. The stocks and bonds held by the ETF's custodian are in a proverbial storage locker. But unlike a storage locker, the issuer doesn't just keep them there collecting dust. A portion of them—one-third to be exact—can be lent out to investors who are looking to short those stocks.

Keep in mind that many ETFs hold securities that no one really wants to borrow, so there may not even be much opportunity in the way of securities lending. On the flip side, there can be cases where the securities an ETF holds are in really high demand to short, such as small caps or solar stocks.

In addition to securities lending, there are little things portfolio managers may be able to do to earn back another basis point or two of the expense ratio simply with their acumen in managing the fund. The index an ETF tracks rebalances its holdings each quarter and is affected by initial public offerings (IPOs), mergers and acquisitions, and the like. All these can help a shrewd manager pick up another little bit of gain to put back into the ETF.

This is the unsung art that goes into effective passive management. The media is obsessed with the "rock star" active managers who have a good run, but gives little to no credit to the passive manager whose work helps put money back into investors' pockets. This is probably because great passive management is about tying an index. And in a culture obsessed with winning, it just doesn't make good copy. But rest assured, inside this ETF world, there is nothing passive about passive portfolio management.

"It's a game of basis points. You want every one of them."

Jim Rowley, Vanguard

There have been some solid arguments that tracking difference is actually more important than expense ratio. In a way, this is true, because expense ratio is one of the inputs into tracking issues. The problem with using tracking difference as the only cost measure is that 99 percent of ETFs are tracking different indices, so it is almost never truly an apples-to-apples comparison.

In the rare cases where there are multiple ETFs tracking the same index, then, yes, tracking should probably be the ultimate decider. But those are rare cases involving a few S&P indices. About 99 percent of the time, competing ETFs will not be tracking the same index, so tracking error and tracking difference is relative. If you really want the exposure a certain index gives you, tracking is more of a checklist item—something to look at to make sure it isn't out of line. If you see an ETF whose exposure you like, with decent liquidity and expense ratio, and the tracking difference is way high, then it means something is going on that you need to look into.

Another good rule of thumb is that the more exotic the underlying holdings, the more tolerance you need to have for tracking difference. For example, a tracking difference of 1.23 percent for the Market Vectors Vietnam ETF (VNM) isn't necessarily that bad given the illiquidity and difficulty of accessing Vietnamese stocks. However, if you see a 1.23 percent in a large-cap U.S. stock ETF, you should run away screaming.

"In most cases with U.S. equities the tracking error will typically be tiny, it's just a very liquid market. But in a less traded area, like fixed income, that's where we will see two ETFs tracking the same index but with different tracking errors. There's a degree of skill. And so when we look at historical tracking errors to see if there were any periods where the two performances are different, we typically will have a call with the PM and the trading team of that particular manager."

Linda Zhang, Windhaven Investment Management

Trading Costs

Investors must also consider how much a round-trip ticket costs when it comes to trading the ETF. Trading costs consist of mainly the bid-ask spread and impact costs. There is also the creation fee which can end up in the spread as well as premiums and discounts to be considered. Much of these costs are variable and depend on a number of things.

Of course, when it comes to trading, many institutions will use a broker or liquidity provider who will make these decisions for them. This gets back to the idea of people liking things to be convenient. Trading is another one of those things. Even if someone else is doing the trading, it can't hurt to learn a bit about your options. This is especially important for active managers who use ETFs a lot. Best execution is crucial since they trade so much.

"At Windhaven, we use ETFs for both strategic long-term investment themes and tactically to express near-term views. Trading efficiency is an important criterion in our ETF selection process, as we view trading efficiency and related costs as a part of the total cost of an ETF."

Linda Zhang, Windhaven Investment Management

Bid-Ask Spread

The bid-ask spread is the difference between what a buyer is willing to pay and what a seller is willing to sell at. In other words, the price you pay for an ETF is more than the price you would sell it at. That difference is what the market middlemen keep for their services.

Unlike the relentless expense ratio termite, the spread is a one-time cost. Most of the big, highly liquid ETFs, such as SPDR S&P 500 Trust (SPY), trade with a bid-ask spread of one cent, sometimes called a *penny wide spread.* This is the best scenario and ends up costing no more than a basis point or two for investors. No big deal.

However, the vast majority of ETFs are not fortunate enough to be in the Penny Wide Club and have bid-ask spreads that are more. One example is the PowerShares FTSE RAFI US 1000 Portfolio (PRF), which is currently trading at a bid-ask spread of 8 cents, as shown in Figure 5.11. That means an extra 0.18 to 0.20 percent of cost if done over the exchange, which is not that bad, but adds a lot to the all-in cost. But PRF's holdings are very liquid, and going through a market maker, you should be able to get a tighter spread than that. More on that in a minute.

FIGURE 5.11 PRF's Quote Monitor Shows an 8 Cent Spread

PRF US $ ↑90.7799 -.39 J90.72/90.79J 9x
At 10:20 d Vol 289,821 O 90.57P H 90.82D L 90.325D Val 2
PRF US Equity 1) Actions 97) Settings Page 1
2) Trade Recap 3) Quote Recap
From 04:00:00 07/06/15 Show Ticks All Cond Code Definitions
To 20:30:00 07/06/15
High 90.82 Low 90.325

Time	BMMKR	E	Bid/Trd/Ask	E	Size (x100)
					<min size>
10:22:22		P	90.71/90.79	J	14x21
10:22:22		Z	90.71/90.79	J	14x21
10:22:22		P	90.71/90.79	J	24x21
10:22:16		P	90.71/90.79	J	14x21
10:22:14		J	90.71/90.79	J	17x21
10:22:14		P	90.71/90.79	J	24x21
10:22:14		P	90.71/90.79	J	14x21
10:22:14		P	90.71/90.79	P	10x2
10:22:14		P	90.71/90.79	P	10x3
10:22:14		P	90.71/90.78	P	10x1
10:22:14		P	90.71/90.78	P	10x2
10:22:12		P	90.71/90.78	P	10x11

Source: Bloomberg

But assuming you did pay the 0.20 percent spread, it is a one-time cost and gets diluted away the longer you hold the ETF. This is why holding period should help inform a total cost analysis. For short holding periods it may make more sense to go with the more expensive ETF if it has a lower spread.

Let's look at example using our buddy EEM versus the cheapest emerging-market ETF on the market, the Schwab Emerging Markets Equity ETF (SCHE). While their exposures are not exactly the same, they are close enough to use an example. Despite SCHE's much cheaper expense ratio of 0.14 percent, there is still a case for holding EEM if your holding period is short because EEM is cheaper to trade. You can use a breakeven holding period calculation to nail down exactly how short that holding period needs to be.[2] Let's apply it to the EEM versus SCHE case.

SCHE has an expense ratio of 0.14 percent and a bid-ask spread of 0.08 percent. Meanwhile, EEM has an expense ratio of 0.67 percent and a trading spread of just 0.02 percent. All you have to do is divide the trading cost difference, 0.06 percent, by the expense ratio difference, 0.53 percent. Your breakeven holding period then is 11 percent of a year. In other words, EEM is a better deal if you're holding period is less than 6 weeks, as shown in Table 5.2.

Of course, the bid-ask spread is also subject to variability. The numbers I'm using are the averages, but not necessarily the ones an investor will get. In fact, investors—especially institutions—have more leverage than they think in getting a good spread from a market maker.

"One of the big things institutional investors don't take advantage of enough in the ETF market is this concept of negotiation. An investor will ask a market maker for a market in an ETF, and they will come back with a bid and offer. Investors take that as a binary event. I can either buy at that price or say no thank you. But you could say to them what you would pay for it, within the spread, and you put the onus back on them to say yes or no. I don't think people take advantage of that process enough."

David Abner, WisdomTree Asset Management

TABLE 5.2 Calculating Breakeven Holding Periods

Ticker	EEM	SCHE	Difference	Breakeven Holding Pd	Breakeven Pd
Expense ratio	0.67%	0.14%	0.53%	11.32% of a year	5.9 weeks
Avg bid-ask spread	0.02%	0.08%	0.06%		

Source: Bloomberg

Impact Costs

Impact cost is basically how much an order adversely moves the execution price. It makes total sense to think your order may drive the price up a bit as you acquire the shares, especially for lesser traded ETFs. While there are many variables at play, it is an important cost to watch out for.

> *"Data shows that two-thirds of your transaction costs come from your order impacting the market, the implicit cost that is not easily seen in your transactions. A fund manager that doesn't measure their implicit market impact cost will underperform their peers following a similar investment strategy. A costly mistake."*
>
> Michael Baradas, Bloomberg Tradebook

If an institution is trading over the exchange, then impact costs are exactly the same as when trading a stock. The standard benchmark used by quantitative analysts is the arrival price or midpoint when an order is sent. For example, say the midpoint between the bid and ask is $10 and the buy order is executed at 10.02; the market impact was thus 0.20 percent.

Market Orders versus Limit Orders

If you are trading over an exchange, it is possible you can control your costs by the type of order you put in. There are two main different types of orders. The first is a market order, which is an order to buy or sell at the best available current price. With a market order you are at the mercy of the market to get filled, but the upshot is the trade will almost definitely get done.

Being at the mercy of the market can turn ugly on occasion, with investors getting prices they may not want—especially with lesser traded ETFs. Figure 5.12 is a look at a graph of the Market Vectors Fallen Angel ETF (ANGL) pricing for the past four years. Can you spot the market order gone bad?

The worst thing you can do is put in a market order in right before the market opens. This is what we saw happen on August 24, 2015, which saw hundreds of ETFs trade at sharp discounts amid a major selloff. The reason for this is that you want to give some time for the ETF's underlying holdings—stocks or bonds—to start trading and pricing. This way, a market maker knows where things stand. In the first few minutes, they may widen out their bid-ask spread to account for unknown risk—especially if the previous day was rough. In addition, many large money managers will place buy and sell orders at the open and close, which can add unnecessary volatility

FIGURE 5.12 Pricing History for the Past Four Years for ANGL

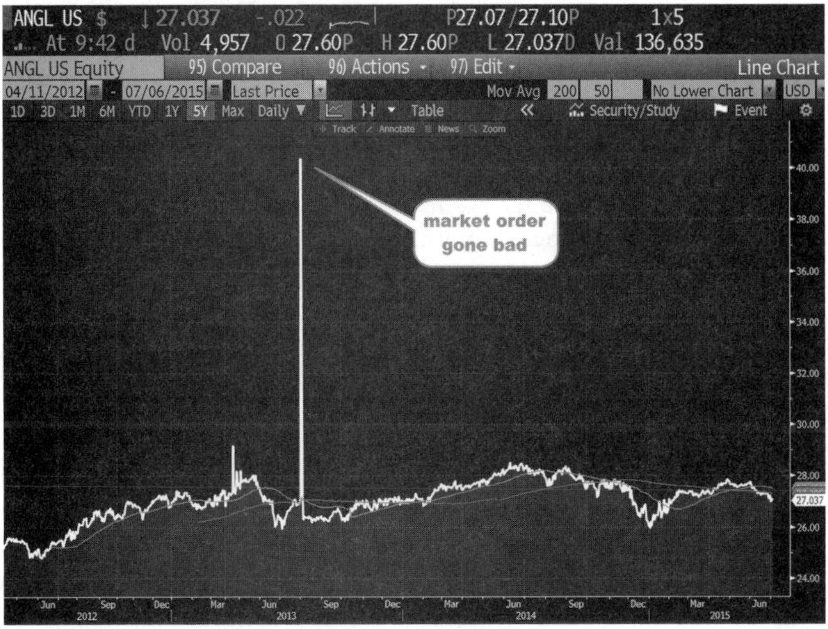

Source: Bloomberg

to the open and close. This is why many will advise not trading in the first 15 minutes of the day and the last 15 minutes.

> *"If you don't know what you are doing, do not use a market order. Or even better, just never throw in a market order."*
>
> Larry Seibert, 780 Riverside Drive, LLC

Alternatively, you can take control and protect yourself by using a limit order. With a limit order you are basically saying, "I will not pay any more or less than the price I want." Limit orders give you complete control, but the downside is that you may not get your order filled.

> *"Using a limit order can be problematic, too, because you can end up taking forever to get your execution. Limit orders make sense when it is a smaller ETF, but if it trades a lot, you can just go in with a market order."*
>
> Gary Stringer, Stringer Asset Management

The good news is that you can always move the limit order up or down to increase the chances of getting filled. The question is how do you know what price to submit? You could look at the midpoint between the bid and the ask or the last price from the last trade. Another option is to use the intraday net asset value (iNAV). However, because of the way it is calculated, it could be useless.

Basically, the iNAV is an index of intraday prices of the securities in a fund's most recent creation unit. In plain English, it is basically trying to tell you what the value of the ETF is right now based on the holdings so you know how much you should pay for the ETF. ETF issuers are required to publish an iNAV every 15 seconds.

It is a noble effort, but by and large creates more confusion than clarity. For U.S.-focused equity ETFs the iNAV is a pretty good indicator of what the underlying stocks are worth. This is because the calculation is running off of stocks that are trading. No problem there. But for international ETFs where the underlying markets are closed, the iNAV is running off of stale data. And with fixed-income ETFs, it is using bonds that may not have priced in a while.

However, institutions that have a large enough order can bypass the exchange altogether by doing a block trade with a market maker who will figure all this out for them. Market makers have their own homemade iNAVs that help them determine the fair value. They can also access authorized participants (APs) to utilize the creation-redemption process. Speaking of creation/redemption, there is also a fee for that too. It gets baked into the spread you pay.

The creation fee is what the ETF issuer charges the AP for each creation unit they make. Creation fees vary from a few hundred dollars to tens of thousands of dollars. The good news for large creations is that the fee is not per unit, but rather a one-time fee no matter how many units you are creating. The creation fees are paid by the AP, although they aren't a charity, so they will pass those fees down the line and it will end up in the bid-ask spread.

Creation fees run the gamut from $0 to $28,000. Figure 5.13 shows the creation fees for the largest ETFs. This will give you an idea of just how different they can be depending on the asset class and strategy.

"For fixed income and international ETFs the creation fee can be very expensive. They can be like $15,000 just to make the phone call to create the order. Then, you are paying a bid-ask spread and then taxes. Then, you are trying to source liquidity to deliver the shares in the basket. It can add up."

Mohit Bajaj, WallachBeth Capital

FIGURE 5.13 Dispersion of Creation Fees among the Very Largest ETFs

<Search name or ticker> 97) Output 98) Actions 99) View Fund Screening
52 funds

Ticker	Name	Creation / Redemption Fee	Tot Asset (M)
1) SPY US	SPDR S&P 500 ETF TRUST	3,000.000	179,049.969
2) IVV US	ISHARES CORE S&P 500 ETF	1,250.000	69,822.883
3) EFA US	ISHARES MSCI EAFE ETF	15,000.000	63,513.031
4) VTI US	VANGUARD TOTAL STOCK MKT ETF	500.000	57,033.840
5) VWO US	VANGUARD FTSE EMERGING MARKE	9,300.000	48,702.816
6) QQQ US	POWERSHARES QQQ TRUST SERIES	1,000.000	39,873.777
7) IWM US	ISHARES RUSSELL 2000 ETF	3,000.000	32,806.328
8) VOO US	VANGUARD S&P 500 ETF	500.000	32,642.625
9) EEM US	ISHARES MSCI EMERGING MARKET	7,700.000	30,414.051
10) IWF US	ISHARES RUSSELL 1000 GROWTH	1,450.000	30,300.934
11) VEA US	VANGUARD FTSE DEVELOPED ETF	10,000.000	28,107.570
12) IJH US	ISHARES CORE S&P MIDCAP ETF	1,000.000	27,689.381
13) BND US	VANGUARD TOTAL BOND MARKET	100.000	27,199.516
14) GLD US	SPDR GOLD SHARES	2,000.000	26,710.039
15) IWD US	ISHARES RUSSELL 1000 VALUE E	1,750.000	26,526.379
16) VNQ US	VANGUARD REIT ETF	250.000	26,017.355
17) AGG US	ISHARES CORE U.S. AGGREGATE	500.000	24,997.939
18) LQD US	ISHARES IBOXX INVESTMENT GRA	500.000	20,816.211
19) VIG US	VANGUARD DIVIDEND APPREC ETF	250.000	20,507.375

Source: Bloomberg

The decision to do creation/redemption is on the market maker's shoulders. It will depend on whether the cost for them to carry a position is more than the cost for them to create it. If it is cheaper to create, they will create it. That's why everyone who is a market maker creates and redeems via APs.

Premiums and Discounts

While not a trading cost per se, investors should understand what it means when an ETF's price is trading above or below its NAV, which is known as a premium or discount. When trading ETFs, premiums and discounts can perplex and even scare investors. For the most part, most ETFs trade close to their NAV, displaying very small premiums typically.

"In normal environments, premiums are just the cost of accessing those markets."

Mohit Bajaj, WallachBeth Capital

The reason most ETF's premiums and discounts are held to a check is due to the arbitrage we talked about earlier. When the price moves to far away from the NAV, market makers will arbitrage away the difference by buying shares of the ETF and then selling the basket or vice versa. This can be a specific trade, but mostly it's just something that happens in the process of making markets.

This is why "premium" and "discount" may not be the right words for it. I think a better name is "arbitrage band" because that is the threshold the price has to hit before arbitrage becomes profitable. The more costly to trade the underlying holdings, the larger the arbitrage band will probably be.

"The width of the arbitrage band for a given ETF is driven by how expensive it is to trade the underlying asset class. A highly efficient asset class like equities will be a very small arbitrage band. When you move into less liquid or more expensive asset classes, you are going to have a larger arbitrage band simply because it costs more to buy and sell high yield securities and execute the arbitrage."

Matt Tucker, Blackrock

Each ETF's arbitrage band is flexible and stretches sometimes due to the winds in the market. If the ETF is tracking something people all want to buy—or sell—at once, it will stretch. But on the vast majority of days it will be within a certain band. The premium/discount history for IWM, as shown in Figure 5.14, shows the 5- to 10-basis-point arbitrage band that it trades within, although on the occasional day it can be as high as 15 basis points.

Ninety-nine percent of the time these arbitrage bands are totally natural and investors should not let them affect their ETF usage. For example, many international ETFs typically trade at a premium or discount simply because the NAV is struck using closing prices of markets that are closed. The NAV

FIGURE 5.14 IWM's Daily Premium/Discount (aka "Arbitrage Band") for the Past 12 Months

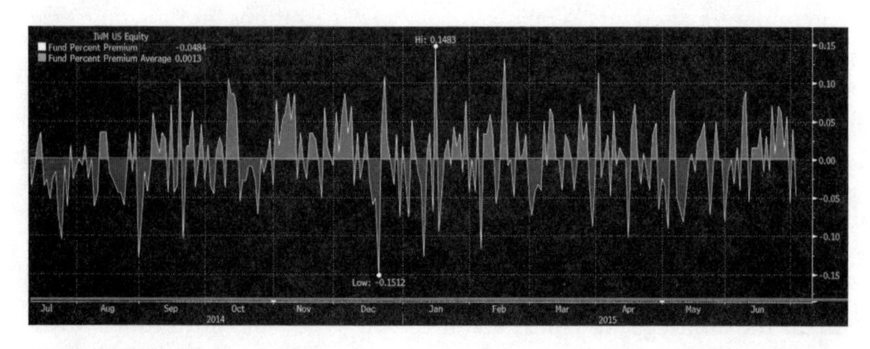

Source: Bloomberg

is stale while the U.S. market is open, so, of course, there will be a variation between the price and the NAV. This means international ETFs can trade a bit like futures. This goes back to how ETFs are price discovery vehicles.

However, there are a few cases internationally where local markets can add their own specific cause for enlarged premiums with local taxes or foreign investment limitations. These local market costs will get baked into the arbitrage band.

In the case of the Market Vectors Vietnam ETF (VNM), the arbitrage band can easily be 2 percent above the NAV and 2 percent below the NAV during normal activity. The reason, though, is logical. This ETF is buying local shares of Vietnamese stocks, which have high foreign ownership limits. As such, the issuer has at times limited creations in order to account for these limits and as well as illiquidity in the Vietnamese markets. If those regulations were lifted you would likely see the arbitrage band narrow.

Brazil is a great example of an ETF that was trading at a persistently high premium thanks to a tax on foreign investors. During that period, the iShares MSCI Brazil Capped ETF (EWZ) operated with an average premium of 1 to 2 percent. After the tax got removed in 2011, the premiums and discounts dropped to roughly 0.50 percent, and a more normal-looking arbitrage band developed, as seen in Figure 5.15.[3]

Fixed-income ETFs will typically trade at a slight premium. The reason comes down to the transaction costs for trading the underlying market—just like with equities—but also can be a result as to how the NAV is calculated. The majority of NAVs for bond ETFs are calculated using the bid price of the bonds, not the mid-price, which is how it is down with equity ETFs. This means the NAV is basically calculated using the most conservative estimated prices of where you could sell all the bonds immediately and thus it is lower

FIGURE 5.15 EWZ's Arbitrage Band Dropped after a Tax Was Lifted on Foreign Investment

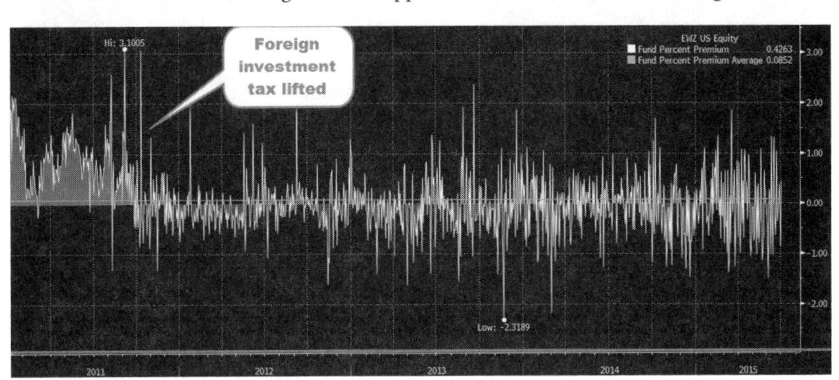

Source: Bloomberg

than reality. Hence, the persistent premium. This is why the price of the ETF will have to rise even further up above the NAV and then above the arbitrage band to make an arbitrage worth it.

It is also important to remember that the arbitrage band generally will be larger the less liquid the market. We saw it with Vietnam above, but it also can be seen in the fixed income category as well. For example, the 52-week average premium for iShares iBoxx $ High Yield Corporate Bond ETF (HYG) is 0.21 percent, while the average for iShares 20+ Year Treasury Bond ETF (TLT) is just 0.02 percent.

Arbitrage bands can also get narrower over time simply because there is more volume in the ETF and more competition among market makers. Figure 5.16 shows HYG's average arbitrage band has come down since its inception as its volume has grown. This feeds into the idea that the more ETFs trade, the cheaper they become to trade.

Your Secret Weapon to Keep Trading Costs Down

All this trading information can get confusing. There is a lot to learn, and it is different for everyone. This is why even institutional investors may want to utilize a free source of help before making an actual ETF trade. Most big issuers have a capital markets desk staffed with folks who know what they are doing and will provide help for customers looking to make a trade in one of their products. The smaller issuers may only have a person or two, but they can also be accessed just the same.

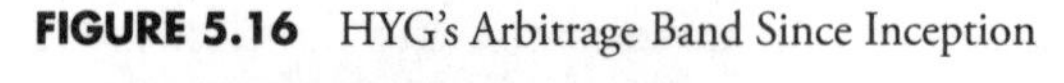

FIGURE 5.16 HYG's Arbitrage Band Since Inception

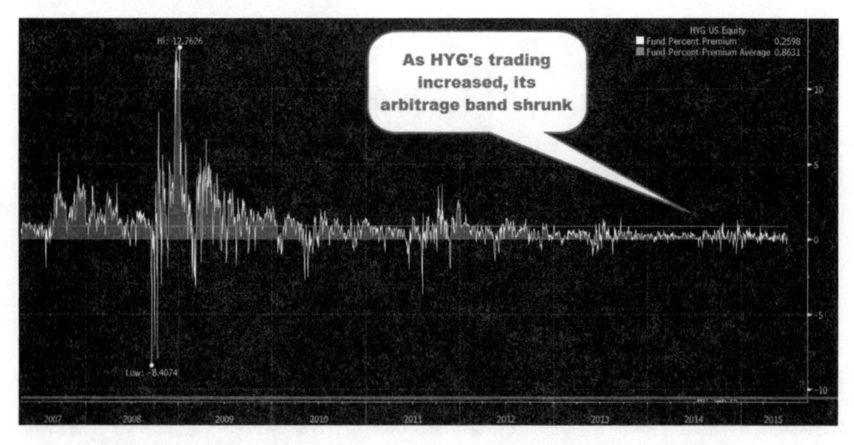

Source: Bloomberg

When it comes to trading ETFs, the issuer can be your ally, as they want you to have pleasant experience in their ETFs. They can educate you on how to trade ETFs and deal with market makers and so on. You can find the phone number on their web site. It's pretty easy and could save you money.

> *"We deal with institutions and investors of all sizes every day explaining the mechanics of ETF trading. We enable them to understand what questions they should be asking their liquidity providers, and we give them a rationale for framing the answers that they are receiving."*
>
> David Abner, WisdomTree Asset Management

Taxes

Many institutions are tax exempt and don't need to worry about taxes. But for everyone else, taxation is another potential cost to be aware of. There are two ways that taxes can become a cost.

Taxes When the ETF Sells Securities

First, an ETF may incur capital gains tax just from the day-to-day management of the fund. It will then pass this on. This is pretty rare, but it can happen.

Ideally, you want an ETF that doesn't pay any capital gains at all. And if it does, you hope it is only long-term capital gains, which are taxed at a lower rate for taxable investors. And if it does pay out capital gains, you hope it is in conjunction with good performance as was the case of HEDJ, a currency-hedged ETF that paid out capital gains as part of income it received from using currency forwards, as shown in Figure 5.17. That income is passed on as gains.[4]

Taxes When You Sell the ETF

Second is how the ETF is taxed when you sell it. The ETF itself may be taxed differently by the IRS. An ETF's taxation is almost always dictated by its holdings. So if an ETF holds a basket of stocks, it is taxed like a stock. If the ETF holds futures contracts, it is taxed like you hold futures contracts. If an ETF holds bars of gold in a vault, then it is taxed as if you hold bars of gold in a vault. While it is a bit more nuanced than that, this is the general idea.

Generally speaking, there is nothing shocking here, as 90 percent of ETFs assets are in ETFs that are taxed just like shares of a U.S. stock. So if

FIGURE 5.17 An ETF Can Pay Both Long-Term and Short-Term Capital Gains

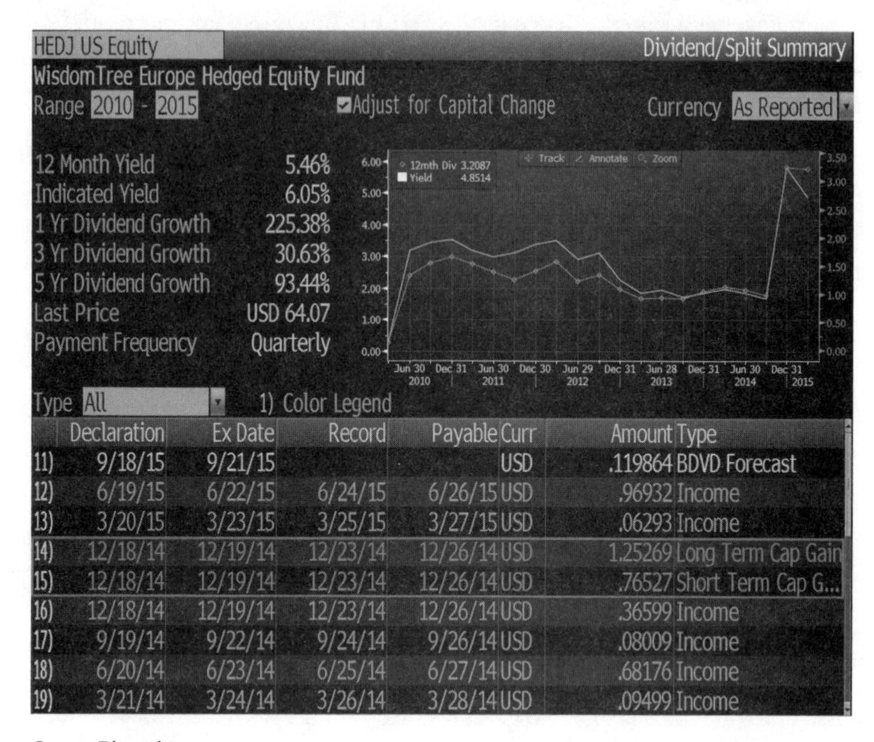

	Declaration	Ex Date	Record	Payable	Curr	Amount	Type
11)	9/18/15	9/21/15			USD	.119864	BDVD Forecast
12)	6/19/15	6/22/15	6/24/15	6/26/15	USD	.96932	Income
13)	3/20/15	3/23/15	3/25/15	3/27/15	USD	.06293	Income
14)	12/18/14	12/19/14	12/23/14	12/26/14	USD	1.25269	Long Term Cap Gain
15)	12/18/14	12/19/14	12/23/14	12/26/14	USD	.76527	Short Term Cap G...
16)	12/18/14	12/19/14	12/23/14	12/26/14	USD	.36599	Income
17)	9/19/14	9/22/14	9/24/14	9/26/14	USD	.08009	Income
18)	6/20/14	6/23/14	6/25/14	6/27/14	USD	.68176	Income
19)	3/21/14	3/24/14	3/26/14	3/28/14	USD	.09499	Income

Source: Bloomberg

you sell at a profit within a year, your gains are taxed at a rate of 39.6 percent, and if you sell at a profit after holding it more than a year, your gains are taxed at 20 percent.

One noteworthy exception is with commodities. Physically backed precious metals ETFs, such as the SPDR Gold Trust (GLD), are taxed like collectibles at a rate of 28 percent. Meanwhile, futures-based commodity ETFs are taxed as if you held futures. This means you are taxed at a blended rate of 28 percent that is marked to market each year, not to mention a Schedule K-1 form to fill out.

Those are the Cliff Notes to ETF taxation. I don't want to get bogged down in taxes since many institutions are tax exempt. Generally speaking, just assume that the tax treatment of the ETF will be informed by what it holds. For taxable investors who want to deep dive into ETF taxation, I recommend checking out the free ETF tax guide that ETF .com puts out.[5]

Lending Revenue

Every cost up until now was, well, a type of cost. As discussed in the long and lend section in the preceding chapter, institutions can offset the expense ratio by lending out the ETF themselves. This isn't an option for retail investors, which is why you don't hear about it in the media much, but for institutional investors, the ability to lend out the ETF to short sellers goes into the total cost of ownership math.

> *"Part of the total cost of ownership calculus is if you potentially lend out your shares. And in the pension, foundation, and endowment space, that's something the early adopters of ETFs have figured out. You might have an S&P 500 strategy that is five basis points and the ETF is nine, but if you can lend the ETF and make back three, then it is really six versus five and the ETF is a lot more flexible so the benefits outweigh the cost."*
>
> Rob Trumbull, State Street Global Advisors

We will explore this idea of lending revenue a few times in the book, as it is something institutions use to factor in when deciding whether to use an ETF or not.

To summarize, unless your holding period is really short, trading costs are not as important as expense ratio and tracking difference since they are a one-time cost that gets diluted over time. In addition, trading costs can also be kept to a minimum by learning how to trade ETFs better and by finding a good trading partner or calling the ETF issuer's capital markets desk.

Liquidity

Liquidity is widely viewed as the amount of trading activity of the ETF. How much does it trade? The idea goes that the more the ETF trades every day, the more liquidity it has and the more you will get in and out of the ETF quickly and easily at a good price. That's basically true. But, unlike stocks, ETFs have additional liquidity that can be sourced. We will look at all sources of liquidity, otherwise known as an ETF's liquidity profile

Volume

The most obvious and popular measure of an ETF's liquidity is its trading volume. A lot of volume is great—no one would argue with that. Many institutional investors won't touch an ETF with volume of less than $100 million a day or that isn't the most traded ETF in the category. If the ETF trades a lot, that is a good thing because it naturally keeps trading costs down since there are so many buyers and sellers and competing firms making markets in it.

Highly traded ETFs that generate massive amounts of exchange liquidity is something that is so coveted by institutions because many of their other investments—such as hedge funds and private equity—are just not liquid like that. The thing with ETF volume is it can't be bought, so to speak. Even the mighty Blackrock can't force the market to trade its ETFs a lot. It is a democratic, organic process decided by the marketplace, not the issuer. But when the marketplace fully accepts an ETF, it produces the kind of liquidity that can make even the largest institutions drool.

There are about 50 or so drool-worthy ETFs that have what can be best described as oceanic liquidity. Figure 5.18 gives a great bird's-eye view of ETF trading. The size of the box is determined by how much it trades. The big blue box in the upper left is SPY, which is the Pacific Ocean in terms of liquidity, trading about $24 billion each day.

There is a phrase in ETF land that "liquidity begets liquidity." The more an ETF trades, the more it attracts bigger investors with bigger trades. I equate it to a snowball rolling downhill. This is evident in the fact that the top 15 most traded ETFs represent *50 percent* of the volume. These are the ETFs that are so well known people put a "the" before their

FIGURE 5.18 ETF by Exchange Volume Showing the Haves and the Have-Nots

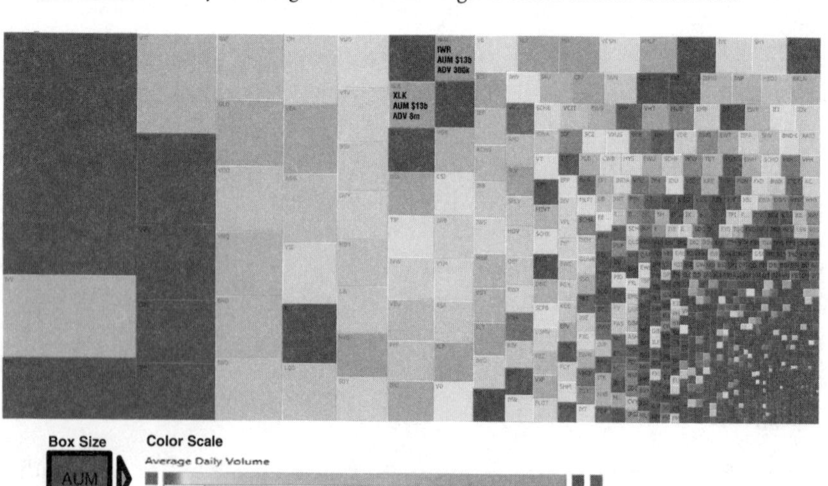

Source: Bloomberg Tradebook

FIGURE 5.19 ETF Exchange Volume Inequality

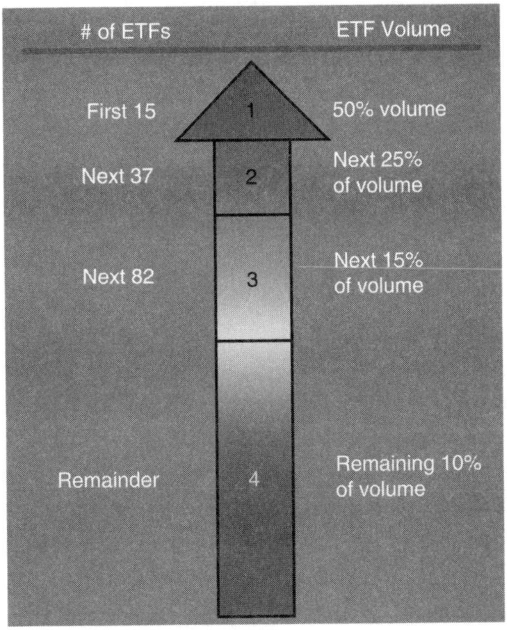

Source: Bloomberg Tradebook

ticker. The SPY. The EEM. The QQQs. The GLD. The next 100 or so account for another 40 percent of the volume, as shown in Figure 5.19. Life is good for these guys.

Implied Liquidity

But what about the 1,600 ETFs that make up just *10 percent* of the volume? Can you use those? Absolutely; you can so long as the holdings of the ETF are liquid. This is called "implied liquidity," and you can tap into it. This other source of liquidity is what makes ETFs different than trading stocks. This is liquidity that can be created on demand, regardless of how much the ETF trades.

"Volume is not liquidity. Low volume means that the ETF doesn't trade often. It doesn't mean that the ETF is illiquid. An ETF is not the same as a stock because liquidity can be manufactured."

Michael Baradas, Bloomberg Tradebook

Thanks to Nate Most's creation/redemption process—where an ETF's basket can be handed in for shares of the ETF and vice versa—the liquidity of the holdings can actually be sourced just like the ETF's trading volume. The reason for this is that if the ETF's holdings are liquid, a market maker can hedge themselves easier in making a market for you, or simply manufacture new shares of the ETF by rounding up the stocks in the basket and handing them into the issuer via the AP. This "implied" liquidity is completely independent of how much the ETF trades on the exchange.

"It really comes down to how deep is that basket."

Reggie Browne, Cantor Fitzgerald

This is why on Bloomberg we have a field called ETF Implied Liquidity™. It is shorthand for "Implied Daily Tradable Shares™," a calculation from David Abner's must-read book *The ETF Handbook.*[6] I read Dave's book and got to know Dave and we started talking about how this calculation would be of great use to the world via a new field on the Bloomberg terminal. The field is designed for investors to quickly figure out how liquid the basket is as part of their pretrade analysis.

"When I first came up with the calculation, I had a market maker viewpoint on it. If I was going to provide liquidity on an ETF, how many shares of the ETF can I trade? But now I think of it from an investor perspective and I think ETF Implied Liquidity™ is critical to understand if you are going to have a large portfolio position in an ETF."

David Abner, WisdomTree Asset Management

Dave's ETF Implied Liquidity™ calculation tells you how many shares of an ETF can be potentially traded as portrayed by the creation unit. It basically looks at the stocks in the creation basket and finds out how many units of the ETF you could trade before becoming 25 percent of the 30-day average volume of any of the stocks in the basket. Once you hit that threshold in any one of the stocks, the formula stops and gives you the total number of shares of the ETF you could have traded or created up until that point.

If that's confusing, I think looking at an example will help. The IQ US Real Estate Small Cap ETF (ROOF) trades a only 20,000 shares/day. But because it tracks a fairly liquid basket of U.S. equities, the implied liquidity is 2,600,000 shares. In other words, you could trade (or create) 2.6 million shares of ROOF without having any significant impact in any of the underlying holdings. See Figure 5.20.

FIGURE 5.20 A Thinly Traded ETF with Plenty of Implied Liquidity

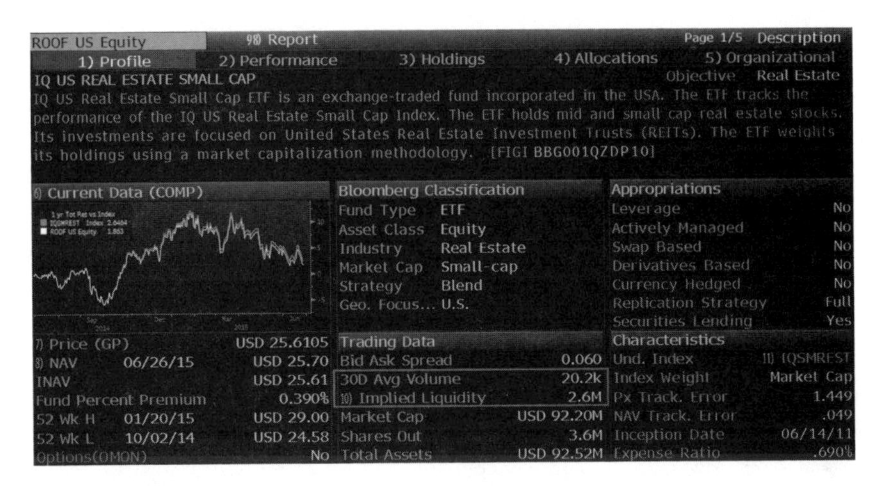

Source: Bloomberg

"When you do trades as a big institution like us, you can't just trade on the secondary market. So the liquidity in the underlying securities of the ETF is important. When we say liquidity we don't just focus on the size of the assets under management of the ETF. We also really focus on the liquidity of the underlying securities in the primary market."

Linda Zhang, Windhaven Investment Management

Whether you are doing an actual creation or calling a market maker to get a quote, this is valuable intel for an investor. This is why my colleagues in Bloomberg Tradebook have gone even further to say that the "E" in ETF is misleading. Because so much of the trading and liquidity is not about the trading activity on an exchange. The most astute users of ETFs get this.

"We start with the volume on the exchange, but after that it is an exercise in understanding the underlying portfolio. Even though you don't see liquidity that you'd like to see traded on the exchange for very desirable ETFs. And if you have enough assets going in there, the AP will create the ETF shares for you. That might even be more expeditious than trying noodle it along trading so much of it a day. That's one of the beauties of the ETF is the fact that with enough assets you can have shares created for you rather than just buying the shares that are available out on the market."

Dave Underwood, Arizona State Retirement System

FIGURE 5.21 Health Care ETFs Volume Compared to Their Implied Liquidity

Ticker	Name	Volume 1 Day Ago	Exchange Traded Fund Implied Liquidity
1) XLV US	HEALTH CARE SELECT SECTOR	9,232,471	25,545,805
2) IBB US	ISHARES NASDAQ BIOTECHNOLOGY	1,506,102	989,800
3) XBI US	SPDR S&P BIOTECH ETF	1,375,493	567,093
4) BIB US	PROSHARES ULTRA NASD BIOTECH	564,462	1,430,873
5) CURE US	DIREXION HEALTHCARE BULL 3X	520,311	3,238,619
6) VHT US	VANGUARD HEALTH CARE ETF	405,350	10,980,555
7) IHF US	ISHARES U.S. HEALTHCARE PROV	305,795	444,157
8) LABU US	DRXN DAILY S&P BIOTECH BULL	302,933	55,878,167
9) IHI US	ISHARES U.S. MEDICAL DEVICES	275,833	1,590,165
10) FXH US	FIRST TRUST HEALTH CARE ALPH	266,930	3,352,957
11) SBIO US	ALPS ETF TRUST-ALPS MEDICAL	243,465	880,294
12) FHLC US	FIDELITY HEALTH CARE ETF	177,817	63,215,958
13) FBT US	FIRST TRUST NYSE ARCA BIOTEC	142,769	726,270
14) IYH US	ISHARES U.S. HEALTHCARE ETF	137,458	12,696,335
15) PJP US	POWERSHARES DYN PHARMACEUTIC	104,971	906,726
16) BBH US	MARKET VECTORS BIOTECH ETF	90,120	1,105,079
17) PBE US	POWERSHARES DYN BIOTECH&GENO	75,232	1,161,510
18) IXJ US	ISHARES GLOBAL HEALTHCARE ET	61,820	21,215,401
19) XPH US	SPDR S&P PHARMACEUTICALS ETF	48,190	703,755

Source: Bloomberg

This brings me to a major point in the book: Implied liquidity is the key to unlocking the toolbox since about 88 percent of ETFs have more liquidity available in their underlying holdings than they do on the exchange. Knowing this is crucial because it may help you get a better ETF for your specific exposure needs instead of just using the one that trades the most.

A good microcosm of this can be found among health care sector ETFs. In Figure 5.21 you will see that for all but two ETFs, the implied liquidity is greater than the secondary market volume. The exceptions are the two popular biotech ETFs. This is because they trade a ton combined with the fact that they are tracking a less liquid area of health care. This is a pattern you will see across all equity ETFs.

Let's look at another example using the Schwab Fundamental U.S. Large Company Index ETF (FNDX). FNDX only trades 231,000 shares (or $3.5 million) a day. That's not horrible, but would probably scare most institutions away. But if you looked at the implied liquidity you'd see that a whopping 142 million shares (or $4.3 billion) of the ETF could be traded or created based on the liquidity in the holdings. Figure 5.22 shows our ETFL<GO> function, which ranks the stocks ranked by their constraint on the implied liquidity. In other words, the first stock that would give you a problem in creating shares is Ingram Micro Inc. (IM).

Where this really comes into play for intuitional investors is in the spread. The bid-ask spread on FNDX is 10 cents wide. If you put in a market order for 10,000 shares you would most likely be paying that

FIGURE 5.22 A Look Inside the Implied Liquidity of an ETF

FNDX US Equity | 5) Export to Excel | ETF Implied Liquidity
SCHWAB FUNDAMENTAL LARGE CAP | Min Portfolio Weight 0 | Variable Percentage 25

Implied Liquidity		Creation Information			
Implied Liquidity (shares)	142.118M	Creation Unit Size	50000	Open For Creations	Yes
Implied Liquidity (USD)	4.319B	Creation Fee (USD)	500	Settlement Cycle	T+3
Liquidity Limiting Holding	IM US	Creation Cutoff Time	16:00 est	Create/Redeem Process	In-kind

Holdings (6/29/2015)	Ticker		IDTS (shares) ↓	Weight (%)	Last (USD)	Volume	30 Day Avg Vol
11) Ingram Micro Inc	IM	US	142,118,097	.12	26.0100	1,631,640	761,753
12) Exxon Mobil Corp	XOM	US	160,074,085	4.47	83.8600	19,023,328	10,155,100
13) World Fuel Services Corp	INT	US	167,118,981	.09	48.5600	422,164	360,977
14) Murphy USA Inc	MUSA	US	180,279,326	.10	58.2100	736,515	374,981
15) Core-Mark Holding Co Inc	CORE	US	209,521,875	.03	59.3600	442,365	134,094
16) Magellan Health Inc	MGLN	US	217,603,125	.04	70.9000	308,985	139,266
17) CST Brands Inc	CST	US	218,567,741	.09	40.9400	502,435	542,048
18) Chevron Corp	CVX	US	232,954,155	2.41	98.6000	10,015,533	6,783,625
19) Domtar Corp	UFS	US	245,356,578	.06	43.7800	671,533	372,942
20) Bunge Ltd	BG	US	252,683,333	.23	89.4400	1,416,276	788,372
21) ConocoPhillips	COP	US	254,229,797	1.13	62.1800	6,684,200	5,511,702
22) Telephone & Data Systems...	TDS	US	263,973,076	.05	30.1700	570,929	549,064
23) Phillips 66	PSX	US	266,194,680	.76	79.6200	8,753,563	3,002,676
24) Leidos Holdings Inc	LDOS	US	289,222,058	.05	41.5000	605,634	393,342
25) Avnet Inc	AVT	US	296,697,348	.09	42.0900	1,857,636	783,281
26) Travelers Cos Inc/The	TRV	US	298,908,450	.47	97.9200	2,061,640	1,697,800
27) Philip Morris International In	PM	US	315,694,303	.86	81.3500	4,584,638	3,990,376

1) Edit Basket

Source: Bloomberg

spread. But for institutions working with a market maker and looking to buy 300,000 shares or 1 million shares, they now have the intel to know the spread they get quoted should be much tighter than 10 cents, since the holdings are so liquid.

In other words, if you know your implied liquidity, you know that FNDX should be just as cheap to trade as one of those top 50 ETFs. Power to the people!

"People don't realize the implied liquidity. They see it only trades 10 cents wide on the screen; it must be illiquid. But they don't understand that if the underlying names are liquid than the ETF will be naturally become liquid as well, from a block level."

Mohit Bajaj, WallachBeth Capital

Implied liquidity is why, for many of the less traded ETFs with liquid baskets but low volume, the majority of their volume is off-exchange. This is driven by market makers creating liquidity though the creation/redemption process. This brings us to block trading, which I felt belongs in the liquidity section—and not the cost section—because it directly shows why implied liquidity is important.

Block Trading

Block trading—also referred to as *upstairs trading*—refers to deals that are executed among large institutions, bypassing the broader market. For institutions that have larger orders, block trading is a luxury that most retail investors can't afford, and it should be utilized.

While some of the fortunate ETFs with oceanic liquidity, like SPY or IWM or EEM, can digest massive orders on the exchange, for the rest of the ETF toolbox institutional investors may want to look at doing a block trade with a market maker. According to my colleague Michael Baradas of Bloomberg Tradebook, when considering whether to do a block trade, it isn't the size of the trade that matters but rather the relative size of the trade.

"If the order is less than 1 percent of the average daily volume, use an algorithm. If it is greater than 1 percent, trade a block."

Michael Baradas, Bloomberg Tradebook

Let's go through an example of how a block trade works. Say you want to buy an ETF where you are definitely going to be over 1 percent of the volume and don't want to trade over the exchange. You call the market maker and get a quote. Assuming you agree to the price, let's look at what happens next.

The market maker—who probably doesn't own the ETF you are interested in—will go out and borrow the ETF and then sell it to you. This makes them short the ETF. In order to balance out the short position, they would have to go long the underlying holdings or some correlated asset. Now they are hedged. But, eventually, they will unwind the position. One way is for them to gather up the securities in the ETFs' basket, if they haven't already, and exchange them for brand new shares of the ETF. Then, they can give those newly created ETF shares back to the person they borrowed the ETF from to begin with. Now they are free and clear. They will do this all day long with many clients.

This ability to create new ETF shares on demand takes the pressure off the market maker of going out and collecting up ETF shares on the exchange. This other source of liquidity is what makes ETFs different than stocks.

Notice how in the above scenario the liquidity of the underlying holdings (the implied liquidity) was more important than the trading volume of the actual ETF.

A real world example of using the liquidity in the holdings to get good execution can be found in iShares Currency Hedged MSCI Germany ETF

FIGURE 5.23 HEWG's Assets Doubled on a Large Creation

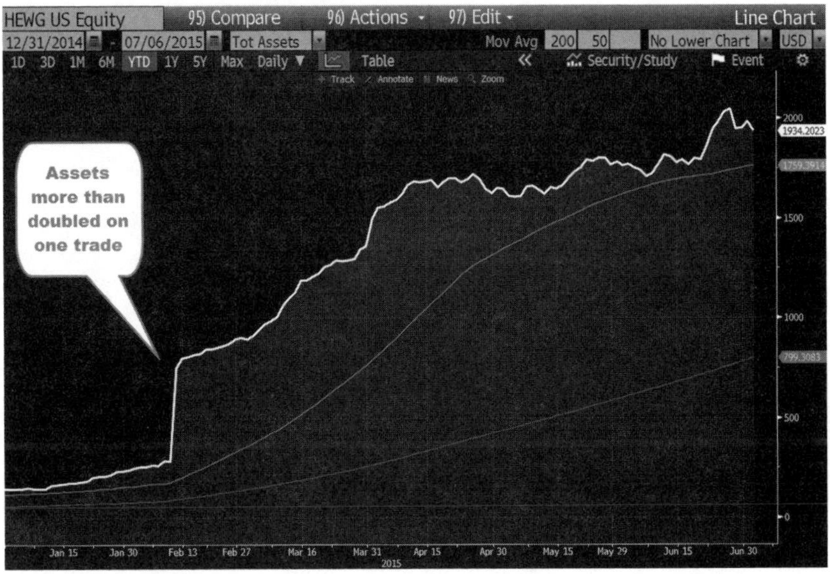

Assets more than doubled on one trade

Source: Bloomberg

(HEWG), where someone wanted more shares than existed at the time. This would be impossible with a stock. But through their market maker they did a creation that was bigger than the existing assets in the fund and they got a price inside the bid-ask spread. See Figure 5.23.

This ability to use the liquidity in the holdings of the ETF is why block trading ETFs is also *cheaper* than block trading individual stocks. Bloomberg Tradebook did a study published in the *Journal of Trading* that found that ETFs have a lower implicit cost of trading largely due to the creation/redemption process.[7] The ability to source the liquidity in the holdings is why an illiquid ETF will have more liquidity and a tighter spread than an illiquid stock.

Tradebook also looked at how the growth in smaller ETF assets is actually correlated to the rise in off-exchange ETF volumes. Figure 5.24 shows that the increase of off-exchange trading goes up as you get into less traded ETFs. This jibes with Baradas's rule of thumb to go off-exchange if you are going to be more than 1 percent of ADV.

It should be noted here that when looking at trading volume and implied liquidity, you may see a few equity ETFs that don't have much of either. These ETFs should be approached with caution. An example is the iShares

FIGURE 5.24 The Smaller the ETF, the More Likely Trading Is Off-Exchange

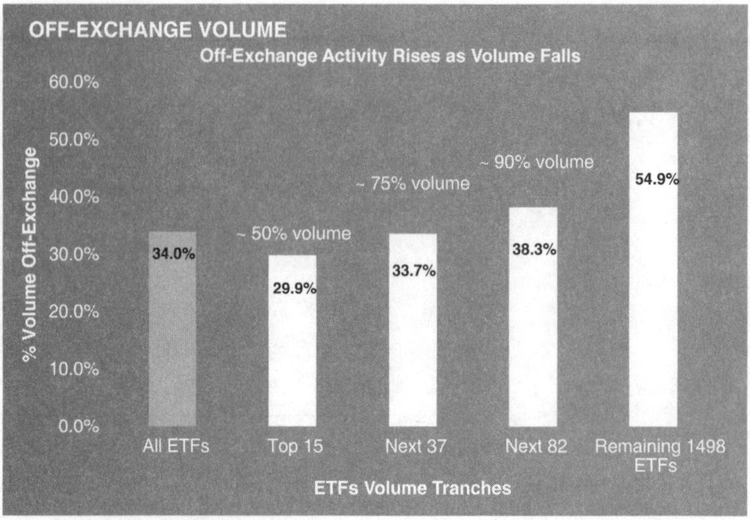

OFF-EXCHANGE VOLUME
Off-Exchange Activity Rises as Volume Falls

ETFs Volume Tranches	% Volume Off-Exchange	Note
All ETFs	34.0%	
Top 15	29.9%	~ 50% volume
Next 37	33.7%	~ 75% volume
Next 82	38.3%	~ 90% volume
Remaining 1498 ETFs	54.9%	

Source: Bloomberg Tradebook

Colombia ETF (ICOL), which trades a mere 13,400 shares ($202,000) a day and has an implied liquidity of only 56,000 shares ($885,000) a day, as seen in Figure 5.25.

FIGURE 5.25 ICOL Is an Example of Low Volume and Low Implied Liquidity

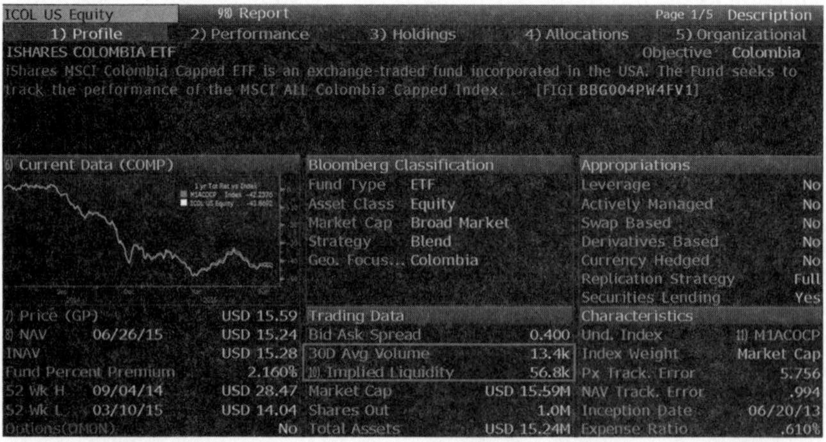

ICOL US Equity 98) Report Page 1/5 Description
1) Profile 2) Performance 3) Holdings 4) Allocations 5) Organizational
ISHARES COLOMBIA ETF Objective Colombia
iShares MSCI Colombia Capped ETF is an exchange-traded fund incorporated in the USA. The Fund seeks to track the performance of the MSCI ALL Colombia Capped Index. [FIGI BBG004PW4FV1]

6) Current Data (COMP)		Bloomberg Classification		Appropriations	
		Fund Type	ETF	Leverage	No
		Asset Class	Equity	Actively Managed	No
		Market Cap	Broad Market	Swap Based	No
		Strategy	Blend	Derivatives Based	No
		Geo. Focus...	Colombia	Currency Hedged	No
				Replication Strategy	Full
				Securities Lending	Yes
7) Price (GP)	USD 15.59	Trading Data		Characteristics	
8) NAV 06/26/15	USD 15.24	Bid Ask Spread	0.400	Und. Index	11) M1ACOCP
INAV	USD 15.28	30D Avg Volume	13.4k	Index Weight	Market Cap
Fund Percent Premium	2.160%	10) Implied Liquidity	56.8k	Px Track. Error	5.756
52 Wk H 09/04/14	USD 28.47	Market Cap	USD 15.59M	NAV Track. Error	.994
52 Wk L 03/10/15	USD 14.04	Shares Out	1.0M	Inception Date	06/20/13
Options(OMON)	No	Total Assets	USD 15.24M	Expense Ratio	.610%

Source: Bloomberg

Ideally, you'd like an ETF with high exchange volume *and* high implied liquidity, like SPY or QQQ. There are about 200 of these lucky dogs. However, you can get good execution if the ETF has either high exchange volume or high implied liquidity. There are about 1,300 in this camp. But if exchange volume and implied liquidity are both low, approach with extreme caution. There are about 300 ETFs with this unfortunate double whammy of illiquidity.

One question you may ponder is how big the trade needs to be to tap into the implied liquidity of an ETF. It really doesn't matter. Let the market maker handle that. The market maker may be able to combine your order with another person and make a creation unit, and you could get a tighter spread than if you were the only one and they had to make up the difference. A lot of this is dependent on many different variables and a bit of luck.

"It is a bit of a misnomer that people think they need a trade big enough to get a creation. Your job is to work with a trading desk that you feel comfortable with that can get you best execution. Because the APs and the market makers on the other side, for all you know, could be aggregating orders."

Jim Rowley, Vanguard

There is also the chance that your order matches up against someone else looking to do the opposite trade. These matchmaking situations are referred to as *naturals.*

"If you are a natural and you are looking to unwind an ETF position and I have a guy who wants to buy it, we can help tighten the spread out."

Mohit Bajaj, WallachBeth Capital

I realize that most institutions have a custody account set up somewhere and they do all their trading. This information still applies. But it is becoming more popular to do "step away" or "step out" trading with a market maker or liquidity provider, who acts as your agent and puts market makers in competition with each other, to help get best execution.

To find out who the best market makers are for a given ETF, you can always call the ETF issuer's capital markets desk and ask them. On Bloomberg, we rank them on a function called RANK<GO>. Figure 5.26 shows the market makers who have reported the most volume on XLF. In other words, if you want XLF, these are the places to call since they trade it the most.

FIGURE 5.26 Market Makers with the Most Reported Volume in XLF

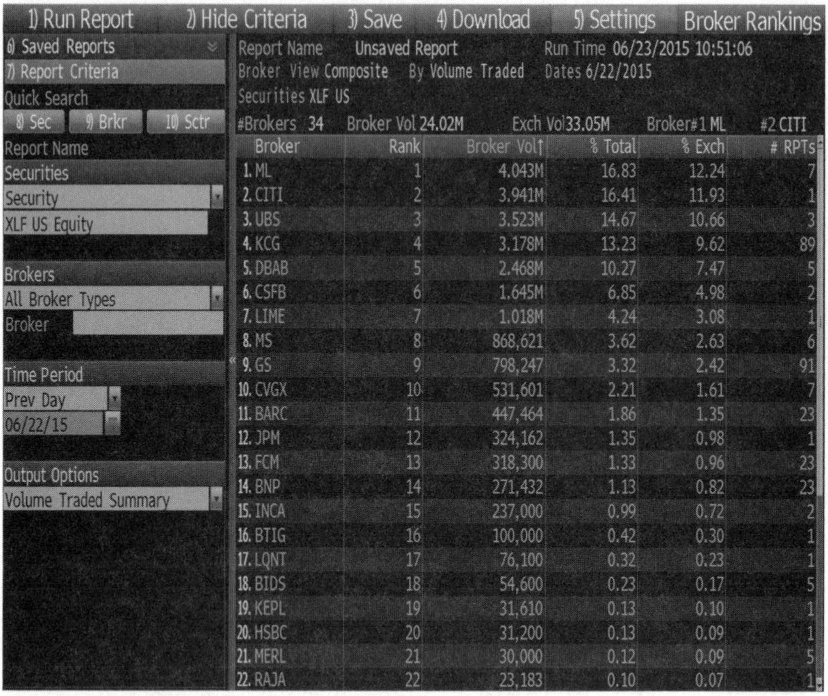

1) Run Report 2) Hide Criteria 3) Save 4) Download 5) Settings Broker Rankings

6) Saved Reports
7) Report Criteria
Quick Search
8) Sec 9) Brkr 10) Sctr
Report Name
Securities
Security
XLF US Equity
Brokers
All Broker Types
Broker
Time Period
Prev Day
06/22/15
Output Options
Volume Traded Summary

Report Name Unsaved Report Run Time 06/23/2015 10:51:06
Broker View Composite By Volume Traded Dates 6/22/2015
Securities XLF US
#Brokers 34 Broker Vol 24.02M Exch Vol 33.05M Broker#1 ML #2 CITI

Broker	Rank	Broker Vol↑	% Total	% Exch	# RPTs
1. ML	1	4.043M	16.83	12.24	7
2. CITI	2	3.941M	16.41	11.93	1
3. UBS	3	3.523M	14.67	10.66	3
4. KCG	4	3.178M	13.23	9.62	89
5. DBAB	5	2.468M	10.27	7.47	5
6. CSFB	6	1.645M	6.85	4.98	2
7. LIME	7	1.018M	4.24	3.08	1
8. MS	8	868,621	3.62	2.63	6
9. GS	9	798,247	3.32	2.42	91
10. CVGX	10	531,601	2.21	1.61	7
11. BARC	11	447,464	1.86	1.35	23
12. JPM	12	324,162	1.35	0.98	1
13. FCM	13	318,300	1.33	0.96	23
14. BNP	14	271,432	1.13	0.82	23
15. INCA	15	237,000	0.99	0.72	2
16. BTIG	16	100,000	0.42	0.30	1
17. LQNT	17	76,100	0.32	0.23	1
18. BIDS	18	54,600	0.23	0.17	5
19. KEPL	19	31,610	0.13	0.10	1
20. HSBC	20	31,200	0.13	0.09	1
21. MERL	21	30,000	0.12	0.09	5
22. RAJA	22	23,183	0.10	0.07	1

Source: Bloomberg

Okay, let's bring it all back home. The bottom line is when evaluating liquidity, it is important to examine the full liquidity profile of the ETF, which includes the volume of the exchange and the implied liquidity of the underlying holdings.

Risk

The riskiness of the ETF is directly informed by its holdings. Risk measures, like the signs before a ski slope, warn of the danger ahead. They will let you know how wild the swings could be in the ETF based on its historical performance. Some ETFs can cause serious face-plants despite having innocent and pleasant-sounding names. Inversely, there are some complex-sounding names that are calmer than a bunny slope. Just checking a few risk metrics will let you know all you need to know about how treacherous the ride will be.

Standard Deviation

Standard deviation is my favorite measure for risk. It tells you how much you can expect the ETFs returns to vary based on its historical returns. Maybe I'm a simpleton, but I have found it to be a reliable informant over the years. For example, the iShares MSCI Japan ETF (EWJ) has a standard deviation of 10.3 percent. This is saying that there is a 2/3 chance that the returns over the next year will be within the range of +/– 10.3 percent.

Table 5.3 is a look at a random mix of ETFs and their standard deviation figures. The standard deviation may be obvious, or it may contrast with the name. For example, the fact that a bond ETF like the Pimco 25+ Year Zero Coupon U.S. Treasury Exchange-Traded Fund (ZROZ) has a higher standard deviation than SPY should make you look further into what exactly ZROZ does. ZROZ moves like a leveraged ETF due to its super-high duration; we will examine why in the fixed-income section.

On the flip side to that, look how low-key and meek the moves are in the IndexIQ Merger Arbitrage Fund (MNA), despite its very complex-sounding name. This is another reason to analyze an ETF regardless of the name. And, of course, there is the Direxion Junior Gold Miners Bull Shares 3X (JNUG), which has the highest standard deviation of any ETF most of the time. It is double that of the volatility index (VIX) and bitcoin. Investors are probably best advised to take a swig of Vodka before buying JNUG. We

TABLE 5.3 Standard Deviations Can Range from Calm to Crazy

Name	Ticker	Stand. Dev.
Vanguard Total Bond ETF	BND	3%
IndexIQ Merger Arbitrage Fund	MNA	3%
SPDR High Yield Bond ETF	JNK	6%
SPDR S&P 500 ETF Trust	SPY	9%
iShares Russell 2000	IWM	15%
Pimco 25+ Yr Zero Coupon ETF	ZROZ	23%
Market Vectors Russia ETF	RSX	42%
iPath Short-Term VIX ETN	VXX	48%
VelocityShares Inverse VIX	XIV	57%
ProShares Ultrashort Nat Gas	KOLD	90%
Direxn Junior Gold Miners 3X	JNUG	146%

Source: Bloomberg

will have more fun looking at the wild and crazy world of leveraged ETFs later in the book.

Of course, there are many other risk measures that can be used, such as beta or even just looking at downside deviation. The point is to look at something that tells you how bumpy the ride is going to be as part of your due diligence.

Closure Risk

A different kind of risk is closure risk. After all, not all ETFs survive. Currently, there are over 500 ETFs pushing up daisies in the proverbial graveyard. Killed off in cruel Darwinism. As with any industry, some products just don't connect with customers and go extinct.

Most likely, an institution won't ever deal with this issue because of their reluctance—right or wrong—to use any ETF that isn't bubbling over with volume. But it is still good to understand the closure process.

For investors, an ETF closure is not the end of the world or your investment, but it can be inconvenient. When an ETF decides to close, it will typically notify investors by way of a prospectus supplement about 30 to 60 days ahead of time so they can sell their shares and find a replacement ETF. Most investors take this route and sell it as soon as possible.

Investors who purposely or unknowingly hold on to the ETF until the day of its death (liquidation) will simply get the cash equivalent of the value of the assets at the time of sale. The bad news in that scenario is it could result in realized capital gains.

Normally, when an ETF closes, there aren't many—if any—investors to notify because the ETF didn't attract assets.

"The majority of the ones we close are the ones where clients just don't want them. We are close to the clients and would never do anything to harm our relationship with them."

Daniel Gamba, Blackrock

But even if an institution is a big chunk of the ownership, a closure can be pretty painless. Larry Seibert's family office once owned an ETF that closed in which they were about 40 percent of the shares outstanding.

> We got a phone call (from the issuer) and they said we are going to close the fund in a month. We said fine. We worked our way out of it. It was fine.

Regulatory Structure

There are many different types of structures of ETFs. In fact, if the "E" in ETF is misleading because not all trading is done on the exchange, then the "F" is just as misleading because not all ETFs are funds.

I think product structures are best grouped by the regulation under which they are approved.

1940 Act

The Investment Company Act of 1940 is what mutual funds are regulated under. It requires an independent board of trustees that has oversight of the ETF. It is more rigorous with safety issues because much of America's retirement money is in funds regulated under this rule. Getting approved under the 1940 Act means the Securities and Exchange Commission (SEC) is basically signing off on it. That's a big deal.

The 1940 Act includes registered investment companies, which is what the vast majority of mutual funds and ETFs are structured as. It also includes UITs, which is what some of the early ETFs were structured as (e.g., SPY). There is little difference between a UIT and an open-end investment company except UITs do not have a board, cannot do securities lending or use derivatives, and can only reinvest dividends quarterly. These limitations are why UITs were abandoned in the mid-1990s in favor of the open-end fund structure.

If you add up the assets in products registered under the 1940 Act, it accounts for 96 percent of the total, as shown in Figure 5.27. So, just like with the taxation issue where, for the most part, it is a nonissue because nearly everything is normal.

It must be said that just because something has been approved under the 1940 Act doesn't mean that it can't be risky from an investment perspective. After all, the most volatile ETF known to man, the Direxion Daily Junior Gold Miners Index Bull 3X Shares (JNUG) is a 1940 Act fund. JNUG and many other leveraged ETFs under the 1940 Act prove that structure doesn't necessarily have anything to do with the riskiness of the actual investment.

1933 Act

In contrast, the Securities Act of 1933 is not nearly as rigorous. In fact, basically all they are saying here is that there is no fraud involved, but that's about it. It is easier to get a product approved under this act.

FIGURE 5.27 ETFs by Regulatory Structure

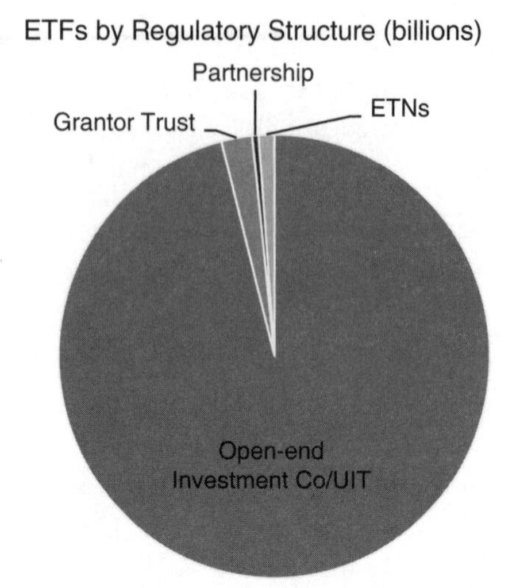

Source: Bloomberg

Here, you will find a disparate grouping of structures including grantor trusts and partnerships, which are sometimes dubbed ETVs, or exchange-traded vehicles, by some. Also under this law are exchange-traded notes, or ETNs. Collectively, these 1933 Act products make up a mere 3 percent of the total ETF assets.

Grantor trusts are typically used for ETFs that physically hold one thing, such as a precious metal or a currency. This is in contrast to, say, an ETF like IVV, which is a diversified basket of securities. The SPDR Gold Trust (GLD) is the most famous grantor trust.

"When you want to put commodities into a fund-like structure, you can't use a '40 Act structure. You have to adopt a different structure, and the one that works for commodities is this grantor trust. It can hold a single asset and doesn't need to be diversified in a way that a '40 Act mutual fund has to be."

Will Rhind, World Gold Council

Commodity and currency ETFs that use futures are structured as a partnership and are regulated as commodity pools by the Commodity Futures Trading Commission (CFTC). In short, these are the products that use futures contracts to get their exposure. The United States Oil Fund (USO) is an example of a partnership.

ETNs

Exchange-traded notes (ETNs) deserve a little explanation. ETNs are unsecured debt obligations issued by a bank or other financial institution. Like ETFs, ETNs trade on an exchange, track and index, and tend to be very tax efficient. Unlike ETFs, they don't hold an underlying basket of securities or futures contracts. Instead, they're a 30-year promise to match the performance of a certain index over a specified period. In this way, ETNs are really more like a bond but one that has daily creation/redemption service.

If the issuer defaults, investors could lose their money. Lehman Brothers had a couple of ETNs that delisted, and investors recovered just 9 percent of their investment.[8] However, there were not many investors, as the ETNs were tiny. While there is legitimate credit risk, over the past 10 years, the asset-weighted default percentage is below 0.1 percent.

What do ETNs do with the money invested in them? They could do whatever they want. They could light it on fire if they wanted. But the truth is that the issuers typically will go out and buy the underlying securities the ETN is tracking, so they are perfectly hedged minus the fee difference, which is how they get paid.

Despite the credit risk that comes along with them, ETNs have a respectable $28 billion in assets, which is just over 1 percent of the total. What makes all this so curious is that almost everything ETNs track you can get in an ETF, with no credit risk. So why on earth have these things captured $28 billion in assets, much less $28?

The answer lies largely in their tax treatment. ETNs are the one exception to the general rule of thumb of looking at the holdings for a clue as to the ETF's tax treatment. ETNs don't hold anything yet have "normal" tax treatment like a plain old equity. So for areas such as commodities and MLPs, which have unusual and costly tax treatment for ETFs, ETNs represent an alternative. That's why most of the assets in ETNs are clustered in a few areas as shown in Figure 5.28.

Master limited partnerships (MLPs), VIX, and commodities represent about three-fourths of ETN assets, as seen in Figure 5.28. These appeal to investors who are looking to get better tax treatment and have decided the credit risk is worth it.

"In most instances, if everything is equal and investors have a choice between an ETN of something and ETF of something, they will pick the ETF. And they rightly should. Why take on credit risk when you don't have to? The reality is the ETN only survives and makes sense when it is delivering some sort of added value,

FIGURE 5.28 Breakdown of ETN Assets

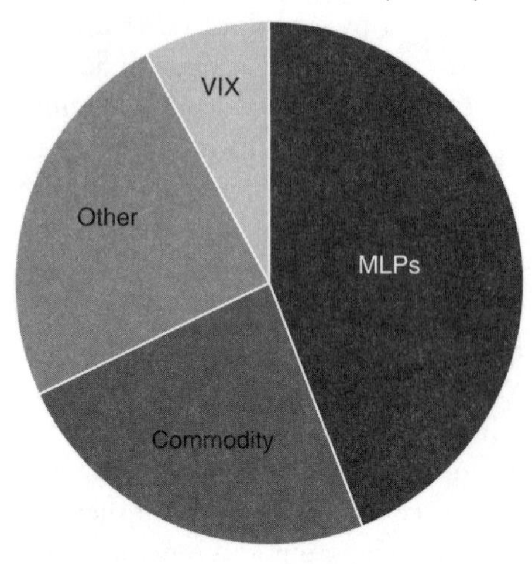

Source: Bloomberg

whether from a tax or regulatory or structural perspective. That's why MLPs and commodities—which really don't work as ETFs—make sense in an ETN."

Chris Yeagley, UBS

ETF Issuers

We just covered my key categories for doing basic due diligence on an ETF. One thing we didn't discuss is the issuer. Personally, I don't worry about who the issuer is all that much because I am trying to be agnostic and nonjudgmental in my analysis. But the reality is that the issuer of the ETF is very important to many investors.

According to a 2014 ETF.com and Brown Brothers Harriman survey of ETF investors, the ETF issuer was the most important factor in selecting an ETF for 20 percent of respondents. While that put it in fourth place, behind exposure, expense ratio, and tracking, it was ranked as more important than trading spreads and historical performance.[9]

We know ETF brands are important considering the fact that 81 percent of the assets are held by just three issuers: Blackrock, Vanguard, and State Street. I call them the "Big Three." A lot of that is due to those issuers having the most traded ETFs, but brand loyalty is part of the equation.

This makes sense from a consumer standpoint. If you bought an iPod and liked it, you are probably more likely to have also bought an iPhone and a Mac, too. ETF investors are comfortable with the salespeople and the capital markets desks, and trust builds.

Each issuer has its own identity and audience. Some issuers appeal more to institutions and some more to retail. One way to tease this out is by looking at the percentage of the issuers' total assets that trade each day. A general rule of thumb is the higher the asset turnover, the more institutional usage going on. Table 5.4 shows the top 10 issuers and the collective daily turnover of their ETFs.

On one side you have ProShares, which issues leveraged ETFs and sees a ton of turnover, indicating nonretail investors. On the other you have Vanguard and Schwab, who have less than half the trading activity of others in the group. This indicates that they are used more by buy-and-hold retail investors.

Of course, there are many, many quality products outside of these top 10 issuers. And investors who know what they want and understand implied liquidity will be the ones most comfortable using a plethora of issuers.

"I don't care about brands. I bought a KraneShares ETF within three months of it launching. The product was unique, fairly priced, and constructed intelligently. That's what I'm looking for. They don't need to be Coke or Pepsi. I drink Dr. Pepper, too."

Josh Brown, Ritholtz Capital Management

TABLE 5.4 Top 10 Issuers by Assets as of June 30, 2015

Issuer	# Funds	# Closures	Mkt Cap ($million)	Turnover/Day
iShares ETFs/USA	388	82	759,417	1.41%
State Street ETF/USA	150	5	454,888	1.85%
Vanguard ETF/USA	67	0	426,872	0.64%
PowerShares ETFs/USA	182	46	96,847	0.82%
WisdomTree ETFs/USA	89	23	39,024	1.50%
First Trust/ETFs	94	0	33,217	1.48%
Guggenheim ETFs/USA	95	23	29,021	1.41%
Schwab ETFs/USA	21	0	26,925	0.70%
ProShares ETFs/USA	158	46	25,057	7.42%
Market Vectors ETFs/USA	62	6	20,433	2.94%

Source: Bloomberg

ETF Ratings

I said earlier that I didn't think star ratings made sense when it comes to ETFs. But I do think that a rating system that alerts investors of any potential surprises could be useful—especially considering that there are now over 1,800 ETFs covering every asset class, sector, industry, region, country, commodity, strategy, currency, and maybe some things you've never even heard of before. They also hold everything from emerging-market bonds to futures contracts to swap agreements. And they keep getting more and more complex.

> *"ETFs are not going to blow up the world, but the complexity—that is going to create a problem."*
>
> Stephen Elgee, Periscope Capital

For this reason, I developed my own shorthand ETF rating system that I can use to easily alert someone as to the potential for a nasty surprise inside an ETF. I modeled it after a rating system we all know very well: movie ratings. Before you dismiss it as absurd or silly, hear me out.

What do movie ratings do? They "provide parents with advance information about the content of movies to help them determine what's appropriate for their children."[10] As such, a rating system for ETFs is needed to provide investors with advance information about what is appropriate for their investment.

While movie ratings look at the levels of things such as violence, nudity, and drug use, my rating system looks at the levels and complexities of the holdings, structure, fees, weightings, and taxation. Basically, it flags all the little bugaboos that can equate to a surprise or bad experience and then adds them together to determine a rating. Perhaps this is more appropriate for a retail audience, but I think given the avalanche of new complex products, anyone doing ETF investing could benefit from it.

This makes more sense to me than putting ETFs into two buckets of "safe" or "dangerous," which is what financial advisors tend to do. But, the dangers are way more nuanced than that. ETFs that invest in senior loans, oil futures, or MLPs or use leverage all have some degree of unwelcome surprises for investors unfamiliar with the terrain.

This isn't to say an ETF with an R rating should be automatically avoided. It just means the ETF has some gremlins in it that could turn nasty if you don't know what you are getting into so you should take time to understand how to use the product correctly. The higher the rating, the more you need to read the fine print.

Following is a general look at my ratings, which I may reference at times in the book. It will hopefully help with shorthand communication and provide some insight into how you should be approaching your own ETF due diligence and maybe creating your own system.

G

Anything that holds developed market stocks or bonds using standard market capitalization–weighted indices. This is for straightforward ETFs with no complications that need explaining. Plain vanilla ETFs. Think Vanguard.

Examples: iShares Core S&P 500 ETF (IVV), Vanguard Short-Term Government Bond ETF (VGSH).

PG

Any ETF that tracks stocks or bonds but uses an index that isn't traditional market cap weighted. This is mostly for ETFs that attempt to outperform the market, like smart beta and actively managed ETFs. This category will also include any plain vanilla ETF where the tax treatment is slightly different, such as physically backed gold ETFs.

Examples: Guggenheim S&P 500 Equal Weight ETF (RSP), SPDR Gold Shares (GLD).

PG-13

ETFs that track slightly more exotic stocks and bonds that could pose liquidity concerns, such as emerging markets or junk bond ETFs. Also, specialized products that involve particularly tricky markets or have big tax consequences, such as China, MLPs, interest rate–hedged ETFs, liquid alternatives, and option-writing strategies.

Examples: iShares MSCI Frontier Markets 100 (FM), PowerShares Senior Loan Portfolio (BKLN), Alerian MLP ETF (AMLP).

R

Not suitable for average investors. Must read fine print. Could get hurt. Any ETF that predominantly holds derivatives such as swaps or futures. This includes all leveraged and inverse ETFs plus all single-commodity ETFs that hold futures contracts. It will also include ETNs, which carry credit risk.

Basically, any product that has high risks, embedded complication, or potential to lose lots of money.

Examples: Direxion Daily Gold Miners Bull 3X Shares (NUGT), United States Oil Fund (USO), JPMorgan Alerian MLP ETN (AMJ).

NC-17

These are the products that make—or should make—even professional investors think twice. Basically, a category reserved for leveraged ETNs that track futures. In other words, you get leverage, roll costs, and credit risk all rolled up into one product.

Examples: VelocityShares Daily 2x VIX Short-Term ETN (TVIX).

While a system using movie ratings will never be used in any official way, there's no reason we can't do it here in this book as a way to reference the level of nasty surprises an ETF has. For those creating their own system, I would recommend a system like this that uses more than two tiers.

As mentioned earlier, some ETFs with high ratings warrant a reading of the "the fine print." By that I mean the prospectus. Prospectuses are brutal, and I'm pretty sure they qualify medically as a cure for insomnia. But they do include things that could go wrong.

Kathleen Moriarty, who writes prospectuses or, as she says, "documents no one reads," thinks investors would be wise to at least give it a quick look-over.

> You should at least read the sections that talk about the expenses and the objective of the fund, what the fund can hold and at least skim over the risks.

In summary, ETF due diligence is about looking at the exposure, cost, liquidity, risk and product structure. Some may include the ETF issuer as well. No matter how you cut it there are several possibilities to be surprised. This is why a homemade rating system based on your needs may be worth the effort.

Well, this officially concludes the first part of the book. You made it! In the next section, we will apply some of this stuff as we take a tour through the ETF toolbox.

Notes

1. Hougan, Matt, "Tracking Difference, the Perfect ETF Metric." ETF.com, July 31, 2015; www.etf.com/sections/blog/tracking-difference-perfect-etf-metric/page/0/1?nopaging=1.

2. Conway, Brendan, "Costs vs Fees in ETF Trading." *Barron's,* November 2, 2013; online.barrons.com/articles/SB500014240531119048971045791576409470 40178.
3. ETF.com Staff, "Brazil ETFs Boosted by Investment Tax Cut." ETF.com, December 7, 2011; www.etf.com/sections/features/10390-brazil-etfs-boosted-by-investment-tax-cut.html.
4. Dieterich, Chris, "Niche ETFs Come with Surprising Tax Bills." *Barron's,* December 13, 2014; www.barrons.com/articles/niche-etfs-come-with-surprising-tax-bills-1418444560.
5. Hudachek, Dennis, "The Definitive Guide to 2014 ETF Taxation." ETF.com, January 9, 2015; www.etf.com/sections/white-papers/definitive-guide-2015-etf-taxation-0.
6. Abner, Dave, *The ETF Handbook: How to Value and Trade Exchange Traded Funds* (Hoboken, NJ: Wiley, 2010).
7. Michael Baradas, "Seeking Optimal ETF Execution in Electronic Markets: Part 1." Bloomberg Tradebook blog, July 10, 2014; www.bloombergtradebook.com/seeking-optimal-etf-execution-electronic-markets-part-1/.
8. Swedroe, Larry, "Swedroe: An ETN Credit Risk Reality Check." ETF.com, July 22, 2013; www.etf.com/sections/index-investor-corner/19350-swedroe-an-etn-credit-risk-reality-check.html?nopaging=1.
9. "Annual Advisor Survey." ETF.com and Brown Brothers Harriman, September 2014; www.bbh.com/wps/wcm/connect/67b8388045e72a0f8fd1efc870621867/ETF+Annual+Advisor+Survey.pdf?MOD=AJPERES&CACHEID=67b8388045e72a0f8fd1efc870621867
10. "Film Ratings." Motion Picture Association of America; www.mpaa.org/film-ratings/.

SECTION II

The ETF Toolbox

CHAPTER 6

U.S. Stock ETFs

Now that we have gotten a look at the ETF phenomenon and how to do due diligence, it is time to meet the ETFs. There are over 1,800 ETFs and close to another 1,400 in registration with the Securities and Exchange Commission (SEC), and they all have to be put into categories. This is part of what I do at Bloomberg.

Even though this book is about a toolbox, a good way to think about the ETF landscape is the metaphor of walking into a department store. When you enter, there are typically about 5 to 10 major departments, such as clothing, furniture, home appliances, toys, cosmetics, gardening, sporting goods, and hardware.

Within each department there are subsections and ultimately aisles. Then, when you eventually find the right shelf with the exact type of product you are looking for, there are many competing brands with products that range in style, quality, and cost.

This is *exactly* how ETFs are categorized. That is exactly how we built our ETF finder tool at Bloomberg. It's just called asset classes instead of departments. Sectors, styles, regions, and market cap are the subsections and aisles, and the competing brands are iShares, Vanguard, SPDRs, and so on. With that metaphor intact, let's have a look around.

Each section will examine some core categories and ETFs. These are the ones that you typically would give a sizable allocation to, as evidenced by their asset size. In addition, we will look at some satellite products as well. These are the more specific-purpose ETFs that you may not allocate a lot, too, but they could come in handy. They include sectors, single countries, smart beta, thematic, volatility, actively managed, currencies, currency-hedged, and interest rate–hedged ETFs, to name a few.

One thing to note is that the asset figures I use are all as of mid-2015, so they may have changed a bit as writing about ETFs is like trying to hit a moving target. But, their relativity to other categories and ETFs is what I'm trying to show and that won't change that much and that is what is important.

In addition, I simply cannot cover every ETF (you wouldn't want me too either). However, I will cover a lot of them and use several examples and case studies in each section that I think highlight a larger analytical point or show a popular dilemma that will give you an analytical edge when evaluating ETFs. There are patterns all over the ETF toolbox. And once you learn the patterns, it can help you in the analysis process. Enough babbling already; let's just get started.

U.S. stock ETFs are the largest, oldest, and most popular category of ETFs. This is the area that people probably know the most about. U.S. stock ETFs have a whopping $930 billion in assets, which is 44 percent of the total pie. They have so much in assets because many of them are used as portfolio building blocks and get large allocations in portfolios. This category is dominated by big brand name issuers tracking big brand name indexes.

U.S. stock ETFs have gotten cheaper and more liquid over time. For example, the S&P 500 Trust (SPY) has an expense ratio of 0.094 percent today, down from the 0.20 percent charged in 1993 when it first launched. SPY's gradually decreased fee is representative of the fee compression in this industry.

Let's look at a couple of ETF examples in the large-cap, mid-cap, small-cap, micro-cap, and broad-market categories. We will also look briefly at ETFs tracking initial public offerings (IPOs), buybacks, spin-offs, and covered call strategies. You can basically capture every phase of a company's life with ETFs.

Large Caps

U.S. large-cap ETFs have just over $600 billion of that $930 billion. The basic choice investors have to make is what index brand you like best and also if you want some kind of tilt, such as growth or value or dividends. Figure 6.1 shows the largest of the large-cap ETFs. Notice how three of the top four are all Standard & Poor's (S&P) 500 trackers. U.S. large cap is the only category where you will see the top 10 ETFs each with assets well north of $10 billion and with such low fees. Life is good here. But, still, there are choices to be made for ETF investors.

FIGURE 6.1 Largest U.S. Large-Cap ETFs by Assets

Ticker	Name	Fund Market Cap Focus	Tot Asset (M)	Expense Ratio
1) SPY US	SPDR S&P 500 ETF TRUST	Large-cap	178,572.297	0.094
2) IVV US	ISHARES CORE S&P 500 ETF	Large-cap	68,701.242	0.070
3) QQQ US	POWERSHARES QQQ TRUST SERIES	Large-cap	40,121.504	0.200
4) VOO US	VANGUARD S&P 500 ETF	Large-cap	32,642.625	0.050
5) VIG US	VANGUARD DIVIDEND APPREC ETF	Large-cap	20,507.375	0.100
6) SDY US	SPDR S&P DIVIDEND ETF	Large-cap	13,204.270	0.350
7) IWB US	ISHARES RUSSELL 1000 ETF	Large-cap	11,499.324	0.150
8) RSP US	GUGGENHEIM S&P 500 EQUAL WEI	Large-cap	11,416.500	0.400
9) DIA US	SPDR DJIA TRUST	Large-cap	11,356.950	0.170
10) VYM US	VANGUARD HIGH DVD YIELD ETF	Large-cap	11,177.820	0.100
11) VV US	VANGUARD LARGE-CAP ETF	Large-cap	6,038.687	0.090
12) USMV US	ISHARES MSCI USA MINIMUM VOL	Large-cap	5,115.259	0.150
13) SPLV US	POWERSHARES S&P 500 LOW VOLA	Large-cap	4,725.611	0.250
14) PRF US	POWERSHARES FTSE RAFI US 1K	Large-cap	4,593.743	0.390
15) SCHX US	SCHWAB US LARGE-CAP ETF	Large-cap	4,527.562	0.040
16) HDV US	ISHARES CORE HIGH DIVIDEND E	Large-cap	4,523.743	0.120
17) OEF US	ISHARES S&P 100 ETF	Large-cap	4,275.452	0.200
18) SCHD US	SCHWAB US DVD EQUITY ETF	Large-cap	2,731.688	0.070
19) FEX US	FIRST TRUST LARGE CAP CORE A	Large-cap	1,931.035	0.660

Source: Bloomberg

S&P 500 ETFs

Incredibly, nearly half of the assets in the category, or $292 billion to be exact, are in ETFs tracking the S&P 500 Index. Since ETFs have existed, the most popular new launch is always an S&P 500 ETF. In the 1990s it was SPY, in the 2000s it was IVV, and in the 2010s so far it is VOO. It goes to show you that despite the explosion of newfangled products and innovation, many investors choose to keep it simple with ETFs.

However, choosing among the three may not be so simple. Even though they literally track the same index, a little due diligence will show you that they aren't exactly equal. This is also a great example of how no two products are exactly the same.

The SPDR S&P 500 Trust (SPY) has many superlatives. It is the oldest ETF, launched in 1993. It is the largest ETF, at $180 billion. It also the most traded ETF in the world, with about $6 trillion worth of shares traded each year, which is more than Japan's gross domestic product (GDP).

But one thing SPY is not: the best-performing ETF tracking the S&P 500. In fact, it's the worst performing of the three ETFs tracking the world famous index.

SPY's main rival, the $46 billion iShares Core S&P 500 ETF (IVV), is beating it by 0.48 percent over 10 years. But both SPY and IVV are being outpaced by the Vanguard S&P 500 Index ETF (VOO) since it came on the scene in 2010. Figure 6.2 shows the performance of all three since VOO's inception.

There are a few reasons for this minor dispersion. The first reason is cost. The returns are almost exactly in order of the cheapness of the ETF. It is no coincidence that the best-performing one is also the cheapest, charging 0.05 percent, while second-place IVV charges 0.07 percent, followed by SPY's 0.095 percent. Again, this goes back to how expense ratio detracts from returns and increases tracking error.

Another lesser known reason SPY trails the other two is that it's structured differently. IVV and VOO are structured as open-end investment companies, like many ETFs and mutual funds, while SPY is a unit investment trust (UIT). The most notable impact of SPY's different structure is that dividends can only be reinvested quarterly, whereas IVV and VOO, as open-end funds, can reinvest daily. This gives SPY a touch of cash drag.

In addition, as a UIT, SPY cannot lend out its securities to short sellers and collect a fee like IVV and VOO can. Such securities lending can bring a tiny bit of revenue that goes back into the fund and helps performance.

So if SPY is the worst performer, why does it have the most money, you ask? It still rakes in the dough because of its freakish liquidity. Even though

FIGURE 6.2 VOO Has Lowest Fee and Highest Return, but Barely

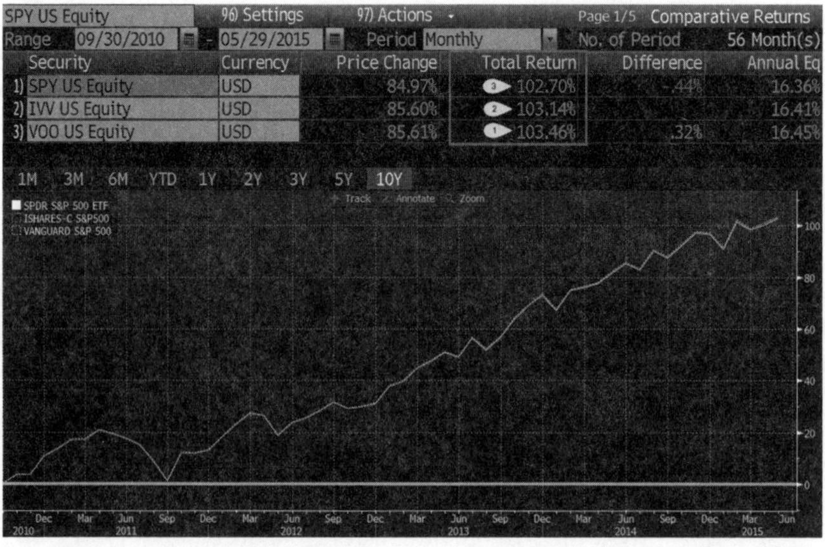
SPY US Equity
96) Settings
97) Actions
Page 1/5 Comparative Returns
Range 09/30/2010 - 05/29/2015
Period Monthly
No. of Period 56 Month(s)
Security | Currency | Price Change | Total Return | Difference | Annual Eq
1) SPY US Equity | USD | 84.97% | 102.70% | -.44% | 16.36%
2) IVV US Equity | USD | 85.60% | 103.14% | | 16.41%
3) VOO US Equity | USD | 85.61% | 103.46% | .32% | 16.45%
1M 3M 6M YTD 1Y 2Y 3Y 5Y 10Y
SPDR S&P 500 ETF
ISHARES C S&P500
VANGUARD S&P 500
Track Annotate Zoom
100
80
60
40
20
0
Dec 2010
Mar
Jun 2011
Sep
Dec
Mar
Jun 2012
Sep
Dec
Mar
Jun 2013
Sep
Dec
Mar
Jun 2014
Sep
Dec
Mar 2015
Jun

Source: Bloomberg

IVV and VOO are plenty liquid by even the most institutional standards, SPY is simply on another planet—a planet that is made of liquid. SPY alone accounts for a good one-third of all ETF trading volume.

The S&P 500 ETFs are a microcosm of a popular dilemma that institutions will face with all ETFs, and that is whether to go with the most liquid ETF (SPY) or the cheapest (VOO) or some kind of a mix of the two (IVV).

The Other S&P 500 ETF

Not to complicate things, but technically there is another ETF that tracks the 500 stocks in the S&P 500 Index, except with one difference: it equal weights them. The Guggenheim S&P Equal Weight ETF (RSP) has handily outperformed SPY et al., by 70 percentage points since it launch in 2003 through the end of May 2015, as shown in Figure 6.3.

RSP's outperformance can be attributed to its equal weighting, which gives each stock a 0.2 percent weight. Launched in 2004, RSP was one of the first-ever "smart-beta" ETFs because it used something other than market cap to weight the stocks. The weighting methodology gives more voice to the smaller-sized large-cap stocks, ones that typically get drowned out in market cap–weighted ETFs like SPY and IVV, which are dominated by a handful of big names.

FIGURE 6.3 RSP Beating SPY Since Inception

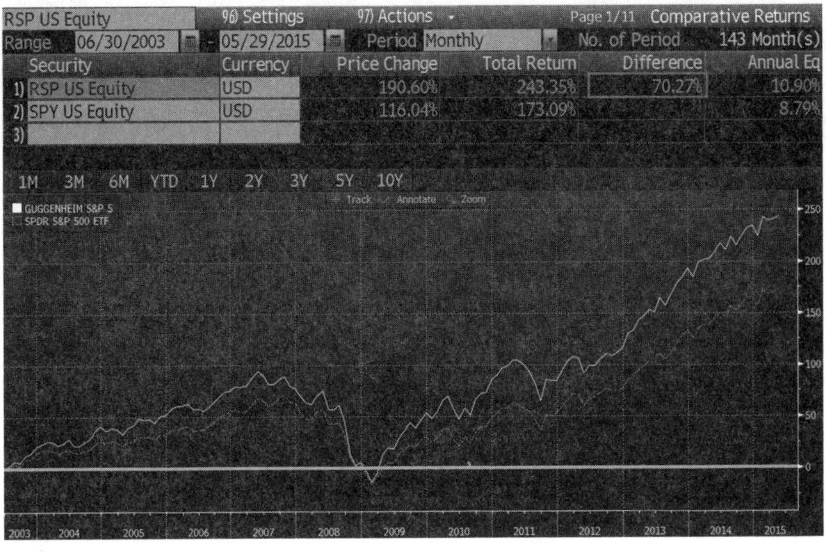

RSP US Equity | 96) Settings | 97) Actions | Page 1/11 Comparative Returns
Range 06/30/2003 - 05/29/2015 | Period Monthly | No. of Period 143 Month(s)

Security	Currency	Price Change	Total Return	Difference	Annual Eq
1) RSP US Equity	USD	190.60%	243.35%	70.27%	10.90%
2) SPY US Equity	USD	116.04%	173.09%		8.79%
3)					

1M 3M 6M YTD 1Y 2Y 3Y 5Y 10Y

GUGGENHEIM S&P 5
SPDR S&P 500 ETF

250 200 150 100 50 0

2003 2004 2005 2006 2007 2008 2009 2010 2011 2012 2013 2014 2015

Source: Bloomberg

One way to think about it is RSP is like the U.S. Senate, where each state gets an equal vote, while the market cap–weighted SPY is like the House of Representatives, where the representation is based on population (although SPY and RSP are both easily much more functional than Congress!).

One example of this difference is a company like Urban Outfitters (URBN US), the clothing store that sells ironic T-shirts to hipsters (yeah, I shop there sometimes). It has a market cap of just $4.5 billion and ranks 490th in size, so it gets an invisible 0.02 percent weighting in SPY. If everyone in America turned hipster tomorrow and bought out everything on the shelves (including the mom jeans and ugly Christmas sweaters) of Urban Outfitters and sales went through the roof, it would have virtually no impact on SPY.

On the flip side, Urban Outfitters is a 0.2 percent weighting—same as every other stock, including Apple. That's still not that much at first glance, but it does amount to RSP giving URBN 10 times more "voice" in the performance of the ETF. And a huge move will be felt more in RSP. Figure 6.4 shows the bottom half of SPY's weightings versus RSP.

FIGURE 6.4 SPY (Port) and RSP (Bmrk) Have Weighting Differences

Name	Ticker	Wgt		
		Port↑	Bmrk	+/-
SPDR S&P 500 ETF TRUST (SPY...		100.00	100.00	0.00
ASSURANT INC	AIZ US	0.03	0.20	-0.18
AUTONATION INC	AN US	0.03	0.20	-0.18
GAMESTOP CORP-CLASS A	GME US	0.03	0.20	-0.18
HUDSON CITY BANCORP INC	HCBK US	0.03	0.20	-0.18
DUN & BRADSTREET CORP	DNB US	0.02	0.20	-0.17
RYDER SYSTEM INC	R US	0.02	0.19	-0.16
FLIR SYSTEMS INC	FLIR US	0.02	0.20	-0.18
PITNEY BOWES INC	PBI US	0.02	0.20	-0.17
TECO ENERGY INC	TE US	0.02	0.20	-0.18
PATTERSON COS INC	PDCO US	0.02	0.20	-0.18
NOBLE CORP PLC	NE US	0.02	0.19	-0.17
OWENS-ILLINOIS INC	OI US	0.02	0.19	-0.17
GENWORTH FINANCIAL INC-CL A	GNW US	0.02	0.20	-0.17
FIRST SOLAR INC	FSLR US	0.02	0.20	-0.18
URBAN OUTFITTERS INC	URBN US	0.02	0.20	-0.18
JOY GLOBAL INC	JOY US	0.02	0.19	-0.17
ALLEGHENY TECHNOLOGIES INC	ATI US	0.02	0.19	-0.17
FOSSIL GROUP INC	FOSL US	0.02	0.20	-0.18
QEP RESOURCES INC	QEP US	0.02	0.20	-0.18
DIAMOND OFFSHORE DRILLING	DO US	0.01	0.19	-0.18

Source: Bloomberg

In addition, RSP's equal weighting mission means that during each quarterly rebalance, it has to sell stocks that have been on a run and reallocate to stocks that haven't been doing well, which effectively means the ETF is selling winners and buying losers. This is known as *disciplined rebalancing* and is one of the selling points for equal-weighted ETFs.

Many critics of equal weight will warn RSP has a "small-cap tilt," even though it holds the S&P 500 stocks, which are large caps. Either way, a tilt toward the smaller-sized large caps over long periods of time is why RSP is about equally correlated to a small-cap index as it is to the S&P 500 Index.

"The S&P 500 is really like the S&P 50 or 100. It is dominated by the top 50 companies and our view is the 500th stock in terms of market cap size is probably more similar to a small- or mid-cap name in characteristics than it is to Apple. So when you equal weight them, you put so much more weight on those names that are 101 to 500 that really are mid- and small-cap in nature in terms of behavior that you get a performance profile that looks very small cap but with typically lower volatility because you are dealing with more liquid names as a whole."

Justin Sibears, Newfound Research

The rub with RSP is that during a steep sell-off or bear market as in 2008, RSP will likely trail SPY. But over the long haul of the past 10 years, though both bull and bear, RSP has proven to be a star performer and legitimate "smart-beta" option within the popular S&P 500 space. There are some institutional owners of RSP, which makes sense since it was really an institutionally driven concept to begin with.

"If you look back at the inception of equal weighting as an investment strategy, it was an institutional investor that really conceived of the best way to own the market was to own it with an equal-weight approach. The support for the strategy has been supported by academic research and institutional adoption."

William Belden, Guggenheim Investments

Russell

The Russell 1000 is another popular index for large-cap ETF investors. Despite getting no attention in the media, the iShares Russell 1000 (IWB) has a respectable $11 billion in assets and is like the S&P 500 except it holds the 1,000 largest stocks. This means you are getting some mid-cap and a tiny dose of small-cap exposure as well. However, despite this minor difference, IWB has a 99 percent correlation to SPY. You could argue you are splitting hairs at this point.

The real-world impact of drilling deeper and including some smaller stocks is that it is more diversified. However, that also means a touch of extra risk. Here is a look at the 360-day volatility of IWB versus SPY. You can see in Figure 6.5 IWB is consistently, although barely, more volatile than SPY. And over the past 10 years, that little bit of extra juice has IWB outpacing SPY by 4.4 percent. IWB charges 0.15 percent, which seems cheap, but is still two to three times more than the S&P 500 ETFs.

IWB isn't even the biggest of the Russell trackers. The iShares Russell 1000 Growth ETF (IWF), which tracks stocks with growth characteristics and the iShares Russell 1000 Value ETF (IWD), which tracks stocks with value characteristics, are both larger at $29 billion and $26 billion, respectively. IWF and IWD both hold 600–700 stocks of the Russell 1000 based on growth and value characteristics. They both charge 0.20 percent. One note is there is a bit of overlap—about 5 percent—between them. Companies like Microsoft, Philip Morris, and Time Warner are on in both the value and growth ETFs.

FIGURE 6.5 IWB's Dip into Mid Caps Gives It Slightly More Volatility than SPY

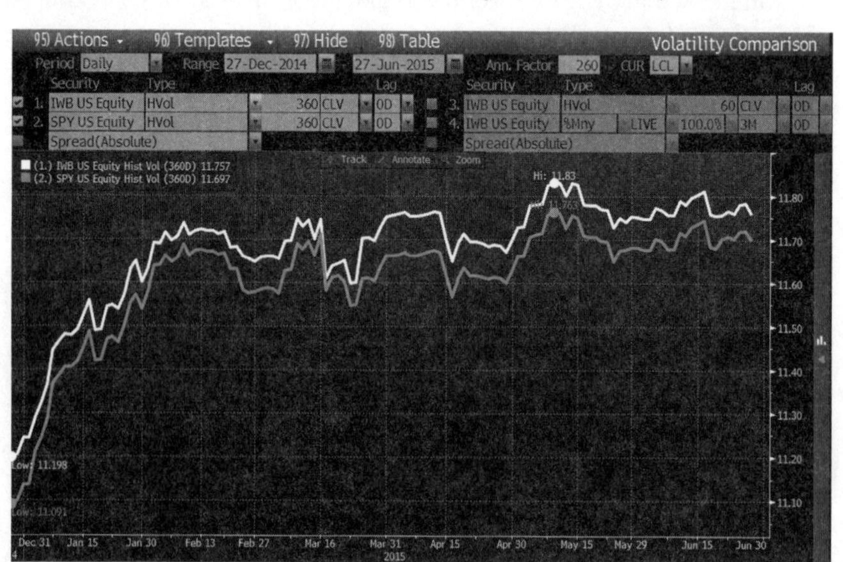

Source: Bloomberg

Vanguard

Vanguard has two unique large cap options—besides VOO—that are massively popular that should be mentioned.

First is the Vanguard Dividend Appreciation ETF (VIG), which tracks companies that have increased their annual dividends for 10 or more consecutive years. VIG holds 180 companies such as Johnson & Johnson, Wal-Mart, and Coca-Cola, but not Apple. VIG's dividend yield as of June 2015 was a microscopic 2.1 percent. VIG's strict rules will draw some investors in and repel others.

> *"One of the classic dilemmas, is what do you do for your dividend-weighted ETF? We looked at a dividend achiever, and the other one is the dividend-weighted methodology ETF. VIG (dividend achiever) waits for 10 years to add a company. So Apple won't be in it until 2022. Is that really the best way to allocate?"*
>
> Adam Grossman, Riverfront

Judging from the $20 billion in assets, investors don't seem to mind VIG's minuscule yield or it not having Apple. It charges 0.10 percent, making it the cheapest dividend ETF on the planet.

Another one is the Vanguard Mega Cap ETF (MGC), which tracks the CRSP U.S. Mega Cap Index. This holds the 300 largest companies in the United States. This alone covers 70 percent of the market capitalization of the U.S. equity market.

Not a whole lot more to it. That's the beauty of Vanguard's G-rated product line. Almost all of them can be explained in a sentence or two.

Beware of the Dow

A highly popular—and quite possibly the most overrated—ETF is the SPDR Dow Jones Industrial Average ETF Trust (DIA). DIA was the 20th ETF, launched back in 1998, and currently has $11.5 billion in assets. It does a great job tracking its index. The problem is that the Dow Jones Industrial Average is the index equivalent of a rotary phone. I'm still not sure why the media bothers quoting it every day.

The Dow tracks just 30 stocks and is price-weighted, which gives the stocks that trade at the highest prices the highest weightings. Right now, Goldman Sachs has the highest weighting of 7.9 percent, which is simply

TABLE 6.1 DIA's Weightings Are Informed by the Stock's Price, Not Size

Name	% Wgt	Px Cls
Goldman Sachs Group Inc	7.90	213.17
Intl Business Machines Corp	6.13	165.46
3M Co	5.82	157.09
Boeing Co/Inc	5.28	142.48
Apple Inc (d)	4.70	126.75
Unitedhealth Group Inc	4.57	123.25
Walt Disney Co/The	4.26	114.99
United Technologies Corp	4.21	113.52
Home Depot Inc	4.17	112.60
Nike Inc-CL B	4.07	109.71

Source: Bloomberg

because it is trading at $213 followed by IBM, which is trading at $165. Microsoft only gets a 1.7 percent weighting because it trades at $46 as shown in Table 6.1. If that seems silly, it is because it is. The index was invented before aspirin was invented and is as outdated as it gets. All this and it charges a rather relatively high fee of .17 percent.

Investors are better served with a big large-cap or broad-market ETF that uses market cap weighting, although one thing you can't take away from DIA is its liquidity. It trades just under $1 billion a day. For some institutions that may very well be enough to overcome all of its flaws.

QQQs

The PowerShares QQQ (QQQ) tracks the Nasdaq 100. This was one of the first ETFs and one of the most liquid. It trades a whopping $2 to $3 billion each day. In terms of QQQ as an investment, it is unique in that it isn't quite a typical large-cap core ETF, nor is it a full-on tech sector play. It is somewhere in between.

As shown in Figure 6.6, tech makes up 55 percent of the portfolio with Apple and Microsoft accounting for over 20 percent of the ETF between them. I have wrestled for a while on where to put this ETF in our database. In the end, since it does have a decent exposure to other sectors, it can't be a sector play, and it isn't a theme per se, thus it is a large-cap equity ETF, albeit one that loves tech stocks.

FIGURE 6.6 Are the QQQs an Equity Large-Cap ETF or a Tech Play?

Name	% Wgt
POWERSHARES QQQ (QQQ US)	100.00
Information Technology	55.24
Consumer Discretionary	19.67
Health Care	15.62
Consumer Staples	6.29
Industrials	2.07
Telecommunication Services	0.78
Materials	0.32

Source: Bloomberg

Mid Caps

Like the Jan Brady of the stock market, mid-cap stocks are often overlooked by the media in favor of large and small caps. But mid-cap ETFs certainly aren't overlooked by investors as they have north of $100 billion, which is nearly 5 percent of total assets and more than most categories. There are about 40 ETFs that aim to give mid-cap exposure.

Just as in the large-cap category, investors prefer using an S&P index. Nearly half of the assets are in the iShares Core S&P Mid-Cap ETF (IJH), which tracks the S&P Mid Cap 400 Index and the SPDR S&P MidCap 400 ETF Trust (MDY), which tracks the same index.

So how do you pick when the top two use the same index and have the same holdings? This is the same deal as the S&P 500 ETFs, with MDY being like SPY—more expensive and a UIT but also more liquid. MDY charges 0.25 percent while IJH charges 0.12 percent. And if you haven't guessed, IJH is outperforming MDY to the tune of about 5 percent over 10 years. MDY trades about $400 million/day, which is four times more than IJH.

So same story here: IJH better as a long-term holding; MDY better for short-term liquidity seekers. For price conscious investors there is also the Schwab U.S. Mid Cap ETF (SCHM) which charges 0.07 percent and the Vanguard Mid-Cap ETF (VO) which charges 0.09 percent.

There are also many flavors of mid cap, such as the WisdomTree Mid-Cap Dividend Fund (DON), which screens and weights mid-cap stocks by their dividend, and the WisdomTree Mid-Cap Earnings Fund (EZM), which screens and weights companies by their earnings. EZM is a good example of always looking under the hood at your allocations. It holds 35 percent exposure to large caps and 4 percent in small caps—not exactly pure in its mid-cap exposure.

This brings us to another popular dilemma, and that is whether to pick an ETF that comes with a twist, otherwise known as smart-beta. Every category pretty much has at least one smart-beta option, if not a dozen. And chances are they will behave differently than the plain vanilla fare. This is something we will discuss more in the next chapter.

Small Caps

There are over 60 U.S. small ETFs with about $100 billion in assets. This category is utterly dominated by the Russell 2000 Index, as shown in Figure 6.7.

IWM and Everyone Else

The largest ETF by far is the iShares Russell 2000 ETF (IWM). It currently has $32 billion in assets, which is about double the next-largest

FIGURE 6.7 IWM Is King of the Small-Cap Category

	Ticker	Name	Fund Market Cap Focus	Tot Asset (M)
1)	IWM US	ISHARES RUSSELL 2000 ETF	Small-cap	31,501.670
2)	IJR US	ISHARES CORE S&P SMALL-CAP E	Small-cap	17,127.805
3)	VB US	VANGUARD SMALL-CAP ETF	Small-cap	11,524.760
4)	IWO US	ISHARES RUSSELL 2000 GROWTH	Small-cap	7,359.419
5)	IWN US	ISHARES RUSSELL 2000 VALUE E	Small-cap	6,156.120
6)	VBR US	VANGUARD SMALL-CAP VALUE ETF	Small-cap	5,614.599
7)	VBK US	VANGUARD SMALL-CAP GRWTH ETF	Small-cap	4,624.670
8)	IJS US	ISHARES S&P SMALL-CAP 600 VA	Small-cap	3,542.671
9)	IJT US	ISHARES S&P SMALL-CAP 600 GR	Small-cap	3,489.623
10)	SCHA US	SCHWAB US SMALL-CAP ETF	Small-cap	3,035.707
11)	DES US	WISDOMTREE SMALLCAP DVD FUND	Small-cap	1,284.007
12)	IWC US	ISHARES MICRO-CAP ETF	Small-cap	962.876
13)	TZA US	DIREXION DLY SM CAP BEAR 3X	Small-cap	775.791
14)	FYX US	FIRST TRUST SMALL CAP CORE A	Small-cap	729.863
15)	SLYG US	SPDR S&P 600 SMALL CAP GROWT	Small-cap	571.721
16)	VTWO US	VANGUARD RUSSELL 2000	Small-cap	526.572
17)	TNA US	DIREXION DLY SM CAP BULL 3X	Small-cap	499.126
18)	FNDA US	SCHWAB FUNDAMENTAL SMALL CAP	Small-cap	458.203
19)	EES US	WISDOMTREE SMALLCAP EARNINGS	Small-cap	445.146

Source: Bloomberg

ETF in the category. It also trades about $2 to $4 billion each day, about the same as Microsoft (MSFT). IWM is a stud by any standard, and more than likely the one most institutions will use regardless of what else I say here.

However, IWM is one of the more expensive options, at 0.20 percent, as well as one of the worst performers among the large small-cap ETFs over nearly every time period. Figure 6.8 shows the past five years.

It is being bested by the iShares Core S&P Small-Cap ETF (IJR) and the Vanguard Small-Cap ETF (VB), both of which have some interesting qualities worth looking at. First, with IJR it tracks only 600 stocks, favoring the more liquid names. It is also half the cost of IWM, at 0.12 percent. That also makes it cheaper than the Vanguard S&P SmallCap 600 ETF (VIOO) and SPDR S&P 600 Small Cap ETF (SLY), which are the other two ETFs in the category that track the same index as IJR.

Besides performance, IJR may hold another appeal over IWM, which is that it doesn't have any micro caps in it. That has attracted some investors to use the primary market (creations and redemptions) when buying and selling their ETFs.

FIGURE 6.8 IWM Has Had the Best Liquidity but Not the Best Performance

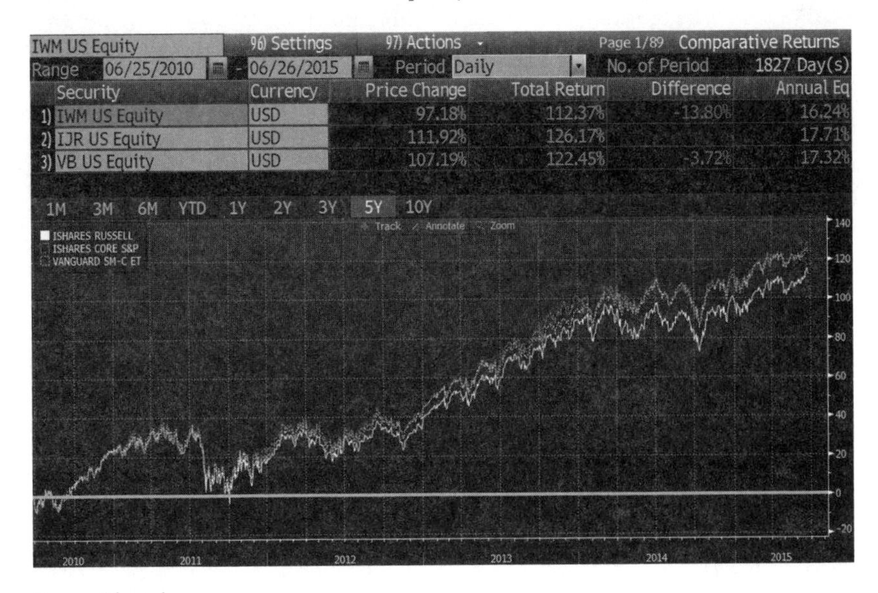

Source: Bloomberg

> *"IWM has half micro caps in it. In a world where you had to get out of it really quick and you have to do a redemption, instead of an open market, IWM is going to be more expensive."*
>
> Adam Grossman, Riverfront Investment Group

Since small caps can be lent out to short-sellers, these ETFs will use that revenue to overcome a chunk of the expense ratio and thus typically only trail their indexes by a few basis points. Both IWM and VB consistently give near-free exposure—and on occasion arguably pay people to own them by beating the index by a few basis points, as shown in Figure 6.9.

Micro Caps

These are the companies that are so small they don't qualify for small-cap status. There are four micro-cap ETFs with about $1 billion in assets. So it isn't exactly a big area.

About 95 percent of the assets are in the iShares MicroCap ETF (IWC), which tracks the Russell Microcap Index. IWC holds 1,400 micro-cap

FIGURE 6.9 VB's Positive Tracking Error Is a Thing of Beauty

Source: Bloomberg

companies you've never heard of. Although bankruptcy is very infrequent, these are pretty risky companies. Perhaps that makes a stronger case for using an ETF which dampens that risk through diversification. About half of IWC's stocks are in the financials and health care sectors. Again, when you are fishing in unchartered waters, you will always find some odd things when you kick the tires on an ETF.

> *"Micro cap was a classic. We spent three or four months looking at them. All completely different in construction and liquidity and focus. They all say micro cap, but it is an incredibly different experience. So what we do is we line that up with our asset allocation and our macro views, and we are saying which one is that one we want to buy. We ended up in IWC, deciding that is the best representation of micro cap. It has the most assets and lines up the closest with our asset allocation work."*
>
> Adam Grossman, Riverfront Investment Group

Speaking of IWC, it charges a whopping 0.60 percent in fees. Are micro caps that much harder to track than small caps that they need to charge triple for it? No, they aren't. The reason they are so expensive is that there is no Vanguard or Schwab with an ETF in the micro-cap category. And if there's no Vanguard or Schwab, there's no reason to lower the fee. IWC isn't alone, either, as the other options in the category are over 0.50 percent, as seen in Table 6.2.

Broad Market

Broad-market exposure is about getting everything in one shot. The good news for investors of all sizes is that you can now get the entire market, including large-, mid- and small-cap stocks, for nearly no cost. There are about 65 broad-market ETFs with over $100 billion in assets.

TABLE 6.2 Micro-Cap ETFs Have Higher Fees with No Vanguard Around

Ticker	Name	Expense Ratio
PZI US	Powershares Zacks Micro Cap	0.930
IWC US	iShares Micro-Cap ETF	0.600
FDM US	First Trust Dow J Select Mic	0.600
WMCR US	Wilshire Micro-Cap ETF	0.500

Source: Bloomberg

Broad-market ETFs have much less turnover, indicating that they are used more by retail investors. For example, large- and small-cap ETFs turn over about 4 percent each day, while broad-market ETFs turn over 0.5 percent a day.

A Perfect ETF?

The broad-market category is where we find what I consider to be the closest thing to a perfect ETF: the Vanguard Total Stock Market ETF (VTI). VTI tracks the CRSP US Total Market Index, which holds over 3,500 securities of all cap sizes, covering 99 percent of the market for the sum total fee of 0.05 percent. Broken down another way, you get exposure to 700 stocks per basis point—the best deal in town.

But it is actually even cheaper than that because of its tight tracking difference. VTI is delivering near-perfect tracking. For example, in 2014, VTI was up 12.56 percent, just two basis points shy of its index, which returned 12.58 percent. In other words, the ETF really costs 0.02 percent, or 1,750 stocks per basis point. And during some stretches it tracks perfectly, which is essentially giving investors free exposure.

The reason for this is that Vanguard utilizes the securities lending that we discussed in the last chapter. Vanguard is able to lend out up to one-third of the securities in the fund to short sellers. It collects a small rental fee for this service and puts all that revenue back into the ETF. This can partly offset the expense ratio, the percentage of assets an ETF issuer takes for managing the fund.

But the securities lending is only part of it. Vanguard's portfolio managers may be able to earn back another basis point or two of the expense ratio simply with their acumen in managing the fund. The index it's based on, the CRSP US Total Market Index, isn't static. It rebalances its holdings each quarter and is affected by IPOs, mergers and acquisitions, and the like. All these can help a shrewd manager pick up a grain of gain, above the index, that can be put back into the fund. This process VTI goes through, of reducing, or outright eliminating, the tracking difference with the index, is how Vanguard's managers are measured and rewarded internally.

VTI is the most liquid in the category (rare for Vanguard) with about $250 million worth of shares exchanging hands each day, about the same as Lockheed Martin stock. That volume helps suppress the cost to trade it. VTI has a spread of just 0.01 percent. Only about 30 to 40 ETFs, out of the universe of 1,700, can boast of average spreads this tight.

The sweet deal that VTI offers isn't lost on investors. It recently became the largest ETF in Vanguard's stable and the fourth-largest ETF overall, at $55 billion in assets. When it comes to fund flows, VTI is a like a giant vacuum cleaner, sucking in an average of $700 million of investor money a month. Figure 6.10 shows about as pretty a flow chart as you will see. VTI has literally never seen a month of outflows.

That money rolls in, rain or shine. Even in January, when VTI lost 2.7 percent as stocks were sold off, it still took in over $1 billion in cash. This, along with its slow turnover, is a big clue that VTI is probably being used by retail buy and hold investors more than institutional traders. They aren't "playing" VTI for short-term gain—they're investing in it for the long haul.

Three Basis Points

This category is where we also find the two ETFs with the lowest expense ratio, the Schwab U.S. Broad Market ETF (SCHB) and the iShares Core S&P Total US Stock Market ETF (ITOT), which charge 0.03 percent.

ETFs have been noted for their innovation and evolution in terms of different exposures and product designs, but the innovation and competition in cost is another frontier altogether. Vanguard started the low-cost trailblazing with its index mutual funds and then on to its ETFs, but it is other issuers such as Schwab and even iShares who have taken it to another (lower) level.

FIGURE 6.10 Months and Months of Inflows for VTI

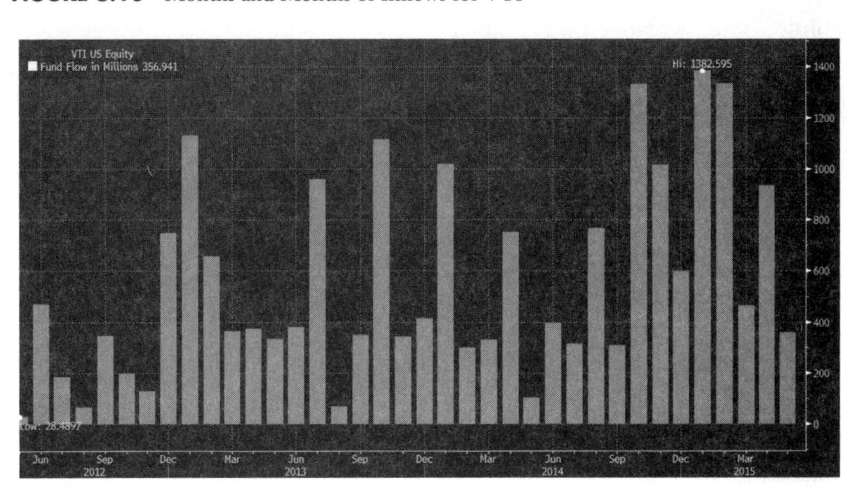

Source: Bloomberg

Whether they are doing it for marketing attention or as a loss leader to get investors onto their platform, the end result is cheaper ETFs, which is a good thing for investors.

There are other broad-market ETFs—namely, the iShares Russell 3000 ETF (IWV). This would most likely be for fans of Russell because, while it is a robust offering with 3,000 securities representing 98 percent of the investable U.S. stock market, it charges 0.20 percent. That is cheap, but still six times more than some of the other broad market ETFs on the market. And the tracking difference in 2014 was 0.20 percent, exactly the expense ratio. But if you like Russell, this is the most popular one.

IPOs

IPO ETFs aim to capture the infant years of a public stock. IPOs don't make their way into the big ETFs, like the ones mentioned above, until many years after they go public. For investors who want to not miss this developing stage of a company's life there are a couple of IPO ETFs.

I equate IPO ETFs to "catch-and-release" fishing, as they hold a new IPO for a short amount of time—squeezing from it any growth spurt it may have early in life—before dumping it back into the figurative stock market sea. At that point, the stock starts to make its way into niche ETFs and perhaps even a small weighting in a big, mainstream ETFs.

The biggest and most liquid IPO ETF is the First Trust U.S. IPO Index Fund (FPX), which typically adds new IPOs and spin-offs within a few months and then keeps them up to 1,000 days. Just doing this one thing has FPX up 192 percent since its inception in 2006, which is 98 percentage points better—or double—that of the large-cap SPY and the small-cap IWM.

Another option in this area is the Renaissance IPO (IPO), which tracks its own index called the Renaissance IPO Index. Renaissance is a leader in IPO research. IPO differs from FPX because it only holds the IPOs for two years before releasing them. It can take in new IPOs after the fifth trading day. And it can take in foreign companies that use the United States to primarily list, such as Alibaba.

Spin-Offs and Buybacks

You can play corporate action themes with ETFs now, too. Since we are getting into the weeds here, I'll keep it brief and just look at the largest from each category. But there are actually multiple options.

FIGURE 6.11 An ETF Tracking IPOs Has Destroyed Large- and Small-Cap ETFs

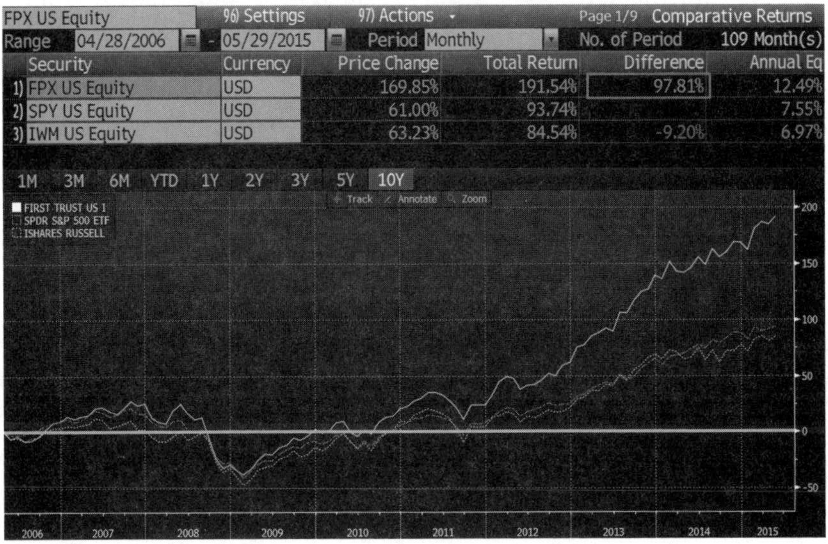

Security	Currency	Price Change	Total Return	Difference	Annual Eq
1) FPX US Equity	USD	169.85%	191.54%	97.81%	12.49%
2) SPY US Equity	USD	61.00%	93.74%		7.55%
3) IWM US Equity	USD	63.23%	84.54%	-9.20%	6.97%

Source: Bloomberg

For spin-offs, there is the Guggenheim Spin-Off ETF (CSD), which tracks recently spun-off companies. Like the IPO ETFs, CSD tries to capture these spun-off companies during a growth spurt between 6 months and 30 months. The ETF is made up of 50 percent small caps and 50 percent mid and large caps.

On the buyback side, the PowerShares Buyback Achievers Portfolio (PKW) is way bigger than you think at $3 billion in assets. PKW simply holds stocks that have reduced net shares outstanding by at least 5 percent in the past year. While that may seem a strict criterion, it nets 171 companies. The portfolio's market cap weighted, so big companies like Oracle, Apple, and Home Depot Inc. dominate.

Covered Call ETFs

One of the more interesting evolutions of the plain vanilla equity ETF is the covered call strategy. Taking the convenience advantage to another level, these ETFs hold a basket of stocks and then write/sell call options on them. The idea is to generate an income stream from the premiums collected from the options. The price you pay for that income stream is giving up the upside gains. This is why they shine best in a sideways market that is exhibiting volatility. The more volatility, the more premium you can make from selling options.

The PowerShares S&P 500 BuyWrite Portfolio (PBP) is one of the bigger examples. PBP writes at-the-money call options. At the time of this writing, PBP was yielding 4.8 percent and was up 4 percent on the year. However, to illustrate the upside that is given up for that yield, one must only look at 2013, where the S&P 500 was up 32 percent, while PBP was up 12 percent.

Another option is the Horizons S&P 500 Covered Call ETF (HSPX), which is like PBP except it writes out-of-the-money options or ones that can only be exercised at prices above the current index level. This means slightly smaller premiums. HSPX is yielding 4.6 percent as of this writing. But you get to enjoy a little more upside if stocks rise. This can be seen in the returns during 2014, where the market was up 14 percent, PBP was up 5 percent, while HSPX was up 7 percent as shown in Figure 6.12.

The methodology difference between PBP and HSPX is a great example in how two similar strategies can actually have a tiny but crucial difference in their designs resulting in substantial differences in performance. Recently,

FIGURE 6.12 Covered Call ETFs Offer Yield but Give Up the Upside

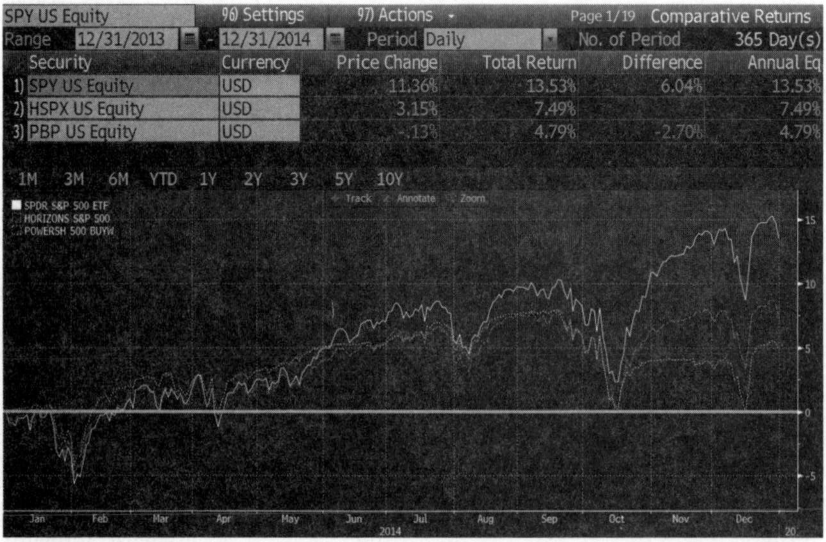
SPY US Equity
96) Settings
97) Actions
Page 1/19 Comparative Returns
Range 12/31/2013 - 12/31/2014
Period Daily
No. of Period 365 Day(s)
Security Currency Price Change Total Return Difference Annual Eq
1) SPY US Equity USD 11.36% 13.53% 6.04% 13.53%
2) HSPX US Equity USD 3.15% 7.49% 7.49%
3) PBP US Equity USD -.13% 4.79% -2.70% 4.79%
1M 3M 6M YTD 1Y 2Y 3Y 5Y 10Y
Track Annotate Zoom
SPDR S&P 500 ETF
HORIZONS S&P 500
POWERSH 500 BUYW
15
10
5
0
-5
Jan Feb Mar Apr May Jun Jul Aug Sep Oct Nov Dec
2014

Source: Bloomberg

a new covered call ETF was launched called the Recon Capital Nasdaq-100 Covered Call ETF (QYLD), which distributes income monthly and has a 9 percent yield as of June 2015.

You may be asking yourself if there are any ETFs that write puts instead of calls? There is one, and it has one of the highest yields of any ETF, at 10 percent. The Alps US Equity High Volatility Put Write Index Fund (HVPW) basically writes put options on the most volatile stocks. This is risky because those stocks are likely to go down and the puts can be exercised, but they also fetch the highest premiums, hence the big yield.

"We bought HVPW and it was working out well for us. Where it really started to struggle is when you had the volatility in biotech and the glamour stocks in the spring of 2014. And that really hurt it. We went in thinking it was picking nickels up in front of a steamroller. We knew we were going to sell it quick and we did."

Gary Stringer, Stringer Asset Management

Sector and Industry ETFs

There are over 350 sector and industry ETFs with over $300 billion in assets. Popular sectors include energy, materials, industrials, consumer discretionary, consumer staples, health care, financials, information technology, telecommunication services, and utilities. Beyond the sectors, there are also many dozens of ETFs tracking industries as well, such as biotech or gold miners.

Sector and industry ETFs can be used in a variety of ways. Many institutions use them both tactically and strategically. Pensions and endowments may use them as part of a tactical equity strategy to overweight a sector or perhaps to complete their portfolio if they don't have a manager for the category.

Hedge funds love to short sector ETFs in order to hedge out market exposure. They currently have north of $20 billion in short sector ETF exposure. For example, they may go long one financial stock and then short the financial-sector ETF in order to try and isolate the returns from that one stock.

Most institutions favor the largest and most liquid sector ETFs, which also happen to be among the cheapest, but there are many to choose from. For example, in the health care sector, there are broad health care ETFs such as the iShares U.S. Healthcare Index ETF (IHF). Then, there are ETFs covering specific sections of the health care sector such as the PowerShares Dynamic Pharmaceuticals Portfolio (PJP) or the SPDR S&P Biotech ETF (XBI). You can also make your health care exposure worldwide with something like the iShares Global Healthcare ETF (IXJ).

Every sector is more or less dominated by ETFs issued by the "Big Three": State Street, Vanguard, and Blackrock. In the tech sector, the Big Three account for 50 percent of the assets and 60 percent of the volume. SPDR in particular dominates this area with 43 percent of the total dollar volume.

This dominance by the Big Three is why if you have done due diligence on one sector's ETF offerings, you basically have done them all. There are easy-to-spot patterns across sectors as to which issuer offers what. While some nuances exist in different sectors, for the most part each sector is similar to the other ones. For this reason we will deep dive into just the tech sector as an example of how to look at the others. Tech is also the largest sector by assets.

The Tech Sector

There are 37 tech-sector ETFs and counting. And they come in many flavors. Figure 6.13 shows the average, minimum, and maximum of the tech-sector ETFs. The variety is so extreme that the range in performance for the first six months of 2015 was 27 percent to –2 percent as shown in Figure 6.13. The 12-month yield ranges from 9 percent to 0 percent. The number of stocks in the holdings ranges from 23 to 401. If this doesn't show why due diligence is important, nothing will.

FIGURE 6.13 A Wide Range of Tech Sector ETFs as of End of June 2015

Selected Criteria 1) Modify Screening Criteri

Exchange: United States X Industry: Technology X

37 matching funds

11) Key Metrics | 12) Cost | 13) Performance | 14) Flow | 15) Liquidity | 16) Allocations | 17) Regulatory Structure

Name	30D Vol	Asset$ (USD)	YTD Return	YTD Flow (USD)	12M Yield	# of Holdings	Index Weight
Average	375.88k	1.04B	+8.48%	27.23M	+1.37%	97	
Minimum	726.93	37.52k	-1.65%	-1.62B	+.05%	23	
Maximum	7.34M	13.38B	+27.05%	1.02B	+9.42%	401	
100) Technology Select Sector SPDR	7.34M	13.38B	+3.08%	-259.60M	+1.79%	73	Market Cap
101) Vanguard Information Technolc	257.96k	7.60B	+3.84%	557.90M	+1.08%	387	Market Cap
102) iShares US Technology ETF	198.23k	3.11B	+2.67%	-1.62B	+1.12%	137	Market Cap
103) First Trust Dow Jones Internet	193.67k	2.99B	+11.45%	747.70M	--	41	Multi Factor
104) iShares North American Tech-S	141.44k	1.23B	+9.61%	-94.95M	+.24%	64	Market Cap
105) PureFunds ISE Cyber Security E	1.29M	1.22B	+21.56%	1.02B	--	32	Market Cap
106) Guggenheim S&P 500 Equal Wei	59.97k	984.08M	+2.23%	186.90M	+1.23%	68	Equal
107) First Trust Technology AlphaDE	255.29k	901.75M	+4.78%	-245.50M	+.54%	85	Fundamentals
108) iShares Global Tech ETF	35.92k	900.57M	+3.75%	76.15M	+1.13%	110	Market Cap

Group By None 2) Select Stats

Source: Bloomberg

Almost every institution is going to choose an ETF from the Big Three, which in this case means the Technology Select Sector SPDR Fund (XLK) or the Vanguard Information Technology ETF (VGT) or the iShares US Technology ETF (IYW). Figure 6.13 is showing the tech-sector ETFs sorted by assets, with these three ETFs at the top.

Most big institutions will simply pick the one with the most exchange volume. However, simply going for the most liquid one or just picking the one all the other institutional managers use may be shortsighted. After all, there is a 7 percent performance difference between just the Big Three's tech sector offerings when you look at the past two years, as shown in Figure 6.14.

So even though they do pretty much the same thing, there are some subtle differences that lead to the performance gap. Let's put these three through the due diligence process to discover the differences.

XLK holds tech stocks that are in the S&P 500 Index. It is fairly concentrated, with 72 large-cap stocks. It is market cap weighted and dominated by a few big names. Apple and Microsoft currently make up 26 percent of the ETF. Additionally, XLK holds telecommunications names as well, with over a 4 percent allocation to both AT&T and Verizon. This is an important difference.

FIGURE 6.14 Return Dispersion among the Big Three's Tech ETFs

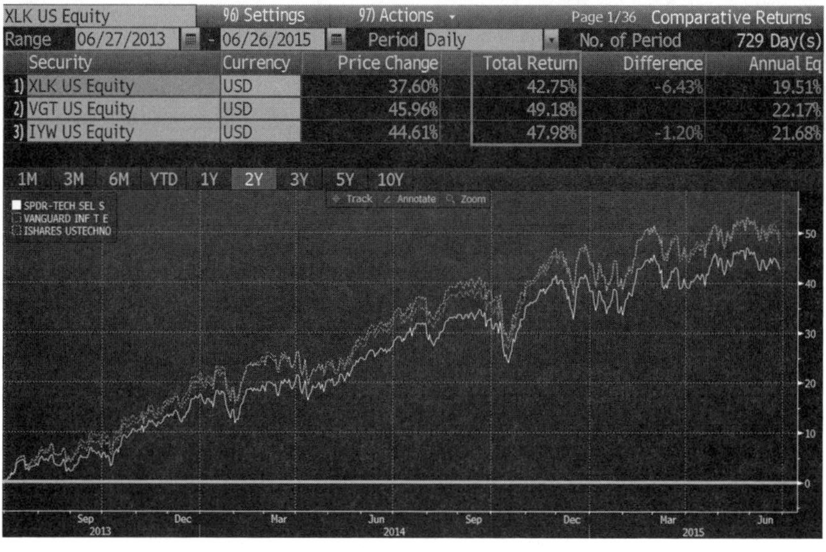
XLK US Equity
96) Settings
97) Actions
Page 1/36 Comparative Returns
Range 06/27/2013 - 06/26/2015 Period Daily
No. of Period 729 Day(s)
Security Currency Price Change Total Return Difference Annual Eq
1) XLK US Equity USD 37.60% 42.75% -6.43% 19.51%
2) VGT US Equity USD 45.96% 49.18% 22.17%
3) IYW US Equity USD 44.61% 47.98% -1.20% 21.68%
1M 3M 6M YTD 1Y 2Y 3Y 5Y 10Y
Track Annotate Zoom
SPDR-TECH SEL S
VANGUARD INF T E
ISHARES USTECHNO
50
40
30
20
10
0
Sep 2013
Dec
Mar
Jun 2014
Sep
Dec
Mar 2015
Jun

Source: Bloomberg

VGT tracks the MSCI U.S. Investable Market Information Technology Index. The first thing I notice is that it holds 393 companies. That's five times the depth of holdings as XLK. As discussed earlier, Vanguard's thing is to be "cheap and deep." Besides holding five times more stocks and having a handful of mid caps, it also doesn't hold those telecom names.

VGT also has small exposures to new tech companies like Twitter and LinkedIn, which are not in XLK. At the end of the day, it is not having these telecom companies that has allowed VGT to outpace XLK, although those names could provide stability to XLK in a wicked tech sell-off.

In terms of exposure, IYW is in between the two. It tracks the Dow Jones US Technology Sector Index. It holds 140 names. Like VGT, it doesn't hold any telecom, which has helped its recent performance. It also doesn't hold companies like VISA, MasterCard, and Western Union, which both XLK and VGT hold.

In terms of cost, IYW is more than three times as expensive as the other two, charging 0.45 percent. It is unclear why iShares can be so competitively cheap in other categories but remain stubbornly expensive in the sector space, especially when they don't have the most traded ETF.

"The iShares sector products on the U.S. side are completely eliminated for us because they are such an outlier cost-wise. When you are talking about double the cost for S&P 500 names, it is just very hard to justify when I can get very similar exposure at 15 basis points instead of 40+."

Justin Sibears, Newfound Research

By contrast, XLK and VGT are much cheaper, charging 0.15 percent and 0.12 percent, respectively. All of them have tight spreads that should add up to no more than 0.02 percent. And they all track extremely well, under 0.05 percent each. So, unless you are going in short term or specifically want the exact exposure of IYW, XLK and VGT certainly have the edge in cost.

In terms of risk (standard deviation), XLK is the least volatile, at 8.9 percent, thanks to its telecom exposure and huge bias toward the largest of the large tech names. VGT and IYW are both slightly higher, at 9.8 percent, due to their exposure to some of the newer tech names and lack of exposure to telecom.

But when it comes to the all-important "L" word—liquidity—none can match XLK in volume. In each and every sector, SPDR's ETFs are the most traded of the group. They all came out in the 1990s and are just the go-to ETF for most people. XLK trades $407 million worth of shares each day. It also has the highest implied liquidity of the three, with potentially $3.2 billion worth of XLK able to be traded based on the underlying holdings' liquidity.

VGT has much less trading volume than XLK with $59 million and an implied liquidity of $2 billion. IYW trades a bit more, at $100 million worth of shares exchanging hands each day. It also has an implied liquidity of $3.2 billion.

In the end, unless you have over $100 million to invest or special liquidity needs, it doesn't really matter—they are all blessed with healthy liquidity. Alas, we know that institutions use XLK from the 13Fs. Here is a look at the plethora of pensions, endowments, insurance companies, and hedge funds that own a piece of XLK, as shown in Figure 6.15. And check out the estimated holding periods. Many have owned XLK for years. Even with these longer horizons, they still choose the most liquid option.

In summary, it depends on what you are looking for. XLK comes with unmatched liquidity and also telecom stocks. VGT casts its net very wide, which adds a spoonful of extra risk. IYW sort of splits the difference between them, but is three times the cost.

Many investors have been slowly moving toward VGT over the past few years. VGT has taken in $3 billion in new cash compared to little or no flows for XLK and IYR. No doubt the fact that it is cheapest and has performed the best with good liquidity is why it has attracted investors of all sizes.

FIGURE 6.15 A Look at the Institutional Owners of XLK

	Portfolio Name	Mkt Val↑	% Portfolio	% Out	Est. Holding	Inst Type
						•[Select Multiple
1.	PROVIDA PENSION FUND ADMINISTRATOR	579.4MLN	11.496	4.33	1.50	Pension Fund
2.	CLAL INSURANCE ENTERPRISE HOLDINGS LTD	70MLN	1.547	0.52	0.50	Insurance Company
3.	ONTARIO TEACHERS PENSION PLAN BOARD	65.5MLN	0.470	0.49	0.25	Pension Fund
4.	US BR SUN LIFE ASSUR CO OF CANADA	56.27MLN	N.A.	0.42	1.75	Insurance Company
5.	--	52.12MLN	N.A.	0.39	1.00	Insurance Company
6.	SPRUCE PRIVATE INVESTORS LLC	46.74MLN	11.724	0.35	1.00	Hedge Fund Mana...
7.	NEW JERSEY MANUFACTURERS INSURANCE COMPANY	40.15MLN	N.A.	0.30	2.00	Insurance Company
8.	INTEGRA F3	29.83MLN	1.175	0.22	0.50	Pension Fund
9.	Multiple Portfolios	28.65MLN	N.A.	0.21	0.75	Insurance Company
10.	Multiple Portfolios	28.4MLN	N.A.	0.21	1.00	Pension Fund
11.	--	27.62MLN	N.A.	0.21	1.00	Hedge Fund Mana...
12.	PARALLAX VOLATILITY ADVISERS LLC	22.74MLN	0.711	0.17	1.00	Hedge Fund Mana...
13.	MILLENNIUM MANAGEMENT LLC	18.74MLN	0.037	0.14	1.00	Hedge Fund Mana...
14.	PUPLAVA FINANCIAL SERVICES	11.68MLN	4.773	0.09	0.50	Hedge Fund Mana...
15.	TEXAS PERMANENT SCHOOL FUND	10.6MLN	0.114	0.08	1.25	Endowment
16.	MOUNT LUCAS MANAGEMENT CORP	8.64MLN	1.492	0.06	3.25	Hedge Fund Mana...
17.	DORINCO REINSURANCE COMPANY	8.42MLN	N.A.	0.06	2.00	Insurance Company
18.	STATE WORKMENS INSURANCE FUND	7.36MLN	N.A.	0.05	2.50	Insurance Company
19.	FOOTHILLS ASSET MANAGEMENT LTD	5.22MLN	4.128	0.04	1.50	Hedge Fund Mana...
20.	STALEY CAPITAL ADVISERS INC	4.01MLN	0.452	0.03	0.25	Hedge Fund Mana...
21.	AMERIHEALTH CASUALTY INSURANCE COMPANY	3.2MLN	N.A.	0.02	2.75	Insurance Company
22.	MARINER WEALTH ADVISORS LLC	2.81MLN	0.233	0.02	2.00	Hedge Fund Mana...
23.	MANUFACTURERS LIFE INSURANCE COMPANY	2.71MLN	0.035	0.02	1.00	Insurance Company

Source: Bloomberg

Regardless, if you are just looking to get some plain vanilla tech exposure, using any of these ETFs will work. What we just did here with these three ETFs you will find paralleled in every sector.

Also paralleled in every sector is the slew of more targeted options. These are the ETFs that you may not have heard of that come with different twists or weighting schemes or lower costs. Let's look at a few.

Smart-Beta Tech

Beyond the Big Three, each sector is going to have some smart-beta options as well. PowerShares, First Trust, and Guggenheim are the most likely issuers of products that offer alternative approaches.

For example, the First Trust Technology AlphaDEX Fund (FXL) employs an elaborate secret sauce that uses both growth and value metrics to select tech stocks from the Russell 1000 Index. Growth factors include 3-, 6-, and 12-month price appreciation, sales to price, and one-year sales growth. Value factors include book value to price, cash flow to price, and return on assets.

After that, the selected stocks are divided into quintiles based on their rankings, and the top-ranked quintiles receive a higher weight within the index. The stocks are equally weighted within each quintile.

I'm sure you are asking yourself right now, does that actually work? Depends on when you look, but since FXL was launched in 2007, it is underperforming XLK by about 10 percentage points. But if we were to isolate, say, 2013, FXL outperformed XLK by 12 percentage points. This gets to the rule of thumb of smart beta: convenience is guaranteed, and outperformance is a bonus. We will look more at smart beta in the next chapter.

You can also put a small-cap tilt on your tech play with the Guggenheim S&P 500 Equal Weight Technology ETF (RYT). RYT is basically an equal-weight version of XLK minus the telecom stocks. RYT's equal weighting means the smaller-sized large caps get an equal voice. So Apple gets the same weighting as Salesforce.com Inc. This equates to increased volatility—about 15 percent more than XLK. Equal weighting sectors is a popular strategy with some who like the increased volatility it brings.

"If you go with market cap–weighted [sector ETFs] you end up with dominant positions in one or two companies. If one of those guys has a hiccup, that has an outsized impact on performance. If we think the theme is strong because of the timing of the trade, we think that volatility [in equal-weighted ETFs] is upside volatility."

Gary Stringer, Stringer Asset Management

One mark against RYT is that it charges 0.40 percent. I'm not sure why something as simple as equal weighting warrants charging more than twice the fees as XLK, which market cap weights. With that said, RYT has nearly $1 billion in assets.

If RYT and FXL are on the edgy side of smart beta, you can also go very conservative. When it comes to playing it safe in tech, no ETF is as conservative as the First Trust Nasdaq Technology Dividend Index Fund (TDIV), which tracks the highest-dividend-paying tech companies. TDIV may be the world's first and only boring tech ETF.

The dividend theme is what keeps the more volatile upstart tech stocks out of the portfolio and leaves TDIV's portfolio with a vintage "I Love the 90s" feel full of large, old-guard tech companies, as seen in Figure 6.16.

Some of the top holdings include Intel, Cisco, and Microsoft—each with an about an 8 percent weighing—and Oracle with a 4 percent weighting. Those four companies had a jaw-dropping average return of 60 percent per year during the 1990s. Those once hot, young 1990s tech companies have matured into more stable adults with tons of cash. Companies like Microsoft, Cisco, Oracle, and Intel are now the anchor tenants of the tech world and give TDIV a lot of stability in a sell-off.

FIGURE 6.16 Top Holdings for TDIV

TDIV US Equity | 97) View Creation Unit | 98) Holdings Analysis | Page 1/7 Mutual Fund Holdings

FT NASDAQ TECH DVD INDEX FD — Portfolio Filing Date 6/26/2015
Fund Type ETF — Cash Position -1.25M USD
Asset Class Equity — Creation/Redemption Fee 500 USD

Name	Ticker		Position	Value(USD)	Change	%Net
1) International Business Machin	IBM	US	335,208	55.46M	unch	8.121
2) Apple Inc	AAPL	US	436,506	55.33M	unch	8.101
3) Microsoft Corp	MSFT	US	1,213,572	54.93M	unch	8.042
4) Cisco Systems Inc	CSCO	US	1,940,225	54.87M	unch	8.034
5) Intel Corp	INTC	US	1,650,261	51.19M	unch	7.496
6) Oracle Corp	ORCL	US	653,806	26.80M	unch	3.924
7) QUALCOMM Inc	QCOM	US	408,065	26.39M	unch	3.864
8) Texas Instruments Inc	TXN	US	402,787	21.31M	unch	3.120
9) Hewlett-Packard Co	HPQ	US	571,223	17.44M	unch	2.554
10) AT&T Inc	T	US	411,610	14.87M	unch	2.177
11) EMC Corp/MA	EMC	US	556,274	14.71M	unch	2.154
12) Rogers Communications Inc	RCI	US	414,248	14.66M	unch	2.147
13) TELUS Corp	TU	US	417,533	14.58M	unch	2.135
14) BCE Inc	BCE	US	324,663	14.29M	unch	2.093
15) Verizon Communications Inc	VZ	US	287,561	13.69M	unch	2.005
16) CenturyLink Inc	CTL	US	427,708	12.83M	unch	1.878
17) Mobile TeleSystems OJSC	MBT	US	1,220,468	11.88M	unch	1.739
18) Seagate Technology PLC	STX	US	232,022	11.62M	unch	1.701

Source: Bloomberg

FIGURE 6.17 TDIV Held Up Well During a Tech Sell-off of Early 2013

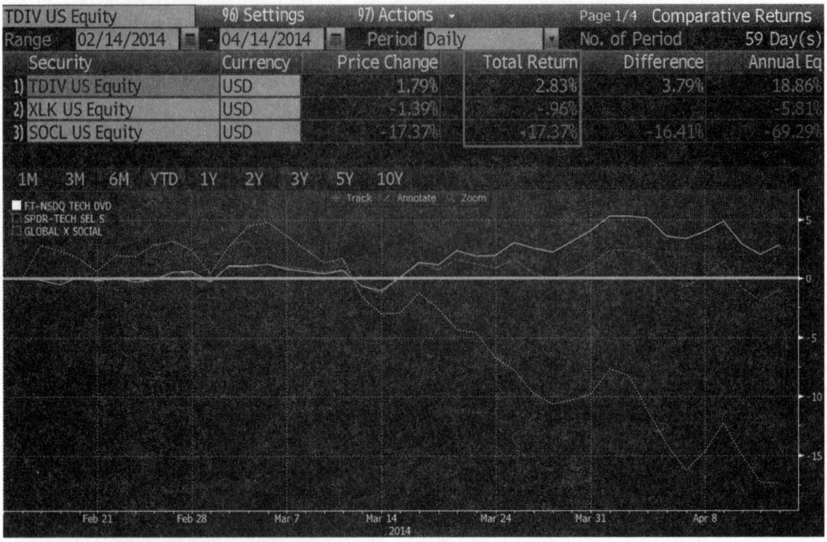
TDIV US Equity
96) Settings
97) Actions
Page 1/4 Comparative Returns
Range 02/14/2014 - 04/14/2014
Period Daily
No. of Period 59 Day(s)
Security
Currency
Price Change
Total Return
Difference
Annual Eq
1) TDIV US Equity USD 1.79% 2.83% 3.79% 18.86%
2) XLK US Equity USD -1.39% -.96% -5.81%
3) SOCL US Equity USD -17.37% -17.37% -16.41% -69.29%
1M 3M 6M YTD 1Y 2Y 3Y 5Y 10Y
FT-NSDQ TECH DVD
SPDR-TECH SEL S
GLOBAL X SOCIAL
Feb 21
Feb 28
Mar 7
Mar 14
2014
Mar 24
Mar 31
Apr 8

Source: Bloomberg

There was a two-month stretch back in 2014 when some of the high flyers in the tech world—like social media and Internet stocks—sold off in a New York minute. TDIV managed to turn in a positive performance. Figure 6.17 shows how it behaved versus XLK and the Global X Social Media ETF (SOCL). This is smart beta paying off. However, since then, up until June 2015, TDIV is lagging XLK by nine percentage points. This is smart beta not paying off. Either way, TDIV is doing as advertised by sporting the highest yield among all the tech ETFs of 2.4 percent.

Small Caps

Traveling even further downtown and away from the safety of portfolio anchors like Apple and Microsoft, we enter Small-Cap Land. These areas can also provide greater diversification benefits and greater returns, but also come with greater risk.

PowerShares S&P SmallCap Information Technology Portfolio (PSCT) is one example of a specific small-cap tech ETF. Unless you are a tech analyst in that sector, you probably haven't heard of any of the holdings. As opposed to something like TDIV, which is full of legendary tech names, it is probably a good thing that your small-cap exposure to be off-the-radar, smaller upstarts. You are hoping to catch the next Microsoft or Apple in one of these names.

FIGURE 6.18 PSCT Is a Mixed Bag of Returns in First Half of 2015

Name	Avg % Wgt	Tot Rtn
POWERSHARES S&P SMALLCAP IN..	100.00	6.75
ADTRAN INC	0.91	-24.28
ADVANCED ENERGY INDUSTRIES	0.87	20.51
AGILYSYS INC	0.13	-27.32
ANIXTER INTERNATIONAL INC	1.78	-25.89
BADGER METER INC	0.76	7.35
BEL FUSE INC-CL B	0.20	-22.90
BENCHMARK ELECTRONICS INC	1.10	-12.93
BLACK BOX CORP	0.28	-11.43
BLACKBAUD INC	1.95	33.46
BLUCORA INC	0.52	19.86
BOTTOMLINE TECHNOLOGIES (...	0.88	12.74
BROOKS AUTOMATION INC	0.69	-2.69
CABOT MICROELECTRONICS CORP	1.00	1.52
CACI INTERNATIONAL INC -CL A	1.82	-2.24
CALAMP CORP	0.58	-0.11
CARDTRONICS INC	1.45	-0.44
CEVA INC	0.35	13.12
CHECKPOINT SYSTEMS INC	0.43	-21.38
CIBER INC	0.23	6.76
CIRRUS LOGIC INC	1.75	46.12
COHERENT INC	1.37	7.23
COHU INC	0.26	11.98
COMSCORE INC	1.49	16.30

Source: Bloomberg

Figure 6.18 shows the holdings sorted alphabetically and gives a wonderful look at just how all over the place the returns of these baby stocks are. Some stocks are up 40 percent and others are down 20 percent, and that's just in the first six months of 2015. If this doesn't make the case for the diversification benefit of an ETF, I don't know what does.

Niche Tech

You can also get your tech in specific groupings or industries or themes, such as Internet, social media, cyber-security, and semiconductors. When perusing any niche industry or thematic ETF, it is important to keep an eye out for increased volatility levels, foreign exposure, and overlap.

One recent example of a niche industry ETF providing some value-add is the surprise smash hit of 2015: the PureFunds ISE Cyber Security ETF (HACK). HACK launched about two weeks prior to the world-famous Sony Pictures Entertainment hack. While unfortunate for some film executives, it was perfect timing for this fledgling ETF.

It tracks 26 companies involved in providing cyber-security software, hardware, and services. About 85 percent of the stocks are based in the United States. About half of the portfolio's stocks are small-cap companies, so investors can expect about double the volatility of the S&P 500, but about half the volatility of the average stock in the holdings.

When using niche products like HACK, though, it's important to check if the portfolio companies are already available in bigger, more mainstream ETFs that you may already own. HACK is pretty good on this front, as it only has a 4 percent overlap with XLK, the world's most-owned tech ETF, as shown in Figure 6.19. XLK will likely rebalance into some cyber-security names as those stocks grow bigger. But that will be a long process. HACK catches those firms way before that time.

FIGURE 6.19 HACK Has Been Crushing the Largest Tech-Sector ETF Since Inception

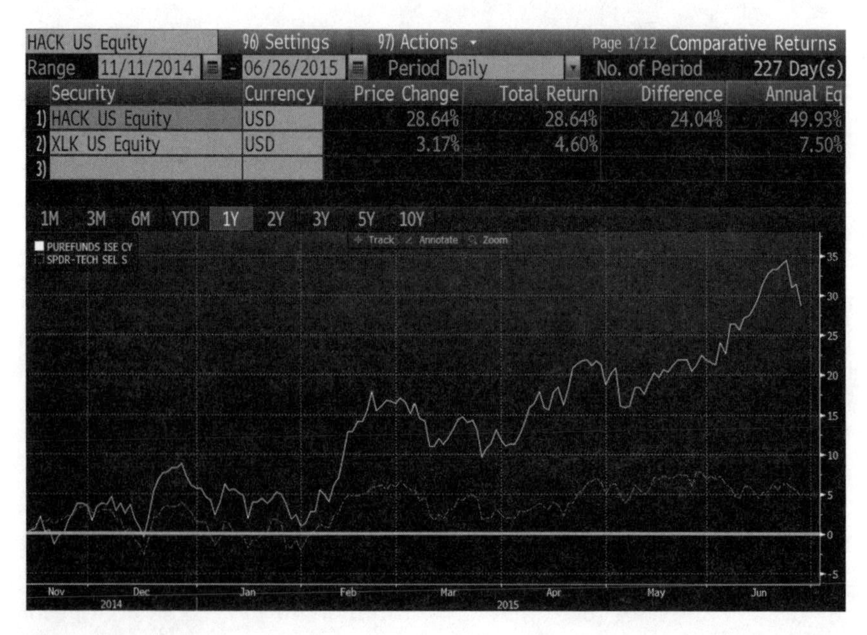

Source: Bloomberg

Industries

Big sectors aside, there are many industries tracked by ETFs such as homebuilders, banks, aerospace and defense, internet, biotech and gold miners. Then there are super-specific industries that people probably forgot existed but have ETFs tracking them, such as nuclear energy and rare earth metals. We don't have the space or time to cover them all, so I will chose a few of the more popular ones.

Homebuilders

Homebuilder ETFs have over $3 billion in assets. There are two big ones to choose from: the iShares Home Construction ETF (ITB) and the SPDR Homebuilders ETF (XHB). While both have similar-sounding names, trade over $50 million a day, and have reasonable expense ratios, they are *very* different when it comes to the exposure they provide, which has them posting wildly different returns over the years.

The heart of the difference comes down to what your definition of "homebuilding" is. Do you think homebuilding is erecting a structure that people will eventually live in, or do you think it is erecting a structure and then furnishing it and making it livable? And by livable I don't mean just hanging a light, but getting things like couches, a fridge, bath towels, and perhaps a hot tub.

If you are in the more conservative camp, then ITB takes the more literal meaning and for the most part tracks companies that bring the wood and put up the walls. ITB has 65 percent homebuilder companies and 15 percent building material companies. Companies like Lennar Corp and Toll Brothers are among the top holdings, with over 8 percent weighting each.

If you are in the more liberal fridge and hot tub camp, then the SPDR ETF may be for you. In fact, XHB has only 31 percent homebuilder companies and 19 percent building materials, as seen in Table 6.3. A good chunk of the rest—19 percent to be exact—is in retail. Another 15 percent is in home furnishing companies like La-Z-Boy and Whirlpool Corp. It is also worth adding that retail companies give XHB a higher correlation to the S&P 500.

That extra exposure to those retail companies can be good or bad, depending on the market environment. In addition, XHB equal weights all of its holdings so that the small- and mid-cap companies have a louder voice in the ETF compared with ITB. These are extra gears in XHB's design that ITB doesn't have.

TABLE 6.3 The Big Difference between ITB and XHB

Industry	ITB	XHB
Homebuilders	64.5%	31.3%
Building Materials	15.9%	19.2%
Retail	9.6%	21.4%
Home Furnishings	2.8%	12.5%

Source: Bloomberg

But these gears can backfire and work against XHB as well, which is why the performance competition of these two is very mixed. They average a 9 percent difference each year, as shown in Table 6.4.

XHB and ITB will probably be going back in forth year after year in a performance slugfest. And while many analysts decry XHB as not being a pure homebuilder ETF, it really comes down to one's view of how you build a home and what you want from your investment. In this way, ETFs are a bit like buying a house: it has to fit your needs and feel right.

In terms of fees, XHB charges .35 percent while ITB charges .43 percent. This is about triple what the cheapest sector ETFs cost. Why? You guessed it, no Vanguard. Vanguard doesn't have any industry ETF offerings so expect to pay more.

TABLE 6.4 Yearly Returns for ITB and XHB

Year	ITB	XHB	Difference
2007	–58%	–48%	10%
2008	–40%	–35%	5%
2009	27%	32%	5%
2010	7%	14%	7%
2011	–9%	–1%	8%
2012	75%	53%	22%
2013	4%	12%	8%
2014	17%	25%	8%
AVERAGE			9%

Source: Bloomberg

Gold Miners

Gold miner ETFs are actually very popular. The category has $8 billion in assets, almost all of which is in the Market Vectors Gold Miners ETF (GDX), which has $6 billion in assets and trades $527 million a day. It is owned by some heavy-hitter hedge funds, such as David Einhorn's Greenlight Capital, which has owned the ETF now for over six years, as seen in Figure 6.20.

Unfortunately for these hedge funds, GDX has been brutal over the past several years. GDX is one of the rare ETFs that has seen massive inflows despite awful performance. This is most likely because many of these hedge funds are trying—and failing—to call a bottom.

FIGURE 6.20 Hedge Fund Owners of GDX

	Portfolio Name	Mkt Val	% Portfolio	% Out	Est. Holding	Inst Type
						Hedge Fund Manag
1.	GREENLIGHT CAPITAL INC	154.09MLN	2.030	2.53	6.50	Hedge Fund Mana...
2.	JANA PARTNERS LLC	123.2MLN	1.083	2.02	0.25	Hedge Fund Mana...
3.	WHITEBOX ADVISORS LLC	24.94MLN	0.961	0.41	3.75	Hedge Fund Mana...
4.	ORCHARD HILL CAPITAL MANAGEMENT LP	14.77MLN	100.000	0.24	0.25	Hedge Fund Mana...
5.	SOROS FUND MANAGEMENT LLC	13.77MLN	0.158	0.23	1.75	Hedge Fund Mana...
6.	STALEY CAPITAL ADVISERS INC	11.66MLN	1.356	0.19	6.00	Hedge Fund Mana...
7.	QS INVESTORS LLC	11.39MLN	0.131	0.19	2.00	Hedge Fund Mana...
8.	CAPSTONE INVESTMENT ADVISORS LLC	11.35MLN	0.506	0.19	0.75	Hedge Fund Mana...
9.	POINT72 ASSET MANAGEMENT LP	9.05MLN	0.072	0.15	0.25	Hedge Fund Mana...
10.	MERU CAPITAL GROUP LP	8.86MLN	2.051	0.15	0.25	Hedge Fund Mana...
11.	CAXTON ASSOCIATES LP	6.33MLN	0.717	0.10	0.50	Hedge Fund Mana...
12.	FIRST EAGLE INVESTMENT MGMT LLC	6MLN	0.014	0.10	6.75	Hedge Fund Mana...
13.	HARVEST CAPITAL STRATEGIES LLC	5.43MLN	0.834	0.09	0.25	Hedge Fund Mana...
14.	CMT TRADING LLC	5.23MLN	9.157	0.09	0.75	Hedge Fund Mana...
15.	GLG PARTNERS LP	5.05MLN	0.191	0.08	0.50	Hedge Fund Mana...
16.	NOKOMIS CAPITAL LLC	4.98MLN	1.526	0.08	3.50	Hedge Fund Mana...
17.	3G CAPITAL PARTNERS LTD	4.98MLN	0.518	0.08	0.25	Hedge Fund Mana...
18.	SCORIA CAPITAL PARTNERS LP	4.52MLN	1.400	0.07	0.25	Hedge Fund Mana...
19.	TWIN TREE MANAGEMENT LP	3.95MLN	1.511	0.06	1.00	Hedge Fund Mana...
20.	PEAK6 INVESTMENTS LP	3.62MLN	0.162	0.06	0.75	Hedge Fund Mana...
21.	ARGENTIERE CAPITAL	3.21MLN	1.591	0.05	0.50	Hedge Fund Mana...
22.	SUN VALLEY GOLD LLC	2.98MLN	2.008	0.05	0.25	Hedge Fund Mana...
23.	GEOLOGIC RESOURCE PARTNERS LLC	2.71MLN	3.272	0.04	0.25	Hedge Fund Mana...
24.	GRAMERCY FUNDS MGMT LLC	2.71MLN	0.782	0.04	1.50	Hedge Fund Mana...

Source: Bloomberg

The temptation of bottom calling is why GDX has taken in $12.5 billion in new cash since it came out, but today it has only $5.5 billion to show for it, as seen in Table 6.5. In other words, $6 billion dollars was lost from enticed investors trying to play a GDX rebound. While there have been a few short-term surges, they never lasted long.

For more daring investors GDX has a mini-me in the Market Vectors Junior Gold Miners ETF (GDXJ), which invests in tiny gold mining stocks that have an average market cap of under $1 billion. This gives it leverage ETF-esque volatility with a standard deviation of 50 percent, or 5 times the S&P 500 Index. However, if an investor is just straight betting on a gold miner surge, GDXJ will give you a greater payoff, such as in the beginning of 2014 when it surged 33 percent in two months compared with 22 percent for GDX.

Master Limited Partnerships

Master limited partnerships (MLPs) aren't an industry per se, but they are a sub-category of the energy sector and hugely popular and worth mentioning. Most MLPs operate toll-road type infrastructure for the transportation of oil and gas. MLPs are used for their big yields and non-correlated returns.

MLPs aren't taxed like normal corporations as long as they pass on income to holders. Many of the MLP products can yield up to 7 percent, which has

TABLE 6.5 GDX Is Among the Top ETF Cash Incinerators

Ticker	Name	Lifetime Inflows	Assets Today	Money Burnt
TBT	Proshares Ultrashort 20+y TR	$8,924.28	$3,002.06	$5,922.22
GDX	Market Vectors Gold Miners	$12,475.20	$6,576.44	$5,898.76
VSS	Vanguard FTSE All Wo X-US SC	$6,760.91	$1,234.23	$5,526.68
SDS	ProShares Ultrashort S&P 500	$6,490.56	$1,210.90	$5,279.66
UNG	US Natural Gas Fund LP	$5,413.46	$649.04	$4,764.41
FAZ	Direxion Daily Finl Bear 3X	$4,859.49	$288.64	$4,570.85
TZA	Direxion Dly Sm Cap Bear 3X	$3,468.62	$740.45	$2,728.17
SRS	ProShares Ultrashort Re	$2,740.26	$35.34	$2,704.92
SH	ProShares Short S&P500	$3,698.05	$1,323.70	$2,374.35
EWZ	iShares MSCI Brazil Capped E	$5,193.24	$3,223.33	$1,969.91

Source: Bloomberg

been very attractive in the low-rate environment from 2009 through 2015. This is why they have over $20 billion in assets—nearly as much as traditional energy-sector ETFs.

However, investing in them through ETFs is a game of picking your poison.

The root of the mess is a rule that says a registered investment company cannot hold more than 25 percent of its portfolio in MLPs. So MLP ETFs are structured as "C" corporations instead to get around the rule. However, in that structure, they are taxed with a corporate tax. This tax treatment that takes a huge bite out of returns—about a 30 percent haircut—and makes it hard for ETFs to track an MLP index.

The Alerian MLP ETF (AMLP) is a good example of how far these ETFs can veer from the return of the index they're trying to track. AMLP has returned 42 percent since its inception in August 2010, as shown in Figure 6.21. Sounds pretty good until you consider the index it tracks is up 77 percent!

This huge, aggravating issue is why many investors use the ETN in this category. ETNs that track MLPs make up 42 percent of total ETN assets, the

FIGURE 6.21 AMLPs Big Tracking Difference Due to Tax Treatment

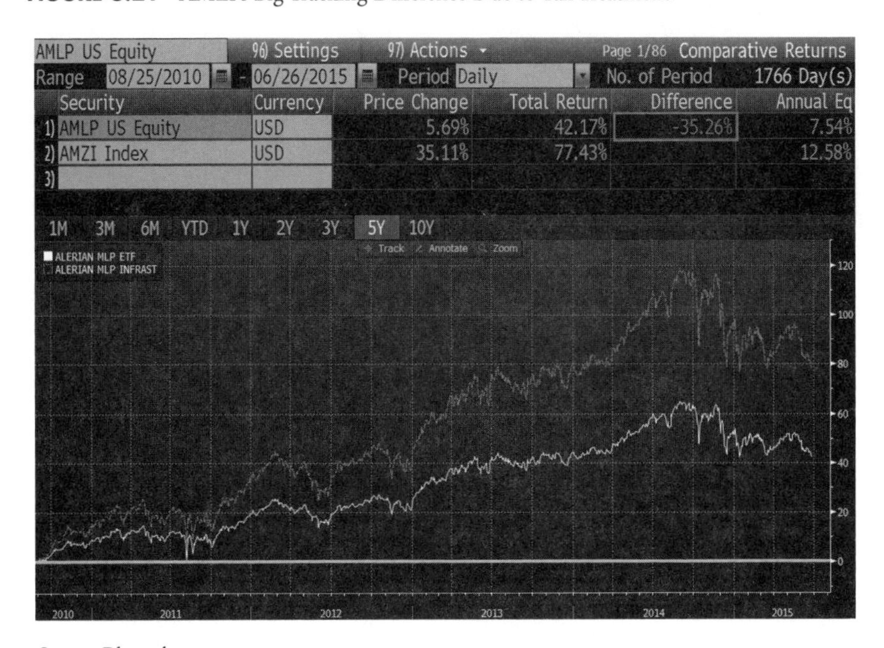

Source: Bloomberg

largest segment of the group. MLP ETNs are way around the tax treatment of MLP ETFs because they're structured as debt obligations and don't have to actually hold the underlying MLPs.

So let's compare AMLP to the UBS ETRACS Alerian MLP Infrastructure ETN (MLPI). It tracks the same index as AMLP but has returned 78 percent. This is why MLPI has grown to $2.5 billion in a couple of years. Or why the JPMorgan Alerian MLP Index ETN (AMJ) is the world's largest exchange-traded note (ETN), at $5.2 billion. Those are unheard of asset levels for an ETN. That speaks volumes as to how concerning the tax is on the ETF side for some investors.

"The tax drag is so large with the ETF and we feel like we can manage the risk around the position with the ETN, so the credit risk is less of a concern for us."

Justin Sibears, Newfound Research

But the ETN structure doesn't get a free pass on this tax issue. Income distributions from ETNs are taxed as ordinary income, since they're considered interest payments. One interesting note is that the issuers take the expense ratio out of the income instead of the NAV in order to minimize what investors get taxed on. This is why ETNs in this area yield a bit less than ETFs.

At the end of the day, with MLPs you have to stomach either taxes or credit risk. A general rule of thumb here is that the ETN is used by investors more interested in a higher total return; investors who are more interested in the income or who don't want to take on credit risk use the ETF.

"We use AMLP. For that space we aren't looking for AMLP for a capital appreciation opportunity. It is more about the income stream than being bullish on MLPs."

Gary Stringer, Stringer Asset Management

Thematic ETFs

Who doesn't love a good story? That's what thematic ETFs offer as they go beyond traditional sector and industry plays by grouping together stocks based on a very specific investment idea such as clean energy or robotics or companies run by women. These ETFs typically reach across multiple sectors to gain their exposure. There are dozens of them with a few billion in assets. But they grab a lot of attention and maybe even a little bit of our imagination.

But when you go beyond the story and actually pop open the hood and look at the engine, many thematic ETFs may have more risk than meets the eye. Many of them equal weight the holdings, which gives them extra volatility. Also, thematic ETF investors need to be on the lookout for overlap, as many of them will hold stocks that overlap with other funds or ETFs.

"That stuff is fun. I have no problem with it. But I'm managing global asset allocation model portfolios. When you start adding thematic stuff in there, it blows up your boxes."

Josh Brown, Ritholtz Capital Management

It is for those reasons that pundits understandably decry—and even mock—many of the thematic ETFs as pointless marketing gimmicks, but the reality is that some investors—even institutional investors—do seek these out. Although, it does tend to be only in very specific cases. For example, the United Nations seeded two thematic ETFs that remove carbon from the portfolio.

While we can't dive into every theme out there, let's go over a few examples and pull the curtain back to reveal what is really going on.

The Guru Theme

Guru ETFs are one of the most popular themes, with $1 billion in assets. These ETFs look at what the largest hedge funds hold and simply copy them.

The biggest one is the Global X Top Guru Holdings Index ETF (GURU), which tracks stocks found in hedge funds' 13F filings. The ETF's index scours the filings and chooses the top stock holdings from each hedge fund for the portfolio.

To be clear, though, this is not a real hedge fund strategy, since only the long equity positions are reported in a 13F. GURU then takes the stocks owned by hedge funds, which can include mid and small caps, from 13Fs and equal-weights them. This last detail is arguably more important than anything else as equal-weighting can be like a performance-enhancing drug for a thematic ETF

GURU became a sort of rock star in 2013 when it crushed the S&P 500, returning 49 percent versus 32 percent for the S&P, which earned it tons of publicity and over $500 million in assets. But if we break down where that mouth-watering excess return of 16 percent is coming from, basically all of it came from its 30 percent weighting in mid- and small-cap stocks. Figure 6.22 shows the contribution to total return (CTR) and how the mid caps contributed 13 percent of the 16 percent return while small caps contributed 6 percent, despite accounting for only one-third of the holdings. This ETF just happened to catch a year like 2013 where small stocks did better.

This extra beta to the market is a big reason why GURU has beaten the market and been written about quite a bit in the press. I'm not saying that there isn't some basic benefit from stock selection based on hedge funds' 13Fs, but there is also a huge element of the extra return coming from extra risk. It's just that simple.

The downside to this extra risk was seen when the market sold off in January 2014, GURU got hit hard. For example, in January 2014 it lost 4.9 percent while the S&P fell 3.4 percent. Why? Because small and mid-caps typically get the worst of a sell off. So GURU lived by the sword, but it also died by the sword.

This is not to take away the real value-add GURU offers of going through the painstaking process of looking through hundreds of SEC filings each quarter and grouping together the high-conviction stock picks from hedge fund managers. This is highly valuable information to certain investors. In one example, an institution was using GURU in tandem with another strategy as a kind of DIY hedge fund.

"The most calls we got from institutions—and this was true pensions primarily out of Europe and a little in the U.S.—was for GURU. The gates on hedge funds are a massive problem for them. And liquidity is an enormous consideration. So they loved GURU because it is liquid and it is replicating hedge funds.

FIGURE 6.22 GURU's Performance Attribution in 2013 versus S&P 500

Name	Avg % Wgt			CTR		
	Port	Bmrk	+/-	Port	Bmrk	+/-
GLOBAL X GURU HOLDINGS INDEX...	100.00	100.00	0.00	48.74	32.31	16.43
Mid Cap	18.79	1.00	17.79	13.43	0.28	13.15
Small Cap	14.46	0.15	14.31	5.74	-0.02	5.76
Cash	0.07	0.38	-0.31	0.00	0.00	0.00
Large Cap	66.68	98.48	-31.80	29.56	32.05	-2.48

Source: Bloomberg

They could overlay with and go long GURU and short the S&P 500 to have a long/short equity product that is 100% liquid. They were replacing 2 and 20 with this."

Bruno del Ama, Global X

GURU is not alone, as many of these thematic ETFs equal weight the holdings. Just be aware that sometimes when it seems like the theme is working, it may just be the small-cap tilt is working.

The Warren Buffet Theme

Is there a Warren Buffett ETF? This is a question I hear occasionally as an analyst.

In the investing world, the brilliance most investors would love to reduce to an imitable strategy is that of Warren Buffett. Unfortunately, there is no straight-up Warren Buffett ETF like there is, say, a Jeffrey Gundlach ETF—the Doubline Tactical Bond ETF (TOTL), where Gundlach is hands-on selecting the holdings. If Buffett did launch an ETF like that, you can bet it would be an instant smash success.

The good news is that Buffett's influence and philosophies are all throughout the ETF space in many different forms. The bad news is that genius can't be reduced to a formula, but that doesn't stop people from trying to connect some ETFs with Warren Buffett. But do these ETFs really have you "investing like Buffett" as some of the articles say?

Let's examine the one that gets connected to Buffett a lot: the Market Vectors Wide Moat ETF (MOAT).

MOAT tracks the Morningstar Wide Moat Index. That index attempts to identify companies with sustainable competitive advantages—or "economic castles protected by unreachable moats," as Buffett calls them.[1] Companies with sustainable moats are able to keep competitors at bay for an extended period of time. Morningstar equity researchers apply their secret sauce criteria to 1,500 stocks to find the 10 percent with the widest moat.

After teasing out that 10 percent, Morningstar analysts identify which stocks are cheapest compared to Morningstar's fair value for them. Then, the top 20 cheapest of those stocks go into the index and subsequently into the ETF. And yes, it then equal weights them. So you have a touch of extra risk along with some overlap since many of the companies in here are prevalent in other ETFs.

Another issue is turnover. Looking at the history of holdings in MOAT it has had about 40 different stocks in and out of the ETF each year, which is a lot for an ETF that can hold only 20 stocks at a time. Many of them stay

FIGURE 6.23 MOAT's History of Holdings for Two Years as of June 30, 2015

Port MARKET VECTO vs Default (None) by None in USD Time Custo 05/29/13 - 06/26/15
Field % Wgt (Port) Freq Quarterly Date Trend

Name	06/30/13	09/30/13	12/31/13	03/31/14	06/30/14	09/30/14	12/31/14	03/31/15	06/26/15
MARKET VECTORS MORNINGSTAR ...	100.00	100.00	100.00	100.00	100.00	100.00	100.00	100.00	100.00
ACCENTURE PLC-CL A			5.28						
ALLERGAN INC		5.07							
ALLERGAN PLC							4.83		
AMAZON.COM INC					4.80	4.93	4.97		
AMERICAN EXPRESS CO									4.91
AMGEN INC	5.10				5.04			5.16	5.01
BANK OF NEW YORK MELLON CORP	4.85	4.84			5.25				
BAXTER INTERNATIONAL INC			4.96	5.36	4.89	4.83	4.93	5.03	
BERKSHIRE HATHAWAY INC-CL B	4.96	4.98	4.95	4.91	4.89				4.89
BLACKBAUD INC									5.33
BLACKROCK INC				5.01	5.09				
C.H. ROBINSON WORLDWIDE INC	5.06	4.97	4.86	4.92					
CATERPILLAR INC	4.93								
COCA-COLA CO/THE		4.91	4.92	4.95	5.14				
COMPASS MINERALS INTERNATION			5.21						
CORE LABORATORIES N.V.				5.04	5.19	4.74	5.34	4.80	
COSTCO WHOLESALE CORP					4.91				
COVIDIEN PLC		4.94							
CSX CORP		4.97							
DISCOVERY COMMUNICATIONS-A							4.93	4.68	5.02
EATON VANCE CORP					5.09				
EBAY INC	5.12	5.14	5.10	4.69	5.08	5.62	4.98		
ELI LILLY & CO			4.87						

Source: Bloomberg

for a quarter or two and are then released. Figure 6.23 shows the Swiss-cheese look of its historical holdings.

In fact, not one stock has been in the ETF for the past two years. This itchy-trigger-finger aspect is inconsistent with the Buffett-osophy of long holding periods. On the upshot, however, all that turnover didn't result in any capital gains, which is testament to the ETF structure and the passive management behind this ETF.

So, again, an interesting concept and decent performer, but not exactly Buffett-esque and reason 61 why investors need to look under the hood before buying an ETF. In the end, though, you could argue that the most Buffett-esque ETF is the "Buffett Special" miniportfolio of VOO and SHY based on his advice.

The Nashville Theme

The Nashville ETF (NASH) was understandably put into the gimmick category by many analysts and the media when it launched one year ago. Its attempt to turn local pride into assets by holding a basket of stocks of companies headquartered in Nashville sounded a bit too cute for the serious business of investing. Thus, it was not a huge surprise that the ETF has failed to attract an audience with just $12 million in assets.

Even though an institution would probably never invest in NASH, it is worth the ink as an example of why looks can be deceiving.

NASH has handily beaten the market since its launch in July 2013, through June 2015, up 38 percent, compared with 30 percent for the S&P 500 Index, as shown in Figure 6.24. Now certainly one good run doesn't make a gimmicky ETF any less gimmicky.

FIGURE 6.24 NASH's Grand Ole Outperformance of the S&P

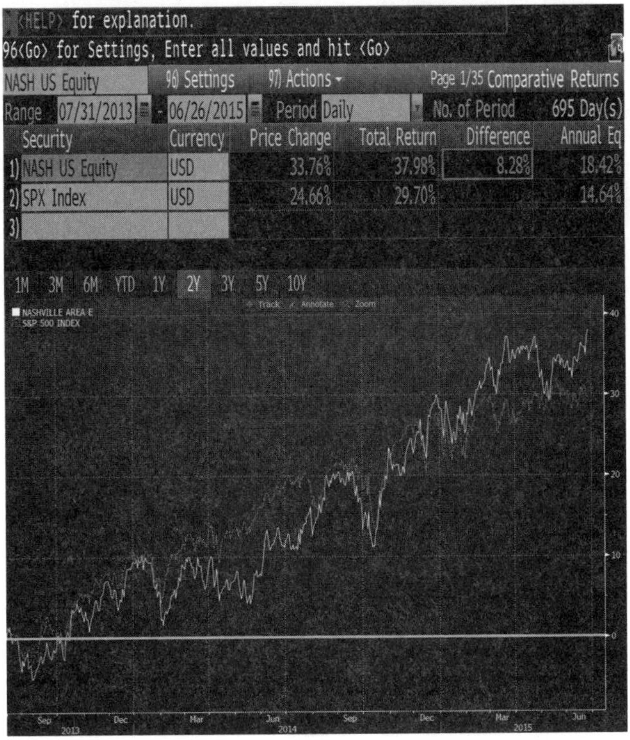
<HELP> for explanation.
96<Go> for Settings, Enter all values and hit <Go>
NASH US Equity
96) Settings
97) Actions
Page 1/35 Comparative Returns
Range 07/31/2013 - 06/26/2015
Period Daily
No. of Period 695 Day(s)
Security
Currency
Price Change
Total Return
Difference
Annual Eq
1) NASH US Equity USD 33.76% 37.98% 8.28% 18.42%
2) SPX Index USD 24.66% 29.70% 14.64%
3)
1M 3M 6M YTD 1Y 2Y 3Y 5Y 10Y
Track Annotate Zoom
NASHVILLE AREA E
S&P 500 INDEX
40
30
20
10
0
Sep
2013
Dec
Mar
Jun
2014
Sep
Dec
Mar
2015
Jun

Source: Bloomberg

However, NASH isn't equal weighted like many thematic ETFs, but rather it uses a factor-based formula to weight the stocks. But that isn't where its juice is coming from. The story here comes down to an outsized exposure to a red-hot industry within the health care sector: hospitals.

NASH has the most exposure to hospitals—nearly 20 percent, as shown in Figure 6.24—of any ETF. Nashville is sometimes called the "Silicon Valley of health care" and is home to more than 250 health care companies.[2] In terms of hospitals, about 60 percent of the for-profit hospitals are headquartered in the Nashville area, according to Bloomberg Intelligence. Hospitals happen to be one of the hottest industries in the past few years thanks to strong earnings seasons and increasing optimism over millions of new paying customers via Obamacare.

FIGURE 6.25 NASH Has Large Weightings in Health Care Service Companies

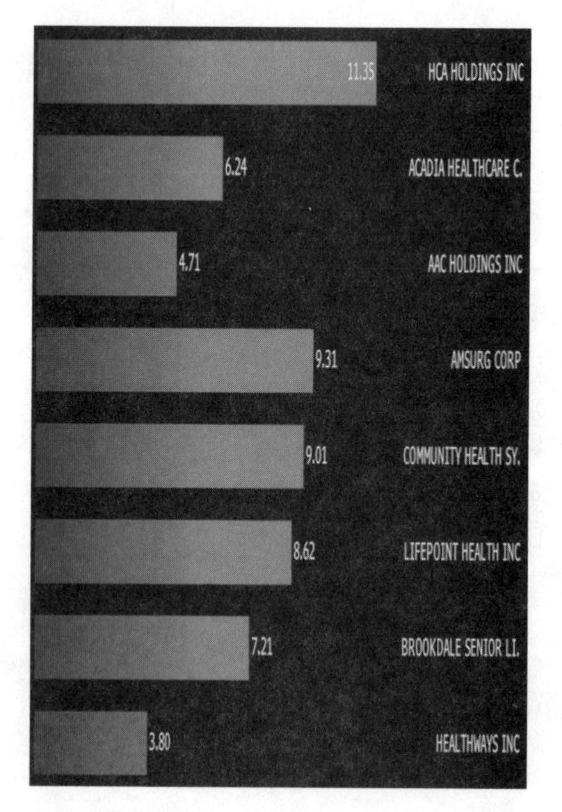

Source: Bloomberg

This leads to the question as to why all of these hospitals are disproportionately headquartered in Nashville, not to mention some other big corporations with over $100 million in market cap, such as Dollar General.

While Nashville is the 25th-largest city by population, it is the seventh-fastest-growing since 2000.[3] And it has one of the nation's overall lowest tax burdens and offers exceptional incentives to relocating or expanding business. Tennessee also has no income tax for citizens—one of only a handful of states.[4]

This is not to say all this makes a company's stock price directly move higher, but certainly it provides a little tailwind to the companies located in Nashville. This is why I'm surprised ETF issuers haven't come out with an ETF that tracks companies with the sweetest tax incentive deals regardless of which city they are in. Nashville isn't the only city doing this, but it is one of the most aggressive. The "cost of doing business" would be an interesting study and possible ETF idea. Why not invest in companies in pro-business, low-tax cities?

Despite all this, it still doesn't necessarily mean there is an investment case for it but perhaps it is enough to debunk the "gimmicky" label put on NASH. Or maybe not. But it is another example of the things you can find when you dig into an ETF's holdings.

Robotics

A more specific surprise-hit theme ETF on the transformative tech tip is the Robo-Stox Global Robotics & Automation Index ETF (ROBO), an intriguing ETF that tracks companies that make all kinds of robots for both institutions and consumers. The ETF's index was designed by a panel of robotics and financial experts from around the world.

The founders of Robo-Stox couldn't find a portfolio tracking robotics on the market, so they decided to make their own index using insights from leaders in the field and eventually turned it into an ETF.[5] The companies in the ETF are creating robots to help with everything from household chores to the military. There is also a swath of 3-D printing companies.

Since its launch in October 2013, ROBO has taken in over $100 million in assets—a huge feat for an outsider thematic ETF. While ROBO has very little overlap with other ETFs it does come with a bit of extra volatility. The ETF uses equal weighting inside a two-tier system in the portfolio and invests in global companies with only 38 percent allocation to the United States. Unfortunately, as futuristic as ROBO's theme is, it carries an archaic expense ratio of 0.95 percent.

Climate Change

There are many environmentally focused ETFs that take on climate change. Climate change and investing are going to get more and more connected in the future.

One example is at Yale University, where David Swensen issued a letter in 2014 asking managers to look at companies with a large greenhouse footprint and "discuss with company managements the financial risks of climate change and the financial implications of current and prospective government policies to reduce greenhouse gas emissions."[6]

This is representative of the grassroots call from clients, constituents, and students who want to know their money isn't going toward something they feel harms the earth. Expect this trend to continue. And expect the ETF issuers to follow suit.

Right now, investors have two options. You can go with an ETF that holds clean energy stocks or an ETF that goes for low-carbon investing. Let's look at an example of the former by analyzing the solar energy ETFs.

Only two "pure play" solar energy ETFs exist and they are a lot alike. The Guggenheim Solar Energy Index ETF (TAN) and the Market Vectors Solar Energy ETF (KWT) both launched within a week of each other in 2008. Both have very similar geographic allocations, with global exposure to the United States, China, Hong Kong, and Germany. Both are about 80 percent tech companies and the rest split between industrials and utilities. But perhaps the key point is that both have a standard deviation of 30 percent, about double the S&P 500.

TAN and KWT are representative of this kind of all-or-nothing performance that is common in ETFs focused on narrow themes. That's because they typically hold some volatile small and mid-cap stocks, as well as foreign stocks. These ETFs are typically used as satellite positions and get smaller weightings in a portfolio.

The second type of way to go green with ETFs is to go with a low-carbon ETF. As discussed in Chapter 4, the United Nations pushed for, and ultimately seeded, two low-carbon ETFs last year.

The funds take a broad market index and remove a big portion of the carbon footprint from it. While TAN and KWT are plays on young clean energy companies, the SPDR MSCI ACWI Low Carbon Target ETF (LOWC) and iShares MSCI ACWI Low Carbon Target ETF (CRBN) are cleaner versions of a popular index.

The carbon emissions of companies in the low-carbon ETFs is 81 percent lower than that of companies in the MSCI ACWI Index, according to MSCI's carbon metrics. It's not that the ETFs remove any of the "dirty" stocks from the index they track. Instead, they shave the weightings of the biggest carbon emitters while trying to still keep the ETF's performance close to its index. For example, the index has a 1 percent weighting to Exxon Mobil, while LOWC and CRBN have 0.13 percent of assets in the company.

I personally think these ETFs have a bright future (pun intended). They essentially help you be green without changing your asset allocation or taking on any extra risk.

Notes

1. Burton, Jonathan, "Follow the Buffett Strategy." *Wall Street Journal,* August 2, 2012; www.wsj.com/articles/SB10001424052702304199804577477012223693628.
2. Nashville Area Chamber of Commerce, Target Industries, Health Care; www.nashvilleareainfo.com/homepage/target-industries/health-care.
3. Boyer, E. J., "Census Data: Nashville among Fastest-Growing U.S. Cities." *Nashville Business Journal,* December 5, 2014; www.bizjournals.com/nashville/blog/2014/12/census-data-nashville-among-fastest-growing-u-s.html.
4. Dzombak, Dan, "These States Have No Income Tax." *USA Today,* April 26, 2014; www.usatoday.com/story/money/personalfinance/2014/04/26/these-states-have-no-income-tax/8116161/.
5. Dorrier, Jason, "Robotics Investors Can Now Buy the Market with New Nasdaq ETF." SingularityHUB, November 5, 2013; singularityhub.com/2013/11/05/robotics-investors-can-now-buy-the-market-with-new-nasdaq-etf/.
6. Fabrikant, Geraldine, "Yale Fund Takes Aim at Climate Change." *New York Times,* September 7, 2014; www.nytimes.com/2014/09/08/business/yale-fund-takes-aim-at-climate-change.html?_r=0.

CHAPTER 7

Smart Beta

Smart beta isn't an asset class or even a section of U.S. equities, but rather a series of twists to the plain vanilla, market cap weighted index. At this point, every equity category of exchange-traded funds (ETFs) has at least one, if not a half a dozen, smart-beta options to choose from. And since smart-beta ETFs are growing faster than ETFs as a whole, it is worth a standalone Chapter.

What is smart beta? Simply put, it is any ETF that purposely deviates from "market return" and tilts the portfolio toward some factor or strategy that has a proven historical record of outperforming or managing risk such as dividends, value, low volatility, momentum, and small caps. It could also involve scoring and weighting stocks by fundamental metrics such as price-to-earnings or revenue as well as technical metrics that show relative strength.

There's nothing new about investing like this. Active managers have been using these screens and tilts for years to generate alpha. The ETF industry just took them and turned them into beta by packaging them into passively managed, low-cost ETFs. In many ways, you could view smart beta as being like artificial intelligence—a robot version of an active manager but with passive rules and lower fees. Essentially, smart beta fills the wide chasm that has always existed between active and passive management. And investors love it.

There are approximately 400 smart-beta ETFs with over $420 billion. They make up 21 percent of the ETF pie, which is up from 12 percent in 2009, as you can see in Figure 7.1.

FIGURE 7.1 Smart-Beta ETFs Growing in Market Share

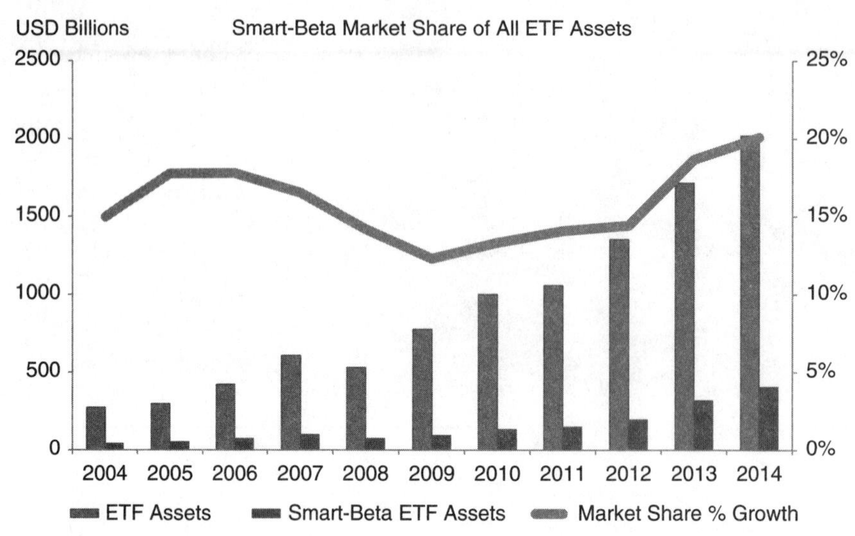

Source: Bloomberg

Controversy

With their growth in popularity has come controversy. While most investors are fine with the concept of smart beta, the terminology is a problem for many. Go to any ETF conference and many panel discussions—no matter the initial topic—often end up debates about smart beta. The heart of the controversy comes from the word *smart.*

"To hook investors on this concept by using the word smart is a problem, and it could be an ethical problem. The true word is additional beta, meaning additional risk, because if you think of a multifactor model, you start out with a beta and you add additional betas. So it's additional risk. Calling that "smart" is a problem."

Rick Ferri, Portfolio Solutions

The origin of the term can be traced to Towers Watson, a leading consultant firm. Towers Watson's Thinking Ahead Group started talking in detail about the area in the early 2000s, with smart beta subsequently evolving into the monster buzzword that we know today. They defined smart beta as "trying to identify good investment ideas that can be structured better. … Smart-beta strategies should be simple, low-cost, transparent and systematic."[1]

I remember being at an ETF conference in Arizona, and hearing a money manager cleverly deconstruct why the term is misleading when he said: "If I buy a smart-beta ETF and short the beta, does that mean I'm long smart?"

The answer is no, you are long a strategy. And the truth is that strategies built into smart-beta ETFs won't always outperform the rest. They can only guarantee convenient, low-cost exposure. Outperformance is a bonus. No shocker to anyone, John Bogle, in a major critique of smart beta, thinks it's just a way to inspire performance chasing:

> The past is not prologue. People think the right thing is what has done well in the past. And they buy it. Even if [smart-beta proponents] are right and there is a permanent bias in favor of an undervalued section of the market. People will bid up the prices and it will be gone.

You can see how this debate could go on and on. This is why many have tried to kill off the term *smart beta*. Many have introduced their own substitute terms, labeling such products strategic beta, advanced beta, scientific beta, alternative beta, factor-based, and—my personal favorite—anti-benchmark.

I agree that some of these terms are no doubt more technically accurate. Unfortunately, they just don't have the zing of smart beta. Smart beta is a little like Obamacare, which is way catchier than the Patient Protection and Affordable Care Act. Obamacare may not be accurate, but everyone calls it that, and we all know what they mean. At this point, the genie is out of the bottle, and we should spend our energy educating investors on what smart beta is all about. Even the president calls it Obamacare now.[2]

Smart Beta versus Active Management

While smart beta is almost always being compared to passive market cap–weighted indexes, it really is much more of a threat to active management. This truly is a rise of the machines.

> *"The whole spectrum of smart beta represents more of a threat to active managers than it does to classic indexing. With smart beta, you are using a disciplined method to sever the link between the price of a stock and its weight in the portfolio."*
>
> Rob Arnott, Research Affiliates

> *"For many institutions, ETFs used to be simply too broad to replace an active manager. But now that the ETFs are getting more narrow and specific (such as smart beta and currency-hedged products), institutions now have more tools to do an apples-to-apples comparison to see if the active manager was worth it."*
>
> Ben Carlson, Ritholtz Wealth Management

One of the biggest institutional users of smart beta is the California Public Employees' Retirement System (CalPERS). CalPERS has $28 billion allocated to smart-beta strategies. They use smart beta as a replacement for active management, not passive. However, CalPERS employs their smart beta via SMAs, not ETFs. Because of their size they can go to a large asset manager to run it in an SMA with just as good tracking and at a fraction of the cost.[3]

> *"What we found is as a placeholder we could use a specific (smart-beta) ETF, but at the end of the day we still can get it run as a physical portfolio. Whether we do it individually or farm it out, we can do it slightly cheaper than the ETF can be done."*
>
> Dave Underwood, Arizona State Retirement System

This brings us to cost. The asset-weighted expense ratio of a smart-beta ETF is 0.34 percent, which is slightly higher than the overall ETF average of 0.30 percent, but is nearly half that of an active mutual fund, which is 0.66 percent. Even though there is no Vanguard around, there has been some cost-compression, albeit no doubt slower without Vanguard there to force the issue. The point is that as smart-beta ETF fees get lower and liquidity increases, the institutions will start adopting them more.

And how are institutions using smart-beta ETFs? Figure 7.2 shows us that among institutional investors currently using smart-beta ETFs, they are employing them as a short-term replacement, a compliment, and in some cases as their only investment, according to a recent Market Strategies International study (sponsored by PowerShares). Clearly, most are using it as complement to their core holdings—especially in equities, where institutions are more likely to have a passive core. Meanwhile, fixed income is the asset class in which they are most likely to use nothing but a smart-beta ETF. Again, this jibes with most institutions employing active strategies when it comes to fixed income.

One final note here is that smart-beta ETFs are the one area of ETF Land where investors evaluate the products much more on their index methodology instead of on the typical liquidity and cost. When it comes to smart-beta ETFs, institutions are applying the similar analysis as they would when evaluating an active manager.

FIGURE 7.2 Application of Smart-Beta ETFs by Institutions

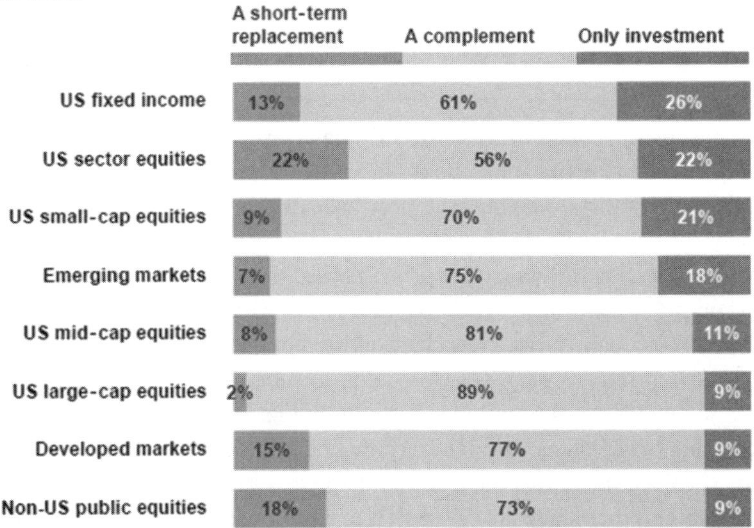

Source: Market Strategies International

Another interesting aspect of the active nature of smart-beta ETFs is their potential appeal to consultants, who many times stand in between ETFs and mid- to small-sized institutions. Not only is a smart-beta ETF a viable option for them to use, it can be a better benchmark to use against their active managers. This can help to weed out closet indexers and determine who is really adding value versus just being exposed to a factor. Moreover, smart beta is active enough to look like a value-add for them to their clients.

"One of the things consultants like is smart beta because it is not passive indexing, which means they still like the ability to say they are delivering some performance relative to say the S&P 500. They get more and more RFPs from ultimate clients, small institutions, family offices, and endowments that want a fully passive solution. Smart beta allows for fully passive but also is sound and robust and potentially has a better Sharpe ratio."

Bruno del Ama, Global X

Okay, enough background on the smart-beta phenomenon; let's look at some ETFs. There are so many flavors of smart beta at this point, so I'm just going to go into a few examples using growth and value, fundamentally weighted and factor-based ETFs. While equal weighting is definitely a form of smart beta since it comes with a small-cap tilt, I'm not covering those here because we covered them multiple times in the chapter on U.S. stock ETFs.

Growth and Value

Given the innovation in smart beta, it may be surprising to know that plain old growth and value make up about half of the smart-beta assets. Even though the newfangled stuff gets all the attention, growth and value are still king. Of course, they had a head start and have been around longer. Growth ETFs focus on companies that show above average growth based on characteristics such as revenues, earnings and cash flow. In short, high flyers. Value ETFs, on the other hand, focus on companies that show characteristics of being undervalued, such as lower price-to-earnings or price-to-book ratios. In short, a good bargain.

When it comes to growth and value ETFs, besides the typical dilemma of choosing between cost and liquidity, there is another dilemma of how narrow to go. There are many that are broad and safe and keep a closer beta to the market at large, and then there are others that make a more concentrated bet and show a little less correlation to the broad market. The choice is probably going to come down to whether you are making a tactical bet or a strategic allocation.

This dilemma can be exemplified using the Vanguard Value ETF (VTV), which holds over 300 stocks, and Guggenheim S&P 500 Pure Value ETF (RPV), which holds about 100 stocks. Here are two strategists explaining why they used each.

"We went for the Vanguard Value ETF (VTV) because we wanted some large-cap exposure, and it was very liquid and very inexpensive. We were looking for cheap beta."

Gary Stringer, Stringer Asset Management

"A lot of the traditional value ETFs out there hold a lot of stocks and market cap weights them so they behave like a broad index. We love RPV because it is such a pure exposure to value. You are only holding 20 percent of the S&P 500 and you are weighting it by value characteristics. That can be good or bad, but it is a behavior we want. We don't want a broad-market index that has value in its name."

Justin Sibears, Newfound Research

FIGURE 7.3 VTV and RPV versus SPY over the Past Two Years

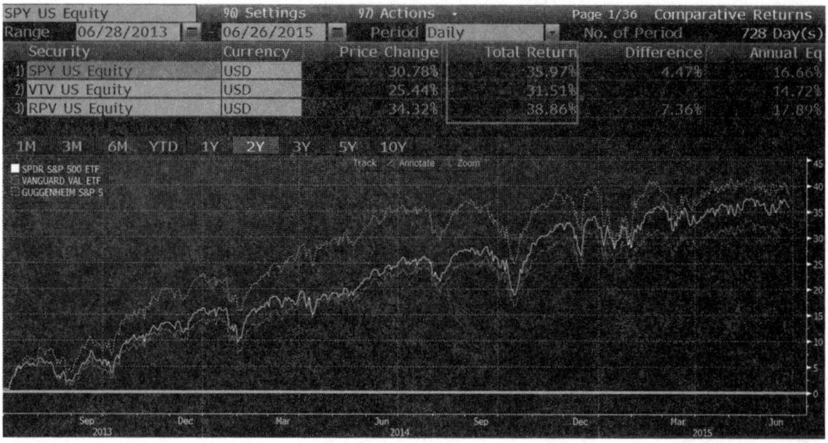

Source: Bloomberg

As mentioned earlier, smart beta can be a replacement for both passive and active. Another way to look at them it is that VTV would be a more fitting replacement for passive—as would the growth and value ETFs we mentioned in the large-cap section—since it is very diversified and has just a slight tilt, while RPV would be a replacement for an active manager since it is making more concentrated bets.

In case you are curious, Figure 7.3 is a chart of their performance over the past couple of years versus the S&P 500 Index. RPV has, in fact, provided some alpha, albeit while sporting a slightly higher standard deviation due to its alternative weighting and slight dip into mid caps.

Fundamentally Weighted ETFs

Back in the day, before smart beta was a term, ETF industry people called them *fundamentally weighted ETFs.* Along with equal-weighed ETFs, these really blazed the trail for smart-beta.

I've always viewed fundamentally weighted stock ETFs as like having your own personal stock-analyst robot around. There are now well over 50 of these funds. While there will continue to be examples of such funds underperforming traditional peers, the two funds below are good examples of classic fundamentals-driven smart-beta ETFs.

One of the oldest and largest of the bunch is the PowerShares FTSE RAFI US 1000 Portfolio (PRF) with $3 billion in assets. The fact that it has a 10-year track record makes it more attractive to the more conservative institutions that are looking at it to replace an active manager. Investors like to see track records with smart beta just as with an actual active manager.

PRF scores each of the 1,000 stocks in the FTSE RAFI US 1000 Index on a combination of five-year trailing book value, cash flow, sales, and dividends. It then weights the stocks by their score and rebalances its portfolio annually. PRF charges 0.39 percent of assets on an annual basis.

Since its start in 2005, PRF is up 86 percent, versus a 68 percent gain for the S&P 500. When investors raced out of financial stocks in 2009, those same stocks became good values, according to PRF's screens. The ETF went from having 16.7 percent of its assets in financials to 25.9 percent, a fearless move that would have seemed crazy at the time. But not crazy for an emotionless, rules-based index just doing what it is designed to do. The move paid off and was a big contributor to PRF's outperformance over the market since then. Figure 7.4 shows that since that rebalance, up until today, financials were responsible for the majority—25 percent to be exact—of the 40 percent in PRF's outperformance over SPX.

FIGURE 7.4 Contribution to Total Return for PRF versus SPY

Port PowerShares FT vs S&P 500 INDEX by GICS Secto
Model Total Return Unit Percentage

Name	CTR		
	Port	Bmrk	+/-
PowerShares FTSE RAFI US 1000...	223.46	183.85	39.61
Financials	51.67	26.19	25.47
Consumer Discretionary	38.87	25.94	12.93
Industrials	27.54	20.12	7.42
Materials	10.10	5.60	4.50
Utilities	7.71	4.82	2.89
Telecommunication Services	6.64	3.82	2.82
Energy	14.86	13.47	1.39
Preferred Shares	0.00		0.00
Options	0.00		0.00
Stocks	-0.03		-0.03
Consumer Staples	18.96	19.15	-0.20
Health Care	25.58	29.20	-3.62
Information Technology	21.55	35.54	-13.98

Source: Bloomberg

"We had a couple of clients for SMAs (in PRF's index) who contacted us and said, "We're believers in the concept, we are here to stay but please don't do this year's rebalance." We recommended against it because the more uncomfortable the rebalance, the more likely it is to be profitable. But it was their money and we respect that. And they finished the year 700 basis points behind the benchmark (and ETF)."

Rob Arnott, Research Affiliates

Another example of using fundamentals is the RevenueShares Large Cap Fund (RWL), whose approach is one of the simplest of the smart-beta set: weight all S&P 500 stocks based on their revenue. According to the company, studies show that industry sectors with lower price-to-sales ratios tend to perform better. The lower the ratio, the less you are paying for the revenue the company generates. The ETF issuer is so into that one metric, they formed a whole company around it.

The way the ETF rebalances every quarter shifts it into stocks with lower price-to-sales ratios. If a stock's price—but not its revenue—went up over the quarter, the ETF buys fewer shares of the stock. If the stock's price went down, but revenues stayed the same or increased, it buys more shares of the stock. The securities in the ETF remain the same, but their weighting in the ETF will likely differ from quarter to quarter.

While we just looked at a couple, there are literally dozens of other ETFs that use fundamental analysis to screen and weight the ETF.

Single Factors

Factors are common characteristics shared by a group of stocks that academics have found explain the excess return of active managers. The six factors according to MSCI are value, size, low volatility, high yield, quality, and momentum. ETFs tracking these factor ETFs are the new, new thing.

"Sometimes when you go fully active, it is less obvious what risks you are taking. So with the factor ETFs you know what risks you are taking. This is really a tool for active investors who want to express their view but with the advantage of low costs and transparency. They need to have a view; otherwise, they should just use a cap-weighted ETF."

Daniel Gamba, Blackrock

Table 7.1 is a nice, clean look at MSCI's definition of each factor.

TABLE 7.1 MSCI's Factor Definitions

Factors	Explanation	Metrics
Value	Captures excess returns to stocks that have low prices relative to their fundamental value	Book to price, earnings to price, book value, sales, earnings, cash earnings, net profit, dividends, cash flow
Low size (small cap)	Captures excess returns of smaller firms (by market capitalization) relative to their larger counterparts	Market capitalization (full or free float)
Momentum	Reflects excess returns to stocks with stronger past performance	Relative returns (3-month, 6-month, 12-month, sometimes with last 1 month excluded), historical alpha
Low volatility	Captures excess returns to stocks with lower than average volatility, beta, and/or idiosyncratic risk	Standard deviation (1 year, 2 years, 3 years), downside standard deviation, standard deviation of idiosyncratic returns, beta
Dividend yield	Captures excess returns to stocks that have higher-than-average dividend yields	Dividend yield
Quality	Captures excess returns to stocks that are characterized by low debt, stable earnings growth, and other "quality" metrics	Return on equity, earnings stability, dividend growth stability, strength of balance sheet, financial leverage, accounting policies, strength of management, accruals, cash flows

Source: MSCI

As you can see, factors are a finer version of the blunt growth and value division of the stocks. While growth and value ETFs still dominate in total assets invested, factors are growing quickly in both number and assets.

To illustrate the growth in this area, of the 95 ETFs based on MSCI indexes that were launched in 2014, 45 percent of those were tied to factors, a seven-fold increase from the year before, according to MSCI. They are a huge priority at MSCI, and you will see this area grow a lot in the coming years. The question is how institutions will choose to access it.

"The main challenge with factor investing isn't so much whether it is in an ETF wrapper or not, it is how do [institutions] deal with this new category in their investment process. Is it the people on the index side? Is it the people on the active side?

Internal management? External management? Those are the big questions. Then the final question is the wrapper. Do they want it in an SMA or in an ETF?"

C. D. Baer Pettit, MSCI

Factor ETFs are used tactically by institutions. For example, an investor may want to ratchet up their exposure to momentum after some positive economic news. This is what asset managers use them for mostly. Each one tends to have its day in the sun. But that day ends so playing them can be an exercise in market timing as well. Here is a look at MSCI's factor indexes over time. If you were to graph all the factors returns over time you would see this obvious return dispersion both short- and long-term.

"Factors are not static. And when so many people allocate to a factor, it will definitely hurt its efficacy going forward. If too many people tilt toward small cap, that premium is then arbitraged away and you don't get it back again until everyone is disgusted with it and sells out. Then what was really popular becomes really unpopular and then it's a good bet it will start working again."

Josh Brown, Ritholtz Wealth Management

Factor ETFs can also be used as portfolio adjustment mechanisms to rebalance a portfolio. This is what some institutions use them for, including the Arizona State Retirement System, the pension that helped seed some of the first factor ETFs from iShares.

"The adjustment of the ETFs allows to richen up or lean out a given factor characteristic. Our intention was not to use the ETFs as an alpha-seeking exercise. Some may want to do that. Our intention was to adjust that set as we need to by buying or selling shares in the ETFs as well as just applying the cash that the ETF throws off and using that as a rebalancing mechanism too. So it's more of a rebalancing exercise than it is a trading exercise."

Dave Underwood, Arizona State Retirement System

Even within single factors, there can multiple ETFs to choose from. As an example, let's dive into the most popular factor category: low volatility.

Low Volatility

As mentioned earlier, low volatility ETFs are quite popular with investors. There are 15 of them with $16 billion in assets—a lot considering they were nonexistent five years ago.

The appeal of the low-vol approach is the promise to take the edge off investing in everything including large caps, mid caps, small caps, emerging markets, and developed markets. Low-volatility ETFs come in two main flavors: low volatility and minimum volatility. They are used for different purposes.

The PowerShares S&P 500 Low Volatility Portfolio (SPLV) holds a collection of low-volatility stocks. The ETF screens for the 100 least volatile stocks in the S&P 500 Index and then weights them inversely by their volatility. This usually leaves the ETF with a massive concentration in one or two sectors, such as utilities or industrials. However, as of this writing, it is financials that has the biggest weighting.

"The problem I have with SPLV is it might be low volatility today, but if it has such a big exposure to one sector like utilities, it is taking a massive amount of interest rate risk, and if the next crisis to hit is rising rate driven, it is a good possibility SPLV could underperform in an environment where it is meant to do the best."

Justin Sibears, Newfound Research

The sector tilt issue is why the iShares MSCI USA Minimum Volatility ETF (USMV) exists. This one is aimed at investors who want a "low-volatility version" of a certain index. They want more standard sector weightings. To do this and keep overall volatility low, USMV's portfolio consists of stocks whose movements neutralize each other. While SPLV is a basket of low volatility stocks, USMV is a low-volatility portfolio.

If you look at the past three years, their performance is nearly identical. For the most part, the real deciding factor is do you care about keeping your sectors similar to the broad market? If so, use the iShares products. Or are you okay with having a few sectors dominate the ETF? Then use the PowerShares products. Again, are you replacing your exposure, in which case you may want the iShares product, or are you complimenting your core exposure with a low-vol tilt, in which case the PowerShares may make more sense?

Performance aside, the simple truth is this: Low-volatility ETFs do deliver on their promise. They will, in fact, provide a smoother ride in a convenient package. If you look at the volatility versus the markets they track, they are indeed less volatile, although not by a ton. While the S&P 500 Index currently has a standard deviation of 8.2 percent, SPLV is slightly higher, at 8.9 percent. Meanwhile, USMV is 9.2 percent.

However, just because they have less volatility doesn't mean they won't underperform. A great recent example is from the summer of 2011; when the

FIGURE 7.5 SPLV versus SPX Since Its Inception Four Years Ago

Source: Bloomberg

European debt crisis rattled U.S. stocks and the S&P 500 lost 11 percent, but SPLV only lost 5 percent. But then, in 2013 when the stock market was on fire with the S&P 500 returning 33 percent, SPLV gave you 23 percent. Figure 7.5 shows you that since its launch SPLV has about tied the S&P 500, but you can see the crisscrossing of the lines indicating the periods of underperformance and outperformance to get there. This is the epitome of smart beta. Which brings me back to my main point on all smart-beta products: *convenience is guaranteed; outperformance is a bonus.*

Multifactor

Picking the right factor at the right time is a bit like playing whack-a-mole. This is why multifactor ETFs were invented. These are relatively new, but investors can now also get ETFs that combine factors, and/or rotate among factors. For example, the SPDR MSCI Emerging Markets Quality Mix ETF (QUAL) combines the more mellow factors together—value, quality, and low volatility—together. This would seem to make sense if you are using multiple-factor ETFs and want someone to handle the weighting of it for you, but for institutions like Arizona who like controlling their own exposure to each single factor, these products don't make sense.

Then there is iShares' multifactor ETFs, such as the iShares FactorSelect MSCI USA ETF (LRGF), which target risk levels similar to the parent index while providing exposure to four factors: quality, value, size, and momentum.

> *"The third generation (of smart beta) is to have a rules-based index that will do this stuff for you. You can become emotionally attached to a company or a factor. As minimum volatility is going up, you can become attached and want to ride the run. But then you have to sell at some point. That's why having much more rules-based mechanics to do the factor rotation for you will be helpful."*
>
> Raman Subramanian, MSCI

In the end, there is no free lunch with smart beta, albeit it is one lengthy menu! We only looked at the tip of the iceberg. Investors will have to figure out what their goals are and then see if smart beta makes sense. But just like the sun sets in the west, there is sure to be a steady stream of performance chasing with smart-beta ETFs. The key for an institution is to figure out what they want. Are they making a bet, or are they allocating? Deciding that is crucial, but then picking the product is no picnic either. However, it is easier if you apply proper ETF due diligence.

Notes

1. Arnott, Rob, and Engin Kose, "What 'Smart Beta' Means to Us." Research Affiliates, August 2014; www.researchaffiliates.com/Our%20Ideas/Insights/Fundamentals/Pages/292_What_Smart_Beta_Means_to_Us.aspx.
2. Cillizza, Chris, and Aaron Blake, "President Obama Embraces 'Obamacare' Label. But Why?" *Washington Post,* March 26, 2012; www.washingtonpost.com/blogs/the-fix/post/president-obama-embraces-obamacare-label-but-why/2012/03/25/gIQARJ5qaS_blog.html.
3. Robert Stowe England, "CalPERS' Journey into Smart Beta Has Boosted Equity Returns." *Institutional Investor,* March 17, 2015; www.institutionalinvestor.com/article/3436895/investors-pensions/calperss-journey-into-smart-beta-has-boosted-equity-returns.html.

CHAPTER 8

International/Global ETFs

There are over 200 international and globally focused exchange-traded funds (ETFs) with about $250 billion in assets. So we are talking well over 10 percent of ETF assets are here. A big reason for the popularity of these ETFs is convenience. You can get exposure to local shares through a U.S.-listed ETF and trade it during U.S. hours.

> *"The reason why people use international ETFs is very simple. They don't need to worry about buying all the local countries. They don't need to get a Sterling account or a euro account or a Hong Kong account. They can just buy the ETF now and gain exposure to those countries."*
>
> Mohit Bajaj, Wallach Beth

Larger institutions with more money and resources may prefer to take on that international exposure and can trade overnight but for everyone else it makes life easier. So expediency certainly drives a lot of big and small institutions to ETFs.

This category is dominated by iShares and Vanguard. iShares will typically have the most liquid option while Vanguard will have lowest cost. Since institutions like their ETFs liquid and cheap, they will have a bit of a dilemma. Throw in the currency-hedged and smart-beta options and you have dilemmas upon dilemmas. Let's look at some examples.

International Developed Markets

Let's start with international ETFs, which are defined as those that invest outside of the United States. This is in contrast to global ETFs, which include the United States.

MSCI EAFE

There are over a dozen ETFs that track some form of the MSCI Europe Australasia Far East (EAFE) Index and they account for just about $100 billion of the $250 billion invested in international and global ETFs as shown in Figure 8.1.

The largest is the iShares MSCI EAFE ETF (EFA) with $63 billion. It is gushing with liquidity with over $1 billion traded each day. This liquidity has attracted a wide variety of big name institutional holders of EFA including Yale, Front Point Capital, IBM Retirement Fund, Northwestern Mutual Life Insurance Company, and the State of New Jersey Common Pension Fund.

> *"We've used ETFs for a long time and some of the earliest kinds of usages were more basic situations where you have some kind of tactical thing that you are wanting to do and it is the quickest and easiest way to do it. Going in and out of certain markets and being able to buy EAFE or S&P 500 ETF to get in something very quickly without disturbing your managers."*
>
> Michael Brakebill, Tennessee Consolidated Retirement System

FIGURE 8.1 ETFs Tracking Some Form of the Popular MSCI EAFE

Ticker	Name	Tot Asset (M)
1) EFA US	ISHARES MSCI EAFE ETF	63,164.457
2) DBEF US	DEUTSCHE X-TRACKERS MSCI EAF	12,581.637
3) IEFA US	ISHARES CORE MSCI EAFE ETF	5,991.094
4) SCZ US	ISHARES MSCI EAFE SMALL-CAP	4,982.582
5) EFV US	ISHARES MSCI EAFE VALUE ETF	2,970.339
6) HEFA US	ISHA CURR HEDGED MSCI EAFE	2,768.180
7) EFAV US	ISHARES MSCI EAFE MINIMUM VO	2,644.669
8) EFG US	ISHARES MSCI EAFE GROWTH ETF	2,051.278
9) DZK US	DIREXION DLY DEV MKT BULL 3X	36.499
10) EFZ US	PROSHARES SHORT MSCI EAFE	31.708
11) EFO US	PROSHARES ULTRA MSCI EAFE	22.662
12) EFAD US	PROSHARES EAFE DVD GROWERS	13.588
13) MFLA US	IPATH LE MSCI EAFE INDEX ETN	5.166
14) EFU US	PROSHARES ULTSHRT MSCI EAFE	4.880

Source: Bloomberg

FIGURE 8.2 A Look at EFA's Allocations

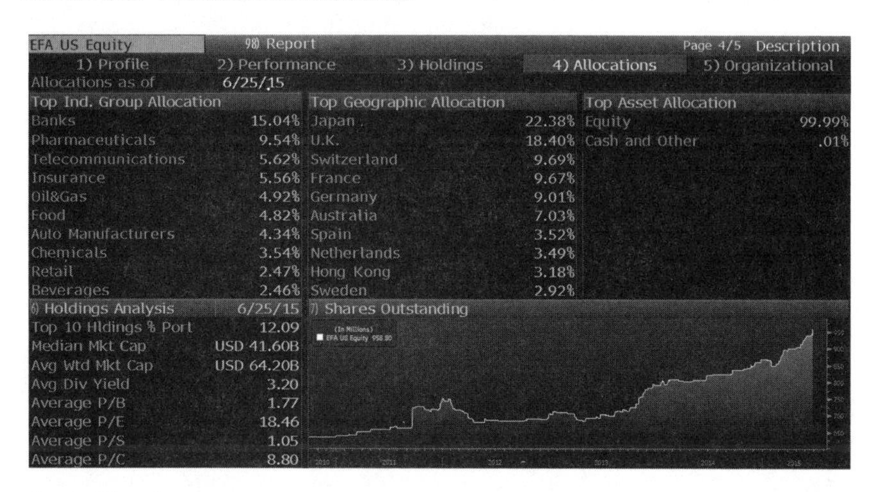

Source: Bloomberg

ETFs tracking the EAFE index serve up the international developed markets in a rational breakdown using market cap weightings, which gives it heavy exposure to Japan and Europe as seen in Figure 8.2. The only odd thing is that it doesn't include Canada. This is because EAFE was built from the perspective of a U.S.-based investor. The U.S. investor already had access to Canadian stocks, since many were already listed on the New York Stock Exchange (NYSE) and American investors were very familiar with Canadian companies and their product and services. Not having Canada is most likely not a deal breaker for most investors however.

The thing about EFA that should give investors pause is the 0.33 percent fee. It isn't that bad, but you can basically get the same thing from the same issuer by using the iShares Core MSCI EAFE ETF (IEFA) for 0.12 percent. iShares rolled out the "core" versions of their popular ETFs to better compete with Vanguard in the retail space. For retail investors, using IEFA over EFA is a no-brainer. But for institutions that need super-charged liquidity, this presents a dilemma.

Judging from the assets, institutions are going to use EFA despite the fee.

"We have $27 million in EFA. That is not a small chunk of change. So if the ETF only has a billion-dollar float, we probably aren't going to use that. We look at the float and ask are we going to move the ETF on a daily basis by getting in and out of it."

Jim Dunn, Verger Capital Management

This speaks to the different needs of institutions. However, this brings us back to whether institutions understand implied liquidity.

"If I am executing big orders and my orders are too big for whatever the secondary market liquidity is anyway, then it kind of becomes irrelevant because I'm going to have to create and redeem anyways, which means my bid-ask that I'm paying is going to be a function of things like underlying security bid-ask, stamp taxes, etc."

Justin Sibears, Newfound Research

Thus, unless secondary volume is your only priority, IEFA just makes more sense, especially for longer-term horizons. And investors are flocking to it. It has grown to over $5 billion in assets in just about two years, which is unheard of.

Just like ice cream, you can get your EAFE in many different flavors. Beyond the plain vanilla EFA, there is also the iShares EAFE Small-Cap ETF (SCZ) and the iShares EAFE Minimum Volatility ETF (EFAV). Sticking to the smart-beta tip, there is also the iShares MSCI EAFE Growth and the ProShares EAFE Dividend Growers ETF (EFAD). Investors can also get their EAFE exposure with the currency taken out in both the Deutsche X-Trackers MSCI EAFE ETF (DBEF) and the iShares Currency-Hedged MSCI EAFE ETF (HEFA).

FTSE

Vanguard doesn't use MSCI indices, so it doesn't have any EAFE products. But it does have a few monster international ETFs tracking the Financial Times Stock Exchange (FTSE) indices. The biggest competitor to EAFE is the Vanguard FTSE Developed ETF (VEA). VEA is pretty similar to EFA minus one major difference. FTSE considered South Korea a developed marked while MSCI considered it an emerging market. Figure 8.3 shows the difference. Basically, by gross domestic product (GDP) standards, South Korea is developed, but other factors that have to do with liquidity and foreign ownership restrictions are what make it emerging market to the more conservative MSCI.

Where VEA shines is in its fee. It sports a very low expense ratio of 0.09 percent. That's nearly four times cheaper than EFA. However, it "only" trades $177 million a day. That is solid liquidity, but much less than the $1 billion that EFA does every day.

FIGURE 8.3 EFA (Port) versus VEA (Bmrk) Shows South Korea as Biggest Difference

Name	% Wgt		
	Port	Bmrk	+/-
iShares MSCI EAFE Index Fund (...	100.00	100.00	0.00
Japan	22.36	23.21	-0.85
United Kingdom	18.40	17.45	0.96
Switzerland	9.73	9.14	0.59
France	9.73	8.58	1.15
Germany	9.04	8.30	0.74
Australia	6.88	6.56	0.33
South Korea		3.85	-3.85
Spain	3.55	3.19	0.36
Netherlands	3.50	3.17	0.32
Hong Kong	3.16	3.06	0.10
Sweden	2.93	2.70	0.23
Italy	2.26	2.13	0.13
Denmark	1.65	1.62	0.03

Source: Bloomberg

Now, there are a few ETFs that combine international developed and emerging markets. The largest is the Vanguard FTSE All-World ex-US ETF (VEU), which is basically VEA but with 10 percent exposure to emerging market countries. And if you want to take this even further, there is the Vanguard Total International Stock Market ETF (VXUS), which serves up exposure to 1,393 stocks from a mind-blowing 55 different countries. This one is like VEU except in includes more small and mid caps. It is the total international exposure.

Global

Global ETFs try to serve up the entire world—including the United States—in one shot. These ETFs have much less in assets than the international ETFs, most likely because people already tend to prefer to pick their pieces more finely. But if killing as many exposure stones with one bird is your goal, these ETFs are for you.

VT and ACWI

I'm just going to jump right into what I think may be two of the best ETFs in the world at tracking the world. The Vanguard Total World Stock ETF (VT)

FIGURE 8.4 VT Serves up the Entire World in One Shot

Name	% Wgt
VANGUARD TOTAL WORLD STOCK ...	100.00
United States	50.18
Japan	8.38
United Kingdom	6.75
Switzerland	3.30
Canada	3.05
France	2.99
Germany	2.94
Australia	2.34
China	1.94
Hong Kong	1.62
Taiwan	1.50
South Korea	1.48
Netherlands	1.24
Spain	1.14
India	1.07

Source: Bloomberg

and the iShares MSCI ACWI Index Fund (ACWI) are both sights to behold. They literally give you everything in one package. And they account for $11 billion, which is about half of the $23 billion in global ETFs.

VT holds 5,500 stocks—the most of any equity ETF—from 60 different countries with 85 percent allocated to large caps and the rest in mid and small caps. This coverage is based on the FTSE Global All Cap Index, which is the broadest equity index in FTSE's lineup.

The geographic breakdown of VT is roughly 50 percent in the United States, 40 percent in international developed markets, and 10 percent in emerging markets. After the United States, Japan and the United Kingdom have the biggest weightings, at 8 percent and 7 percent, respectively, as shown in Figure 8.4. Further down, past the BRICs (Brazil, Russia, India, and China), smaller countries like Mexico and Malaysia both get a 0.50 percent weighting. The expense ratio for VT is 0.18 percent, which is well below average for an ETF and roughly 10 times less than the average global mutual fund.

VT's biggest rival in the space is the ACWI, which has a similar geographic breakdown with 50 countries, albeit with 1,200 stocks in portfolio. When you compare the performance of VT and ACWI, both were up around 50 percent from 2010 through July 2015 and exhibit a 99 percent correlation with each other. The big difference again comes down to liquidity and cost. VT is 0.18 percent and trades $19 million a day, while ACWI is charges

0.33 percent but trades $70 million a day. Again, the dilemma of liquidity versus cost.

An investor of any size could make a decent case for a portfolio consisting of one of these ETFs and an aggregate bond ETF and simply rebalance every couple years and be done with it. Simple, cheap, and powerful. You have to wonder why smaller institutions just don't do this instead of hiring all the consultants and managers.

"We are looking to get exposure to the world's asset classes. So we are looking at the MSCI All World Index. It's 44 countries and about 85 percent of the world's investable opportunity. Okay, so maybe we don't get Tibet in there."

Josh Brown, Ritholtz Capital Management

Beyond VT and ACWI

Coming in at a distant third is the iShares MSCI All Country World Minimum Volatility ETF (ACWV). This smart-beta product is designed for investors who want their global equities but with a smoother ride. ACWV lowers the volatility by using offsetting stocks to create a less volatile version of ACWI. As you can see in Figure 8.5, the weightings aren't exactly the same, but pretty close.

FIGURE 8.5 ACWV (Port) Keeps Fairly Close Adherence to the Allocations of ACWI (Bmrk)

Name	% Wgt		
	Port	Bmrk	+/-
ISHARES MSCI ALL COUNTRY WO...	100.00	100.00	0.00
United States	53.13	50.31	2.82
Japan	12.56	7.81	4.75
Canada	5.99	3.01	2.98
Hong Kong	5.26	1.78	3.48
Taiwan	4.10	1.43	2.67
Switzerland	3.59	3.70	-0.11
China	3.54	1.99	1.55
United Kingdom	1.88	6.61	-4.72
Bermuda	1.69	0.06	1.64
Singapore	1.40	0.54	0.87
Malaysia	1.00	0.34	0.66
Indonesia	0.77	0.28	0.50
Thailand	0.66	0.23	0.44

Source: Bloomberg

Then there is the iShares Global 100 ETF (IOO). This one goes the other direction from the likes of VT and ACQI which hold thousands of stocks. Instead, IOO tried to capture the performance of 100 large transnational companies selected by an S&P committee. You get 56 percent U.S. mega-cap stocks like Apple and Microsoft.

A surprise hit in this category that quietly gathered a billion dollars in assets is the Global X SuperDividend ETF (SDIV). SDIV has a simple strategy of holding the 100 highest-dividend-seeking companies in the world. This thing is a dividend-seeking missile. And it appears to be working as SDIV kicks out a 6.3 percent yield, which is amongst the highest of any dividend themed ETF.

However, SDIV will take you far away from a normal-looking global ETF, as it has 30 percent exposure to REITs and includes some master limited partnerships (MLPs). It also has 60 percent of its holdings in mid and small caps. In other words, this isn't your grandfather's dividend fund, but a notable option nonetheless.

Emerging Markets

Emerging markets represent an incredibly diverse group of countries that are progressing toward being a developed market but are not quite there. They are in the on-deck circle if you will. At this point, most investors have some kind of exposure to the emerging markets.

Believe it or not, there are nearly 70 emerging-market equity ETFs. They have $110 billion in assets, just over 5 percent of the total assets in ETFs. The space has a wide variety of products but is utterly dominated by the Vanguard FTSE Emerging Markets ETF (VWO) and the iShares MSCI Emerging Markets ETF (EEM). EEM and VWO have $83 billion in combined assets, or about 75 percent of the total. While this is a lot, it is down from over 90 percent just a couple of years ago.

Emerging-market ETFs really evolved in three waves, or generations, of products.

The First Movers

EEM came out first in 2003 and dominated for years. It accumulated over $10 billion in assets by the end of 2005—a massive amount for a new ETF. It was used by hedge funds, endowments, pensions, and asset managers alike. EEM offered a fast, liquid, and tax-efficient way to dart in and out of the emerging markets.

All was well for EEM until the new kid on the block, VWO, came out in 2005 and disrupted EEM's sweet gig. For investors, VWO was a welcome launch because it was so much cheaper than EEM. It was originally called the Vanguard Emerging Markets VIPERs, and it charged 0.30 percent. That was less than half the cost of EEM, which charged 0.75 percent. (Today, VWO is 0.15 percent to EEM's 0.67 percent)

VWO was a game-changer when it was launched in 2005. It showed both retail investors and institutions that you can have exotic exposure like emerging markets (EMs) at a similar cost to what the largest institutions were used to. Not to mention, all the other benefits, such as tax efficiency.

Not surprisingly, VWO slowly started to steal away EEM's assets. VWO's eating of EEM's lunch peaked in 2011 when VWO took in $7.9 billion in new cash, while EEM lost $6.6 billion. That made VWO the flow champ and put EEM in last place.[1] In other words, EEM was seeing investors defect to VWO in the billions. VWO also passed EEM in size that year, as shown in Figure 8.6.

EEM's Mini-Me

Blackrock's response to this—and Vanguard in general—was to launch a series of "Core" ETFs that would be priced at Vanguard-ian levels for retail clients and advisors. These are effectively mini-me ETFs based on popular existing ETFs.

FIGURE 8.6 VWO's Assets Passing EEM's Assets in 2011

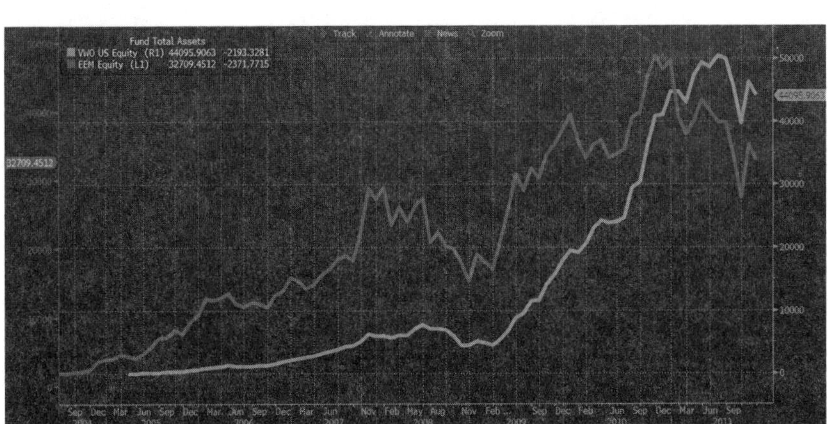

Source: Bloomberg

The iShares Core MSCI Emerging Markets ETF (IEMG) was launched in 2012 with an expense ratio of 0.18 percent. That is four times cheaper than EEM. It is also a wider and deeper ETF holding double the number of stocks and going into a touch of small caps. If EEM was an iPhone 1, then IEMG is an iPhone 5. The move worked smashingly. Since then, IEMG has hauled in $7.6 billion in assets—three times more than any other EM ETF during that stretch.

And what about EEM? Well, it is still very expensive for an EM ETF at 0.67 percent. iShares figured that the unbelievable amount of liquidity that EEM offered was so good that some investors would still use it and keep paying up. And they were right, as some investors—or shall I say traders—don't seem to care because it still has over $20 billion in assets and trades over $1 billion worth of shares a day. That is more than six times what VWO or any other EM ETF trades. And again, that kind of liquidity can erase all other flaws for an ETF.

"We use EEM. Right now liquidity is a big deal. Those other ones are pretty small."

Jim Dunn, Verger Capital Management

Given that investors are hooked on EEM's liquidity, should iShares have just lowered the fee on EEM instead of launching a new product? In an altruistic sense, yes. But they are trying to run a business here. For institutions that prefer ETFs with EEM's oceanic liquidity, however, it is a bummer that EEM didn't get IEMG's fee.

The South Korea Difference

Remember the South Korea difference between EFA and VEA? Well, with EEM and VWO it is the reciprocal situation, with MSCI considering South Korea an EM, while FTSE does not. This is a big difference because it represents a 14 percent allocation in EEM, as shown in Figure 8.7.

Is this good or bad? Well, it depends on how South Korea performs or if it overlaps other parts of your portfolio. However, with no South Korea, VWO has put more weighting into India, China, and Taiwan. Still, both ETFs match up pretty closely in terms of regional exposure, though. All this can be seen in Figure 8.7, which compares the country allocation of EEM and VWO.

FIGURE 8.7 EEM (Port) versus VWO (Bmrk) Shows South Korea Difference

Name	% Wgt		
	Port ↑	Bmrk	+/-
ISHARES MSCI EMERGING MARKE...	100.00	100.00	0.00
China	19.37	21.77	-2.40
South Korea	14.19		14.19
Taiwan	13.20	14.97	-1.77
South Africa	7.69	9.24	-1.55
India	7.62	11.84	-4.22
Brazil	7.53	9.01	-1.49
Hong Kong	5.46	5.97	-0.51
Mexico	4.66	5.31	-0.65
Russia	3.70	3.36	0.33
Malaysia	3.14	4.06	-0.92
Indonesia	2.31	2.40	-0.09
Thailand	2.18	2.66	-0.48
Poland	1.46	1.73	-0.28

Source: Bloomberg

But before you let this one thing concern you too much, the truth is EEM and VWO are 98 percent correlated. So, it is more likely going to come down the cost (VWO or IEMG) or liquidity (EEM) for most institutional investors more than South Korea. It will also probably mean that investors use EFA and EEM as a pair or VEA and VWO as a pair or risk having no South Korea or being overweight.

As I was editing this chapter, Vanguard upped the ante with iShares by announcing that it was going to add mid and small caps, as well as China A-shares, to VWO. They are also adding small and mid caps to several of their ETFs. In one way, this is good because it means you get more in one shot and don't need to purchase multiple ETFs to get the same thing. However, it may mess with institutions looking to track a global benchmark.

> *"Where Vanguard is maybe taking it to a strange place is by adding in small caps into all their indices. You are getting further and further away from the benchmarks, and you are putting your own style tilts on them. The challenge with having, say, 5 percent of your portfolio in small caps is that's not enough to matter., and it's enough to wreck tracking error if you are institutional."*
>
> Adam Grossman, Riverfront Investment Group

Meanwhile, MSCI is holding off on adding A-shares to its popular EM index. MSCI is still waiting for China to open up access even more because, after all, they have just under $2 trillion benchmarked to the index.

"The absolutely critical question [on A-share inclusion] is: Can international investors access China with a relatively level playing field so that everyone can get access in more or less the same way commensurate to their size. Leaving everything else aside, that is the big issue."

C. D. Baer Pettit, MSCI

All of this will unfold over next couple of years. And I'm sure EEM and/or IEMG will respond. Blackrock and Vanguard will be at it for many years to come always trying to one-up each other. And this isn't just an inside industry thing either—it is something investors should stay on top of.

"The process by which index publishers add countries to international ETFs, and the impact that timing has on market performance, is important for investors to understand. Markets tend to inflate right before the index inclusion and then they sort of underperform for several months after. If you are not smart about how that works, forget about saving transaction costs and management fees, you can really wipe that out if you are not careful with what you are doing. It can have fairly significant impact. So it's not part of your fundamental analysis, but it is part of your trading and toolbox usage that's important to consider in the international ETFs."

Jeffrey Davis, LMCG Investments

The BRICs

There are some other, older-generation EM ETFs that just focus on the BRIC (Brazil, Russia, India, China) countries. They barely need any explanation, as they simply hold four countries. These ETFs have largely been ignored by investors as they make up just 0.2 percent of emerging market ETF assets.

Why do I bring them up then? Because they are the perfect example of the Vanguard Effect, or lack thereof. Vanguard doesn't offer a BRIC-specific ETF, and as such the cheapest BRIC ETF charges 0.59 percent—much more than the .14 percent that the cheapest EM ETF charges and which tracks way more stocks! You would think a BRIC ETF would be easier to run—and subsequently cheaper—than running an entire EM ETF. Figure 8.8 shows how everyone should feel about this.

FIGURE 8.8 Unnecessarily Costly BRIC ETFs

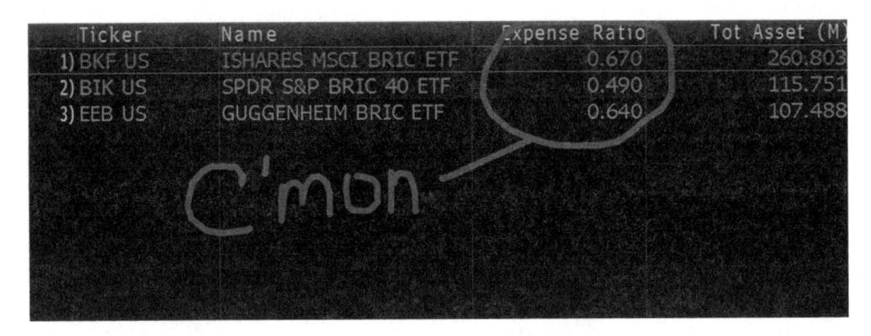

Ticker	Name	Expense Ratio	Tot Asset (M)
1) BKF US	ISHARES MSCI BRIC ETF	0.670	260.803
2) BIK US	SPDR S&P BRIC 40 ETF	0.490	115.751
3) EEB US	GUGGENHEIM BRIC ETF	0.640	107.488

Source: Bloomberg

Second-Generation EM

While first-generation ETFs like EEM and VWO all serve up broad exposure to EM, a new breed of ETFs has come out slicing and dicing EM up to offer more precise exposure. This is the normal progression for any ETF category. Many of these ETFs take the first-generation product and add a wrinkle to it.

Low Vol

One example is the iShares MSCI Emerging Markets Minimum Volatility ETF (EEMV). If IEMG is a cheaper and deeper version of EEM, then EEMV is a less volatile version of that mega-fund. This newly popular ETF keeps its country and sector allocations similar to EEM's. To damp volatility, it creates a portfolio of stocks that offset each other. While outperformance will come and go, EEMV has delivered on the promise of a smoother ride. It has a standard deviation of about 10 percent compared to 14 percent for EEM. So it is definitely serving up what the label says.

EM Dividend ETFs

Emerging-market dividend ETFs are a hit. Investors like the idea of going into EM and focusing on dividend paying companies. This seems like a safer way to play EMs than a broad-market ETF, and it can be, but these should be used with caution because following a trail of dividends can lead the ETF into overweighting certain countries.

One of the most popular is the WisdomTree Emerging Markets Equity Income Fund (DEM). A possibly surprising scenario for investors is the

FIGURE 8.9 DEM's 18 Percent Russia Exposure Contributed –9 Percent of Return in 2014

Name	Avg % Wgt	Tot Rtn	CTR
WISDOMTREE EMERGING MARKETS..	100.00	-10.22	-10.22
Russia	18.62	-42.12	-9.33
China	17.48	16.56	2.66
Taiwan	13.50	-3.29	-0.49
Brazil	11.90	-22.28	-2.54
South Africa	9.80	-5.91	-0.61
Poland	5.78	-10.27	-0.38
Thailand	5.70	10.04	0.45
Malaysia	5.05	-0.04	-0.14
Turkey	2.58	11.26	0.25
Czech Republic	2.13	-3.17	-0.06
South Korea	2.01	7.58	0.16
Indonesia	1.90	6.15	0.10
Chile	1.64	-16.56	-0.25
Philippines	1.35	8.64	0.11

Source: Bloomberg

ETF's oversized weighting to Russia, as shown in Figure 8.9. In 2014, Russia had an abysmal year, and the ETF was hit hard by that. But Russia kicks out high dividends. The Russian stocks in DEM were yielding over 6 percent—normally a good thing for a dividend fund. But if you were expecting a dividend *version* of EEM, you'd be in for a big surprise. That's the point.

In the case of the iShares Emerging Markets Dividend ETF (DIVY), nearly half of the exposure is in Taiwan and Brazil. Those two countries are more than double the weight they would get in the MSCI Emerging Markets Index. That is the mandate of the ETF, but it is still worth noting.

WisdomTree also has the WisdomTree Emerging Markets SmallCap Dividend Fund (DGS). DGS holds 570 small-cap stocks across the emerging markets and weights them based on their dividends. That dividend focus actually manages to make DGS calm despite being small caps. It has a standard deviation of 11 percent, while EEM is 14 percent—something you wouldn't expect, since EEM focuses on large-cap stocks, which tend to be more stable than small-caps.

DGS is another great example of needing to look under the hood. Because it focuses on small caps and dividends, the holdings produce a sort-of "beyond BRICs" portfolio. Some 77 percent of its country exposure is in Taiwan, South Korea, Malaysia, South Africa, and Thailand. It has

30 percent in consumer stocks. That's a play on the potential growth in emerging economies from domestic demand rather than from more export-reliant multinational companies. DGS charges a fee of 0.63 percent.

> *"We use a lot of the new EM small cap because it cuts out the commodity exposure and cuts it down to more basic direct emerging markets investing. You get the good and the bad with EM small, and a significant change in regional weights, so you have to think about all those factors. But with that in mind, it has worked pretty well and as far as excluding the commodity exposure, it does it nicely."*
>
> Jeffrey Davis, LMCG Investments

The Consumer Story

Another example of a successful second–generation EM ETF is the EGShares Emerging Markets Consumer ETF (ECON). This surprisingly successful ETF tries to capture a subplot in the emerging markets, which is the rise of the middle class and an economic shift away from commodities exports and towards consumer goods and services.[2]

To do this, ECON basically pools together consumer staples and consumer discretionary stocks in EM countries. Unlike IEMG and DGS, which take more of a shotgun approach to investing, ECON's strategy is more like a rifle shot. It invests only in consumer stocks and holds just 30 of them. Ten of those make up 50 percent of the portfolio, which has large weightings in South Africa, China, and Mexico.

For such a small number of holdings, it has a very high expense ratio of 0.85 percent, although anyone invested in it probably doesn't care because it has absolutely destroyed the broad emerging markets by nearly 30 percentage point since it launched and through the end of 2014, as shown in Figure 8.10.

On the flip side—and there's always a flip side—if and when it underperforms, the expense ratio will just add insult to injury.

Following the Heat

The PowerShares DWA Emerging Markets Technical Leaders Portfolio (PIE) is a unique take on the EM space. It tracks the Dorsey Wright Emerging Markets Technical Leaders Index, developed by Tom Dorsey's firm, which

FIGURE 8.10 Since Launching in 2010, ECON Has Utterly Destroyed EEM

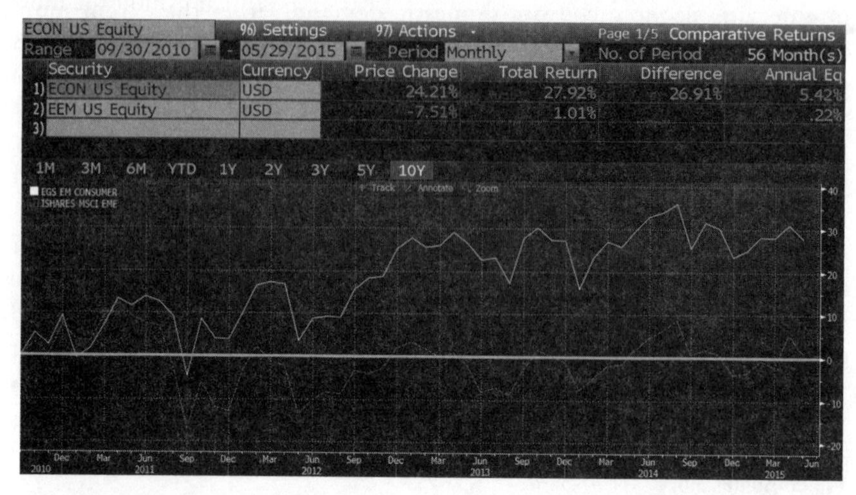

Source: Bloomberg

FIGURE 8.11 PIE's Historical Country Allocations Are Literally All Over the Map

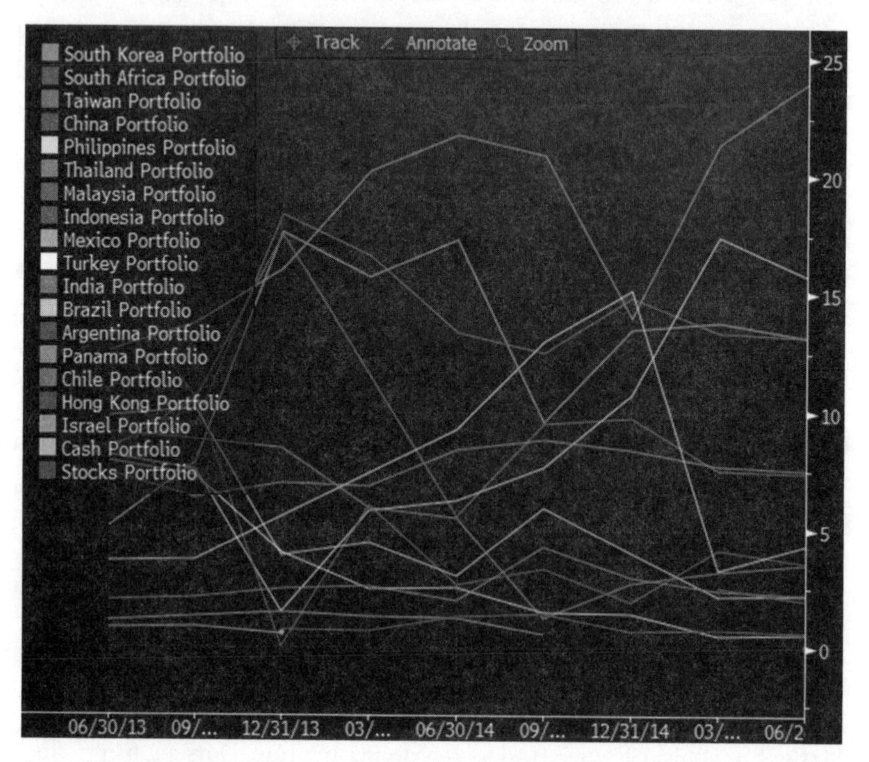

Source: Bloomberg

specializes in technical analysis. Here's how it works: Every quarter the index looks through over 2,000 EM stocks and picks the 100 that exhibit the most relative strength to the group over the past 6–12 months.

So what you end up with is something that changes a lot. Indonesia can be 15 percent one quarter and then 0 percent six months later. Figure 8.11 shows a wild chart of the country allocations over the past two years for PIE. It's all over the map, literally. This is not your grandfather's EM ETF. But again, it's doing exactly what it says it is going to do.

So how has this method performed against a conservative old-timer like EEM? Well, since it launched in 2007, it is down 22 percent, while EEM is down 6 percent over same time period. However, it launched right before the financial crisis and got hit harder than EEM in 2008. But since June 2009, it is up 76 percent versus EEM's 42 percent return. It's also one of the rare EM ETFs that makes EEM look cheap. PIE charges 0.90 percent.

Next-Generation EM ETFs

Since the beginning of 2014, there have been well over a dozen new EM ETFs launched. Many of them take it to another level and offer a twist upon a twist. Here's a look at some of those and should also give you a feel for where things are headed.

Economic Exposure

The EGShares Blue Chip ETF (BCHP) doesn't hold any EM stocks. Rather, it tracks companies in the developed world that have "quality, meaningful and growing revenue from emerging markets," according to the fund's prospectus. BCHP looks at "economic exposure" to the emerging markets. The 30 stocks in BCHP get an average of 47 percent of their revenue from emerging markets.

This ETF gets investors exposure to emerging-market consumer growth through bigger, less volatile, developed-market companies. By contrast, some of the companies tracked by the big EM ETFs are giant multinationals that get large portions of their revenue from developed markets. This sort of plays to the opposite of that. One example of a holding is Las Vegas Sands, which gets the majority of its revenue from casinos in the Chinese enclave of Macau.

So far, BCHP hasn't been able to attract many investors, as it has only $8 million in assets.

Futuristic EM

If you want a peek into what broad EM ETFs may look like years from now, just check out the allocations in the KraneShares FTSE Emerging Markets Plus ETF (KEMP), as shown in Table 8.1. Yes, China will be that big. Even bigger if countries like South Korea and Taiwan were to get promoted to developed-market status by MSCI.

Some would argue that's how it should be. There are two reasons for the heavy China exposure. Beyond the obvious Hong Kong–listed China exposure, KEMP includes China A-shares, which at the time of this writing had a market cap of over $7 trillion and was not yet being included in the MSCI Emerging Markets Index. It also includes U.S.-listed China stocks (N-shares), such as Alibaba. Throw all that together and you get a truer picture of China's true size. KEMP's futuristic design comes with a cost of 0.68 percent and limited volume of only a few thousand shares a day.

Removing Socialism

One of the raps against EM ETFs is how they hold a lot of state-owned companies. For investors who want to remove this socialist element from their emerging markets, enter the WisdomTree Emerging Markets ex-State-Owned Enterprises Fund (XSOE), which provides exposure to EM stocks

TABLE 8.1 KEMP's China-Heavy Look Is What EM ETFs Will Look Like in the Future

Top Geographic Allocation	
China	43.37%
India	16.41%
Brazil	5.06%
Hong Kong	4.79%
Mexico	4.34%
Russia	4.25%
Turkey	3.49%
Indonesia	2.99%
Taiwan	2.14%
Poland	1.58%

Source: Bloomberg

where government ownership does not exceed 20 percent of the shares outstanding.

The country weightings are not that out of whack for EM ETFs. Where you do see some difference is in the sectors. Perhaps not surprisingly, it gets you more tech and consumer companies and less utilities and financials.

> *"We also like to have ETFs that will eliminate things. The WisdomTree product I thought was conceptually very interesting, where they try to take out state-owned enterprises. As U.S. investors increase international exposure, more and more they are going to be conscious that they don't want to buy dead companies that are basically government bureaucracies exploiting their equity markets. That is kind of what we like to do."*
>
> Jeffrey Davis, LMCG Investments

Frontier Markets

Beyond emerging markets lie frontier markets. *Frontier markets* is an economic term used to describe countries in the developing world that are smaller and less accessible. These "pre-emerging" countries can offer high reward but come with liquidity and geopolitical risk. Some of these countries include Argentina, Nigeria, Kuwait, Pakistan, Kenya, and Vietnam.

One of the attractive features of frontier ETFs is their low correlation with other markets, which can offer increased diversification for a portfolio, much more so than emerging markets. For example, the iShares Emerging Markets ETF (EEM) has a five-year correlation to the S&P 500 Index of 0.78 (on a scale of –1 to 1), while the MSCI Frontier 100 Index (M1FM10) has a 0.56 correlation, as shown in Table 8.2. I threw GLD in there as a reference point.

TABLE 8.2 5-Year Monthly Correlation of EEM, Frontier Markets, and Gold to SPY

Security	Corr to SPY
SPY	1.000
EEM	0.778
M1FM10	0.556
GLD	0.141

Source: Bloomberg

You can get frontier markets in different ways—including broadly and by going into a region or continent.

The most popular broad market frontier ETF out there is the iShares MSCI Frontier 100 (FM), which is market cap weighted and holds local shares of 100 frontier stocks. The country weightings lean toward the Middle East, as over half of its country allocation is in that region. Following its launch in 2012, FM went on a two-year 60 percent tear during which the EEM was up only 14 percent. It has cooled off lately, but the initial run out of the gate showed investors what frontier markets are capable of and their independence from the emerging markets.

Africa

Africa is fascinating—a continent full of both potential and turmoil. Rapid economic growth in Africa has the terms *African lions* and *Asian tigers* being used in the same breath. The Market Vectors Africa ETF (AFK) is the sole continent-wide ETF play and a unique product. AFK weights its portfolio exposure to countries based on their gross domestic product—one of the first ETFs to ever do this. That translates into 25 percent in South Africa, 20 percent in Nigeria and Egypt, 10 percent in Morocco, and 4 percent in Kenya—so a chunk of frontier markets.

The remaining 30-odd percent of the portfolio is in companies that are based outside of Africa but derive over 50 percent of revenues from, or in some cases, hold over 50 percent of their assets in, smaller African countries where direct investing isn't possible or practical. That strategy brings exposure to countries such as Zambia, Mozambique, and Tanzania, mostly through energy and mining companies based in the United Kingdom, Canada, and Australia. AFK charges investors an annual fee of 0.78 percent, which is pricey for an ETF.

Investors may assume their emerging-market or frontier-country ETF or mutual fund has exposure to Africa. This is likely true, but only for South Africa. For example, the Vanguard Emerging Markets ETF (VWO) has 9.6 percent of its assets in Africa, with nearly all of that coming from South Africa. Egypt is a 0.13 percent weighting. Nigeria, Kenya, and Morocco are considered frontier countries, so they aren't in emerging-market ETFs.

AFK has a few institutional users. One noteworthy one is the Commonwealth Africa Fund (CAFRX), a mutual fund. Its largest holding is the Market Vectors Africa ETF (AFK). If that isn't a ringing endorsement for ETFs, I don't know what is.

FIGURE 8.12 CAFRX's ETF Holdings

Port COMMONWEALTH vs None by Security Type in USD

Name	Ticker	% Wgt	Mkt Val
COMMONWEALTH AFRICA FUND (CAFRX US)		100.00	2,282,815
Common Stocks		57.85	1,320,642
ETFs		24.94	569,301
MARKET VECTORS AFRICA INDEX	AFK US	11.06	252,399
ISHARES MSCI SOUTH AFRICA ET	EZA US	10.64	242,905
GLOBAL X MSCI NIGERIA ETF	NGE US	3.24	73,997
Depository Receipts		14.01	319,893
Open-End Funds		3.14	71,685
Cash		0.06	1,293
Sovereign Debt		0.00	

Source: Bloomberg

Currency-Hedged ETFs

Currency-hedged ETFs serve up different international stock market exposures while neutralizing the effects of the currency. They basically allow an investor to own foreign stocks in the local market's currency- essentially removing the dollar from the equation.

Currency-hedged ETFs shine when the dollar is strong relative to other currencies. In a strong dollar environment, you can see your foreign stocks rally, only to have all the gains eviscerated when you convert them to dollars, because you get fewer of them. This is the problem currency-hedged ETFs are trying to solve.

There are now over 30 currency-hedged ETFs with over $50 billion in assets. Just a few years ago, no one really cared about currency-hedged ETFs. There were only a couple of them, and they pretty much lived in oblivion thanks to a weak dollar. But then other countries and regions, namely Japan and Europe, started to weaken their own currencies on purpose, by printing money and buying assets. This is why I sometimes refer to currency-hedged ETFs as central bank surfboards because they have allowed investors to ride waves of liquidity.

Of course, the very real flip side is that a weak dollar can be a benefit and rack up extra returns. Over long stretches of time, studies have shown that the currency effects are a mixed bag and by and large even out over very long periods. Table 8.3 looks at the past 10 years' worth of performance and risk of different MSCI indices, unhedged versus hedged. Generally speaking, it has been better to be hedged in developed-market regions and unhedged in the emerging markets, although this could all change in the next 10 years.

TABLE 8.3 10-Year Returns of Major MSCI Indices Unhedged Versus Hedged with Brazil (Yellow) on a 9-Year Basis

	10Y Jan 2005—Jan 2015	
Performance	Unhedged	Hedged
EAFE	4.68%	7.84%
EM	8.47%	8.33%
Brazil	8.92%	–0.32%
Germany	7.10%	9.69%
Japan	2.77%	4.68%
United Kingdom	4.57%	6.77%
Europe	4.79%	6.68%
AC Asia Pacific ex Japan	8.98%	7.84%
Korea 25/50	8.11%	9.42%
Mexico IMI 25/50	9.84%	9.80%
ACWI ex USA	5.30%	6.54%
EMU IMI	3.78%	6.38%

Source: MSCI

"We are very skeptical of the currency-hedged movement in the equity space. It is a tactical trade; you are taking a bet. There is a view that somehow risk is being lowered by hedging currency, and in a way it is, but in a way some of that currency exposure is a lot of what's good about holding international companies in the first place."

Justin Sibears, Newfound Research

Tactically hedging against the dollar is nothing new for institutions, but now you can get the trade in one easy-to-access package in a Securities and Exchange Commission (SEC)-approved wrapper. This is in contrast to using derivatives, which some institutions may not be able to use depending on their mandates.

One of the selling points for currency-hedged ETFs is that they decrease volatility in international investing. If you look at the numbers, this is in fact the case, at least in the past 10 years, as shown in Table 8.4.

In terms of ratings, I give the entire lot of currency-hedged ETF a PG-13 rating because they use derivatives. In order to hedge out the currency, they enter into a currency forward agreement. There's nothing too wild about selling

TABLE 8.4 10-Year Standard Deviation of Major MSCI Indices Unhedged Versus Hedged with Brazil (Yellow) on a 9-Year Basis

	10Y Jan 2005—Jan 2015	
Annualized Stand. Dev.	Unhedged	Hedged
EAFE	18.15%	16.89%
EM	23.74%	17.96%
Brazil	33.02%	20.98%
Germany	23.92%	18.40%
Japan	15.51%	19.24%
United Kingdom	17.86%	13.72%
Europe	19.96%	14.64%
AC Asia Pacific ex Japan	22.24%	16.89%
Korea 25/50	28.12%	19.80%
Mexico IMI 25/50	24.59%	17.48%
ACWI ex USA	18.82%	14.35%
EMU IMI	23.06%	20.53%

Source: MSCI

a currency forward, but it does take them to another level of complexity that requires a little extra reading on the investor's part.

Let's take a look at some examples of currency-hedged ETFs.

Japan

Japan put currency-hedged ETFs on the map in late 2012 when Shinzo Abe was elected in 2012 to try and get Japan out of its long economic funk.[3] Abe announced he would make a purposeful move to weaken the yen, which would make it cheaper for Japanese companies to export goods. Abe had created the perfect situation for the WisdomTree Japan Hedge Equity ETF (DXJ). It was born for this moment.

Falling currency + rising stock market = currency-hedged ETFs' sweet spot. You can see in Figure 8.13 how DXJ came to life in both performance and flows right after Abe's election in 2012.

In addition to the currency-hedge, DXJ has a screen to include only companies who get at least half of their revenue from outside of Japan. The idea is that exporters would benefit most from a weaker yen. It then weights them

FIGURE 8.13 DXJ Performance (Top) and Flows (Bottom) All Changed When Abe Was Elected

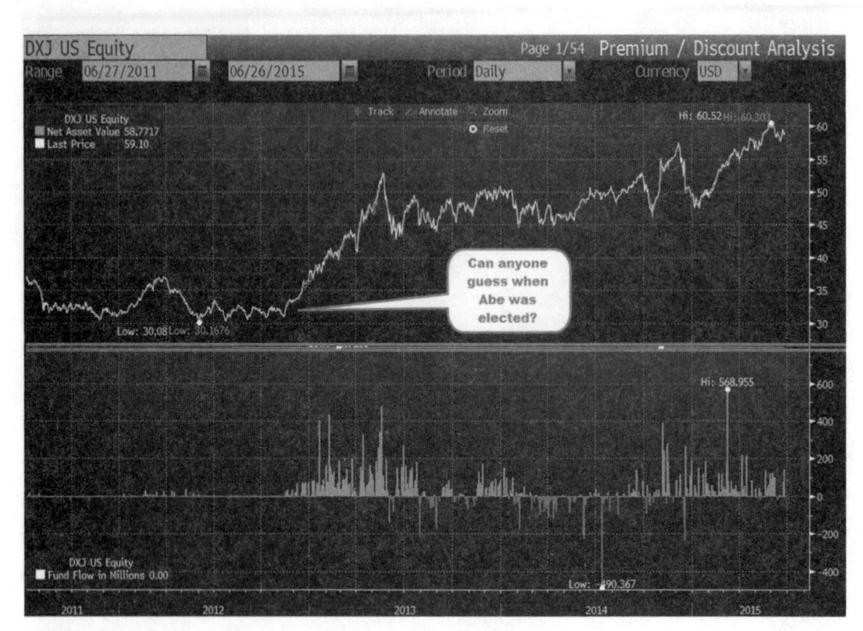

Source: Bloomberg

by dividend yield to take a little of the volatility out. It uses currency forwards to hedge out the yen. The cost of this hedge is dependent on the interest rate in the country. And in Japan's case it is currently nil.

By the end of 2013, DXJ has taken in $10 billion in new cash making it the second most successful ETF in 2013 in terms of flows only behind SPY. In terms of performance, it was up 42 percent compared to 26 percent for the unhedged iShares Japan ETF (EWJ) as shown in Figure 8.14.

But DXJ was only partially a case of "build it and they will come." It also showed the power of marketing. There was actually another product that did the same thing called the Deutsche X-trackers MSCI Japan Hedged Equity ETF (DBJP), and in fact, it performed better—by a lot. DBJP was up 52 percent in 2013 versus DXJ's 42 percent. A big reason DBJP did better is that it had more traditional sector weightings. WisdomTree, which was tracking a WisdomTree index, had underweighted financials to 7 percent, because of its unique screen for exporters.

Meanwhile, DBJP tracks MSCI's currency-hedged version of its MSCI Japan Index and so it had a much more traditional weighting to financials of 21 percent, which turned out to be a good thing. Not only that, but it is a touch cheaper, too. DBJP charges 0.45 percent compared to DXJ's 0.48 percent.

FIGURE 8.14 Performance of Hedged DXJ versus Unhedged EWJ Since Abe's Election

Security	Currency	Price Change	Total Return	Difference	Annual Eq
1) DXJ US Equity	USD	84.59%	113.98%	64.83%	33.22%
2) EWJ US Equity	USD	43.27%	49.15%		16.27%

Source: Bloomberg

I'm guessing many of the investors who rushed into DXJ probably didn't understand the differences or were even aware there was another choice.

However, the DB folks didn't get the word out as well or as fast as WisdomTree did. WisdomTree seemingly stopped everything and put all their promotion behind DXJ. They knew immediately that Abe's election was the moment of a lifetime for them. They went nuts marketing DXJ, which included TV commercials and print ads all featuring the same slogan: "Take the yen out of Japan." They sent their best people out to speak at industry conferences. They had PR e-mails going out. They blogged about it. They did everything short of skywriting. As a midsized issuer, WisdomTree is more like a speed boat than a cruise ship and is able to rally around a hot ETF very quickly.

As soon as DXJ got a little liquidity, more people started using it. Liquidity begets liquidity, and before long it started to attract bigger and bigger institutional investors, such as pension plans, insurance companies, and endowments, as shown in Figure 8.15—not to mention retail and advisors. I remember being in Houston, Texas, at a Bloomberg ETF event talking to an advisor who had a thick Southern accent, who said, "The boss really likes the DXJ." That's when I knew DXJ—and currency-hedged ETFs—had arrived.

FIGURE 8.15 DXJ's Institutional Ownership Includes Pensions, Endowments, Insurance Companies, and Hedge Funds Alike

	Portfolio Name	Mkt Val	% Portfolio	% Out	Est. Holding	Inst Type
						•[Select Multiple]
1.	EMPLOYEES RETIREMENT SYSTEM OF TEXAS	337.82MLN	4.052	1.80	2.25	Pension Fund
2.	CLAL INSURANCE ENTERPRISE HOLDINGS LTD	278.01MLN	5.837	1.48	0.50	Insurance Company
3.	LIBERTY MUTUAL GROUP ASSET MANAGEMENT INC	132.98MLN	3.812	0.71	0.75	Insurance Company
4.	SAFECO INSURANCE COMPANY OF AMERICA	75.07MLN	N.A.	0.40	0.75	Insurance Company
5.	STATE OF NJ COMMON PENSION FUND D	75.06MLN	0.272	0.40	0.50	Pension Fund
6.	NATIONWIDE MUTUAL INSURANCE COMPANY	70.33MLN	N.A.	0.38	2.00	Insurance Company
7.	UNIVERSITY OF NOTRE DAME DU LAC	59.5MLN	89.173	0.32	0.50	Endowment
8.	PARALLAX VOLATILITY ADVISERS LLC	52.62MLN	1.562	0.28	1.00	Hedge Fund Manager
9.	NEW YORK STATE COMMON RETIREMENT FUND	52.6MLN	0.071	0.28	1.75	Pension Fund
10.	RMB CAPITAL MANAGEMENT LLC	35.01MLN	2.062	0.19	0.75	Hedge Fund Manager
11.	NEW YORK LIFE INSURANCE & ANNUITY CORPORATION	29.86MLN	N.A.	0.16	1.75	Insurance Company
12.	PERMANENS CAPITAL LP	25.28MLN	23.107	0.13	1.50	Hedge Fund Manager
13.	SPRUCE PRIVATE INVESTORS LLC	23.02MLN	5.485	0.12	4.25	Hedge Fund Manager
14.	PANNING CAPITAL MANAGEMENT LP	20.69MLN	9.338	0.11	0.25	Hedge Fund Manager
15.	COBALT CAPITAL MANAGEMENT INCORPORATED	18.79MLN	1.866	0.10	0.50	Hedge Fund Manager
16.	PENNSYLVANIA TRUST CO	14.9MLN	0.893	0.08	2.25	Insurance Company
17.	BEAUMONT FINANCIAL PARTNERS LLC	14MLN	0.469	0.07	0.25	Hedge Fund Manager
18.	LMCG INVESTMENTS LLC	13.69MLN	0.266	0.07	0.50	Hedge Fund Manager
19.	--	13.16MLN	N.A.	0.07	2.75	Insurance Company
20.	HARVEST CAPITAL MANAGEMENT INC	12.79MLN	5.215	0.07	2.00	Hedge Fund Manager
21.	VOLLERO BEACH CAPITAL PARTNERS LLC	11.6MLN	1.358	0.06	0.25	Hedge Fund Manager
22.	MARINER WEALTH ADVISORS LLC	10.42MLN	0.822	0.06	2.00	Hedge Fund Manager
23.	SEABRIDGE INVESTMENT ADVISORS LLC	10.2MLN	1.906	0.05	2.25	Hedge Fund Manager
24.		8.75MLN	N.A.	0.05	2.25	Insurance Company

Source: Bloomberg

Once an ETF is known as the one to use, many investors carelessly throw out all other due diligence and just follow the herd. But the irony is that if investors had done homework and understood how to exploit implied liquidity, they may have chosen DBJP. DBJP has implied liquidity of nearly $1 billion. In all fairness, some people do use DBJP, as it has $726 million in assets. Sizable for any ETF, but nickel-and-dime compared to DXJ's $13.3 billion.

Europe

Japan was just the beginning. In 2014, Europe's central bank announced it was going to jump on the bond-buying train with plans to buy asset-backed securities. This was also combined with the Fed's decision to end its quantitative easing program. All this equated to a weaker euro and a stronger dollar. Another perfect situation for currency-hedged ETFs.

Again, the one everyone turned to was the WisdomTree product. The WisdomTree Europe Hedged Equity (HEDJ) goes long eurozone exporters mostly in France, Germany, and Spain, while shorting the euro to eliminate the currency effect. HEDJ followed DXJ in setting the world on fire by going from $1 billion to $10 billion in under a year—a super-rare feat for any ETF.

Developed Markets

Many investors have decided to blanket the entire developed world in one shot. Deutsche X-trackers MSCI EAFE Hedged Equity ETF (DBEF) give exposure to Europe and Japan together with a bit of Australia and Hong Kong thrown in. It hedges out all currencies. It also charges just 0.35 percent. This shows that the competition hitting the currency-hedged space is starting to compress fees. DBEF is up to $4 billion in assets.

Taking this even farther, DB recently launched Deutsche X-trackers MSCI All World ex US Hedged Equity ETF (DBAW), which hedges out basically everything in the world against the dollar—both developed and emerging markets. This ETF would be used if you are bullish on the dollar or you want to hedge up your global holdings in one shot.

Emerging Markets

While currency hedging works the same way in emerging markets as it does in developed markets, there is one big difference: the cost of hedging. When the ETF issuer is hedging out a currency using a currency forward, it is short the currency. The party on the other end of the trade needs to be compensated for the interest they could have earned by simply sticking that money in the local country's bank. This makes each country's interest crucial.

Unlike developed markets, where interest rates have been near zero, emerging-market countries have high interest rates, generally speaking. A back-of-the-envelope calculation of the cost of hedging can be done by taking the weighted average interest rate of the countries in the holdings minus the interest rate in the United States. Table 8.5 shows the top countries in DBEM and their interest rates.

As it stands now, DBEM has to overcome about a 4 percent headwind. This cost of hedging is something you won't see in the expense ratio, but you will see it in the returns. Alas, if you did this trade yourself, you would also be paying that fee. So it's not sneaky at all—but something to be aware of nonetheless.

Currency-Hedged Gold

A new litter of currency-hedged gold ETFs was launched carrying the Dennis Gartman name. The AdvisorShares Gartman Gold/Yen ETF (GYEN) basically goes long gold futures while selling yen futures, which simply

TABLE 8.5 Interest Rates in DBEM's Countries

Country	% Weight	Interest Rate
China	19.76	2.09
South Korea	15.24	1.56
Taiwan	12.16	0.66
Brazil	7.54	13.99
South Africa	7.20	6.13
Hong Kong	5.90	0.01
India	5.14	7.56
Mexico	4.86	3.17
Average		4.40

Source: Bloomberg

provides access to gold in a foreign currency. The case for doing this is that sometimes other currencies depreciate more than the dollar so you can get more out of your gold investment. In fact, in 2014, gold in dollars was down 29 percent, but gold in yen was down only 6 percent because the yen lost so much value. AdvisorShares rolled out Gold/British Pound and Gold/Euro as well.

In summary, currency-hedged ETFs provide great tactical opportunities for investors to "ride" a trend, namely central bank monetary policy. As long as anything like the currency wars is going on, these products will shine. Their long-term use is more debatable. Some have argued a 50–50 hedged-unhedged allocation is the sweet spot. As I write this, IndexIQ just launched a few ETFs that go 50% hedged and 50% unhedged while iShares filed for ones that change the currency-hedging percentage based on market signals. (This is what I meant when I said writing a book on ETFs was like hitting a moving target)

If there was one issue with currency-hedged ETFs, it is that they are a bit pricey. The average expense ratio is 0.50 percent. This cost—while cheap for retail investors and advisors—may keep some large institutions away. Gee, I wonder what could happen to bring fees down in this category.

"I would love for Vanguard to release a currency-hedged product because it would bring fees down."

Adam Grossman, Riverfront Investment Group

Single-Country ETFs

Single-country ETFs are a way for investors to get targeted exposure to areas of the world during U.S. trading hours. Most institutions use them tactically or in transitions, although some buy and hold as well. It just depends. Some institutional investors I spoke with mentioned using single-country ETFs to "reduce an underweight" in a portfolio so as to make sure you are keeping up with your global benchmark.

There are over 200 single-country ETFs with over $100 billion in assets, representing over 50 countries. The largest ones by ETF assets are Japan, Germany, and China, as shown in Figure 8.16. While those are the most popular ones, the fastest growing include Germany and India, which have seen assets double in the past three years.

> *"We hear a lot of discussions like 'next time I rebalance I will put some more money in the iShares MSCI Germany ETF (EWG).' There's that type of discussion. There's a lot of use of [single-country ETFs] as tools, particularly in the context of working around core holdings and adjusting weights of core holdings."*
>
> C. D. Baer Pettit, MSCI

FIGURE 8.16 The Largest Single-Country ETFs by Assets

Ticker	Name	Fund Geographical Focus	Tot Asset (M)	Expense Ratio
3) FXI US	ISHARES CHINA LARGE-CAP ETF	China	8,332.811	0.740
4) EWG US	ISHARES MSCI GERMANY ETF	Germany	7,516.945	0.510
5) EWT US	ISHARES MSCI TAIWAN ETF	Taiwan	4,268.567	0.610
6) EWY US	ISHARES MSCI SOUTH KOREA CAP	South Korea	4,139.910	0.610
7) INDA US	ISHARES MSCI INDIA ETF	India	3,851.145	0.670
8) EWH US	ISHARES MSCI HONG KONG ETF	Hong Kong	3,759.281	0.510
9) EWU US	ISHARES MSCI UNITED KINGDOM	United Kingdom	3,573.601	0.510
10) EWZ US	ISHARES MSCI BRAZIL CAPPED E	Brazil	2,783.319	0.610
11) EPI US	WISDOMTREE INDIA EARNINGS	India	2,562.717	0.830
12) EWC US	ISHARES MSCI CANADA ETF	Canada	2,528.307	0.510
13) MCHI US	ISHARES MSCI CHINA ETF	China	2,334.816	0.610
14) RSX US	MARKET VECTORS RUSSIA ETF	Russia	2,074.278	0.620
15) HEWG US	ISHA HEDGED MSCI GERMANY	Germany	2,028.825	0.530
16) EWP US	ISHARES MSCI SPAIN CAPPED ET	Spain	1,852.150	0.510
17) EWA US	ISHARES MSCI AUSTRALIA ETF	Australia	1,600.257	0.510
18) EWW US	ISHARES MSCI MEXICO CAPPED	Mexico	1,537.309	0.500
19) DBJP US	DEUTSCHE X-TRACKERS MSCI JAP	Japan	1,354.814	0.450
20) GXC US	SPDR S&P CHINA ETF	China	1,336.399	0.590

Source: Bloomberg

Single-country ETFs are ideal tools for institutions because they allow for pinpoint exposure to a single country while dampening the volatility that single stock investing brings. In addition, almost all of them invest in local shares, which can be logistically difficult—even for an institution—because you need a brokerage account and custodian in that country. Prior to the ETFs, many institutions would enter into a total return swap with a bank for various fees. Now they can just buy the ETF.

"We brought the Portugal ETF to market because the banks were telling us that we're getting a lot of demand for Portuguese swaps. The ETF was a more cost effective tool."

Bruno del Ama, Global X

Many single-country ETFs are used for short-term trading as well. You can tell because of the turnover. For example, the iShares MSCI Brazil Capped ETF (EWZ) has a market cap of $3.8 billion, but trades $750 million worth of shares every day, which equates to daily asset turnover of about 20 percent a day. Anything over 4-5 percent is a sign that there is a lot of short-term trading going on by all kinds of investors, including institutions doing everything from tactical moves to portfolio rebalancing.

Single-country ETFs can be used for big institutions doing manager transitions as well.

"When we were getting ready to hire a Japan manager, we would buy EWJ until we got them hired. No question that works."

Mark Yusko, Morgan Creek Capital Management

Volume inequality is a way of life when it comes to single-country ETFs. This can be seen in nearly every single-country category where one or two ETFs trade 10 to 20 times more than the rest of the pack. While that is ideal, the implied liquidity of the underlying holdings is also important to consider and can make many of the lesser traded ETFs just as usable.

For example, in Russia, there are four ETF options for investors, but the Market Vectors Russia ETF (RSX) trades over 20 times more than the other ones. However, it actually has the least amount of implied liquidity among its peers, namely, the iShares MSCI Russia Capped ETF (ERUS), which is sitting on over 1 million shares of implied liquidity—not to mention also trading at a penny spread as shown in Figure 8.17. Not that RSX is the wrong

FIGURE 8.17 Implied Liquidity Is Important Consideration for Single-Country ETFs

Selected Criteria
Exchange: United States X Geo Focus: Russia X
1) Modify Screening Criteria

6 matching funds

11) Key Metrics | 12) Cost | 13) Performance | 14) Flow | 15) Liquidity | 16) Allocations | 17) Regulatory Structure

Name	Today Vol↑	30D Vol	Implied Liquidity	Bid Ask Spread	Short Interest%	Open Interest
Median	568.28k	465.67k	17.16k	.04	3.30	12.66k
100) Market Vectors Russia ETF	5.51M	9.52M	1.68k	.01	13.45	567.96k
101) iShares MSCI Russia Capped ET	900.93k	430.83k	1.44M	.01	1.12	--
102) Direxion Daily Russia Bull 3x	827.43k	1.13M	11.01M	.03	5.49	12.66k
103) Direxion Daily Russia Bear 3x	309.12k	500.50k	--	.05	10.06	7.26k
104) Market Vectors Russia Small-C	8.25k	22.01k	5.27k	.09	.35	--
105) SPDR S&P Russia ETF	1.58k	9.55k	17.16k	.09	.09	--

Source: Bloomberg

one to use, but just that investors can use other options if that exposure is more up their alley.

DIY EM

Now that there are so many single-country ETFs with more and more liquidity, an institution is now able to do it themselves and custom-build an international position to their exact weighting and liking.

This is what the Tennessee Consolidated Retirement System did. They have reconstructed an EM position using over a dozen single-country ETFs to fit their exact vision. With millions allocated to ETFs, such as the MSCI Brazil Capped ETF (EWZ), iShares MSCI South Africa ETF (EZA), iShares MSCI Indonesia ETF (EIDO), and the iShares MSCI Thailand Capped ETF (THD). You can see the extent of it in Figure 8.18.

"We put together an emerging markets strategy where we avoid countries that we felt had political or underlying governance issues. We essentially get rid of countries that are undemocratic and corrupt. And the easiest way to do that was through single-country ETFs."

Michael Brakebill, Tennessee Consolidated Retirement System

The reason to do this was to allay people's fears that they were investing public money into countries where they weren't happy with their political or economic situations. Tennessee essentially created its own ETF really. I wouldn't be surprised if we see an Emerging Markets Ex-Corruption ETF at some point in the future.

FIGURE 8.18 State of Tennessee's DIY Single-Country ETF Portfolio as of June 30, 2015

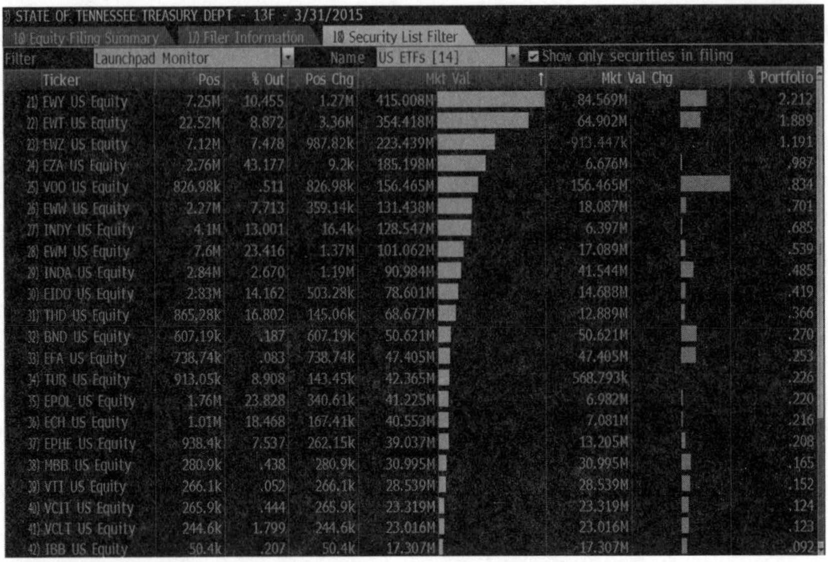

STATE OF TENNESSEE TREASURY DEPT - 13F - 3/31/2015

16) Equity Filing Summary | 17) Filer Information | 18) Security List Filter

Filter: Launchpad Monitor | Name: US ETFs [14] | Show only securities in filing

Ticker	Pos	% Out	Pos Chg	Mkt Val	Mkt Val Chg	% Portfolio
21) EWY US Equity	7.25M	10.455	1.27M	415.008M	84.569M	2.212
22) EWT US Equity	22.52M	8.872	3.36M	354.418M	64.902M	1.889
23) EWZ US Equity	7.12M	7.478	987.82k	223.439M	-913.447k	1.191
24) EZA US Equity	2.76M	43.177	9.2k	185.198M	6.676M	.987
25) VOO US Equity	826.98k	.511	826.98k	156.465M	156.465M	.834
26) EWW US Equity	2.27M	7.713	359.14k	131.438M	18.087M	.701
27) INDY US Equity	4.1M	13.001	16.4k	128.547M	6.397M	.685
28) EWM US Equity	7.6M	23.416	1.37M	101.062M	17.089M	.539
29) INDA US Equity	2.84M	2.670	1.19M	90.984M	41.544M	.485
30) EIDO US Equity	2.83M	14.162	503.28k	78.601M	14.688M	.419
31) THD US Equity	865.28k	16.802	145.06k	68.677M	12.889M	.366
32) BND US Equity	607.19k	.187	607.19k	50.621M	50.621M	.270
33) EFA US Equity	738.74k	.083	738.74k	47.405M	47.405M	.253
34) TUR US Equity	913.05k	8.908	143.45k	42.365M	568.793k	.226
35) EPOL US Equity	1.76M	23.828	340.61k	41.225M	6.982M	.220
36) ECH US Equity	1.01M	18.468	167.41k	40.553M	7.081M	.216
37) EPHE US Equity	938.4k	7.537	262.15k	39.037M	13.205M	.208
38) MBB US Equity	280.9k	.438	280.9k	30.995M	30.995M	.165
39) VTI US Equity	266.1k	.052	266.1k	28.539M	28.539M	.152
40) VCIT US Equity	265.9k	.444	265.9k	23.319M	23.319M	.124
41) VCLT US Equity	244.6k	1.799	244.6k	23.016M	23.016M	.123
42) IBB US Equity	50.4k	.207	50.4k	17.307M	17.307M	.092

Source: Bloomberg

Playing Elections

Another growing purpose for single-country ETFs is playing elections. There is nothing like a regime change to make a single-country ETF come to life. This is evident in the fact that *more than half* of the flows into single-country ETFs since 2012 is related to elections, namely, with Japan and India.

Japan

Japan-focused ETFs took in $17.7 billion in 2013 solely on the election of Shinzo Abe. That was 13 times more than the second-place United Kingdom, which took in $1.8 billion. And if we needed further proof that it was the election, Japan ETFs took in literally $0 the year before. Before Abe won, Japan ETFs had $5.7 billion in assets. Since then, they have quadrupled to $30 billion.

One needs only to chart the historical volume and flows of the WisdomTree Japan Hedged Equity ETF (DXJ). DXJ barely showed a pulse for years, and then boom—Abe gets elected and it jolted to life and, ultimately, rock stardom. DXJ took in $9.8 billion in new cash and traded $66 billion worth of shares in 2013. This was the perfect ETF for that particular election since it is currency hedged and fits Abe's accommodative monetary policy.

India

After years of the Gandhi family dynasty, the new pro-reform, pro-business Narendra Modi was elected prime minister in 2014 in a landslide, with a majority rule in the government. Investors went wild trying to play this regime change with ETFs. Assets in India ETFs literally tripled after Modi was elected, going from $2.3 billion to $7.3 billion. Investors who rushed into these ETFs were rewarded, as India ETFs rose by over 30 percent in the year after he was elected.

India is also one of those areas where an ETF may be easier than going out and trying to find an active manager, especially if it is a fluid situation you are trying to take advantage of.

"INDA (iShares MSCI India ETF) has been useful for and pretty heavily used by our emerging markets manager. Who in certain new funds that are open we have to park it into an MSCI India. So we will have a large concentration in that."

Jeffrey Davis, LMCG Investments

Lost Countries

Any single-country ETF can be bought to increase or tilt a portfolio toward a country. For example, if you own Vanguard FTSE Emerging Markets ETF (VWO), then you have a 12 percent exposure to India. If you buy an India ETF on top of that, you just added on, or overweight, your existing India position.

But for many countries in the world, they have little or no weighting in the bigger international and EM indices. They sort of slip through the cracks. These lost-country ETFs provide decent opportunities for tactical moves or portfolio add-ons. Here are a few examples.

Ireland

Ireland has had a run like no other, returning 110 percent from the end of 2010 through the end of 2015. Yet, it didn't really impact many big international or even European ETFs. For example, the Vanguard FTSE Europe ETF (VGK) only gives it Ireland a miniscule 1 percent weighting. Although in all fairness, Ireland is only 1 percent of Europe's population. And inside the big international ETF like EFA, Ireland is basically invisible with a weighting of less than 1 percent. This may explain why the iShares MSCI Ireland Capped ETF (EIRL) has a healthy $150 million in assets.

Israel

When Israel graduated from EM status to developed market, it disappeared from big indices, just like a star college basketball player going to the NBA only to be forgotten. A small fish in a big pond, Israel is a tiny 0.60 percent weighting in the iShares MSCI EAFE ETF (EFA), as shown in Figure 8.19.

There are two single-country ETFs that track nothing but Israel. One is the traditional single-country tracker the iShares MSCI Israel ETF (EIS), which tracks 52 local Israel-listed stocks. The other is the more globally minded Market Vectors Israel ETF (ISRA), which include Israel companies with primary listings in U.S.- or London- and Israel-linked companies. With that more liberal criteria, ISRA tracks 115 stocks, 39 percent of them are Israeli companies that are listed in the United States or London.

Peru

In the emerging markets area, Peru is an example of a country that gets lost in the shuffle. Peru is a small country but an intriguing mining play. While

FIGURE 8.19 Israel Is Down Near the Bottom of the Weightings in the EAFE Index

Name	% Wgt
iShares MSCI EAFE Index Fund ...	100.00
Sweden	2.92
Italy	2.24
Denmark	1.64
Singapore	1.36
Belgium	1.31
Ireland	0.91
Finland	0.82
Norway	0.59
Israel	0.57
Luxembourg	0.37
Austria	0.18
Portugal	0.15
New Zealand	0.12
Macau	0.10
South Africa	0.10

Source: Bloomberg

Peru ranks 52nd in terms of GDP, according to the International Monetary Fund (IMF), it ranks near the top among countries in the production of gold (number 6), silver (number 3), and copper (number 3). Peru is right up there with the big boys—China, Australia, and Russia. They are like the little mining country that could.

Peru gets a microscopic 0.3 percent weighting in the iShares MSCI Emerging Markets ETF (EEM) and an invisible 0.05 percent weighting in Vanguard Total International Stock ETF (VXUS).

The only way to get any real exposure to Peru is through the iShares MSCI All Peru Capped ETF (EPU), which tracks 25 stocks, half of which are in the materials sector. The big question though to investing in these lost countries is how you would actually use them in a real portfolio. Unless you made a huge bet, it may not do too much.

"The allocations of a small country would just create noise for us. How much would you really allocate to Peru? A percent or two? If it works out for you, great. But that's not going to have huge impact when you think about the contribution to return on that portfolio. And with small countries, there's all kinds of other esoteric risks that are out there."

Gary Stringer, Stringer Asset Management

DM versus EM

One interesting trend you see when you look at the data in Figure 8.20 is that some investors are choosing to unbundle their emerging markets and just pick single-county EM ETFs a la carte style. This is in contrast to the international developed markets, where investors largely tend to use the broad-reaching ETFs.

"There is no real difference between Portugal and Spain. Portugal is like diet Spain. But there is a huge difference between Russia and India. One is a commodity exporter, one is an importer. Their demographics are racing in different directions. This is why I bet we smash the BRIC idea completely. The whole idea of EM/DM has very little to do with each other. We only own them in a packager because it is easy. But it is probably not the best way to invest."

Josh Brown, Ritholtz Wealth Management

FIGURE 8.20 Single-Country EM Seeing More Flows Relative to the Regional EM through April 2015

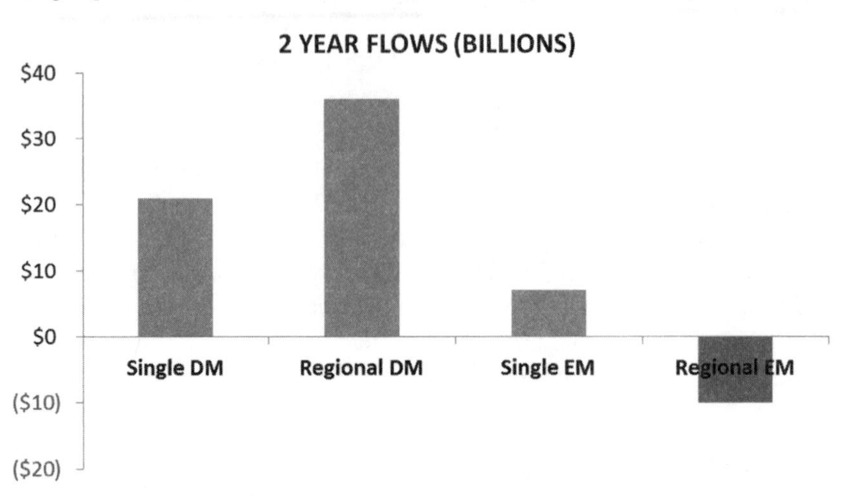

Source: Bloomberg

Single-Country Frontier ETFs

Speaking of countries that get lost in the big indices, frontier countries are basically nonexistent in the big emerging and international ETFs. That's because these are countries that are categorized as preemerging. These are countries that have to get their act together in order to "graduate" to the emerging markets. That is why these are at once intriguing and a bit scary. The four available in ETF wrappers currently are Vietnam, Argentina, Nigeria, and, most recently, Pakistan.

Generally speaking, frontier markets should be approached with caution. The obvious reasons are that these are that are less developed, less liquid, and typically more volatile.

Beside those obvious risks, there is also a lesser-known risk of *launch timing.*

For example, the Global X MSCI Pakistan ETF (PAK) was launched after the MSCI Pakistan Index was up 150 percent in the past five years. Like every other frontier-country ETF, PAK was launched after the country went on a nice run. I'm not saying it is done on purpose, but it definitely helps the marketing if the country shows good returns when the ETF launches. But it can hurt the investment potential—at least for a little while after the launch.

For example, Nigeria was on an 85 percent one-year run when the Global X Nigeria ETF (NGE) launched. But in the year after the ETF launch, it dropped 32 percent. Another example is the Market Vectors Vietnam ETF (VNM), which was launched in 2009 on the heels of a 109 percent six-month tear, only to drop 12 percent in the year after VNM's launch. Finally, the Global X Argentina ETF (ARGT) was launched after a 93 percent run, only to fall 12 percent in the six months afterwards.

We will continue to see a slew of additional single-country ETFs launched in the future as well as ETF issuers ETF-ize the world, country by country like a game of Risk. It all starts with the index, though.

"There will continue to be markets that open and become more liquid."

C. D. Baer Pettit, MSCI

But, with that said, many countries are still in the waiting room, held back by liquidity issues.

"A good example (of one not ready) is Sri Lanka. It is a good market. There's potential to make money with the right mkt conditions. It's just too illiquid. But when that changes, there's actually a decent amount of people who would want access."

Bruno del Ama, Global X

China

In my opinion, China is more than just a single country—it is an entire investment planet unto itself and worthy of its own separate section. China's market cap is in the neighborhood of $7 trillion, although as I write this, the stock market is moving so dramatically it could be way less or more by the time you read this. Regardless, China is a massive entity and a world superpower.

"In the next five years, I predict most asset allocation models include a China slug just like they do Japan."

Josh Brown, Ritholtz Wealth Management

It is also a communist country where the government has a lot of control over the markets. This makes investing in it a bit different. As an ETF analyst, I can tell you that China is the one of the most complex areas of ETFs. It makes VIX futures seem like a walk in the park. I have taken the deep dive into this area multiple times, only to learn more each time. I am by no means a China expert, but I will share with you how I have learned to simplify things for myself.

China can be broken down into two distinct sections: onshore and offshore. Go ahead and imagine the Great Wall of China separating the two sections. But instead of bricks, the wall is made of the Chinese government's regulations and restrictions. Some of these regulations are being loosened and each time it is like a few bricks getting removed from the wall. This opening up process is the long-term story underlying the day to day rise and fall of the stock market.

In terms of ETFs, there are 42 ETFs focusing purely on China. They have about $10 billion in assets, and no two are the same. Let's take a look at the ETFs on each side of the wall.

Onshore

The onshore equity market is called A-shares, and these are Chinese companies incorporated on the mainland and traded on the Shanghai Stock Exchange and the Shenzhen Stock Exchange. This market is massive. On the equity side, there are about 2,500 stocks with a market cap of $7 trillion (as of July 2015). Only about 100 of those are dual-listed outside of the mainland.

This is illustrated by the fact that only about 2 to 3 percent of the onshore market is owned by foreigner investors.[4] So the markets there are driven almost entirely by the locals in China.

Investors cannot tap into this previously untapped market with ETFs. Issuers found a way to offer this exposure by teaming up with Hong Kong companies that China has given quota to trade a limited amount of A-shares. It's the start of a long-term effort by the Chinese government to open up to foreign investors. The hope is that more such steps will eventually lead the big global index providers to integrate A-shares into their indexes, which would increase demand since they have trillions benchmarked to them. I estimate that $200 to $300 billion worth of foreign demand comes with full inclusion of A-shares, albeit slowly over years.

One advantage of China A-shares is their lack of correlation with the U.S. market, which can add diversification to a portfolio. To put this into perspective, over the past 10 years the correlation of A-shares to U.S. stocks has been zero—about the same as gold. Lack of correlation has become increasingly difficult to find in this ever-connected world. Nowadays, even emerging markets and offshore China stocks are up around 0.69 (or 69 percent), as shown in Table 8.6.

TABLE 8.6 Correlations of Offshore China Shares (FXI) Compared with Onshore Shares (SHSZ30)

Security	SPY
SPY	1.000
FXI (offshore)	0.686
SHSZ30 (onshore)	0.074

Source: Bloomberg

There are obvious risks to A-shares. There are the overall worries about the Chinese government's unpredictability and heavy hand. Some investors shy away from investing directly in China because of concerns over corporate governance and accounting. There's also the fear that China's economy will suffer a sharp slowdown after a period of rapid growth.

Regardless of the bull and bear cases, ETFs stand ready and waiting to provide this access. The first China A-share ETF to physically hold the shares came out in November 2013. The db X-trackers Harvest CSI 300 China A-Shares Fund (ASHR) tracks the 300 largest companies on the two main exchanges in China. ASHR is by far the most liquid as well with over $200 million worth of shares exchanging hands each day.

KraneShares Bosera MSCI China A Shares (KBA) differentiates itself by offering broader exposure to A-shares. It holds 442 stocks, including more mid and small caps. The fund, with just $3 million in assets, charges investors 0.85 percent of assets annually.

Investors can also get deep into China with something like the Market Vectors ChinaAMC SME-ChiNext ETF (CNXT), which tracks the 100 most liquid names on the SME and Chi-Next exchange, which are the junior boards of the Shenzhen exchange. These are the smaller, more privately owned, tech-oriented type companies inside China. In short, this is like China's Nasdaq. Although you won't find tech names like Alibaba in here because those companies have their primary listing in the United States.

CNXT has a 35 percent allocation to tech, compared with 5 percent for ASHR. Those kinds of differences can really affect returns. CNXT also has sizable weightings to health care and consumer sectors. Many have called those sectors China's new economy. This is where the Chinese government wants to see the Chinese economy grow. CNXT also comes in as the cheapest China ETF at 0.68 percent. However, it doesn't trade a whole lot and it is very, very volatile as seen in Figure 8.21.

That is a look at just a couple of A-share ETFs. Get ready for more and more to come out. There are several waiting in registration with the SEC.

FIGURE 8.21 CNXT Quick Start Since Inception

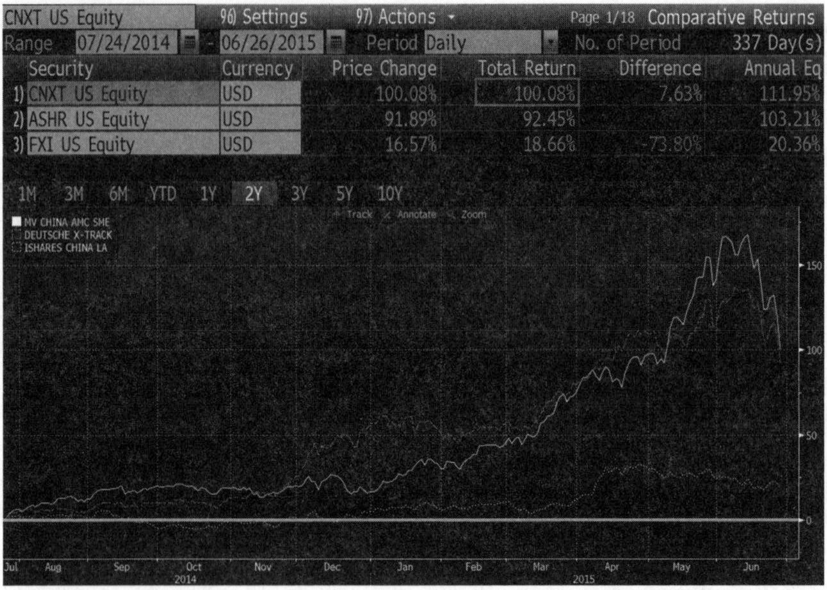
CNXT US Equity
96) Settings
97) Actions
Page 1/18 Comparative Returns
Range 07/24/2014 - 06/26/2015
Period Daily
No. of Period 337 Day(s)
Security Currency Price Change Total Return Difference Annual Eq
1) CNXT US Equity USD 100.08% 100.08% 7.63% 111.95%
2) ASHR US Equity USD 91.89% 92.45% 103.21%
3) FXI US Equity USD 16.57% 18.66% -73.80% 20.36%
1M 3M 6M YTD 1Y 2Y 3Y 5Y 10Y
Track Annotate Zoom
MV CHINA AMC SME
DEUTSCHE X-TRACK
ISHARES CHINA LA
150
100
50
0
Jul Aug Sep Oct Nov Dec Jan Feb Mar Apr May Jun
2014
2015

Source: Bloomberg

Fixed Income

The onshore bond market in China is gargantuan. With a total market size of $6.5 trillion it is the world's third largest and has only about 2 percent foreign ownership. And yes, you can now get onshore China bonds in an ETF wrapper as well. While they are newer to the market than the A-share ETFs, there are four of them as of this writing.

Getting this exposure in the past—even for an institution—would have been a bit difficult. The good news here is that all of them are relatively cheap for providing such exotic exposure. All have expense ratios between 0.40 percent and 0.56 percent. The onshore bonds yield more and have less correlation than the offshore bonds. Onshore bonds also make up 35 percent of total emerging-market debt, which is consistent with China's outsized market cap relative to emerging-market equities.

The Global X GF Bond ETF (CHNB) holds onshore China debt through its sub advisor's quota, similar to how the China A-Shares ETFs CHNB only holds investment grade bonds issued by the Chinese government and agencies plus state-owned enterprises. There is also the Market Vectors ChinaAMC China Bond ETF (CBON), which is very similar to CHNB and tracks investment-grade government and corporate bonds.

Then, there is the KraneShares E Fund China Commercial Paper ETF (KCNY), which holds mainland commercial paper like money market funds hold. The reasoning here is that the Chinese yield curve is incredibly flat, so why not lower your duration to nothing while maintaining a similar yield. KCNY and the others are also a backdoor way of getting exposure to China's mainland currency.

Offshore

The offshore Chinese market is even more complex than the onshore, unfortunately. This is the China market that most investors probably own a piece of either through a China fund or via an EM fund.

First, a quick rundown of the different types of offshore shares:

H-shares: Chinese companies incorporated on the mainland and traded in Hong Kong.

Red chips: State-owned Chinese companies incorporated outside the mainland (mostly in Hong Kong) and traded in Hong Kong.

P-chips: Non-state-owned Chinese companies incorporated outside the mainland, most often in foreign jurisdictions such as the Cayman Islands and Bermuda, and traded in Hong Kong.

N-shares: Chinese companies incorporated outside the mainland, most often in certain foreign jurisdictions (see above), and U.S.-listed on the NYSE or Nasdaq (American depositary receipts of H-shares and red chips are sometimes referred to as *N-shares*).[5]

Yes, there will be a quiz on all of this later.

Most institutions reach for the iShares China Large Cap ETF (FXI), which is the largest China ETF three times over, at $6.3 billion, and trades in the neighborhood of $1 billion a day—or as much as big blue-chip stocks. FXI tracks a pretty concentrated portfolio of just 50 stocks consisting of H-shares and P-chips. Some of its institutional owners include Harvard's endowment, Nationwide, and New Jersey's and Ohio's pension funds. It is also owned by dozens of hedge funds as well, including Jim Chanos' fund.

However, every ETF analyst out there would agree FXI is not the best broad China ETF. Most wouldn't even rank it in the top 10. It holds only 50 stocks and has a disproportionate 48 percent allocation to the financial sector. And then there's the 0.74 percent expense ratio—on the high side for a China ETF and astronomical compared to the average ETF. It also doesn't include

U.S.-listed Chinese companies like Alibaba, which tend to be more innovative tech companies. But because it got oceanic liquidity, institutions use it.

Even iShares knows this, which is why they launched the iShares MSCI China ETF (MCHI). MCHI is a cheaper and deeper version of FXI and tracks China more broadly with 140 stocks that include all the share types, except U.S.-listed China shares. It is also cheaper, at 0.61 percent.

As popular as MCHI is, the SPDR S&P China ETF (GXC) takes it one step farther by also including U.S.-listed China companies. GXC is essentially a fully loaded offshore China play. GXC costs 0.59 percent and tracks 240 stocks giving it broad and cheap coverage. It is comparable to MCHI as the most liquid alternative to FXI.

Investors also have access to offshore small caps in the Guggenheim China Small Cap Index ETF (HAO), which tracks 300 China small caps listed offshore. Like GXC, it includes U.S.-listed as well. It is decent size and liquidity but certainly not anywhere near the FXI levels.

One more China ETF worth mention is the PowerShares Golden Dragon Halter USX China Portfolio (PGJ). This one is unique because it holds U.S.-listed China companies. When it launched it was meant to fill out the gap left by FXI, which covers only Hong Kong–listed China companies. So FXI and PGJ would give you a more complete offshore China position.

China Tech

When it comes to capturing China's fast-growing tech sector, the KraneShares CSI China Internet Fund (KWEB) will serve up unique exposure that doesn't have much overlap with existing China ETFs. KWEB tracks 58 China technology companies, most of which have their primary listing on a U.S. exchange (N-shares). KWEB is full of rising-star China tech companies such as Alibaba, Tencent Holdings, and Baidu.

Tech is a big potential growth area for China, where only half of all citizens are online, compared to around 90 percent for the United States. Its launch in August 2013, was well timed as China tech companies were among the country's best performers. KWEB has gained 65 percent since it launched in July 2013 through the end of June 2015.

Josh Brown, CEO of Ritholtz Wealth Management, stated:

> The story in China is the rise of the consumer. China hasn't spent 30 years building Wal-Marts and chain stores, so now when that rising consumer wants to shop, the way they are doing it is online. If you're somebody looking for exposure to that trend, buying FXI—which is

essentially state-owned banks and oil companies—is not really getting the benefit of what's happening.

KWEB's index has rules that will allow it to add new IPOs to its portfolio quickly—after the stock's eleventh trading day, to be precise. KraneShares worked with index makers to be sure the ETF could include U.S.-listed China companies On the flip side, when you add new, young companies, you get more volatility and higher valuations. So back to the due diligence process; KWEB shows why it is important to look at risk. KWEB has a standard deviation of 28 percent, which is more than twice as much as MCHI, at 11 percent.

Fixed Income

The PowerShares Chinese Yuan (DSUM) is the oldest and largest China offshore bond ETF. It tracks the offshore dim sum bond market, which are China's government and corporate bonds—of all credit quality—issued outside of mainland China. This market is only about 1 percent the size of the China's onshore bond market. It also holds some non-Chinese company bonds as well. It is sort of the China bond equivalent to FXI in that it was first to market but newer products have come along that are better.

Both Sides of the Wall in One ETF

You may be asking yourself right about now, why isn't there an ETF that just covers the whole China market so as to avoid dealing with the complicated alphabet soup of different types of shares. Good news! There is. The Deutsche X-trackers Harvest MSCI All China Equity ETF (CN) gives you all the China shares in one shot via mid- and large-cap stocks.

It breaks down like this:

A-shares: 63.58%
H-shares: 17.10%
P chips: 8.39%
Red chips: 7.20%
N-shares: 3.54%
B-shares: 0.12%

A nice feature of CN is its multitude of technology stocks, something often lacking in the more popular China ETFs. CN is able to include U.S.-listed

FIGURE 8.22 CN's Lackluster Assets Contrasts the Value-Add of the ETF

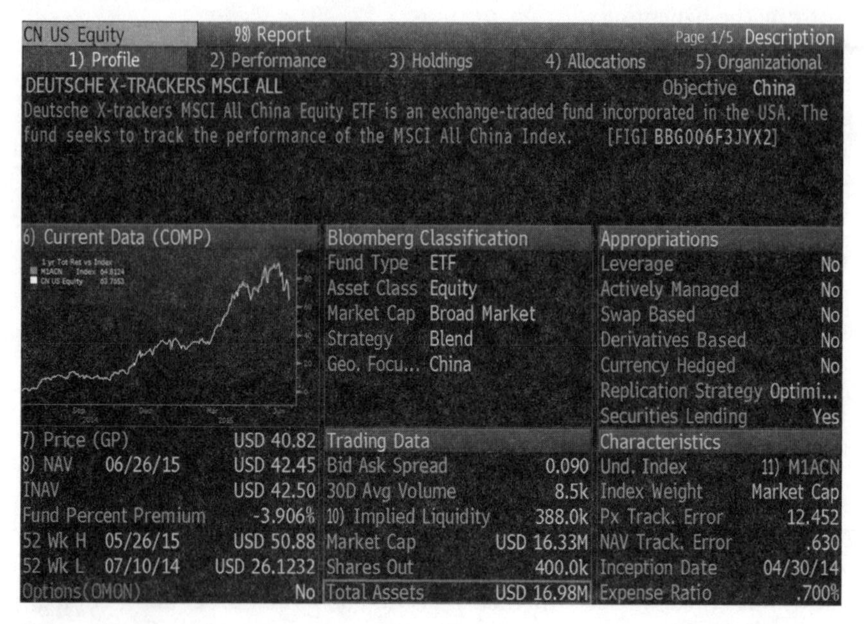

Source: Bloomberg

China stocks, such as Alibaba. Many of the most popular China ETFs will never hold Alibaba, which makes no sense, since it was the biggest tech initial public offering (IPO) in history. CN has also had great performance since its launch. It is up 74 percent since April 2014 (through June 2015).

The bad news is that it barely has any assets or volume. It is one of the great mysteries of ETFs as to why CN doesn't have any more than $10 million in assets as shown in Figure 8.22. CN is like a movie all the critics love but makes no money. I have two theories on why this is. One is that investors already own an offshore tracker like FXI or MCHI, so they then go and buy a China A-share ETF to fill in the rest, which means something like CN is not necessary. Or they just don't know, or aren't ready for it. CN may just be years ahead of its time.

Notes

1. ETF.com Staff, "2011 ETF Flows: EEM Bleeds, VWO Exceeds." ETF.com, January 3, 2012; http://www.etf.com/sections/features/10661--2011-etf-flows-eem-bleeds-vwo-exceeds.html.

2. Hougan, Matt, "Argument for Emerging Global's ECON," ETF.com, July 18, 2013; www.etf.com/sections/blog/19326-argument-for-emerging-globals-econ.html?nopaging=1&qt-etf_related_articles=2.
3. Fackler, Martin, "Ex-Premier Is Chosen to Govern Japan Again." *New York Times,* December 26, 2012; www.nytimes.com/2012/12/27/world/asia/shinzo-abe-selected-as-japans-prime-minister.html.
4. Riley, Charles, "Why China's Crazy Stock Market Is Getting Scary." *CNN Money,* July 5, 2015; money.cnn.com/2015/07/02/investing/china-stock-markets/.
5. Hudachek, Dennis, "Definitive China ETF Guide 2015." ETF.com, February 2015; www.etf.com/sections/features-and-news/definitive-china-etf-guide#sharedescriptions.

CHAPTER 9

Fixed Income

Bonds are not only a source of income but can be used to diversify a portfolio by helping to absorb shocks from the equity market. Like three-dimensional objects, bonds can also be more difficult to understand and analyze than stocks because they come with cash flow and an expiration date. They also don't trade on a central exchange, so buying or selling them is done dealer to dealer over the counter.

Enter the fixed-income exchange-traded fund (ETF). When fixed-income ETFs came along, they instantly made bond investing more convenient. You could now buy or sell a basket of bonds on an exchange just like you would buy or sell an individual stock. Bond ETFs brought price transparency to investors. This is a big reason—along with some of the other advantages of the ETF structure—why assets in bond ETFs are have grown from nothing to $335 billion in ten years as shown in Figure 9.1.

The advantage of bond ETFs trading like stocks is also a big reason people *worry* about them. When you take a prehistoric, over-the-counter market like bonds and put them into a lightening speed, equity-trading vehicle like an ETF, you can have liquidity mismatch. Whether this is a permanent evolution that we all should praise or a *Jurassic Park*-esque disaster waiting to happen or somewhere in between is up for debate. I lean toward the former, but I do think certain pockets of this category are a concern.

Fixed-income ETFs have been one of the biggest drivers of increasing institutional usage of ETFs, according to a Greenwich Associates study. They found that a third of institutions surveyed are planning to use them even

FIGURE 9.1 Asset Growth of Fixed-Income ETFs

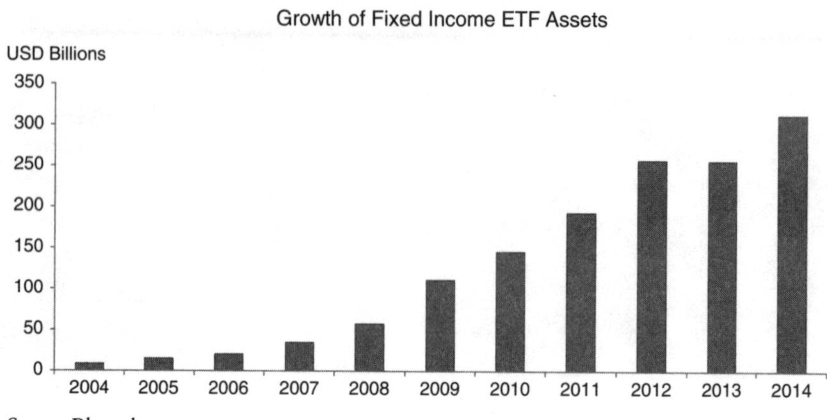

Source: Bloomberg

more next year. Institutions like them for ease of use, liquidity, lower trading costs, quick access and single-trade diversification.

"Investors are cleaning up their portfolios. It is easier to monitor four or five positions instead of 10,000. Even at the larger institutional level in something like high yield, it is easier to buy the ETF wrapper because it is tradable, it has a marketplace, it's tighter than the underlying bonds, and you aren't calling around to multiple dealers to try and sell an entire basket. You don't need to trade or have exposure to a thousand line items."

Reggie Browne, Cantor Fitzgerald

While all institution types are warming up to fixed-income ETFs, the biggest potential may be with insurance companies. They have $4 trillion in their general accounts, which are the assets that they need for liabilities. They typically invest this money very conservatively, and as such, roughly 80 percent of that is allocated to fixed-income investments. And right now they have only about $15 billion of that in ETFs, according to Blackrock. That's way less than the 1 percent norm for institutions.

The big reason insurance companies have been trailing other institution types in ETF adoption is that fixed-income ETFs were being designated as equities by the National Association of Insurance Commissioners (NAIC). That was a problem because equities require bigger risk-level capital requirements than bonds. That held up things for a long time, but the issue has been resolved, and now insurance companies can use fixed-income ETFs as if they were bonds.

"For the first 10 years that fixed-income ETFs existed, it didn't make sense for insurance companies to own them as they were penalized by holding them as common stock. Now that the artificial barrier has been removed for the past few years, utilization of fixed income ETFs by insurers is on the rise."

Rob Trumbull, State Street Global Advisors

But it isn't just insurance companies, as nearly everyone I spoke with was pretty enthusiastic about the potential for fixed-income ETFs and thought this was in the very early days in terms of growth.

"I think the big horizon, the real interesting space, is bond ETFs. And the things that can be done there. Think about the liquidity in the corporate bond market and how the access to actual specific instruments has waned because of Dodd-Frank and other dynamics. Here, ETFs can give you very good representation in the market whether you are using it as a placeholder while you are reallocating or using it as a specific strategy."

Dave Underwood, Arizona State Retirement System

Regulations

Bond ETFs have in fact been the beneficiary of increased Wall Street regulation. Regulatory reforms, such as the Dodd-Frank Wall Street Reform Act and Basel III, have resulted in greater capital and liquidity requirements for banks and hamstrung their ability to keep large inventories of bonds. In addition, the Volcker Rule has restricted proprietary trading, which has sucked out some of the liquidity from the bond market.[1]

In addition, some of the biggest players have simply gone away.

"As a result of the financial crisis, we saw six major broker dealers go out of business or be acquired in some way. So the population of institutions that can supply liquidity on the sell side decreased. At the same time you had a number of new regulations come into play. Meanwhile, the supply of bonds has been exploding. So the size of the corporate bond market has approximately doubled since the end of 2007."

Matthew Tucker, Blackrock

FIGURE 9.2 Ownership of Corporate Bonds

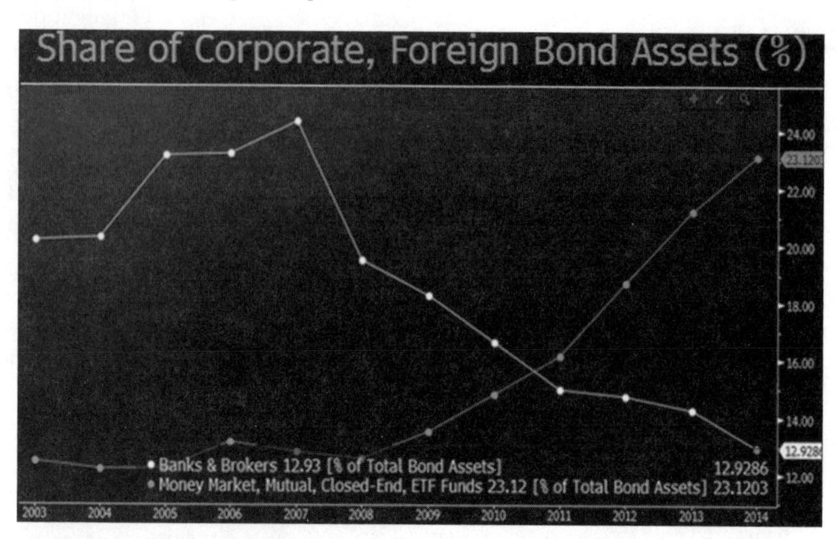

Sources: Bloomberg Intelligence, Blackrock, Federal Reserve Bank of New York as of March 2013

Figure 9.2 shows that the inventory of corporate bonds by banks and brokers is falling as the ownership of bonds by funds—including ETFs—rises.

This environment has helped increase bond ETF trading as well. Total dollar volume for fixed-income ETFs grew from $2 trillion in 2010 to over $5 trillion in 2014. This volume has in effect resulted in the spreads of ETF becoming tighter than the underlying basket of bonds. In some cases, it is a lot cheaper. For example, the SPDR Barclays High Yield Bond ETF (JNK) and the iShares iBoxx Investment Grade Corporate Bond ETF (LQD) both trade at bid-ask spreads of less than 0.05 percent, while their respective baskets trade over 0.40 percent.

Liquidity Concerns

Of course, an increase in bond ETF liquidity is not without some concern, especially when you see liquidity in the actual bond market decreasing. One of the concerns with fixed-income ETFs is that they will freeze up in a fire sale–type scenario and make it hard to exit the ETF—much harder than it was to get in. This is based on the notion that you have a super-liquid vehicle wrapping up something that isn't as liquid. While this may be overblown sometimes in the media, it is a legit issue as well with a good 80 percent of institutions reported this as being a concern, according to the Greenwich survey.

For example, most of the bonds held by junk bond ETFs don't trade every day. So if there's a huge sell-off in the bond market, the ETF will appear as though it is trading lower than its stated net asset value (NAV), or the value of its underlying portfolio. However, this is partially due to the NAV having been calculated the previous night before the sell-off.

Meanwhile, the ETF is trades real time as news breaks. This is why Blackrock referred to the ETF as the "true market" in a letter to shareholders in 2013. While that is true to an extent, the discount may also have a cost of liquidity baked in since everyone wants to sell. However, you'd be facing a similar situation if you tried to sell individual bonds as well.

> *"Try selling bonds when the credit markets freeze up like in '08. Now you might not like the price you get for an ETF, but at least you can trade it."*
>
> Sharon Snow, Metropolitan Capital

That's why even on these rare stressful occasions, you can sell your ETF, but you will probably get less than you'd want, since the firms that step in to make liquid markets for the ETFs have more difficulty pricing, hedging, and arbitraging the underlying securities. Really what the premiums and discounts are showing you is an "arbitrage band" or a natural result of making markets in the ETF and hedging with the underlying. Arbitrage bands stretch in times of crisis and snap back to normal in times of calm.

> *"ETFs tend to trade like the part of the market that's trading. What that means is if you have a sharp dislocation and high-yield markets are selling off, the bonds that trade in the market are going to sell off, and most likely ETFs are going to sell off, too. They are not really different than the individual bond exposure that investors are used to acquiring."*
>
> Matthew Tucker, Blackrock

So here is a good rule of thumb: the more exotic a bond ETF's underlying holdings, the more you'll see the arbitrage band stretch in times of market stress. Treasuries and investment grade corporate bonds probably won't get too rattled, but junk bond and senior loan ETFs could see increased stretching. ETFs can only promise convenient, low-cost exposure to different areas of the bond market, but they're not magic. And they can't protect anyone from horrible sell-offs. Like owning a beach house, you should go in expecting stormy days and the occasional hurricane.

These bond market hurricanes are nothing new either. There have been dozens of them in the past 10 years alone. The latest, most recently publicized mass sell-off was during the "taper tantrum" of mid-2013. When the Fed spoke of eventually ending its bond-buying program, rates rose 1 percent over 43 trading days. Things got ugly in the bond market, and iShares iBoxx $ High Yield Corporate Bond ETF (HYG) closed at discounts on 20 days. It also closed at premiums on 23 days. On June 19—one of the worst days—it closed 0.91 percent below its NAV.

The ETF bounced back the next day and closed at a 0.34 percent discount. These were some rough days, but really this was nothing for HYG, relatively speaking. In fact, it was only the 43rd worst discount of HYG's life, as shown in Figure 9.3. It traded less back then and had less

FIGURE 9.3 HYG's Daily Premium/Discount Since 2007

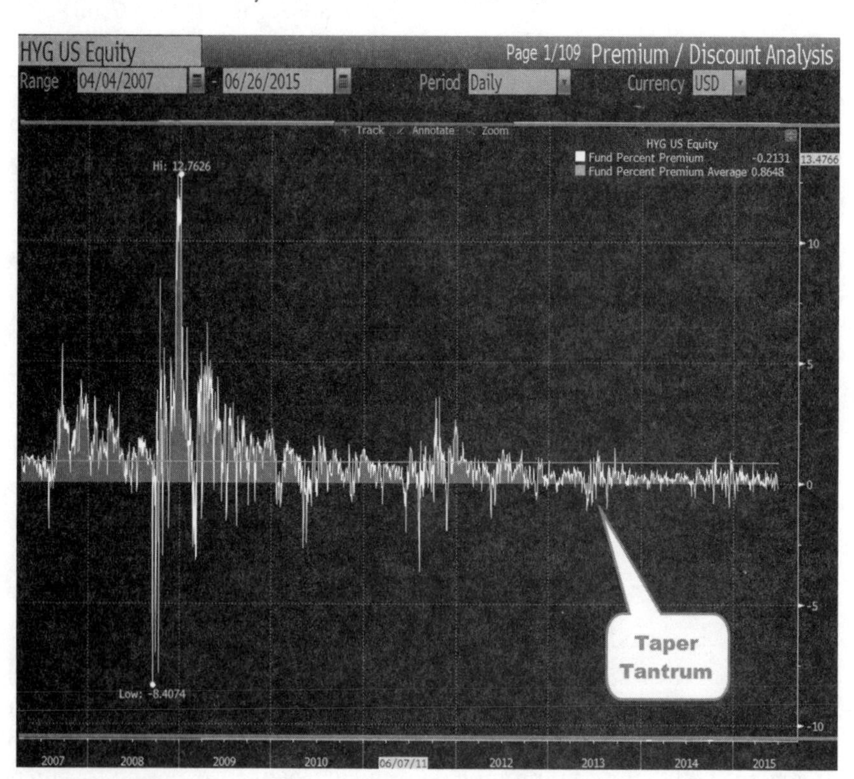

Source: Bloomberg

liquidity, but still it puts things into perspective. These bad days are not that uncommon.

Another interesting note about HYG is that it traded approximately $500 million a day during the taper tantrum. The volume on the exchange outnumbered the redemptions by six to one. While it normally has a 12-to-1 ratio, it meant that for every $6 of trading on the exchange, only $1 resulted in redemptions that impacted the underlying bonds. This means the ETF did act as a liquidity buffer, taking some pressure off of the bond market.

"ETFs are not the cause of lack of liquidity. They are the only thing keeping liquidity in the market. Dodd-Frank is the cause for lack of liquidity. You put a lot of trading desks out of the game. You did it for the best interest of the banking system, but that might not have been in the best interest of the bond market. But we'll see."

Josh Brown, Ritholtz Wealth Management

And investors who fight the urge to sell on these rare rough days have been rewarded—at least historically speaking. Even when we include the horrible taper tantrum, HYG's return in 2013 was 5.90 percent, while the index was up 5.93 percent. That's almost perfect tracking, which means investors essentially got *free exposure* to high-yield bonds. In short, an ETF can deliver on its promise in spades despite a nasty day or series of days.

This battle toughness and proven track record is drawing in more investors. As bond ETF liquidity continues to rise and costs keep coming down, you can expect some larger institutions to start using them more. The lack of liquidity and expenses are two of the top three reasons that institutions have quoted for not using ETFs, as seen in Figure 9.4. Also note that investment guidelines are the top reason. Those can change, too, but as mentioned in my intro, it takes time with institutions.

Okay, so that was a long intro. But fixed-income ETFs—as boring as they may seem—are actually one of the most controversial areas of ETF Land and investors must understand these debates before using them. While nearly everything in here is G or PG in my rating system, there are a couple of areas such as senior loans and zero-coupon bond ETFs that are PG-13. Let's take a look at some of these.

FIGURE 9.4 Why Institutions Don't Use Fixed-Income ETFs

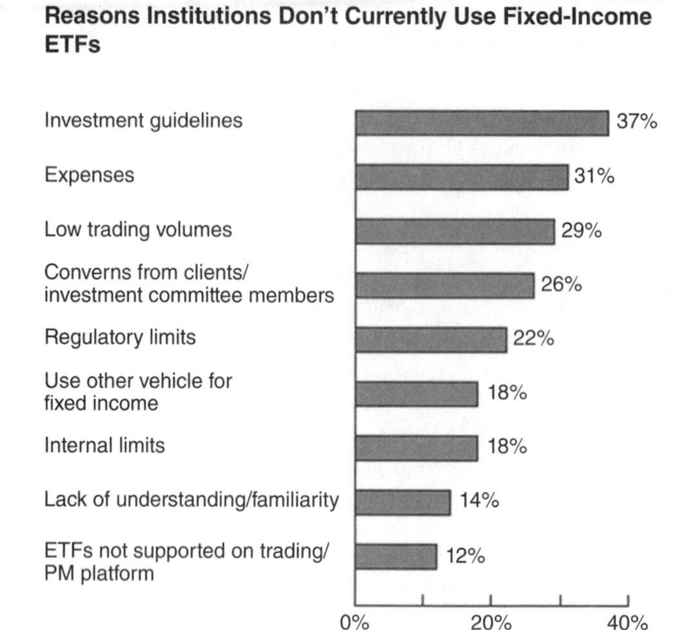

Source: Greenwich Associates

Aggregate Bond ETFs

Let's start with the ETFs that attempt to give you everything in one shot. There are 24 aggregate bond ETFs with $82 billion in assets, and most of that money revolves around one index.

The "Agg"

Barclays Capital U.S. Aggregate Bond Index (formerly called the Lehman Aggregate Bond Index) is the most popular bond index and is the standard to which many active bond managers are held. Otherwise known as the "The Agg," it has $54 billion in ETF money tracking it, or 65 percent of the total in this category.

It is made up of investment-grade bonds including Treasuries, mortgage-backed securities, corporates, and a tiny number of municipals. Those bonds are then market value weighted, which means those issuers with the most

FIGURE 9.5 Cross-Section of AGG's Bonds

AGG US Equity | 98) Report | Page 4/5 Description

1) Profile | 2) Performance | 3) Holdings | 4) Allocations | 5) Organizational

Allocations as of 6/25/15

Top Ind. Group Allocation		Top Geographic Allocation		Top Asset Allocation	
Sovereign	42.36%	U.S.	91.07%	Government	42.800%
FNMA Collateral	15.26%	Canada	1.36%	Mortgage	29.460%
FGLMC Collateral	6.36%	U.K.	.82%	Corporate	26.904%
Banks	5.82%	Germany	.80%	Municipal	.837%
GNMA2 Collateral	5.09%	Mexico	.54%	Preferred	.000%
Oil&Gas	2.14%	Netherlands	.52%	Equity	.000%
Electric	1.71%	Australia	.38%	Cash and Other	.000%
Multi-National	1.63%	France	.35%		
Commercial MBS	1.60%	Turkey	.24%		
Telecommunications	1.47%	Switzerland	.22%		
6) Holdings Analysis	**6/25/15**	**Bloomberg Composite Rating**		**Maturity Allocation**	
Top 10 Hldings % Port	12.62	AAA	41.35%	3 - 5 yrs	25.85%
		NR	28.29%	1 - 3 yrs	20.62%
		BBB	12.68%	5 - 7 yrs	20.44%
		A	11.20%	7 - 10 yrs	14.77%
		AA	6.17%	+ 10 yrs	13.96%
		BB	.32%	0 - 1 yr	4.37%

Source: Bloomberg

debt get the largest weighting. This fact is used a lot in critiques against the Barclays Agg, as not everyone is a fan of this mega-popular index.

"The aggregate bond index for bonds is bullshit. It was invented by a guy from Lehman Brothers and if you ask him why he came up with it, he'll tell you it was to sell bonds: 'If we index these things, people will have to buy them.' It's not like Moses came down from Mt. Sinai and handed us the Barclays Agg. It's a product itself. Also, the biggest debtors are going to make up the largest part of the index. So when you know that, you are way less centered on this idea that you need to be neck and neck with the Barclays Agg."

Josh Brown, Ritholtz Wealth Management

"What we know is that historically a lot of investors—especially institutions—have looked at the Agg as an appropriate benchmark for the core of the

fixed-income exposure. Yes, issuers that have more debt have a larger percentage of the benchmark, but people have to remember that having more debt doesn't mean you are a more risky borrower."

Matthew Tucker, Blackrock

Regardless of the debate over the index, one thing that can't be denied is just how popular the ETFs are that track it. AGG is a huge hit with investors at $24 billion. It trades a healthy $100 million a day and charges a low 0.08 percent—a cost that makes it competitive with separately managed accounts.

The same goes for the $27 billion Vanguard Total Bond ETF (BND), which also tracks the Barclays Agg. It is a float-adjusted version that slightly limits the mortgage bond exposure, charges 0.08 percent, and also trades about $100 million a day.

In the end, the differences between them is outweighed by their similarities. Both BND and AGG track the index well, and when you put their long-term returns on top of one another, as in Figure 9.6, they are pretty

FIGURE 9.6 AGG and BND's Total Return from May 17, 2010, to June 29, 2015

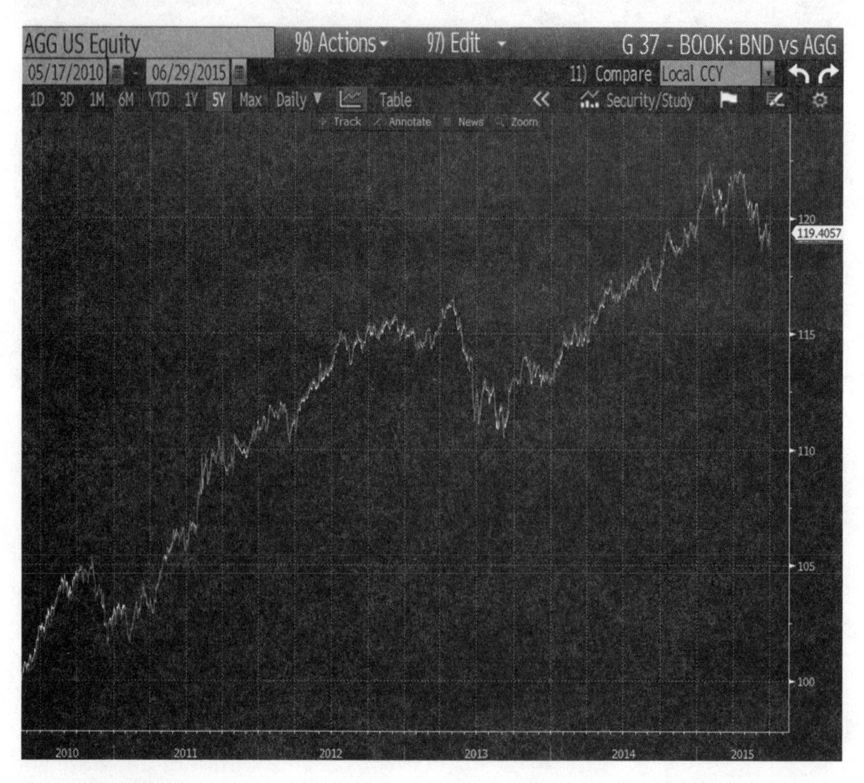

Source: Bloomberg

indistinguishable. So there really is no dilemma here; either one will get job done. The choice may ultimately come down to which issuer you like better or have a relationship with.

The other two ETFs tracking the Barclays Agg are the Schwab U.S. Aggregate Bond ETF (SCHZ) and the SPDR Barclays Aggregate Bond ETF (LAG). They do same thing and but trade less. So is there any point in using either of them? Probably not for LAG, but SCHZ is actually cheaper. The only one who consistently out-Vanguards Vanguard by undercutting costs is Schwab.

SCHZ charges 0.05 percent, making it the bond ETF with the lowest expense ratio. However, it trades $1 million a day, which will definitely scare some large institutions away. But the bonds are liquid, so the implied liquidity is good. So if an investor is going in long-term, it may be worth it to execute a trade in SCHZ using a block order just for the utter cheapness of the ETF.

And, of course, this is a popular category for actively managed ETFs, such as the PIMCO Total Return Active ETF (BOND) and the SPDR Double-Line Total Return Tactical ETF (TOTL). We will cover these in the actively managed ETF section.

This category also has one of the first of what will probably be many smart-beta fixed-income ETFs. The iShares U.S. Fixed Income Balanced Risk ETF (INC) is weighted and rebalanced based on risk to keep it at 50 percent credit risk and 50 percent interest rate risk. This product was a response to some of the feedback on their hugely popular iShares Core Aggregate Bond ETF (AGG) which is 90 percent interest rate risk while kicking out a low yield.

INC is sort of the goldilocks option that combines AGG's stability with some of HYG's juice and balances out the risk. A true solutions-oriented product and the beginning of smart-beta in fixed income. The fixed-income ETF world is going to see more and more of these types of ETFs.

Treasuries

These ETFs track debt issued by the United States Treasury. There are over 40 of them with about $45 billion in assets. They all pretty much do the same thing which is hold a basket of treasuries. You couldn't get more G rated than that.

The value-add here for an institution is that some of these ETFs trade so much that they offer cheaper transaction costs—via minuscule spreads—than buying the Treasuries directly. So while advisors and retail have always found these ETFs useful as cheaper asset allocation tools, institutions are more and more interested in them as a result of their growing liquidity.

This growing liquidity really is only in the iShares ETFs, as they utterly dominate the treasury ETF category with over 80 percent of the assets and volume. So, yeah, volume inequality is in full form here with only a select few iShares ETFs getting all the action.

"You tend to see ETF volume growth has an exponential curve to it. As you start seeing volume pick up other investors are drawn to it, and you see volume increase at an increasing rate. What you end up with is funds that tend to corner the market on liquidity. A lot of the reason you haven't seen more treasury ETFs come into the market is existing funds in market have a lot of liquidity and are heavily used."

Matthew Tucker, Blackrock

In terms of due diligence, this is one of the simplest areas to deal with. The key thing here is just eyeballing the maturity differences between the ETFs and whether it is holding bonds (long-term), notes (intermediate-term and short-term) and bills (ultra-short-term). The big dilemma is whether to use the super-liquid iShares product versus perhaps the slightly cheaper Vanguard or Schwab offering.

Bonds (Long Term)

Treasury bonds have the longest maturity, from 20 to 30 years. When it comes to a Treasury bond ETF, the iShares 20+ Year Treasury ETF (TLT) is beyond dominant, with $5 billion in assets. There is really nothing to TLT, it basically holds about 20 or so Treasury bonds that mature in 20 years or more. It charges 0.15 percent and trades around $1 billion a day, making it the most traded bond ETF in the world. TLT has a duration of 17.7 years, so it is very sensitive to interest rates.

TLT also serves as a potentially underrated portfolio diversifier as well. Unlike portfolio hedges that use derivatives, such as leverage and VIX products, TLT is "organic" and simply made up of a little basket of Treasury bonds. Yet it has also displayed less correlation to the stock market than gold and corporate bond ETFs, which are frequently used for diversification.

TLT proved its diversification chops back in 2008, the last time the stock market tanked. Back then, SPY went down 37 percent. TLT gained 33 percent,

FIGURE 9.7 TLT's Compared to Other Diversifiers in 2008 When the S&P 500 Was Down 36 Percent

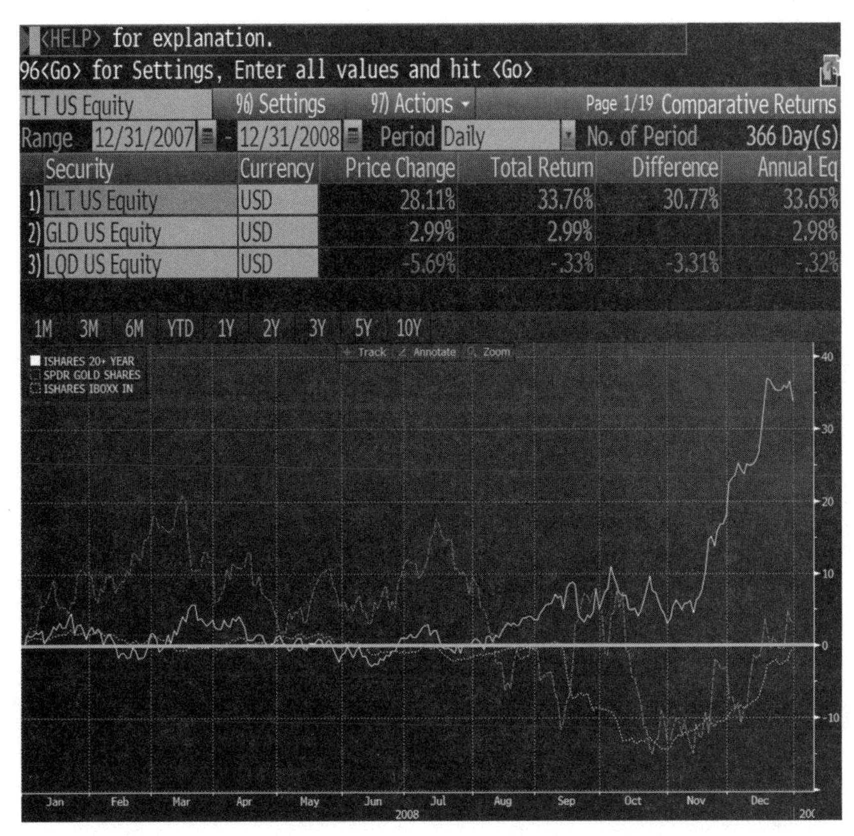

Source: Bloomberg

offsetting nearly all the losses of the S&P 500. GLD rose 3 percent and LQD was flat as seen in Figure 9.7.

And when you look at more recent downturns, such as the 3.4 percent stock market drop in January 2013, TLT gained 6 percent. I also did a study for an article where I divided the past six years through August 2014 into 26 quarters and TLT moved in the opposite direction as SPY in 19 quarters. GLD did so for 13, and LQD for 12.

Granted, it was a different world in 2008 and since. The Federal Reserve hadn't started a program that keeps rates artificially low, and 30-year Treasuries were yielding 4.8 percent. But still, TLT is a popular diversifier, which is something not lost on institutions.

"We see some Treasury ETF usage by endowments as a risk balancer in their portfolio. A lot of them will actually employ Treasury investments as a way to balance out some of those more risky investments they have and try to improve their risk-adjusted returns through time."

Matthew Tucker, Blackrock

Notes (Intermediate Term)

Treasury notes mature in 2 to 10 years. There are about a dozen ETFs with $10 billion in assets. The most popular two products are the iShares 7–10 Year Treasury Bond ETF (IEF) and the iShares 3–7 Year Treasury Bond ETF (IEI). IEF charges 0.15 percent and trades about $100 million worth of shares per day, while IEI also charges 0.15 percent but trades much less—about $20 million a day.

An intriguing non-iShares option in this category is the SPDR Barclays Intermediate Term Treasury ETF (ITE), which sort of combines both IEF and IEI together by tracking Treasuries with maturities between 1 and 10 years. ITE is also cheaper than all of the iShares products, with an expense ratio of 0.10 percent. But keep in mind it tends to favor the shorter-term side of that range and has a duration of 3.7 years.

Notes (Short Term)

In between these intermediate notes and treasury bills which we will get to in the next section is short-term Treasury ETFs. The one everyone uses here is the iShares 1–3 Year Treasury Bond ETF (SHY). SHY has an apropos ticker, as this is a popular ETF for investors who are feeling shy and want to hide away from the market. SHY is used as a parking spot for cash by both large and small investors alike. SHY charges 0.15 percent.

There are also some other options here, including the Schwab Short-Term U.S. Treasury ETF (SCHO), which is cheaper, at 0.08 percent, and the Pimco 1–3 Year U.S. Treasury ETF (TUZ), one of their few passively managed funds. The performance between the ETFs at this level is so close that most investors end up just using SHY because it trades the most.

Bills (Ultra-Short Term)

Treasury bills mature in one year or less. These ETFs act like money market mutual funds. These are ETFs that are so stable they are basically like

FIGURE 9.8 SHV's Price Barely Changed Over Five Years

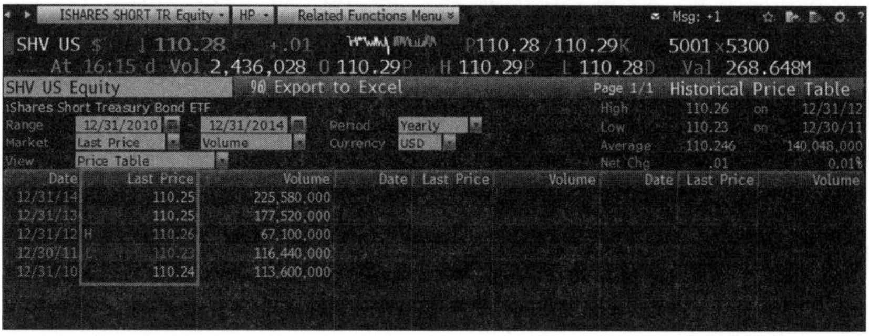

Date		Last Price	Volume
12/31/14		110.25	225,580,000
12/31/13		110.25	177,520,000
12/31/12	H	110.26	67,100,000
12/30/11	L	110.23	116,440,000
12/31/10		110.24	113,600,000

Source: Bloomberg

mattresses—a place to park cash. Like money market funds, they don't really yield anything or return anything, but that's sort of the point.

The most popular one is the iShares Short Treasury Bond ETF (SHV), which tracks Treasuries with remaining maturities between one month and one year. It has a yield and return of 0 percent. It has basically had the same price for the past five years, give or take a penny, as shown in Figure 9.8. It has $4 billion in assets and trades about $50 million a day, though. So investors clearly are using it. It charges 0.15 percent in fees.

Another option is the SPDR Barclays 1–3 Month T-Bill ETF (BIL). It goes a step further and tracks only Treasury bills maturing within one to three months. It yields nothing and returns nothing and has literally no standard deviation; just like a real money market fund, it is a mattress—albeit one with over $1 billion under it.

TIPS

Treasury inflation-protected securities (TIPS) are issued by the Treasury as a way for investors to get income that is protected from inflation. They are an alternative to Treasury bonds by providing a guaranteed real rate of return. The principal and interest payments of a TIPS increases with inflation and decreases with deflation.

There are about a dozen TIPS ETFs with about $18 billion in assets. The monster in the space is the iShares TIPS Bond ETF (TIP). It tracks about 40 inflation-protected Treasury securities maturing in at least a year or more. It has $13 billion in assets, more than quadruple the next largest ETF in the category. It is also one of the most expensive, charging 0.20 percent in annual fees.

While TIP has most of the assets, there are three other ETFs with over $1 billion, including the Vanguard Short-Term Inflation-Protected Securities Index Fund (VTIP), which is a bit cheaper than TIP, at 0.10 percent.

Another billion-dollar option is the FlexShares iBoxx 3-Year Target Duration TIPS Index Fund (TDTT). The twist here is that TDTT looks to keep its duration at exactly three years. This is less than the other ones, which all hover around four years. For investors looking for a cheaper option, there is the Schwab U.S. TIPs ETF (SCHP), which is the cheapest in the group by far, with a fee of .07 percent.

Zero-Coupon Bond ETFs

Another slice of the Treasury bond market is zero-coupon bonds. But be warned—these are not your grandfather's Treasury bond ETFs. These are more like power tools. This is the one section of treasury ETFs this not rated G.

Even though *Treasury* is in their name, they're way riskier than other bond ETFs. The Pimco 25+ Year Zero US Treasury Index Exchange-Traded Fund (ZROZ) is like long-dated bonds on steroids because they have had their coupon payments stripped out, hence their street names of *strips* and *zeros.* Behind every zero-coupon bond, there used to exist a plain vanilla Treasury bond.

Back in the early 1980s, investment bankers got the idea to strip out the interest payments on the bonds and sell them as two separate revenue streams. Because the strips pay no interest, they are sold at a deep discount to face value. For example, you could buy a $1,000 bond for $200. Pay $200 now and collect your $1,000 in 20 years.

Removing the coupon payments makes them extra-sensitive to interest rate moves. They both have a duration of over 26 years—the most among bond ETFs—which means they can gain or lose a ton in any given day/month/year if rates move. For example, in 2014 when rates fell, ZROZ returned 49 percent for the year.

But look out when rates rise—even a little—as these bond ETFs are essentially the canaries in the coal mine. For example, in 2013 when rates rose from 1.7 to 3 percent, ZROZ and EDV took a beating and lost 22 percent and 21 percent, respectively. This made them the worst-performing bond ETFs that year.

Their interest rate sensitivity makes these bond ETFs have nearly twice the volatility of junk bonds and the Standard & Poor's (S&P) 500. In short, these two ETFs get a PG-13 based on the unique potential for a nasty surprise due to the high duration and volatility. Figure 9.9 shows EDV and ZROZ

FIGURE 9.9 ZROZ and EDV's Volatile Historical Returns Contrasted to IEF, a More Typical Treasury Bond ETF

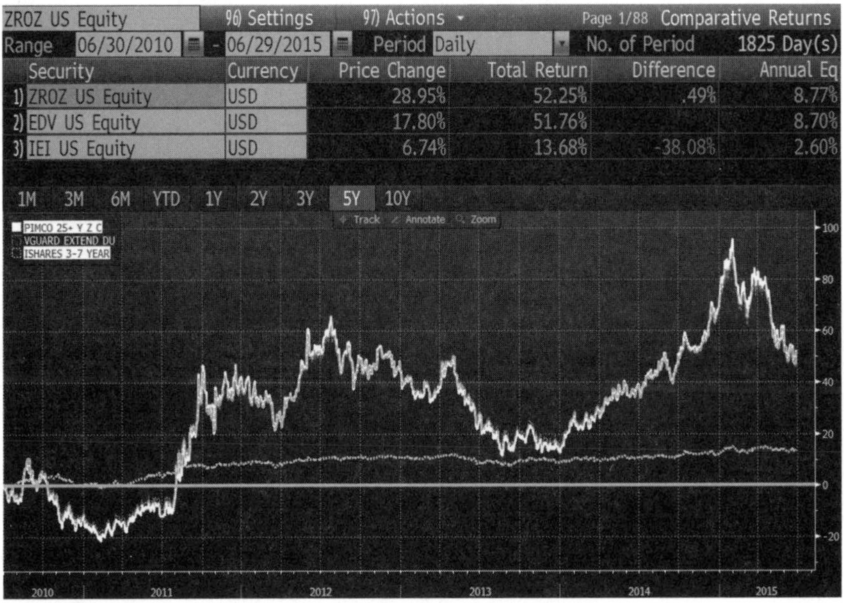
ZROZ US Equity
96) Settings
97) Actions
Page 1/88 Comparative Returns
Range 06/30/2010 - 06/29/2015
Period Daily
No. of Period 1825 Day(s)
Security
Currency
Price Change
Total Return
Difference
Annual Eq
1) ZROZ US Equity USD 28.95% 52.25% .49% 8.77%
2) EDV US Equity USD 17.80% 51.76% 8.70%
3) IEI US Equity USD 6.74% 13.68% -38.08% 2.60%
1M 3M 6M YTD 1Y 2Y 3Y 5Y 10Y
Track Annotate Zoom
PIMCO 25+ Y Z C
VGUARD EXTEND DU
ISHARES 3-7 YEAR
100
80
60
40
20
0
-20
2010
2011
2012
2013
2014
2015

Source: Bloomberg

versus a more typical treasury ETF the iShares 3–7 Year Treasury Bond ETF (IEI). The chart speaks volumes as to their behavioral differences.

The other thing investors should know about ZROZ and EDV is that even though the bonds pay no interest during their life, the owners of the bonds are taxed every year as if income was paid out. This is known as *phantom interest.* Heads up on that.

Both EDV and ZROZ are very similar. EDV trades a bit more and has a lower expense ratio. It charges 0.12 percent compared to ZROZ's 0.15 percent. But for someone looking for the high-octane exposure to zero-coupon bonds, either will do.

Mortgage-Backed Securities

Mortgage-backed securities (MBSs) are created as loans and are pooled together and made into tradable securities. These are typically pass-through securities guaranteed by government agencies such as Ginnie Mae, Freddie Mac, and Fannie Mae.

In terms of ETFs, there are about a half dozen of them providing this exposure. The largest in the group is the iShares Barclays Bond ETF (MBB), which holds about 500 AAA-rated investment-grade MBS. It has a duration of 2.6 years. In other words, not really too much credit risk or interest rate risk despite the reputational issues surrounding the name.

"MBB is mostly agency-backed that are frankly going to have directly or indirectly have the full faith and credit of the U.S. government behind them. If you look in 2008, MBB didn't get killed in 2008 because that wasn't the type of mortgage security that got killed."

Justin Sibears, Newfound Research

MBB trades about $40 million worth of shares a day and charges 0.27 percent. MBB has had a stellar run since the down days of the financial crisis. In the five year span between 2010 through 2015, MBB is up 19 percent while exhibiting a miniscule standard deviation of 1.7 percent.

A big competitor to MBB is the Vanguard Mortgage-Backed Securities ETF (VMBS), which boasts an expense ratio of just 0.12 percent, more than twice as cheap as MBB. In addition, iShares also takes MBSs to another level down by offering the iShares GNMA Bond ETF (GNMA), which holds just securities issued by one agency, Ginnie Mae. Although, judging from the asset level of $55 million, investors don't seem to need to get that granular with it.

Municipals

There are over 30 municipal bond ETFs. They slice up the muni market in more ways than you can imagine. You've got big, broad ones like the iShares National AMT-Free Municipal Bond ETF (MUB) and then ones that focus on a specific state, such as California and New York, like the SPDR Nuveen Barclays California Municipal Bond ETF (CXA). Muni bond ETFs may not yield a lot at first glance, but because they are tax exempt, their tax-equivalent yield is much higher.

It is easy to get distracted by the credit quality and yield with muni bond ETFs, but don't forget about the duration. Many times I've analyzed an impressive performer in this space only to find out it was mostly due to the increased duration, not necessarily the types of munis it held.

One example of that is the muni bond ETFs tracking Build America Bonds. Remember those? They were only issued between 2009 and 2010 as taxable municipal bonds that carry special tax credits and federal subsidies. The purpose behind them was to reduce borrowing costs for state and local governments.

The SPDR Nuveen Barclays Build America Bond ETF (BABS) is one of the best performers in the category in the three years from 2011 to 2014. It has more than doubled the performance of MUB, as seen in Figure 9.10, even though both of them are investment-grade bond ETFs.

At first you think, well it must be something about Build America Bonds. But, it turns out the reason is that BABS holds much longer-term debt and has a duration of 12.7 years, while MUB has less than half that rate risk with a duration of 4.5 years. And investors will see that if rates start to rise, that performance will flip and they will suffer much more than MUB. This was the case in February of 2015: when rates rose, BABS lost 2.5 percent versus 1.2 percent for MUB.

FIGURE 9.10 BAB's Duration Gives It Extra Volatility

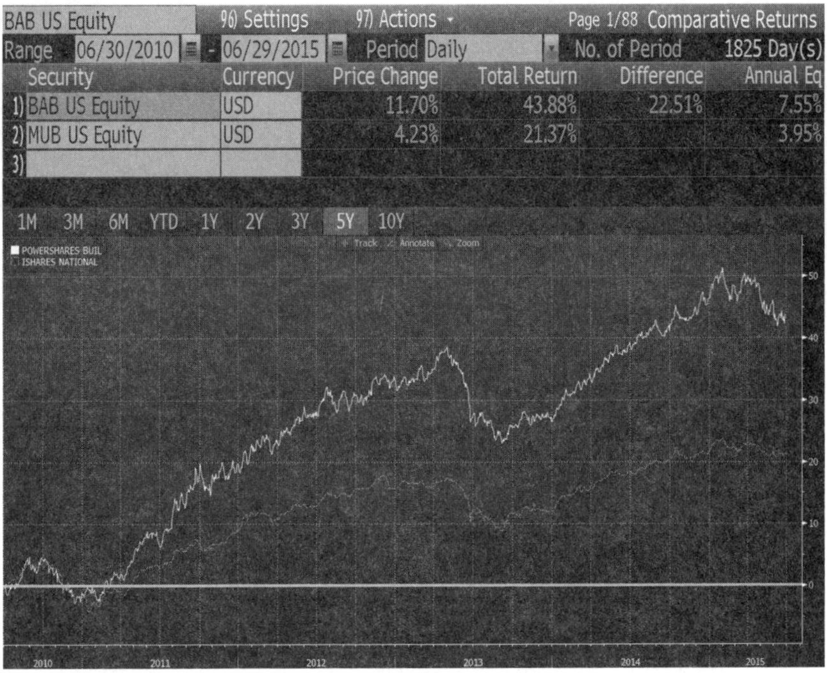
BAB US Equity
96) Settings
97) Actions
Page 1/88 Comparative Returns
Range 06/30/2010 - 06/29/2015
Period Daily
No. of Period 1825 Day(s)
Security
Currency
Price Change
Total Return
Difference
Annual Eq
1) BAB US Equity USD 11.70% 43.88% 22.51% 7.55%
2) MUB US Equity USD 4.23% 21.37% 3.95%
3)
1M 3M 6M YTD 1Y 2Y 3Y 5Y 10Y
POWERSHARES BUIL
ISHARES NATIONAL
50
40
30
20
10
0
2010
2011
2012
2013
2014
2015

Source: Bloomberg

You can also get municipals of the high-yield variety. For example, the Market Vectors High Yield Municipal Index ETF (HYD) tracks higher-yielding—but higher risk of defaulting—municipal bonds. It has about double the yield of MUB. And if you want to eliminate some interest rate risk there is the Market Vectors Short High-Yield Municipal Index Fund ETF (SHYD). This is like HYD except it only picks bonds with shorter maturities, making it less prone to interest rate risk. The two ETFs have $1.6 billion in assets.

The fact that you can get a short-term, high-yield municipal bond ETF is emblematic of just how precise fixed-income ETFs have gotten over the past few years.

Corporates

One of the fastest-growing categories, there are now over 80 ETFs that track U.S. corporate bonds with $110 billion in assets. They account for nearly one-third of all fixed-income ETF assets.

Between 2007 and 2013, the corporate bond market grew 81 percent, from $2.6 trillion to $4.7 trillion. During that time, corporate bond ETFs jumped from $3.9 billion to $100 billion, which is a 25-fold increase.[2] However, even with this growth inside the ETF world, corporate bond ETFs own just a tiny sliver—about 2 percent—of all corporate bonds.

Anyhow, let's have a look at a few pockets of corporate bond ETFs.

Investment Grade

The big fish is the iShares iBoxx $ Investment Grade Corporate Bond ETF (LQD), which has $22 billion in assets. LQD was the very first bond ETF; it launched back in July 2002. It holds 1,300 bonds from many of America's most beloved companies, such as General Electric, Apple, and Verizon.

LQD trades $400 million worth of shares per day, making it one of the most liquid bond ETFs. It is also cheap, at 0.15 percent. That is the kind of liquidity and cheapness that can attract even the largest of institutions, such as the New York State Common Retirement Fund, which has a $193 million holding in LQD.

Vanguard also has two popular corporate bond ETFs that slice up the market by maturity. The Vanguard Intermediate-Term Corporate Bond ETF (VCIT) and the Vanguard Short-Term Corporate Bond ETF (VCSH) offer both intermediate and short-term corporate bonds for the tiny cost of 0.12 percent.

High Yield

High-yield, or junk bond, ETFs rose in popularity during the period after the 2008 financial crisis as investors became more desperate for yield with interest rates so low. There are 43 ETFs that hold junk bonds, and they have $50 billion in assets. Half of those assets are in just two ETFs—the SPDR Barclays High Yield Bond ETF (JNK) and the iShares iBoxx $ High Yield Corporate Bond ETF (HYG).

They are very similar except JNK will include a bit more lower quality junk bonds, which gives it a bit of extra yield but also a bit of extra credit risk. Both of them trade around $300 million a day and their 5-year returns are within 80 basis points of each other. Both should serve an institutional investor just fine. JNK is a hair cheaper, at 0.40 percent to HYG's 0.50 percent.

Both JNK and HYG have short-duration mini-me's as well. The SPDR Barclays Short-Term High Yield ETF (SJNK) is the short-term version to JNK. SJNK posts a duration of two years compared to JNK's four years. They both yield around 5 to 6 percent. Some investors use these short-term high-yield ETFs instead of JNK and the like.

"The reason we are in short duration high yield instead of long duration, if you look at the yield differential, there isn't that much difference."

Adam Grossman, Riverfront Investment Group

HYG's mini-me is the iShares 0–5 Year High Yield Corporate Bond ETF (SHYG). SHYG takes on a little less of the really junky stuff than SJNK, but yields a little less as well, at 3.9 percent. This is a parallel to the HYG/JNK differences. SHYG is also the cheapest on the market, charging 0.30 percent in annual fees. It has $500 million in assets.

Another popular one from the short-term junk category is the Pimco 0–5 Year High Yield Corporate Bond Index ETF (HYS), which has a duration of two years. Many people assume this one is actively managed because it is Pimco, but it isn't. Even though Pimco runs it, it is a passive ETF.

Despite all usage and seeming normality of high-yield bond ETFs, investors shouldn't forget that these bonds are rated junk for a reason and approach this area with extreme caution.

"We've seen people try and come out with more sophisticated strategies in the fixed-income realm, and it's typically just an amount of time before people hurt themselves. Fixed income tends to be an asymmetrical thing—either you get your money back at par or you don't."

Gary Stringer, Stringer Asset Management

Hedge funds love to short junk bond ETFs. Both HYG and JNK made the Top 25 list of net short ETFs. Like the sector ETFs, hedge funds are known to short a high-yield ETF in order to hedge out the market in order to isolate something else that they are betting on. It can get more complicated than that as well.

"We also see hedge funds using ETFs—especially large liquid funds like an HYG or LQD—as a way to make a relative value bet about different segments of the fixed-income market. For example, they may look at current valuations in bonds but also look at CDX versus ETFs and going long or short different pairs or to extract some relative value."

Matthew Tucker, Blackrock

Fallen Angels

Living in the purgatory between investment grade and high yield are fallen angel bonds. These are the bonds that lost their footing and have been downgraded to junk status from investment-grade credit rating.

This bond purgatory is what is tracked by two ETFs, the Market Vectors Fallen Angel High Yield Bond ETF (ANGL) and the SPDR BofA Merrill Lynch Crossover Corporate Bond ETF (CJNK). Some examples of popular companies with bonds that fell from grace include Goldman Sachs, Dell, and Alcoa. Of course, by the time you read this, they may have gotten back up to investment grade.

"The biggest risk-adjusted outperformance that historically has existed in high yield has been at the BB credit rating. The fallen angels ETF focuses exclusively on those bonds."

Justin Sibears, Newfound Research

It is true that the performance of ANGL has been far superior to both investment grade and junk bond ETFs. It is up 32 percent since inception through May 2015, while HYG is up 20 percent during the same stretch, as shown in Figure 9.11.

The performance is partially due to a value factor in bonds that ANGL has tapped into. When these bonds get downgraded from investment grade to high-yield, they tend to get oversold leading up to the downgrade. Much of this selling is from active managers and institutions getting rid of these

FIGURE 9.11 ANGL Outpacing HYG Since Inception

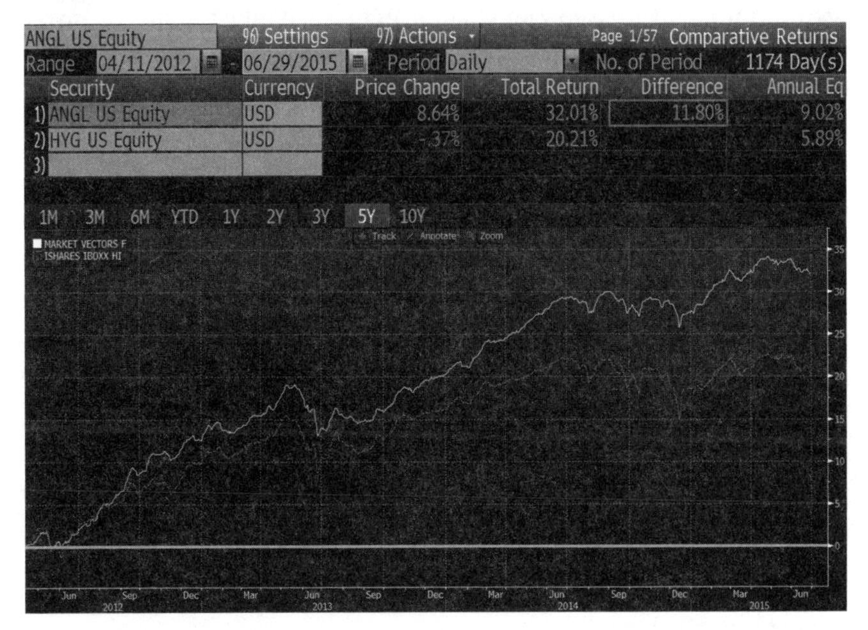

Source: Bloomberg

bonds that they owned to keep up with their investment-grade benchmarks. This means extra selling pressure that may not be justified by the fundamentals. ANGL is picking these bonds after the dust has settled during its monthly rebalance. The hope is that ANGL scoops them up and harvests profits as they move back to those justified levels.

Senior Loans

Senior loans are debt obligations issued by financial institutions that hold legal claim to the borrower's assets above all other debt obligations, hence the "senior." The reason investors like them is that they are basically high-yielding bonds with floating rates, which makes them very popular for investors starved for yield while at the same time nervous about rising interest rates. There are five senior loan ETFs, with over $6 billion in assets with the PowerShares Senior Loan ETF (BKLN) accounting for nearly all of it with $5.7 billion in assets. It also trades about $40 million worth of shares a day.

Before ETFs, an investor would have to use an active bond manager or distressed fund manager to gain senior loan that exposure through an investment vehicle like a hedge fund. It wouldn't have been as direct. However, senior loans are a very illiquid class of securities. They are even less liquid than junk bonds. They may take weeks to settle. There have been concerns that a rush to the exits would cause problems.

Many investors have accepted this risk and are okay with it for the sheer convenience and attributes that a senior loan ETF brings.

"We use BKLN. But we are very sensitive to the liquidity in the underlying. You gotta be quick on your trigger finger and get out because you don't want to be the last one holding the bag on that sort of thing. It's not set-it-and-forget-it."

Gary Stringer, Stringer Asset Management

PowerShares—recognizing the liquidity mismatch and a potential issue—has gone as far as taken out a line of credit for BKLN to help deal with a very bad day and mass redemptions if need be. Some others aren't as much worried about liquidity issues in a fire sale but rather the simple riskiness of holding high-yield bonds.

"I don't need alpha in my fixed income. No, thank you. When the shit hits the fan, I need my bonds to act like bonds. Bank loan ETFs are not going to do it. Asset allocation doesn't work if you turn your bonds into equities. ETFs are allowing a lot of people to do that."

Josh Brown, Ritholtz Wealth Management

Unfortunately for investors, Vanguard doesn't have a product in this category, so the average fee is pretty high. BKLN charges 0.65 percent. The cheapest in the category is the Highland/iBoxx Senior Loan ETF (SNLN), which charges 0.55 percent.

Enhanced Short-Maturity ETFs

These are ultra-short-term aggregate bond ETFs, which are designed to be somewhat spicier version of a money market fund. They generally hold all investment-grade bonds from a variety of issuers with weighted average maturities of around a year or less. It is a growing area and now has $6 billion in assets, as investors like a little bit of yield when they park their cash.

The largest of the bunch is the Pimco Enhanced Short Maturity Active Exchange-Traded Fund (MINT). It is actively managed with 70 percent of its assets in corporate bonds and 16 percent in mortgage bonds; the rest is in U.S. Treasuries and municipal bonds. Half of its holdings are outside the United States, in bonds from South Korea, the United Kingdom, and Switzerland.

That mix of holdings adds up to a yield of 0.80 percent, and the ETF returned 0.60 percent in the past year, after fees. That's not a lot, but it's considerable for something that holds investment-grade debt maturing in less than a year. MINT charges 0.35 percent in annual fees.

Further out on the risk spectrum is Guggenheim Enhanced Short Duration ETF (GSY), which invests in mostly investment-grade corporate and government bonds that mature in less than a year. It charges investors 0.27 percent of assets under management.

"Really, what MINT and GSY are doing is they are recognizing that when you look in the ETF market at the short-term part of the curve, there are limited options. But there are all of these fixed-income instruments that offer more yield that are pretty safe that aren't even a part of any other types of ETFs like commercial paper, repo agreements. Because of these tools, they can get 60 to 100 basis points right now with really minimal risk compared to, say, SHY, which might be 30 basis points and BIL might be zero."

Justin Sibears, Newfound Research

The counterargument for these products is that unlike money market mutual funds, they have trading costs associated with them, albeit only if you are trading in and out of them That can start to add up and cut into the whole point of using it in the first place. Add in the fact that it is not a guaranteed NAV like a money market fund and it starts to look like less of a good deal.

However, it should be noted that the SEC has recently wrote new rules that will require money market funds that invest in nongovernment securities (prime funds) and are aimed at institutions to have a floating share price and impose redemption fees and gates in times of market stress.[3] These new rules, which will be in effect in October 2016, may put ETFs on a more level playing field with money market funds, which could bode well for them, as $1.4 trillion is currently sitting in prime money market funds, according to the Investment Company Institute. However, many institutions may just end up moving to government-only money market funds instead of ETFs. We will see.

Floaters

Floaters is slang for floating-rate notes, which are debt instruments with a variable interest rate tied to a benchmark like the London interbank offered rate (LIBOR). There are only three floating-rate note ETFs, with about $3.5 billion in assets. They don't yield that much, but they also don't have any interest rate risk.

The iShares Floating Rate Note (FLOT) has $3 billion, or 90 percent of the assets in this category. FLOT holds about 300 short-term, investment-grade corporate bonds that are pegged to LIBOR. This floating feature is why they come with low yields. The current 12-month yield of FLOT is 0.65 percent. This may seem like nothing, but it is six times more than the approximately 0.10 percent that money market mutual funds yield.

There's also the iShares Treasury Floating Rate ETF (TFLO), which is floating-rate Treasuries, quite possibly the safest ETF known to man. It has a duration of 0.01 years and is AAA-rated Treasuries. It is pretty small still, at $15 million in assets.

Target Date Bond ETFs

Target date maturity bond ETFs are ETFs that have a maturity date just like an individual bond. They hold a group of similar bonds that all mature in the same year. And when that year comes the ETF liquidates. So unlike, say, AGG or BND, which have perpetual maturities, these all have a defined maturity. This is one of the fastest-growing areas, as there are now 50 of them with over $8 billion in assets.

The purpose of these ETFs is to mimic an individual bond and allow for laddering, which is to divide your fixed-income allocation among bonds with different maturities. As each one matures, you would replace it with a new one equal to the longest maturity in your portfolio. So if rates rise, you will buy the next year out at the new higher rates as you redeem the maturing year at the lower rates. After all the bells and whistles, it may be one of the simplest and most proven ways to cope in a rising rate environment.

"You ladder. Same way your grandfather did it."

Josh Brown, Ritholtz Wealth Management

Normally, in a category you have a couple of ETFs that hog all the inflows and the rest are left for dead. But in this category, the love is spread around.

FIGURE 9.12 Target Date Bond ETFs Sorted by Assets

Ticker	Name	Fund Strategy	Tot Asset (M)	Expense Ratio
1) BSCH US	GUGGENHEIM BULLETSHARES 2017	Corporate	876.269	0.250
2) BSJG US	GUGGENHEIM BULLETSHARES 2016	Corporate	792.719	0.440
3) BSJF US	GUGGENHEIM BULLETSHARES 2015	Corporate	726.394	0.440
4) BSCG US	GUGGENHEIM BULLETSHARES 2016	Corporate	721.966	0.250
5) BSCI US	GUGGENHEIM BULLETSHARES 2018	Corporate	654.997	0.250
6) BSJH US	GUGGENHEIM BULLETSHARES 2017	Corporate	534.213	0.430
7) BSCF US	GUGGENHEIM BULLETSHARES 2015	Corporate	433.116	0.250
8) BSJI US	GUGGENHEIM BULLETSHARES 2018	Corporate	421.020	0.440
9) BSCJ US	GUGGENHEIM BULLETSHARES 2019	Corporate	346.929	0.250
10) BSCK US	GUGGENHEIM BULLETSHARES 2020	Corporate	323.801	0.250
11) BSCM US	GUGGENHEIM BULLET 2022 CORP	Corporate	170.193	0.250
12) IBCC US	ISHARES IBONDS MAR 2018 CORP	Corporate	167.831	0.100
13) BSCL US	GUGGENHEIM BULLET 2021 COR	Corporate	165.509	0.240
14) IBMF US	ISHARES IBONDS SEP 2017 AMT-	Municipals	156.225	0.180

Source: Bloomberg

There are no target date maturity bond ETFs over $1 billion, but there are a dozen or so over $100 million, as seen in Figure 9.12. This is because these are typically used as a set, with each one representing one rung on the ladder.

This is one way to protect against rising rates because you are always in a process of buying bonds at new interest rates as the old ones mature. Guggenheim leads the category, as seen in Figure 9.12, with a huge product line of these, which they call "BulletShares." For example, the Guggenheim BulletShares 2018 Corporate Bond ETF (BSCI) holds 285 investment-grade corporate bonds and will mature in 2018; the Guggenheim BulletShares High Yield 2022 holds high-yield corporate bonds that mature in 2022.

iShares also has a bunch of these it dubs "iBonds" like the iShares iBonds Sep 2016 AMT-Free Muni Bond ETF (IBMF), which holds 614 investment-grade U.S. municipal bonds maturing between the end of May and the end of August. All of the assets will then be distributed on August 31, 2017. iShares has two dozen of these, mostly munis and corporates, spanning all the way into 2023. They have seen some institutional interest in these products.

"We've had a number of institutional investors into our term maturity bond ETFs. They are typically investors that have a liability of some sort. So if you have an institution that is trying to hedge a liability, this can be a very efficient way of doing it. Before, they would have had to go out and hire an asset manager to build a separate account that created a similar hedge."

Matthew Tucker, Blackrock

The liquidity in these ETFs is so-so at best. But that is because these aren't really something you trade. You could, but normally these are used as part of a laddering strategy for the long term. Institutions may not love the liquidity, but the costs are institutional level. The iShares products are all 0.18 percent, and the Guggenheim ones charge 0.25 percent.

Interest Rate–Hedged ETFs

Remember when I referred to currency hedged ETFs as "central bank surfboards"? Well, you could argue that interest rate–hedged ETFs are central bank lifeboats. As currency-hedged ETFs are designed to let you surf central bank liquidity waves, these products are designed to keep you afloat in an era where central banks are raising interest rates.

Interest rate–hedged ETFs, like their currency-hedged cousins, serve up something investors want (bond exposure) while eliminating something they don't (rate risk). They effectively let you keep your bond exposure and yield while not having to worry about rising rates. They come in many flavors, such as U.S. investment grade, high yield, and even emerging markets.

Institutions listed these types of ETFs as the top area where they expect to see increased usage among fixed-income asset classes, as seen in Figure 9.13. That is fascinating considering they have only a few hundred million in assets. This tells me they are going to explode in size as soon as rates start rising.

They do this essentially by shorting Treasury futures that parallel the maturities of the bond in the portfolio. By betting against Treasuries, the ETF gets a lift when the prices of those bonds fall, which is what happens when rates rise. That's how the risk of rising rates is dampened.

However, the catch is when you short Treasury futures, you are responsible for the coupon payment. So all of these products have an embedded cost that drags on performance. Right now, it is roughly 2 to 3 percent per year, but would go up with rates. Now if rates were to go down and there were also concerns about bond defaults, these ETFs would be hit from both sides.

This kind of rate hedging is nothing new for institutions. These ETFs essentially isolate credit risk and allow you a bet on credit spreads between treasuries and corporate bonds. If spreads widen, these ETFs suffer; if they narrow, you profit. What is new is the packaging of it in a convenient, low-cost product that trades like a stock. These products are under three years old and, like currency-hedged ETFs, were built for a certain environment. We have yet to see this environment form for any extended period, though.

FIGURE 9.13 Greenwich Survey Shows Investors Most Concerned with Interest Rates

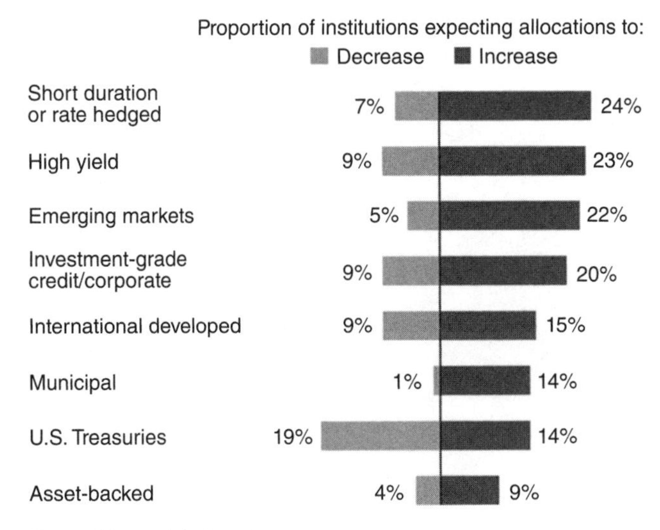

Source: Greenwich Associates

However, we have seen small windows of time when rates rose and each time they do indeed outperform. Looking at the month of February 2014, yields on the 10-year rose from 1.6 percent to 2 percent, a 25 percent jump. During that stretch, all of the rate-hedged ETFs outperformed their unhedged brothers, as exemplified in Figure 9.14. If this kind of performance persists over a long period, there is no doubt they will gather assets.

There are many to choose from. ProShares launched the first ones. The ProShares Investment Grade-Interest Rate Hedged ETF (IGHG) and the ProShares High Yield-Interest Rate Hedged ETF (HYHG) track corporate bonds while shorting Treasury futures with matching durations. ProShares are leaders in inverse ETF products, so it is natural they launched first.

iShares followed suit and came out with rate-hedged versions of their popular bond products. So if you own HYG and you want to hedge, they have iShares Interest Rate Hedged High Yield Bond ETF (HYGH), which simply holds HYG and then shorts Treasury futures. So you retain the exact exposure and yield you had with HYG. Same with LQD when it comes to the iShares Interest Rate Hedged Corporate Bond ETF (LQDH). Since HYG and LQD have a combined $35 billion in assets, it isn't hard to imagine some of that moving over to these products when rates rise.

FIGURE 9.14 LQDH Beat LQD in February 2015 When Interest Rates Rose

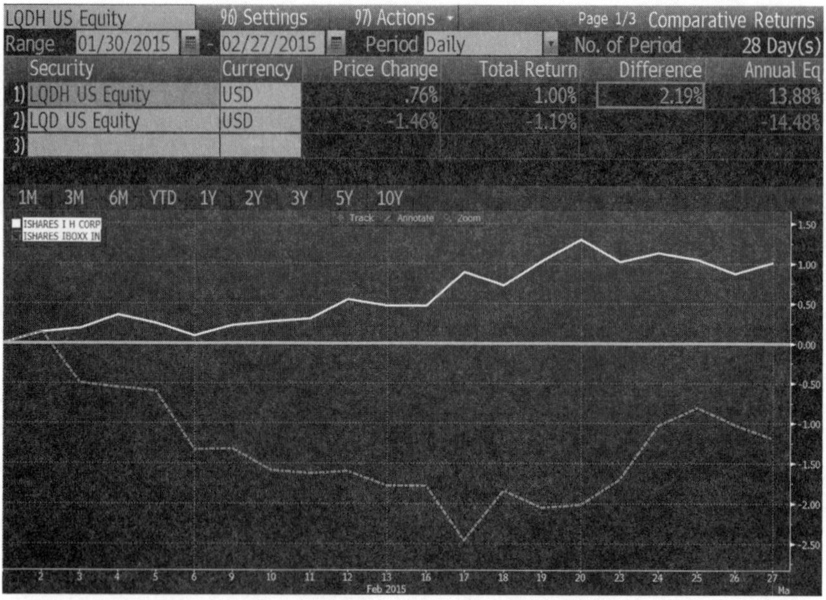
LQDH US Equity
96) Settings
97) Actions
Page 1/3 Comparative Returns
Range 01/30/2015 - 02/27/2015
Period Daily
No. of Period 28 Day(s)
Security
Currency
Price Change
Total Return
Difference
Annual Eq
1) LQDH US Equity USD .76% 1.00% 2.19% 13.88%
2) LQD US Equity USD -1.46% -1.19% -14.48%
3)
1M 3M 6M YTD 1Y 2Y 3Y 5Y 10Y
Feb 2015

Source: Bloomberg

WisdomTree also has some products including the WisdomTree BofA Merrill Lynch High Yield Bond Negative Duration Fund Fund (HYND). This one takes it a step further by shorting more long-dated Treasuries to achieve a duration in the ballpark of -7 years. The reason for this is, as a portfolio manager, if you want to hedge your rate risk, while actually bringing down the duration of your overall portfolio of bonds, this will do it.

As shown in Figure 9.15, many of the issuers of interest rate–hedged ETFs are the top issuers of currency-hedged ETFs. They are ready and waiting for the same type of investor looking to take a chance and capture a trend, although maybe not as big a deal as currency-hedged ETFs due to the cost of the hedge and the fact that they have more competition.

"Interest rate hedging is just one of many tools that investors have for managing interest rate risk. So in an environment where we see short term rates rise and investors concerned about the impact of rising rates, I think we'll see investors using a number of different types of ETFs. Some will use interest rate–hedged ETFs, some will use floating-rate ETFs, some will use term-maturity funds, and some will use short-maturity funds."

Matthew Tucker, Blackrock

FIGURE 9.15 A Small Army of Rate-Hedged ETFs Is Waiting for Their Moment in the Sun

Ticker	Name	Fund Strategy	Tot Asset (M)	Expense Ratio
1) IGHG US	PROSHARES IG HEDGED	Corporate	163.639	0.300
2) HYHG US	PROSHARES HIGH YIELD INTERES	Corporate	136.654	0.500
3) HYGH US	ISHARES INT RATE HEDG HY ETF	Corporate	105.253	0.550
4) AGZD US	WISDOMTREE BARC US AGG BD ZE	Aggregate	58.358	0.230
5) AGND US	WISDOMTREE BARC US AGG BD NE	Aggregate	36.279	0.280
6) LQDH US	ISHARES INT HEDG CORP BD ETF	Corporate	23.588	0.250
7) HYZD US	WISDOMTREE BOFA ML HY BD ZER	Corporate	14.320	0.430
8) HYND US	WISDOMTREE BOFA ML HY BD NEG	Corporate	10.894	0.480
9) HYIH US	DBX HY CORP BOND INT RATE HD	Corporate	9.651	0.450
10) EMSH US	PROSHARES SHORT TERM USD EME	Aggregate	7.614	0.500
11) EMIH US	DBX EM BOND INT RATE HEDGED	Government	6.164	0.500
12) IGIH US	DBX INV GRADE BOND INT RATE	Corporate	4.876	0.250

Source: Bloomberg

Multi-Asset Income ETFs

Multi-Asset income ETFs merge fixed income along with other high-yielding areas such as MLPs and dividend-paying stocks into on one ETF. These ETFs are like choosing "all of the above" for yield. Not surprisingly, in a low-rate environment, this area is quietly growing in size and number of ETFs and is now over $2 billion in assets.

Here is a look at two of the best ones in terms of yield, return, asset growth, and true diversification across asset classes.

On example is the First Trust Multi-Asset Diversified Income Index Fund (MDIV), which is one of the broadest of the bunch with well-rounded and nearly equal-weighted exposure to dividend-paying stocks (25 percent), master limited partnerships (MLPs; 20 percent), preferred securities (20 percent), real estate investment trusts (REITs; 20 percent) and high-yield bonds (15 percent). In addition, its REIT exposure is half made up of mortgage REITs, which are some of the most unknown yet high-yielding securities around. As of this writing, MDIV yields around 5 to 6 percent.

Another example in this category is the iShares Morningstar Multi-Asset Income Index ETF (IYLD), which is broad in scope as well but tilted more to the bond side, with 60 percent of its allocation going to fixed income. It is also global in scope, allocating 30 percent overseas. The full breakdown is high-yield bonds (20 percent), emerging-market bonds (20 percent), Treasury bonds (15 percent), mortgage REITs (15 percent), dividend-paying stocks (20 percent), corporate bonds (5 percent), and international REITs (5 percent).

IYLD achieves its exposure by investing in several other iShares ETFs. It charges an expense ratio of 0.60 percent, which is all-inclusive of the fees of the underlying ETFs. IYLD has grown assets by 20 percent in the past year and now sits at $250 million.

While those two examples, there are about 10 multiasset income ETFs on the market. Some other notables include the Guggenheim Multi-Asset Income ETF (CVY), the SPDR SSgA Income Allocation (INKM), and the Arrow Dow Jones Global Yield ETF (NYSEArca: GYLD)

International Debt

ETFs allow access to bonds all over the world in one click. And this is typically an underweighted area of a portfolio. These ETFs may be some of the most attractive to an institution as portfolio completion tools as it is a fairly exotic area where they may have any manager but want the exposure.

Let's take a look at the most popular options.

International Developed-Market Debt

There are not many international developed-market debt ETFs out there. It is definitely a growing area. By far, the most popular ETF in this area is Vanguard Total International Bond ETF (BNDX). One of the most successful new ETFs of the past few years, accumulating over $3 billion in just over two years on the market, it already towers above the rest. It looks a lot like any international developed-market equity ETF in terms of country allocations, with the majority of it in investment grade government and corporate bonds in Europe and Japan. BNDX is 75 percent government debt and 25 percent corporate debt. It also hedges the currency out.

The second biggest is the SPDR Barclays International Treasury Bond ETF (BWX), which is a Treasury-only play and has nearly 25 percent Japan. It isn't currency hedged, so it will be much more affected by moves in the currency markets than BNDX.

Emerging-Market Debt

There are 17 emerging-market debt ETFs with a respectable $10 billion in assets. These are the kind of ETFs that may appeal to an institution that needs to complete a portfolio or complement an active manager. The big dilemma in this category is the currency. You can buy your emerging-market debt issued in U.S. dollars or the local currency.

The two biggest in the category are U.S. dollar denominated. The iShares J.P. Morgan USD Emerging Markets Bond ETF (EMB) trades a decent $78 million a day and charges 0.40 percent. Meanwhile, PowerShares Emerging Markets Sovereign Debt Portfolio (PCY) trades about $21 million a day and charges 0.50 percent. The big difference between them is that EMB is a little heavier in Asia and much lighter in Eastern Europe.

The country allocations can be concentrated or wide-reaching like PCY as shown in Figure 9.16,. Digging through the specific country allocations will be crucial for any investor considering this category.

"We went and did the PCY because we liked the structure and the country exposure. Many of them are made up in different ways and you end up getting exposures to countries. And at the time, that one in particular had country exposure that we favored."

Gary Stringer, Stringer Asset Management

The local currency versions are the path less traveled, as they have only about $2 billion in total assets compared to about $10 billion for the U.S. dollar versions. They are a real evolution in ETFs, as getting this kind of

FIGURE 9.16 A Partial Look at PCY's Country Allocation Shows It Going to All Corners of the World to Fetch Bonds

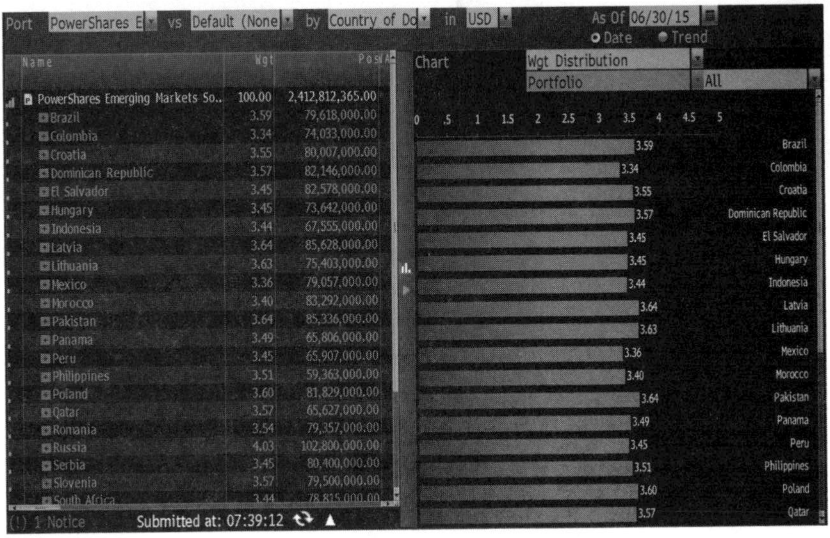
Port PowerShares E vs Default (None by Country of Do in USD
As Of 06/30/15
Date Trend
Name Wgt Pos
Chart
Wgt Distribution
Portfolio
All
PowerShares Emerging Markets So.. 100.00 2,412,812,365.00
Brazil 3.59 79,618,000.00
Colombia 3.34 74,033,000.00
Croatia 3.55 80,007,000.00
Dominican Republic 3.57 82,146,000.00
El Salvador 3.45 82,578,000.00
Hungary 3.45 73,642,000.00
Indonesia 3.44 67,555,000.00
Latvia 3.64 85,628,000.00
Lithuania 3.63 75,403,000.00
Mexico 3.36 79,057,000.00
Morocco 3.40 83,292,000.00
Pakistan 3.64 85,336,000.00
Panama 3.49 65,806,000.00
Peru 3.45 65,907,000.00
Philippines 3.51 59,363,000.00
Poland 3.60 81,829,000.00
Qatar 3.57 65,627,000.00
Romania 3.54 79,357,000.00
Russia 4.03 102,800,000.00
Serbia 3.45 80,400,000.00
Slovenia 3.57 79,500,000.00
South Africa 3.44 78,815,000.00
0 .5 1 1.5 2 2.5 3 3.5 4 4.5 5
3.59 Brazil
3.34 Colombia
3.55 Croatia
3.57 Dominican Republic
3.45 El Salvador
3.45 Hungary
3.44 Indonesia
3.64 Latvia
3.63 Lithuania
3.36 Mexico
3.40 Morocco
3.64 Pakistan
3.49 Panama
3.45 Peru
3.51 Philippines
3.60 Poland
3.57 Qatar
(!) 1 Notice
Submitted at: 07:39:12

Source: Bloomberg

exposure was very difficult before ETFs came along. The local versions also tend to yield a bit more as well.

The most popular one is the Market Vectors Emerging Markets Local Currency Bond ETF (EMLC) and the actively managed WisdomTree Emerging Markets Local Debt Fund (ELD). Both are lightly traded but competitive cost-wise, with EMLC charging 0.47 percent versus 0.55 percent for ELD.

"People are viewing the U.S. dollar–denominated one to be safer because it doesn't have the currency. The local currency version appears riskier. But the local currency version of the bond is less risky for the issuer. If I'm an EM country and I issue a bond in my local currency, I know I can always pay it because I can just print more money. The U.S. dollar versions have the problem where if all of a sudden one of these EM countries' currency collapses, to make my dollar-denominated interest payments it might be 4 times or 10 times more expensive because they don't have that natural hedge, so there is an additional credit risk."

Justin Sibears, Newfound Research

Notes

1. Novick, Barbara, Richie Prager, Supurna VedBrat, Kashif Riaz, Joanne Medero, and Alexis Rosenblum, "Corporate Bond Market Structure: The Time for Reform Is Now," Blackrock white paper, September 2014.
2. Tucker, Matt, and Stephen Laipply, "Fixed Income ETFs and the Corporate Bond Liquidity Challenge," Blackrock white paper, 2014.
3. Stein, Charles, "Blackrock Plans Money Fund Changes to Meet New SEC Regulations." Bloomberg, April 6, 2015; www.bloomberg.com/news/articles/2015–04–06/blackrock-plans-money-fund-changes-to-meet-new-sec-regulations.

CHAPTER 10

Alternatives

Alternatives is a broad term that includes hedge funds, private equity, commodities, real assets, and real estate. Over the past 10 years, more and more institutions have turned to alternatives as a way to diversify their portfolio and pick up extra return. Perhaps inspired by the "Yale Model," which is an alternatives-heavy strategy that has produced superior returns for Yale, many institutions have beefed up their alternatives exposure as well. Some institutional funds now have over 50 percent of their portfolio in alternative investments. Pension funds as a group have gone from having an 11 percent allocation to alternatives in 2006 to a 23 percent allocation in 2012.[1]

It is highly debatable whether using alternatives this heavily in a portfolio really works for everyone or is worth the costs. Some have argued that the Yale Model and its highly promoted success has been a curse to the entire institutional investing world since it requires spending billions on hedge funds and consultants and many times doesn't produce the returns that Yale has. That's a worthy debate, but one beyond the scope of this book.

Although I will note that our little "Buffett Special" ETF portfolio beats the average endowment and pension fund returns over the past ten years just like Uncle Warren said it would. And, for a fraction of the cost of an alternative-heavy institutional portfolio. Regardless, the fact is institutions love their alternatives and so we will look at some ETFs trying to serve up this exposure.

The two areas within alternatives where exchange-traded funds (ETFs) have the most value-add are hedge fund ETFs and commodity ETFs. They can actually compete with what an institution is currently using.

For real estate and private equity these are typically private investments. While there are ETFs tracking these areas, such as the PowerShares Global Listed Private Equity Portfolio (PSP), the Vanguard REIT ETF (VNQ), or the Guggenheim Timber Index ETF (CUT), they hold a basket of stocks of companies in that area. They are much more an equity-sector play that behaves much more like the stock market than a real alternative investment. However, they can be used as transition tools to equitize cash if an institution is waiting for the private investment to get started since many private investments can take a while to get into.

With that said, let's dive into hedge funds and commodities.

Hedge Fund Strategies (aka "Liquid Alts")

Most people think hedge funds aim to shoot the lights out and return a zillion percent. The funds are routinely mocked by the media's for not beating the Standard & Poor's (S&P) 500 Index during a bull market.[2] This is not what the vast majority of hedge funds do. The media's misunderstanding of this was in full display in 2014 with multiple stories that gleefully pointed out how the average hedge fund returned just 3 percent. That's like saying the average animal can run at a speed of just seven miles per hour. It makes no sense to lump together wildly different species when calculating an average. In fact, if you lumped together all ETFs, their average return for 2014 was 2.8 percent—less than hedge funds!

The truth is most hedge funds are trying to provide positive returns with limited risk regardless of market conditions—so-called absolute return. They do this by hedging out risks they don't want and isolating risks they do want. This is why they do not move in tandem with other asset classes, such as equity and fixed income.

"With alternatives, the potential return is higher than what we might get from traditional fixed income, but probably less than we'd expect from traditional equity, but with less volatility and with a low correlation to both."

Gary Stringer, Stringer Asset Management

I have a few theories on why the media misses the boat on hedge funds: they don't understand risk metrics such as standard deviation and fail to take that into consideration when comparing them to equity indexes. Or, they understand and simply find it too irresistible to take a shot at them. To the media, hedge funds are like the Republicans of the financial industry. A reporter will receive many compliments and retweets on Twitter for a take-down of hedge funds, even if it is not an accurate portrayal.

Not saying that hedge funds deserve our sympathy, believe me, but the truth is hedge funds are designed to not move in lockstep with the broad markets. That is why they are called a "hedge" fund. Institutions buy them for positive risk-adjusted returns and for lack of correlation to stocks and bonds.

So while I will defend hedge funds from being miscast in the media, where they do deserve to be dinged is on their fees, lock-up periods, and capital gains distributions. While institutions love the noncorrelated returns hedge funds can provide, they would like to see improvements.

According to a recent study, 68 percent of institutional investors want to see an improvement in the level of management fees of hedge funds.[3] This is one reason why the California Public Employees' Retirement System (CalPERS) decided to eliminate all of its hedge fund investments in 2014 because it was not happy with the performance and the fees.[4]

Enter liquid alt ETFs. The *liquid* refers to the ability of investors to get in and out of the fund whenever they want, as opposed to hedge funds, which use lock-up periods and redemptions schedules. In some cases, lockups can contain tranches that take years to get your money out completely. The *alternative* refers to the fact that the strategies march to the beat of their own drummer and provide low correlation to the stock and bond markets.

When it comes to liquid alt ETFs, you aren't getting the real thing, but you are getting a generic, robotic version of the real thing for less than half the cost and with better tax efficiency. While the total assets are a mere $2 billion, the issuers of such products have high hopes for these ETFs in the future.

"The hedge fund market has evolved a lot, and it has matured and it looks a lot like the mutual fund market now. In essence how many people are actually getting access to those tremendous alpha drivers on a consistent basis? The answer is very few. So now the thought is evolving to getting the right exposure and then analyzing the fees, both management fees and embedded fees."

Adam Patti, IndexIQ

Because of the high fees, the hedge fund has to return a bit more to overcome their management fees and other hidden fees as a result of turnover. If liquid alts take root with institutions as a replacement for hedge funds, the days of billion-dollar salaries and glorious compensations for hedge fund managers that seem to repulse most of society will go away. Pensions and other institutions firing their hedge fund managers—not political rhetoric—will be how to end the days where the top 25 highest-earning hedge fund managers make more than all the kindergarten teachers in the country combined.[5]

But don't hold your breath. Institutions probably aren't going to be using liquid alts anytime soon. The ones I spoke with weren't really moved by the concept of liquid alts at all, regardless of the return stream and cost savings.

"I think the whole concept of hedge fund replication is crazy. Especially the way it's done. When you look at all the managers and net all their positions, you just get oatmeal. Just get mush. And it's just useless. There are certain strategies that are more open to replication. Merger arbitrage, for example, can be replicated. But so many strategies really rely on judgment and judgment can't be quantifiably modeled."

Mark Yusko, Morgan Creek Capital Management

At least for now, institutions will probably never use liquid alts, since they can afford the real thing. And even if an institution may have been burned by an overpriced hedge fund, there could be other factors at play to keep them coming back for more—such as ego.

"It will be a while before we start seeing liquid alts factor into institutional portfolio. There is a prestige factor with hedge funds that I think you don't get on the liquid alt side, right or wrong. I think it is an ego-driven thing where it is going to be hard for people to admit they can't pick the best hedge funds. Maybe it will take years of bad performance and if they don't lower fees a bit."

Ben Carlson, Ritholtz Wealth Management

Intuitional managers and/or consultant may feel they need to pick an active manager, not some generic ETF, because that is their job. Many of them have the time and resources to do it as well. But they should rest easy because picking a liquid alt ETF or mutual fund is no walk in the park. As an ETF analyst, I assure you, this is one of the most complicated areas of ETF Land.

Due diligence is needed here more than most places. Nearly all of these liquid alt ETFs get my PG-13 rating mostly due to the sheer complexity of some of the strategies. Plus, some have embedded costs depending on the strategy that can include the cost of shorting and roll costs. Although one thing most of them are not is risky in terms of volatility. Despite their complexities, they are mostly half as volatile as the S&P 500 Index, as seen in Table 10.1.

TABLE 10.1 Table of Liquid Alts Compared to SPY

Name	Ticker	Assets ($million)	2014 Ret	Strd Dev	Corr to SPX
SPDR S&P 500 Trust (SPY)	SPY	171740	13%	9%	1.0
IndexIQ ETF Trust—IQ Hedge M	QAI US	1036	2%	5%	0.76
WisdomTree Managed Futures Str	WDTI US	225	5%	5%	-0.05
IQ Merger Arbitrage ETF	MNA US	138	5%	3%	0.35
ProShares RAFI Long/ Short	RALS US	47	0%	4%	0.15
ProShares Hedge Replication ET	HDG US	40	1%	3%	0.84
IQ Hedge Macro Tracker ETF	MCRO US	20	–1%	3%	0.47
PowerShares Multi-Strategy Alt	LALT US	16	–3%	5%	0.14
ProShares Merger ETF	MRGR US	6	–2%	3%	0.07

Source: Bloomberg

Let's jump into some examples of ETFs using the different strategies. Given the depth of this category contrasted with the minuscule amount of assets. Let's check out a few examples.

Multi-Strategy

Multi-Strategy is self-explanatory as it combines many strategies together—the hedge fund equivalent of the color gray. This is the strategy that Mark Yusko was describing above as "oatmeal." It isn't an actual hedge fund strategy per se like long/short or event-driven, but rather a combination of many of them. The ETFs in this category study the risk and returns of a multi-strategy hedge fund index and then replicate the return stream using other ETFs. One thing to point out is that multi-strategy ETFs are all based on historical performance, so if there are big shifts in the market, the ETF's tracking difference can increase.

The largest of the bunch with about half of the assets of the group is the IQ Hedge Multi-Strategy Tracker (QAI), which has $1 billion. QAI replicates its index using a mathematical model that analyzes hedge fund performance

FIGURE 10.1 QAI Holds Other ETFs to Replicate the Risk and Return of a Multi-Strategy Hedge Fund

Name	Ticker	Wgt
IQ HEDGE MULTI-STRATEGY TRACKER ETF...		100.00
VANGUARD SHORT-TERM BOND ETF	BSV US	25.08
VANGUARD TOTAL BOND MARKET	BND US	18.97
ISHARES 1-3 YEAR TREASURY BO	SHY US	14.42
MARKET VECTORS EMERGING MARK	EMLC US	4.74
ISHARES CORE U.S. AGGREGATE	AGG US	4.64
CURRENCYSHARES EURO TRUST	FXE US	4.43
ISHARES SHORT TREASURY BOND	SHV US	3.80
SPDR S&P EMERGING MKTS SMALL	EWX US	2.68
SPDR BARCLAYS 1-3 MONTH T-BI	BIL US	2.24
WISDOMTREE EMRG MKTS DEBT	ELD US	2.13
VANGUARD SMALL-CAP VALUE ETF	VBR US	2.01
POWERSHARES DB G10 CURR HARV	DBV US	2.00
ISHARES MSCI EAFE SMALL-CAP	SCZ US	1.99
ISHARES CHINA LARGE-CAP ETF	FXI US	1.79
CURRENCYSHARES JAPANESE YEN	FXY US	1.41
VANGUARD REIT ETF	VNQ US	1.37
VANGUARD FTSE EUROPE ETF	VGK US	1.14
ISHARES MSCI EMU ETF	EZU US	0.80
SPDR BARCLAYS AGGREGATE BOND	LAG US	0.70
ISHARES MSCI CHINA ETF	MCHI US	0.55

Source: Bloomberg

patterns to identify the asset classes being used by hedge funds. The ETF then invests in liquid proxies—broad-based ETFs—for those asset classes to get similar performance. Figure 10.1 shows the ETFs held by QAI.

It has returned 28 percent since its launch in 2009 and through June 2015 and with about half the volatility of the S&P 500. Not bad if that's the kind of stability you are looking for. One note is that QAI's correlation to the stock market is 76 percent, which is probably much higher what most people would want out of an alternative. It also charges 0.94 percent of assets annually—low compared to a real hedge fund, but astronomical compared to the average ETF.

Managed Futures

This strategy goes long and short futures contracts in areas like commodities, currencies, and bonds. The term *managed futures* refers to a 30-year-old industry made up of professional money managers known as *commodity trading advisors* or CTAs.

The big one in the category is the actively-managed WisdomTree Managed Funds (WDTI), which has $156 million in assets. Unlike QAI which replicates a return stream, WDTI directly implements this hedge fund strategy as if it were a hedge fund manager. The ETF looks for momentum signals in the markets to determine its long and short positions in futures contracts connected to commodities, currencies and interest rates. WDTI lives up to the "alternative" label as it exhibits a correlation of basically 0 percent to the S&P 500 and has about one-third the volatility. WDTI charges 0.95 percent and is the second largest of the group with $206 million.

WDTI is also one of the few ETFs that hold futures that gets normal equity-like tax treatment because it invests in a Cayman Islands subsidiary that holds the futures. Clever trick, but why not? Investors avoid the tax treatment that comes with holding futures contracts. This is something we've seen more and more of with the newer commodities ETFs.

Merger Arbitrage

Merger arbitrage involves buying the stock of a company being acquired while selling short the stock of the acquirer at the same time. Because deals can fall through, the stock of the target will initially trade for slightly less than the deal's closing price. Arbitrageurs hope to capitalize on a valuation gap when the target's price rises as the deal moves closer to being done.

Like WDTI, these ETFs directly implement the hedge fund strategy as if they were merger arb managers. The largest in the space is the $100 million IQ Merger Arbitrage ETF (MNA). MNA is close to a real merger arb fund but has two important differences. While it goes long target companies, it doesn't short the acquirer stock, but rather it partially hedges using different stock market indices.

Note the word *partially* because that is the second difference. This product, while useful, could easily surprise you if you were expecting straight merger arbitrage. The partial hedging gives MNA more long stock exposure and thus double the volatility of a normal merger arbitrage hedge fund, not to mention double the correlation to the S&P 500 Index.

This extra volatility and correlation is a big part of why it's up 16 percent in the past three years, compared with 10 percent for the HFR Merger Arbitrage Index, as shown in Figure 10.2. This chart will have the opposite look if the market has sustained negative performance. Some investors are totally aware of this and like that MNA doesn't do true merger arbitrage.

FIGURE 10.2 The HFR Merger Arbitrage Index Getting Beat by Riskier MNA

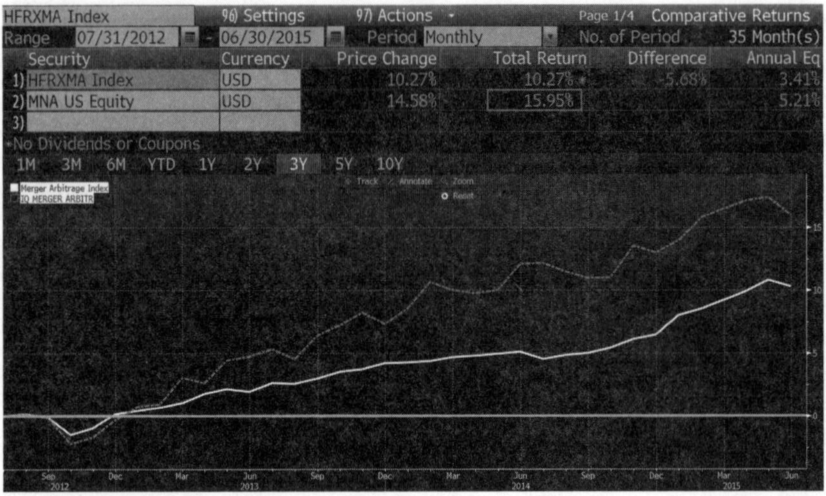

Source: Bloomberg

"We like MNA because it does lean towards some directionality. It gives it a little more upside. Especially if we are using it as an alternative equity allocation."

Gary Stringer, Stringer Asset Management

Now for investors who want that more true merger arb strategy, there is the ProShares Merger ETF (MRGR). MRGR shorts the acquiring companies directly in an effort to be more precise in shorting the alpha in the deal. It also rebalances on a daily basis instead of monthly in hopes of getting to the target companies faster after the deals are announced. They also hedge the currency exposure for the international portion of the portfolio. And if you haven't guessed it, MRGR's volatility is much lower than MNA's. It is much closer to what the HFR Merger Arbitrage Index is.

This is a great example of how two ETFs with the same name can have such subtle but important differences that cannot be seen from the name or even the descriptive information on various financial web sites. Liquid alts are definitely one area where reading the dreaded prospectus is a good idea.

That was just a taste of some of the liquid alt ETFs. There are ETFs covering other hedge fund strategies such as long/short and event driven. And there's going to be a lot of product innovation over the next couple of years. Plus, we may see actual hedge funds and big Wall Street banks start launching liquid alt ETFs. These big fish could turn this small pond into a hot area.

> *"I think (liquid alts) has potential. I think the burden is on us to figure which hedge fund strategies are really beta strategies that people are charging alpha fees for. I would say private equity and liquid alts are the last two havens for the asset management world that the ETF industry hasn't figured out a way quite how to penetrate yet."*
>
> Luciano Siracusano, Wisdom Tree Asset Management

Commodity ETFs

There are over 150 commodity ETFs on the market with about $61 billion in assets. They break down into these categories: precious metals, agriculture, energy, industrial metals, livestock, and broad based.

Another important way commodity ETFs are broken down is by how they replicate the commodity. On one side you have "physically backed" commodity ETFs that physically store the commodity in a storage facility such as gold and silver. On the other side is "futures-based" commodity ETFs, which use futures contracts to obtain the exposure such as with oil and corn. That's how we will break them down in this section.

Physically Backed Commodity ETFs

Investors overwhelmingly prefer the physically backed commodity ETFs. While there are only 11 that are physically backed, they have $40 billion and account for 65 percent of the assets. Physically backed commodity ETFs are also more straightforward and safer for investors not to mention better at tracking the actual "spot" price of the commodity. Let's start with Gold, since that is where the majority of the assets are.

Gold

Gold and religion have a lot in common. Both are thousands of years old. Both provide a light in times of crisis when darkness descends but are easy to forget about when everything is looking up. And both gold and religion spark emotion and passion from believers and skeptics. In fact, much of the gold commentary can be divided into two camps: gold bugs that own gold and practically worship the metal and gold haters who think it is a lousy investment and seem to find the very concept of gold offensive. In this way, it's kind of like the debate between Christians and atheists or Republicans and Democrats with no one ever convincing the other side of anything.

"Everybody on the planet knows what gold is. That is both a blessing and a challenge at the same time. It's a blessing that you are selling and marketing a product that everybody knows what it is. But it can be a challenge because everybody has an opinion on gold and its value regardless of how much they understand about gold."

William Rhind, World Gold Council

And when all hell breaks loose and the you-know-what hits the fan gold, like religion, tends to be a light in the dark. At least there is something investors can turn to that has thousands of years of history and human value behind it. That is why saying gold is "just a rock" is like saying a church is "just a building."

But when it comes to actual portfolio management, it could be best to be more of a gold agnostic. Because whether you love gold or hate, you cannot deny its attractive 0 percent correlation to stocks and low 20 percent correlation to bonds. In a social-media, 24-hour-news world with increasing amounts of groupthink driving up correlations, zero correlation is a valuable attribute for portfolio diversification no matter how you slice it.

Besides its role as a crisis hedge and diversifier, the fact is many people around the world buy gold, especially those in the emerging markets entering the middle class for the first time. The long-term drivers of gold aren't speculators or central banks; it is consumers around the world. Still, many investors simply say no to gold.

"Gold is not additive to returns. It doesn't hedge against inflation. It is noncorrelated sometimes. It is prone to tremendous boom and bust cycles. I've spent most of the past five years selling people out of it."

Josh Brown, Ritholtz Wealth Management

Whether you are a gold lover or hater or fall in between, there are now a slew of gold ETFs that have made gold easier to own than ever before. This is one area where even institutions prefer using the ETF in many cases compared to other options. Let's look at some of the offerings.

"The GLD"

The most popular choice in this category by far is the legendary SPDR Gold Shares (GLD), which launched in 2004. GLD accounts for 80 percent of the gold ETF market in the United States. It is massively popular with between 750,000 and 1 million holders, according to the World Gold Council.

The SPDR Gold Trust (GLD) is designed to track a tenth of an ounce of gold. It does this by literally storing gold bars in a vault in London. GLD holders range from retail to hedge funds to pensions and insurance companies, as seen in Figure 10.3. Notice that nearly all of them have held it for multiple years as well.

GLD has had an up-and-down life so far. When it launched in November 2004, GLD was the very first commodity ETF. It kicked open the door for other kinds of ETFs outside of the standard stock and bond asset classes. There are now 154 commodity ETFs. GLD became part of an exclusive club of ETFs that are so popular—so accepted as the standard in their area—that traders put a "the" before the ticker. The SPY. The EEM. The GLD.

It still holds the all-time ETF record for the fastest to get to $1 billion. It did it in just three days. This DiMaggio-esque record will probably never be broken. The next fastest was when Bill Gross's Pimco Total Return ETF (BOND) reached the $1 billion mark in two and a half months.

While GLD recently hit the decade mark, it isn't half the exchange-traded fund it used to be. Assets stand at $27 billion today, down from $76.7 billion

FIGURE 10.3 Institutional Holders of GLD

	Portfolio Name	Mkt Val	% Portfolio	% Out	Est. Holding I	Inst Type
						•[Select Multiple]
1.	PAULSON & CO	1.15BLN	5.923	4.29	6.50	Hedge Fund Manager
2.	FIRST EAGLE INVESTMENT MGMT LLC	463.87MLN	1.122	1.74	8.50	Hedge Fund Manager
3.	D E SHAW & CO	227.66MLN	0.451	0.85	0.50	Hedge Fund Manager
4.	STEADFAST CAPITAL MANAGEMENT LP	171.29MLN	2.549	0.64	0.75	Hedge Fund Manager
5.	ADAGE CAPITAL PARTNERS GP LLC	95.18MLN	0.236	0.36	1.75	Hedge Fund Manager
6.	IVORY INVESTMENT MANAGEMENT LP	67.72MLN	1.934	0.25	1.50	Hedge Fund Manager
7.	COMMONWEALTH OF PENNSYLVANIA PUBLIC SCHOOL	57.62MLN	1.046	0.22	8.25	Pension Fund
8.	WS MANAGEMENT LLP	53.97MLN	2.285	0.20	8.50	Hedge Fund Manager
9.	MOON CAPITAL MANAGEMENT LP	36.28MLN	21.008	0.14	7.00	Hedge Fund Manager
10.	TEACHER RETIREMENT SYSTEM OF TEXAS	36.26MLN	0.286	0.14	6.00	Pension Fund
11.	BLUEMOUNTAIN CAPITAL MANAGEMENT LLC	34.55MLN	0.787	0.13	1.75	Hedge Fund Manager
12.	COBALT CAPITAL MANAGEMENT INCORPORATED	34.31MLN	3.729	0.13	4.25	Hedge Fund Manager
13.	PARALLAX VOLATILITY ADVISERS LLC	33.93MLN	1.103	0.13	1.25	Hedge Fund Manager
14.	STATE OF NJ COMMON PENSION FUND D	33.59MLN	0.133	0.13	5.75	Pension Fund
15.	CNA FINANCIAL CORPORATION	28MLN	6.621	0.10	7.00	Insurance Company
16.	--	26.39MLN	N.A.	0.10	6.75	Insurance Company
17.	ARROWPOINT ASSET MANAGEMENT LLC	22.4MLN	0.590	0.08	5.75	Hedge Fund Manager
18.	LITESPEED MANAGEMENT LLC	18.64MLN	1.543	0.07	1.50	Hedge Fund Manager
19.	RMB CAPITAL MANAGEMENT LLC	18.56MLN	1.196	0.07	0.50	Hedge Fund Manager
20.	MILLENNIUM MANAGEMENT LLC	13.3MLN	0.027	0.05	4.75	Hedge Fund Manager
21.	TOCQUEVILLE ASSET MANAGEMENT LP	12.96MLN	0.155	0.05	0.75	Hedge Fund Manager
22.	STALEY CAPITAL ADVISERS INC	12.85MLN	1.504	0.05	8.50	Hedge Fund Manager
23.	LEVIN CAPITAL STRATEGIES LP	12.38MLN	0.188	0.05	8.50	Hedge Fund Manager

Source: Bloomberg

FIGURE 10.4 Assets Since 2003 for SPY and GLD

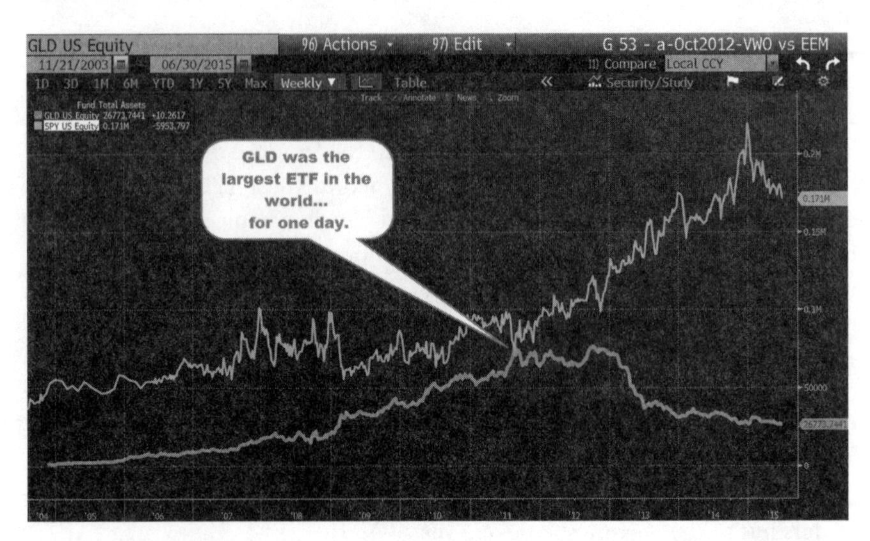

Source: Bloomberg

three years ago, when for one day, on August 19, 2011, it was larger than SPY, as shown in Figure 10.4. The only time SPY has ever been dethroned. As of this writing, it is now the 17th-largest ETF.

GLD was one of those products that got institutions excited from the beginning. They bought it up in droves early on because this was not something they could get anywhere else unless they stored gold themselves. Anthony Rochte who works at Fidelity but used to work at State Street during some of the early years of GLD saw many adopters that included hedge funds and endowments and calls GLD one of the "point of the spear" ETFs.

GLD's rapid growth raised concerns that its stockpile would distort the metal's price. While the inflows into GLD have added to demand for gold, GLD really doesn't hold that much gold. Its 700 metric tons is 1 percent of the 66,000 metric tons of gold bars and coins owned by central banks, and just 0.4 percent of 183,000 metric tons in the world. While all the world's gold would fit into two and a half Olympic swimming pools, the gold in GLD's London vault would fit in a small bedroom, according to data from the World Gold Council.

Some conspiracy theorists posited that the gold bars weren't really in storage and wouldn't be available in a crisis. However, in 2013 assets in GLD were cut from $72 billion to $31 billion as investors redeemed physical gold in droves without a glitch. This type of mass redemption would have been more than a bit tricky if there were no actual gold in storage.

"The conspiracy theories were all completely unfounded and have almost entirely gone away since 2013."

Will Rhind, World Gold Council

While many view gold as a hedge against the stock market, GLD has handily beaten the market since inception through the middle of 2015, as shown in Figure 10.5. If you had invested in GLD when it launched, your investment would be up 149 percent. That's 37 percentage points better than the S&P 500 Index's 112 percent return ending June 2015, and it includes GLD's 34 percent loss over the past two years.

The other upshot to holding something like GLD is that there are people who want to short it, and thus an institution can pick up some extra income by doing a long and lend. This sort of defies the myth that gold is an unproductive asset, as institutional investors have the ways and means to turn gold into a productive asset.

One important note about GLD—and why it gets my PG rating instead of G—and that is that is it's unusual tax treatment. GLD is considered a

FIGURE 10.5 Despite the Tough Times, GLD Still Outperforming SPY Since Inception

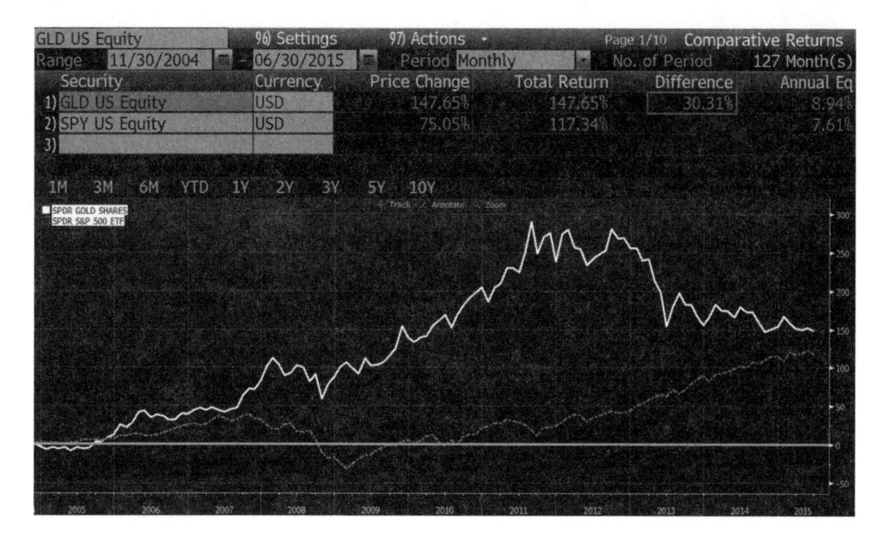

Source: Bloomberg

"collectible" by the IRS. That means it's taxed at the special collectibles tax rate of 28 percent for long-term gains as if you held gold bars yourself. Again, back to the ETF's taxation being driven by what it holds.

In terms of cost, GLD is the most expensive of the physically backed ETFs, charging 0.40 percent in annual fees. While it definitely is the cheapest to trade due to its oceanic liquidity it is considerably more expensive than another ETF that basically does the same thing. Let's meet some of GLD's competitors.

The Other Gold ETF

The other sizable gold ETF is the iShares Gold Trust (IAU), which has $25 billion in assets. IAU is similar to GLD except for two things. First, it is the cheaper of the two, with an expense ratio of 0.25 percent, which is $25 in annual fees for every $10,000 invested. This doesn't seem like a lot, but it is 37% cheaper. Since fees come out of the NAV, this gives IAU the performance edge over the long term. In any given 12-month stretch, you will see IAU outperform GLD by almost exactly 0.15 percent, which is the difference in expense ratios. However, long term this adds up, so since IAU launched in January 2005, it is up 175 percent versus 173 percent for GLD, as shown in Figure 10.6.

FIGURE 10.6 IAU versus GLD Since Inception

Source: Bloomberg

On the flip side, IAU could see slightly higher trading costs. While GLD trades about $700 million worth of shares each day, IAU averages about $50 million. However, the bid-ask spread on both is a penny.

The other way IAU differs from GLD is that it diversifies where it stores the gold, spreading it out between vaults in London, New York, and Toronto. That may seem unnecessary to some, but to others it doesn't go far enough. After all, back in 1933 President Franklin Roosevelt issued an executive order criminalizing the possession of monetary gold by an individual, partnership, association, or corporation.[6]

For the Paranoid

For those extra-paranoid gold investors, there's always the ETF Securities Physical Swiss Gold Shares (SGOL), which stores its gold in a vault in Switzerland (gold bugs like Switzerland's long history as a safe haven for capital).[7] SGOL charges a 0.39 percent expense ratio. Just sticking the gold bars in a Swiss vault was enough to attract $1 billion in assets for SGOL. In many ways, this is one of the most ingenious ETFs ever made. I wish I had thought of it!

And then there is the Merk Gold Trust (OUNZ). OUNZ is the first gold ETF to let investors take physical delivery of gold when they sell their shares. That's right—someone will deliver gold bars and coins to your door.

Investors who opt to take delivery of the gold will need to fill out an application, which their broker submits to the fund's trustee bank. Once that's done, the gold arrives, in most cases, UPS next-day delivery. And yes, there have been many deliveries so far. As Seinfeld would say, who are these people?

While delivery is covered for anyone in the continental United States, there's an "exchange fee" that runs about 2 percent to 7 percent, depending on the transaction size and the type of gold. One of the selling points for OUNZ is that investors won't incur tax, because no money is exchanged. They are merely taking possession of what they already own. If there were a Ron Paul ETF, it would have to be OUNZ since it involves two of his biggest campaign themes: gold and no taxes.

Gold as Yield Play?

Income is the last thing people think of when they think of gold, but the Credit Suisse Gold Shares Covered Call ETN (GLDI) sports a yield of 11 percent. GLDI essentially holds GLD and then writes monthly call options that are 6 percent out of the money.

This means that if the price of GLD rises 6 percent higher than where it is the option may be exercised. This effectively means you give up your upside in gold for the income received from the premiums from the call options. This has actually been a good play since it came out as not only has it yielded so much but that income has helped it not sink as low as GLD. GLDI is beating GLD by about five percentage points since its January 2013 inception.

Silver

Gold gets all the glory, but silver is no slouch. And I'm including it here because, like gold, silver can be stored in a vault. It is the other big physically backed commodity ETF.

About half of silver's demand comes from industrial uses, according to the Silver Institute. It is in everything from cell phones to solar panels. The other half of silver's demand is like gold—a precious metal used for jewelry and to store value. Silver's versatility can put it in the sweet spot as something that can add diversity for investors weary of stocks, while at the same time benefiting from improvements in the global economy.

The most popular silver ETF by far is the iShares Silver Trust (SLV) with $5 billion in assets. It is essentially a silver version of IAU, except it is twice as expensive, at 0.50 percent. An alternative to that is the ETFS Physical Silver Shares (SIVR), which does same thing, except it charges 0.30 percent a year in fees versus 0.50 percent for SLV. That may not seem like much, but over time it can add up. For example, SIVR outperformed SLV by 1.5 percent over the past five years, which can be attributed to SLV's higher cost. SIVR has $400 million in assets and trades just under 100,000 shares a day.

There is also an ETF that serves up all the storable precious metals—gold, silver, platinum, and palladium—in one shot: Physical Precious Metals Basket Shares (GLTR), which is approximately 50 percent gold, 33 percent silver, and the rest platinum and palladium. The metals are stored in London and Zurich. GLTR, like all of the ETFs in this section, is pretty straightforward with no big surprises lying beneath the surface. The same can't be said for ETFs that hold futures.

Futures-Based Commodity ETFs

Futures-based ETFs do not store the commodity, but rather maintain exposure by using derivatives. While there are 140 of them, they only have about $21 billion in assets, which is about a third what the physically backed commodity ETFs have.

Within the futures-based commodities category investors tend to use the single-commodity ETFs, such as oil and natural gas, for short-term tactical trading, while using the broad-market commodity ETFs more for strategic allocations and portfolio diversification.

Let's start with a look at the highly traded single-commodity ETFs. We'll use energy as an example since that is where a lot of the action is.

Energy

There are 34 ETFs that track popular energy-related futures such as oil and natural gas. These ETFs have about $8.5 billion in assets, or about a third of the total for the futures-based commodity ETFs, but less than 25 percent what GLD alone has.

While these ETFs aren't huge in the way of asset size, some do trade a ton. As a group, they trade about $1.5 billion in shares each day. In other words, they turn over about 20 percent a day, or 100 percent each week. To put that into perspective, Vanguard ETFs as a whole turn over about 0.5 percent a day, or 40 times less!

This is as it should be. You want to see high turnover in futures-based energy ETFs and low turnover in Vanguard, because the longer you hold Vanguard ETFs, the better off you are. But for these, the longer you hold, the more chance you have of losing money simply due to the cost of carry associated with maintaining futures positions, especially with the ETFs that maintain front-month positions.

Because no one wants to take delivery of the commodity—including the ETF issuer—the front month contract decays as the contract get closer to expiration. So when it comes time to sell out before expiration and buy the next month out, many times the next month is less decayed and, ipso facto, more expensive. Repeated jumping from decay to freshness, otherwise known as "rolling," can wreak havoc on the ETF's total return. Of course, there are occasions where the opposite happens, like in a shortage, where everyone wants the front month contract and you actually make money by rolling. It is nice when it happens, but it is rare.

The largest in the group, the United States Oil Fund (USO), which holds front-month crude oil futures, is down 71 percent since its inception in 2006 through the end of 2014, even though spot oil is down only 26 percent, as shown in Figure 10.7. The difference is the roll costs.

Of course, you would incur these costs if you were holding the futures yourself, but it can be a nasty surprise for an unsuspecting investor, not to mention a complex concept. This is why I give futures-based commodities

FIGURE 10.7 USO Return versus WTI Crude Oil Spot Price Since Inception

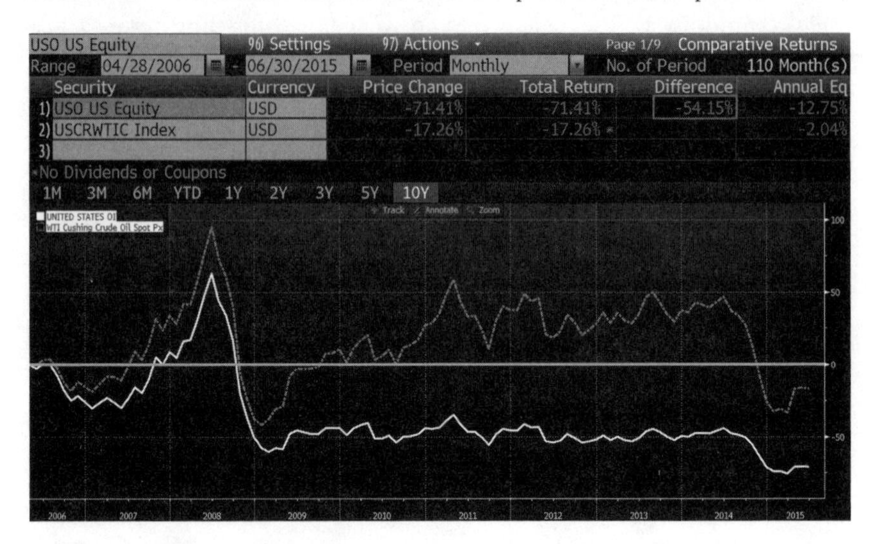

Source: Bloomberg

an R rating in my system. Judging from the high turnover in some of these futures-based ETFs—especially the single-commodity ones—it is clear that they are being used mostly by institutions anyway.

> *"We've always told people as far as we can tell, 80 to 90 percent of the shares and trading of a fund like USO (oil) or UNG (nat gas) is being done by non-retail. The bulk of the trading is being done by institutional or professional players like hedge funds, prop desks, energy trading desks, etc."*
>
> John Hyland, former CIO of United States Commodity Funds

Over 35 hedge funds reported ownership of it- some of which can be seen in Figure 10.8. Notice how short the estimated holding periods are. That is great to see since USO is not an ETF you want to hold long-term due to the cost of carry inside the ETF. So it looks like this tool is being used by the right clientele in the right way.

The reason everyone uses USO is that it has high sensitivity to the price of a barrel of oil in the short term. So if you are going in purely speculative and looking at a day or week horizon, USO will get the job done. For example, in the first two weeks of April 2015, spot oil rallied 18.5 percent while USO was up 17.6 percent. That sensitivity however, breaks down over longer holding periods due to the corroding roll costs.

FIGURE 10.8 USO's Heavy Hedge Fund User Base

	Portfolio Name	Mkt Val	% Portfolio	% Out	Est. Holding	Inst Type
						Hedge Fund Manager
2.	POINT72 ASSET MANAGEMENT LP	24.7MLN	0.174	1.14	0.50	Hedge Fund Manager
3.	POLAR SECURITIES INC	10.41MLN	0.616	0.48	0.75	Hedge Fund Manager
4.	DG CAPITAL MANAGEMENT LLC	9.47MLN	9.456	0.44	0.50	Hedge Fund Manager
5.	KYNIKOS ASSOCIATES LP	8.7MLN	3.719	0.40	0.75	Hedge Fund Manager
6.	PEAK6 INVESTMENTS LP	6.63MLN	0.261	0.31	3.25	Hedge Fund Manager
7.	WOLVERINE ASSET MANAGEMENT	6.15MLN	0.118	0.28	1.00	Hedge Fund Manager
8.	WHITEBOX ADVISORS LLC	4.62MLN	0.157	0.21	0.50	Hedge Fund Manager
9.	CITADEL ADVISORS LLC	2.09MLN	0.003	0.10	1.50	Hedge Fund Manager
10.	MADISON STREET PARTNERS LLC	1.89MLN	1.698	0.09	0.50	Hedge Fund Manager
11.	UBS O'CONNOR LLC	1.89MLN	0.036	0.09	0.75	Hedge Fund Manager
12.	JUMP TRADING LLC	1.3MLN	0.722	0.06	0.50	Hedge Fund Manager
13.	FIRST NEW YORK SECURITIES LLC	1.14MLN	1.040	0.05	0.75	Hedge Fund Manager
14.	GRAHAM CAPITAL MANAGEMENT LP	946,500	0.074	0.04	0.50	Hedge Fund Manager
15.	QUINTIUM ADVISORS LLC	889,615.35	0.673	0.04	1.75	Hedge Fund Manager
16.	CMT TRADING LLC	637,657.05	0.986	0.03	0.50	Hedge Fund Manager
17.	HILLSDALE INVESTMENT MANAGEMENT INC	478,929	0.109	0.02	0.50	Hedge Fund Manager
18.	TIPP HILL CAPITAL MANAGEMENT LLC	378,600	0.295	0.02	0.50	Hedge Fund Manager
19.	SPROTT INC	306,666	0.034	0.01	0.50	Hedge Fund Manager
20.	MYCIO WEALTH PARTNERS LLC	290,575.5	0.053	0.01	0.75	Hedge Fund Manager
21.	BERKSHIRE ASSET MANAGEMENT INC	283,950	0.042	0.01	0.75	Hedge Fund Manager
22.	PARALLAX VOLATILITY ADVISERS LLC	253,056.24	0.007	0.01	1.00	Hedge Fund Manager
23.	CQS CAYMAN LP	238,518	0.011	0.01	0.75	Hedge Fund Manager
24.	RAMIUS LLC	236,625	0.019	0.01	0.50	Hedge Fund Manager

Source: Bloomberg

USO is just one of many oil ETFs. There are ETFs that track other types of oil besides West Texas Intermediate, such as Brent Crude and even heating oil. There's even the United States Gasoline ETF (UGA), which tracks unleaded gasoline futures. And in each category you will find some ETFs that are designed to try and minimize roll costs by picking certain futures contracts that minimize that cost. These products are used more by longer-term investors who are willing to give up sensitivity to spot price in order to minimize roll costs.

You can also get all 12 months' worth of futures in one shot like with the United States 12 Month Oil Fund LP (USL). Although judging from the assets, by and large investors prefer the front-month trackers which tend to pop the most when oil does.

One question in all this is why do hedge funds—or any institution—choose to trade commodity ETFs rather than just invest in futures? With futures you can pick your month and you don't have to pay the expense ratio.

Basically, it comes down to one that same word again: *convenience.*

"I would always tell my employees, 'Let's not confuse ourselves. What we are doing is not rocket science. All we are really selling is convenience. All we've done with USO or UNG is take the front month futures contract and turn it into an equity.'"

John Hyland, former CIO of United States Commodity Funds

"It is much cheaper to buy futures than use an ETF, but you have to know how to roll them or you get killed. I personally would much rather have someone do that for me."

Larry Seibert, 780 Riverside Drive, LLC

Beyond the convenience, there are some other reasons that hedge funds use these products. If a hedge fund's back office and portfolio management system may be set up to only handle stocks and bonds and not derivatives, according to Hyland. So even though these ETFs hold futures, they would show up as equities on the books.

Further, contrary to popular belief, not all hedge funds can just own anything they want. They can only own what their investing partners have agreed to. So if in the offering docs the fund didn't specify that that it would be buying commodity futures and it wants to, it would have to amend the docs or use the ETF.

ETNs

Commodities is where you will see some ETNs getting some action. For example, the iPath Goldman Sachs Crude Oil ETN (OIL) has over $1 billion and is the second-biggest product in the category. This is a good example of where some investors are choosing the ETN structure over the ETF structure. And there is really only one reason for this: taxes.

Commodity ETFs, like USO, that buy and sell futures contracts, are taxed as partnerships, which means a different tax rate and tax form as discussed in Chapter 5. ETNs on the other are taxed like a regular old equity ETF because they don't actually hold futures contracts. We don't know what they hold. They are unsecured debt obligations. Thus, there is credit risk with them, but you get taxed normally as if you held SPY shares, meaning you are taxed only when you sell shares.

Another part of this story is that with commodity ETFs you also get an additional tax form called a Schedule K-1, which no one likes because they are different, plus they are sent out late—after April 15—and can mean additional taxes even if you didn't sell the security. One asset manager I spoke with compared the tax treatment to a paper cut. It isn't terminal, but it is annoying.

ETNs, on the other hand, distribute the normal 1099 form. This brings us to the big dilemma for investors in the commodity space. Do you want to stomach credit risk or tax annoyance? Figure 10.9 shows the dilemma between the energy ETFs and the ETNs and their respective tax forms. It is a game of picking your poison.

FIGURE 10.9 Energy ETFs and ETNs Have Different Tax Treatments and Forms

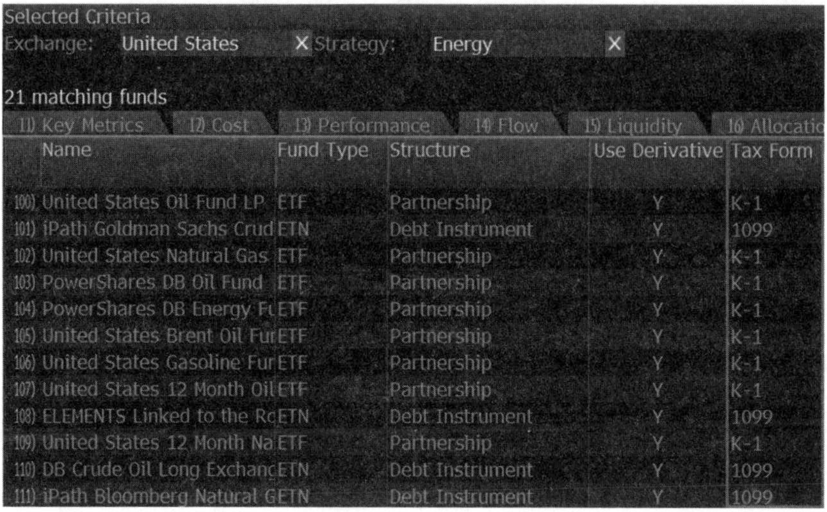

Selected Criteria
Exchange: United States X Strategy: Energy X

21 matching funds

11) Key Metrics 12) Cost 13) Performance 14) Flow 15) Liquidity 16) Allocatio

Name	Fund Type	Structure	Use Derivative	Tax Form
100) United States Oil Fund LP	ETF	Partnership	Y	K-1
101) iPath Goldman Sachs Crud	ETN	Debt Instrument	Y	1099
102) United States Natural Gas	ETF	Partnership	Y	K-1
103) PowerShares DB Oil Fund	ETF	Partnership	Y	K-1
104) PowerShares DB Energy Fu	ETF	Partnership	Y	K-1
105) United States Brent Oil Fur	ETF	Partnership	Y	K-1
106) United States Gasoline Fur	ETF	Partnership	Y	K-1
107) United States 12 Month Oil	ETF	Partnership	Y	K-1
108) ELEMENTS Linked to the Rc	ETN	Debt Instrument	Y	1099
109) United States 12 Month Na	ETF	Partnership	Y	K-1
110) DB Crude Oil Long Exchanc	ETN	Debt Instrument	Y	1099
111) iPath Bloomberg Natural G	ETN	Debt Instrument	Y	1099

Source: Bloomberg

The Rest of the Commodities

Beyond energy there are several diverse groups of ETFs and ETNs tracking all kinds of commodities, such as industrial metals (copper, aluminum, lead, tin, and nickel), agriculture (cocoa, corn, cotton, soybeans, sugar, and wheat) and livestock. However, even though there are over 50 ETFs and ETNs, they have just $2 billion in assets. These are rarely used. And most of them probably are not going to have the kind of volume to interest the average institution.

Broad Based

There are about two dozen broad-based commodity ETFs that have about $8 billion of the assets. The broad-based commodity ETFs are used much more strategically as long-term allocations. We know this because their turnover is about 0.5 percent a day—about the same as a Vanguard ETF.

The most popular choice with about $3 billion in assets is the PowerShares DB Commodity Index Tracking Fund (DBC). It holds 14 different commodities. Right off the bat, the big thing to know here is it has 60 percent energy exposure. But energy is the biggest commodities market, so this is similar to a market-cap weighted take on commodities. It also selects futures contracts in a way that minimizes roll costs. It is also very liquid, trading just under $30 million worth of shares per day—by far the most of any broad-based commodity ETF. It has an expense ratio of 0.85 percent.

The second biggest one is the iPath Bloomberg Commodity Index Total Return ETN (DJP) with $1.2 billion in assets. Big difference here is that DJP doesn't go as heavy into energy because it caps each commodity sector at 33 percent. This means less energy and more agriculture and metals than DBC. Being an ETN, it also is taxed like a normal stock position.

The DBC versus DJP battle for the top shows that, just as in the energy category, investors are a bit split on which poison they'd rather accept: the credit risk or the tax annoyance.

Smart-Beta Commodities

Smart-beta isn't relegated to just equities. There are a few smart-beta commodity ETFs. One example is the GreenHaven Continuous Commodity Index Fund (GCC) which holds futures contracts on 17 commodities, the most among its peers, and weights them equally—each commodity makes up about 5.8 percent of the portfolio. It's like you are betting the same amount on each horse in the Commodity Derby.

Its portfolio breaks down into six agricultural commodities (corn, wheat, soybeans, soy oil, live cattle, and lean hogs), four "softs" (coffee, cocoa, sugar, and cotton), four metals (gold, silver, platinum, and copper) and three energy commodities (natural gas, crude oil, and heating oil).

A popular criticism of GCC is that its equal weighting of commodities doesn't match reality. After all, oil is a much bigger portion of the commodities market than, say, lean hogs or cotton. On the flip side, when one of those smaller commodities—like coffee or cocoa—go on a tear, you feel it in GCC as opposed to the broad based ETFs. GCC is what smart-beta is all about: an alternative.

Another example is the United States Commodity Index Fund (USCI), which is the largest, at $560 million in assets. What makes it smart beta is the way it picks the contract. Each month it selects 14 commodities out of 27 choices from six sectors—energy, precious metals, industrial metals, grains, livestock, and softs—based on price signals and which commodities' futures market offers the best chance to make money from the roll. Then it takes those 14 commodities and equal weights them.

This strategy is working lately as USCI is well ahead of its largest broad-based commodity peers since inception with a return of –5.7 percent. This sounds pretty blah but is a big deal considering its two biggest competitors the PowerShares DB Commodity Tracking ETF (DBC) and iPath Dow Jones-UBS Commodities ETN (DJP) are both down over 20 percent as seen in Figure 10.10.

FIGURE 10.10 USCI Return Since Inception versus DBC and DJP

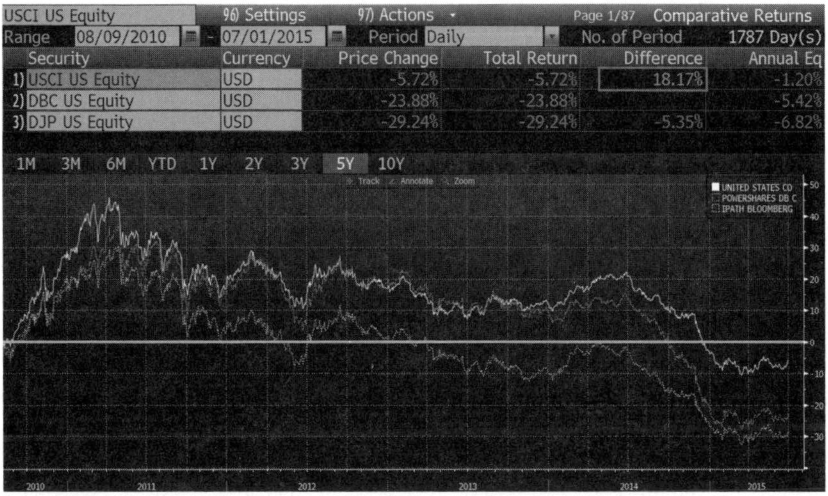
USCI US Equity
96) Settings
97) Actions
Page 1/87 Comparative Returns
Range 08/09/2010 - 07/01/2015
Period Daily
No. of Period 1787 Day(s)
Security
Currency
Price Change
Total Return
Difference
Annual Eq
1) USCI US Equity USD -5.72% -5.72% 18.17% -1.20%
2) DBC US Equity USD -23.88% -23.88% -5.42%
3) DJP US Equity USD -29.24% -29.24% -5.35% -6.82%
1M 3M 6M YTD 1Y 2Y 3Y 5Y 10Y
UNITED STATES CO
POWERSHARES DB C
IPATH BLOOMBERG
50
40
30
20
10
0
-10
-20
-30
2010
2011
2012
2013
2014
2015

Source: Bloomberg

40 Act Commodity ETFs

First Trust Global Tactical Commodity Strategy Fund (FTGC) initiated a "third way" type of commodities ETF that was able to launch as an ETF but avoid the tax treatment of a futures-based commodities ETF. FTGC was able to set register as an open-end investment company because it holds futures contracts through a subsidiary in the Cayman Islands, so no credit risk and no alternative tax treatment or K-1 form. This is the same deal as WDTI, the managed futures ETF we discussed earlier in the chapter.

In addition, as opposed to traditional commodity ETFs that weight the holdings based on liquidity or production, FTGC favors commodities exhibiting less volatility and lower correlation to other commodities. Its active management also allows it to choose futures contracts that exhibit the least amount of roll cost. Its current top holdings include silver, wheat, nickel, and coffee. It is down 1 percent since its launch. The downside is that it charges 0.95 percent a year.

Another example of a 40 Act commodities fund the iShares Commodities Select Strategy ETF (COMT). It is not only 40 Act, but it blends futures with actual commodity-producing companies. So investors are playing energy futures and energy stocks at the same time. FTGC and COMT are both next-generation commodity ETFs that you will probably see more of.

"By blending in equity commodity producers, the newer generation products bring in long-term diversification enhancement and alleviate near-term contango issues that those purely futures-based products have."

Linda Zhang, Windhaven Investment Management

Notes

1. The Pew Charitable Trusts, "State Public Pension Investments Shift Over Past 30 Years," June 3, 2014; www.pewtrusts.org/en/research-and-analysis/reports/2014/06/03/state-public-pension-investments-shift-over-past-30-years.
2. Kolhatkar, Sheelah, "Hedge Funds Are for Suckers." Bloomberg, July 11, 2013; www.bloomberg.com/bw/articles/2013--07--11/why-hedge-funds-glory-days-may-be-gone-for-good.
3. Preqin, "Preqin Investor Outlook: Hedge Funds H1 2015," 2015; www.preqin.com/docs/reports/Preqin-Investor-Outlook-Hedge-Funds-H1--2015.pdf.
4. Stevenson, Alexandra, and Michael Corkery, "Calpers, Nation's Biggest Pension Fund, to End Hedge Fund Investments." *New York Times,* September 15, 2014; dealbook.nytimes.com/2014/09/15/nations-biggest-pension-fund-to-end-hedge-fund-investments/?_r=0.
5. Strauss, Valerie, "Hillary Clinton: 'You See the Top 25 Hedge Fund Managers Making More than All of America's Kindergarten Teachers Combined." *Washington Post,* June 13, 2015; www.washingtonpost.com/blogs/answer-sheet/wp/2015/06/13/hillary-clinton-you-see-the-top-25-hedge-fund-managers-making-more-than-all-of-americas-kindergarten-teachers-combined/.
6. Traynor, Ben, "Roosevelt's Gold Confiscation: Could It Happen Again?" *The Telegraph,* April 3, 2013; www.telegraph.co.uk/finance/personalfinance/investing/gold/9968494/Roosevelts-gold-confiscation-could-it-happen-again.html.
7. Lydon, Tom, "Swiss Gold: Does It Matter Where ETFs Store Their Bullion?" *ETF Trends,* September 22, 2012; www.etftrends.com/2012/09/swiss-gold-does-it-matter-where-etfs-store-their-bullion/.

CHAPTER 11

Leveraged, Inverse, and VIX

Leveraged, inverse, and VIX products are the bad boys of the ETF world. Most of them get a hard R rating in my system, while some are even (gasp) NC-17. With that said, this is one of the most fascinating categories of ETFs full of unreal returns, trapdoors, and crazy math.

Leveraged ETFs

Leveraged exchange-traded funds (ETFs) can return in a day what most people would call a good year. The problem is they can also lose just as much in a day. They can be used for straight up gambling or they can actually be used to hedge a portfolio. Leveraged and inverse ETFs are like power tools; in the hands of the trained professional they can be helpful and precise. In the hands of a novice they can cut your hand off.

I recently participated in a StockTwits Q&A session as a China ETF expert. I was expecting people to ask about the new China A-share phenomenon that was in full swing at the time. Instead, almost every question I got was on triple-leveraged China ETFs. So people are clearly using them, and people have questions about them.

There are currently about 240 of them and with $42 billion in assets, which is about 2 percent of total. Unlike other areas of the ETF landscape, they really haven't grown too much in the past five years. Part of the reason is the Securities and Exchange Commission's (SEC's) freeze on granting exemptive relief to any new companies wanting to issue them (although that doesn't cover exchange-traded notes [ETNs]).[1] So you will only see new leverage products from ProShares, Direxion, and/or in an ETN wrapper. It probably comes to no shock to anyone that these products have a more narrow appeal than say traditional stock and bond ETFs.

"They have always been and always will be a niche-type product. They're essentially used as short-term trading vehicles. You don't see assets sticking around in these. You see a lot of turnover, and that's why assets haven't grown more."

Mike Eschmann, Direxion Investments

You can get your leveraged and inverse in many varieties such as 1x short, 2x long and short, and 3x long and short. There is even some "diet leveraged" ETFs that go 1.25x long as well. While exotic and dangerous, some of these ETFs trade quite a bit. As shown in Table 11.1, nearly 15 of them trade more than $100 million a day, which is about the level even the largest institutions are comfortable with.

TABLE 11.1 Notional Daily Volume of Inverse/Leveraged ETFs

Ticker	Name	Volume/Day ($million)
TNA US	Direxion Dly Sm Cap Bull 3X	405.51
SSO US	ProShares Ultra S&P500	267.99
TBT US	ProShares Ultrashort 20+Y TR	189.69
SDS US	ProShares Ultrashort S&P500	181.60
UPRO US	ProShares Ultrapro S&P 500	166.00
DWTI US	VelocityShares 3X Inverse Crude	151.67
SPXU US	ProShares Ultrapro Short S&P 500	150.60
SQQQ US	ProShares Ultrapro Short QQQ	146.87
NUGT US	Direxion Daily 3X Gold Miners	122.84
UGAZ US	VelocityShares 3X Long Nat Gas	107.93
SCO US	ProShares Ultrashort Crude Oil	103.41
SPXL US	Direxion Daily S&P 500 Bull	101.85
DUST US	Direxion Daily 3X Inverse Gold Min	100.02

Source: Bloomberg

> *"My core is an active equity selection, then I use leverage ETFs around that. I can use inverse or even triple long exposure to things that I think will move more quickly. I even day trade the triple long and short S&P 500 ETFs. On a tactical basis, they are awesome because they are so easy to trade."*
>
> Larry Seibert, 780 Riverside Drive LLC

From an investor's standpoint, it is crucial to understand how they work before using them. Let's start with the ones that are bullish, which we will call "leveraged long." With these, each dollar you invest in them provides—synthetically—either $2 or $3 of exposure to the performance of a benchmark for one day. Leverage at its core isn't that unusual. Many parts of our life are leveraged, such as vehicles, houses, and education. It is just that you are outsourcing the borrowing and logistics to another company by using the ETF.

The ETF issuer can provide this exposure by holding the securities in the index, or a corresponding ETF, and then using some of the cash to finance over-the-counter total return swaps. The total return swap is an agreement where one party makes payments based on the return of an underlying asset in exchange for a fee—typically a spread above the London interbank offered rate (LIBOR).

On the flip side, there are leveraged inverse ETFs, which essentially do the opposite of the leveraged long side. Basically, the ETF is buying the exposure on the long side and selling the exposure on the short side. It is important to note that swaps come with counterparty risk that the other side could default. This is why leveraged ETF issuers typically go to great lengths to minimize this risk, by using multiple swaps from different banks. So far, there haven't been any issues at all in this department.

Most leveraged long ETFs have a twin that does the exact opposite. Many call them "mirror pairs." For example, the leveraged ProShares Ultra Bloomberg Natural Gas (BOIL) is a mirror pair with the ProShares UltraShort Bloomberg Natural Gas (KOLD). And the Direxion Daily Gold Miners Bull 3X Shares (NUGT) is a mirror pair with the Direxion Daily Gold Miners Bear 3X Shares (DUST).

The big devil in the details of all this—and what I meant by "crazy math"—is the fact that the leverage is reset daily. This is the one thing that must be known before using these tools. The reason they reset each day is so investors buying in tomorrow get the correct 2x and 3x beta and aren't buying into leverage at yesterday's share price.

What this means is that leverage ETFs only promise the 2x or 3x exposure for one day and that's it. The longer you hold the product, the more chance that the daily-resetting corrodes returns and you get less than that. This is why Direxion went so far as to put the word "Daily" in the name of their products. This shows that they don't want people mis-using their products either.

A simple example will show how daily resetting of leverage can mess you up. Say you make a $100 investment into a double long leveraged ETF. On the first day, the index gains 10 percent. The index is now at $110. The double long ETF adds 20 percent to close at $120.[2]

The next day the index loses 10 percent and closes at $99. The double long ETF closes at $96 because it started the day at $120, so the loss on the day is $24. So even though the index is down 1 percent, the double long is down 4 percent. You can imagine if this kind of volatility went on for multiple days or months; it would leave you with a nasty surprise if you weren't paying attention to it. However, the opposite can happen as well.

In short, volatility is the enemy of leverage products, and momentum is their friend. This is why they say that leveraged ETFs are "path dependent," which means the straighter the path, the better the outcome. Let's look at this using two 5-day scenarios using Direxion Daily FTSE China Bull 3X Shares (YINN).

Volatility Drag

In the first scenario, YINN's index, the FTSE China 50 Index was up 5.1 percent over five days between April 9, 2015 and April 16, 2015. Meanwhile, YINN was up only a hair more, at 6.4 percent, nowhere near the 15 percent you may have expected.

The reason is that the path to get to that 5.1 percent consisted of an up day, then a down day and then another up day, as you can see in Figure 11.1. And when the ETF resets the leverage after a down day, it will decrease the impact of the next day's gains. A continued pattern of this will decay the longer-term returns of the fund. This is called volatility drag and can hurt returns.

This is why leveraged products are controversial and dangerous if you don't know how they work. One of the most extreme and famous examples of volatility drag is with the leveraged long and short financials ETF during the financial crisis in 2008 through June 2009, when the Financial Select Sector SPDR Fund (XLF) was down 56 percent, but it was a very volatile trip to get there. Due to the decay that volatility drag produces, the ProShares Ultra Financials (SKF), which is 2x leveraged long, was down 90 percent, while the ProShares UltraShort Financials (UYG), which is 2x leveraged short, was down 58 percent, as shown in Figure 11.2. In other words, even if you made the right call, you may have lost money due to the volatility drag.

FIGURE 11.1 YINN versus Its Index April 9, 2015 to April 16 2015

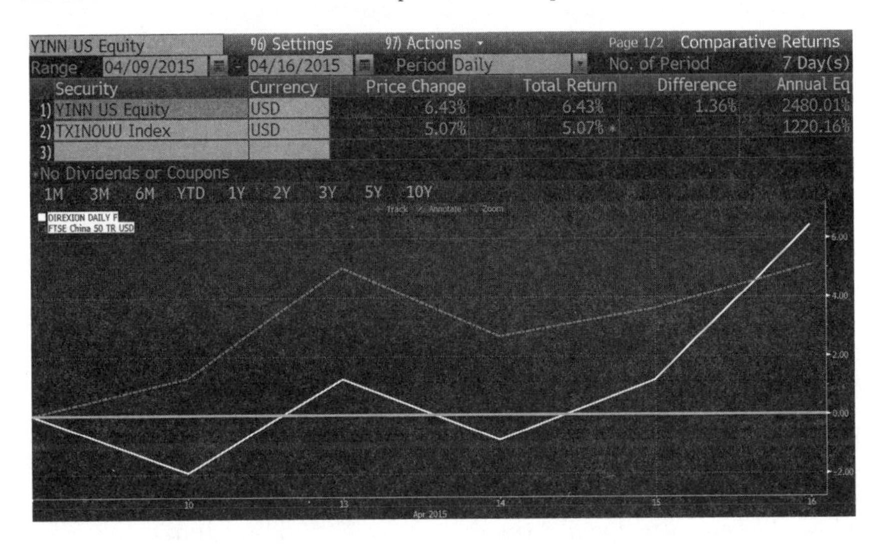

Source: Bloomberg

FIGURE 11.2 Leveraged Long and Short Financials Were Both Down during Financial Crisis

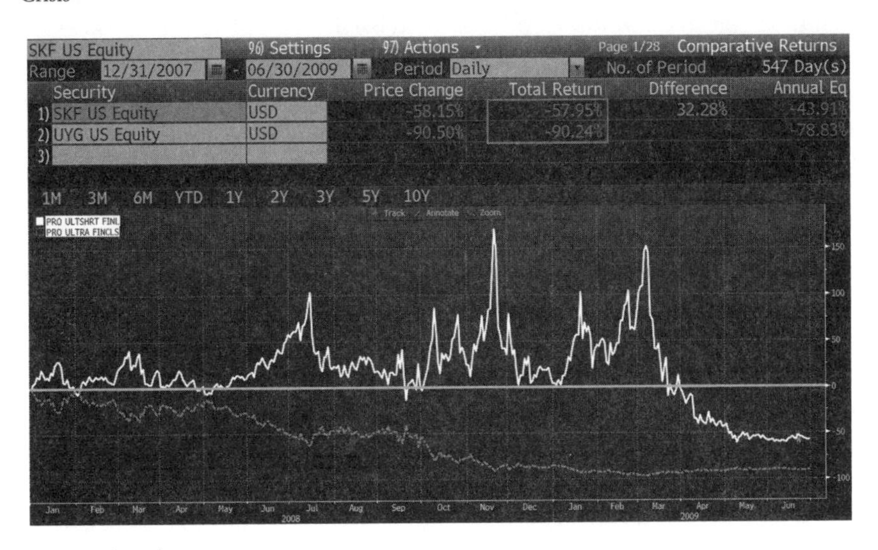

Source: Bloomberg

"You can't use these products in volatile time periods. I think that's the biggest misunderstanding with the advisor world. So if you can't identify periods of time with high confidence that the market is going to have a strong rise, you shouldn't touch these things."

Sharon Snow, Metropolitan Capital

Understandably, the media tends to look only at the type of scenarios in Figures 11.1 and 11.2 where 2x (or 3x) don't deliver 2x over the holding periods longer than a day. But what you don't hear about is the other side of the coin and how the Devil of Daily Resetting can turn into the Angel of Compounding and multiply your returns beyond the 2x or 3x.

The Compounding Effect

For this scenario we are going to look at another example using YINN, except using a five day period which saw the index rise steadily each day. This is less likely but can happen and is good for leveraged ETF holders. In this case you are actually up more than 3x the index. This is because each day the fund takes the gains and resets the leverage from a higher point, which increases your gains.

Here we see that between March 31, 2015, and April 8, 2015, which is five trading days, the index closed higher each day as seen in Figure 11.3 and booked a five-day return of 8.53 percent. You would think the YINN would then be up 25.6 percent, but it is up 34.2 percent. In this case, you did better thanks to the compounding effect of the rebalance. Not bad for one week!

Just to be clear, though, this is the best-case scenario and not the norm. But it can happen. For many, this type of exaggerated returns is exactly what you want for high-conviction bets. You expect them to go up; otherwise, you wouldn't bet on it.

Unfortunately, the key to this blissful state of extra returns is knowing when the market will go up *and* that it will take a steady path to get there. This requires two levels of market timing, which can be very difficult if not impossible. I equate the compounding effect in a leveraged ETF to a full moon. It is pretty when it happens, but is much more the exception than the rule.

However, even if it isn't a full moon scenario, they can still be used effectively and serve a valuable purpose by those who are highly convicted.

"When we are convicted, a levered ETFs allow us to stay in for 60 to 80 percent of the move, and we don't have to try and squeeze out every ounce of the upside move. You can get out before the upside has peaked, hitting your goal. We could

FIGURE 11.3 YINN versus Its Index March 31, 2015, to April 8, 2015

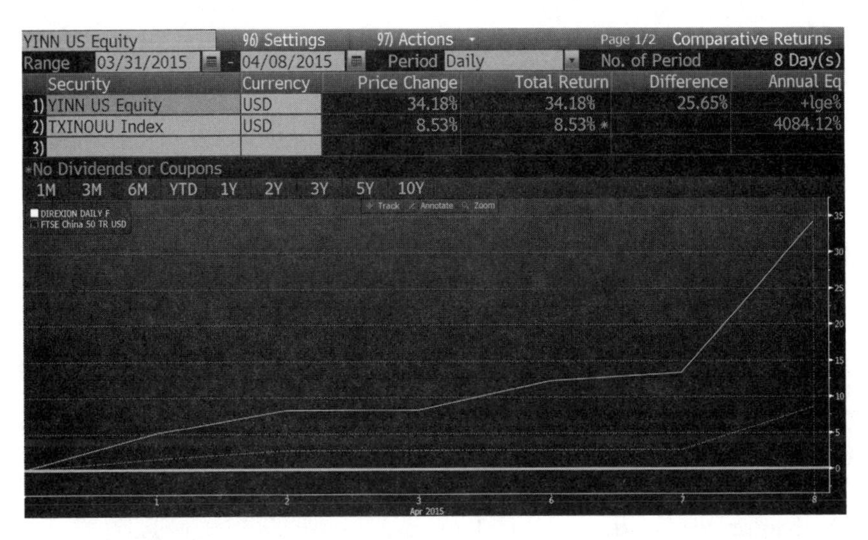

Source: Bloomberg

write options, there are other strategies that we could use. We could lever our hedge fund, we could use margin. We don't do that. We prefer to buy the leveraged ETFs because you can get out of that trade with one click or one call. It's the easiest way to express our trades. To us, they're a godsend."

Sharon Snow, Metropolitan Capital

However, she says they hold them for short periods of time and only when they have the highest investment conviction based on their extensive review of both fundamental and technical analysis.

While hedge funds like Snow's seem like a natural fit, what about other more conservative institutions? Again, it is hard to tell given the minimalist 13F filings so you have to rely on anecdotal information.

"We have seen large pension funds use the products as well as name brand hedge funds. One way they use them is an alternative to doing swaps or futures. They are using them to overweight allocations. If I'm a pension or hedge fund and I believe in a certain part of the market without selling something else, I can overweight an allocation. Conversely, we see people using the short products as a classic hedge. Now you do have the compounding issue. But the institutions know how the compounding works."

Michael Sapir, ProShares

The Double Short

One of the most interesting usages of leverage ETFs by institutions—namely, hedge funds—includes a trade called the *double short.* This trade, which accounts for about 5-10 percent of the volume in leveraged ETFs, involves shorting both the long and short version of a leveraged ETF in order to profit from the compounding decay that volatility drag produces. As we stated earlier, leveraged ETFs are path dependent, and volatility is the enemy. The double short is basically a creative way to turn an enemy into a friend.

Of course, this also involves market timing and has a lot of downside risk. Back in 2010, Credit Suisse looked at the double short trade for rolling three-month periods over several years and found that the trade works about 70 percent of the time.[3] But it also had the potential for large negative returns when those full moons happen and the compounding effect is in effect.

A recent case where the double short would have paid off big time is the first half of 2015 with the two triple leveraged oil ETFs. Crude oil was up around 11 percent through early June. Meanwhile, because of the volatile route it took to get there, the VelocityShares Daily 3X Long Crude ETN (UWTI) was down 31 percent while the VelocityShares Daily 3X Inverse Crude ETN (DWTI) was down 46 percent, as shown in Figure 11.4.

FIGURE 11.4 UWTI and DWTI Both Down Big in First Half of 2015

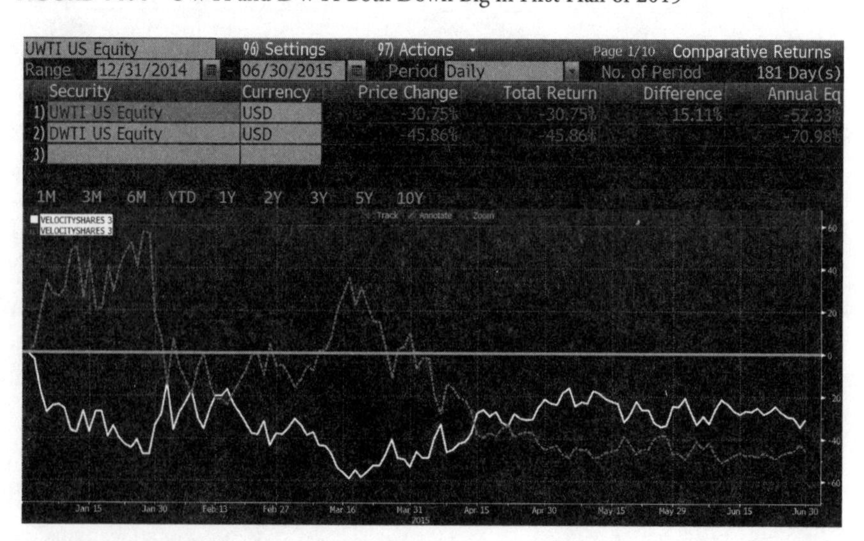

Source: Bloomberg

A quick note here is that borrowing costs can be high for leveraged ETFs. They average about 4 percent, according to Direxion. This is about four times more than something like IWM and eight times more than SPY. Borrowing costs and tail risk make the double short a dangerous, but fascinating endeavor.

Another move done by asset managers using leverage products is portable alpha. For example, if an investor is looking for $100,000 worth of S&P 500 exposure, he could buy SPY or IVV. Or he could buy $33,000 worth of Direxion Daily S&P 500 Bull 3X Shares (SPXL), then use the remaining $67,000 to invest in something that brings down his risk profile, such as in cash or a noncorrelated asset.

Cash Incinerators

Notice that all of the preceding use cases are professionals with short-term goals, using the ETFs like a technician. To drive home a final point on why you don't want to hold them long-term, I will share with you a list that I call ETF "cash incinerators." Basically, it ranks which ETFs with the biggest gap between inflows and current total assets. In other words, total assets minus lifetime flows equals cash burned. At any given time about half of the list is leveraged products. The last time I pulled it in mid-2015, over half of the top 10 were leveraged ETFs, as shown in Table 11.2.

The top dog, or bottom dog, depending on how you look at it, is the ProShares UltraShort 20+ Year Treasury (TBT), which is the largest leveraged ETF, which provides twice the daily inverse exposure to 20-year Treasury bonds. In effect, TBT allows you to bet on rising rates, or lower duration in a portfolio. TBT has burned through nearly $6 billion and is proof just how wrong investors were about when rates would rise.

The ETF took in an astonishing $9 billion while losing 76 percent of its value since inception in 2008. Like the Sirens in Homer's Odyssey, TBT has lured countless investors with its sweet song of huge profits when rates rise, only to dash them against the rocks repeatedly as rising interest rates failed to materialize.

With that said, TBT's potential is scary. Think about it, if TBT can become the largest leverage ETF during a time when the trade *wasn't* working, imagine if interest rates start a long rise up and the trade starts working. TBT could become the next hot ETF you never stop hearing about.

"We think TBT could be our best trade ever, when it occurs."

Sharon Snow, Metropolitan Capital

TABLE 11.2 Leveraged ETFs Dominate List of ETFs that Have Burned through the Most Cash in Their Lifetime

Top 10 Incinerators (USD)				
Ticker	Name	Lifetime Inflows	Assets Today	Money Burnt
TBT	ProShares Ultrashort 20+Y TR	$ 8,924.28	$ 3,002.06	$ 5,922.22
GDX	Market Vectors Gold Miners	$ 12,475.20	$ 6,576.44	$ 5,898.76
VSS	Vanguard FTSE All Wo X-US SC	$ 6,760.91	$ 1,234.23	$ 5,526.68
SDS	ProShares Ultrashort S&P500	$ 6,490.56	$ 1,210.90	$ 5,279.66
UNG	US Natural Gas Fund LP	$ 5,413.46	$ 649.04	$ 4,764.41
FAZ	Direxion Daily Finl Bear 3X	$ 4,859.49	$ 288.64	$ 4,570.85
TZA	Direxion Dly Sm Cap Bear 3X	$ 3,468.62	$ 740.45	$ 2,728.17
SRS	ProShares Ultrashort Re	$ 2,740.26	$ 35.34	$ 2,704.92
SH	ProShares Short S&P500	$ 3,698.05	$ 1,323.70	$ 2,374.35
EWZ	iShares MSCI Brazil Capped E	$ 5,193.24	$ 3,223.33	$ 1,969.91

Source: Bloomberg

The VIX

Despite their outlaw reputation, some of the VIX ETFs trade a lot, especially on bad days in the market. When the market tanks, these ETFs and ETNs get snatched up like people buying umbrellas from the that guy on the street when it rains. This space is largely institutional as evidenced by the incredibly high turnover. As a group, these ETPs turnover about 71 percent of their assets each day-by far the most of any category. In contrast, Vanguard ETFs turn over about 0.5 percent a day.

The Chicago Board Options Exchange Volatility Index, known as the VIX or "fear index," measures the intensity of put and call buying for the S&P 500 Index for a 30-day period. If the intensity around buying puts and calls is going up, it indicates investors are nervous and thinking about protection on their portfolio. As a barometer of fear in the market, it is great.

The problem with it is you can't actually invest in it. The VIX lives in a vacuum. The best you can do is VIX futures. For that, there are about 20 products and they have $3.2 billion in assets. And they trade about $1 billion a day. The most popular by far is the iPath S&P 500 VIX Short-Term Futures Exchange-Traded Note (VXX). It trades more than Oracle Corp. every day and does a great job of tracking VIX short-term futures.

The problem is that VIX short-term futures do a poor job of tracking the VIX Index. That's due to crippling costs from managing futures contracts as they roll from one month to the next. These roll costs average 37 percent each year for short-term VIX futures trackers. This is why VXX is down 99.7 percent since inception, as seen in Figure 11.5. And you thought roll costs in commodities were bad!

FIGURE 11.5 VXX Total Return Since Inception versus the VIX

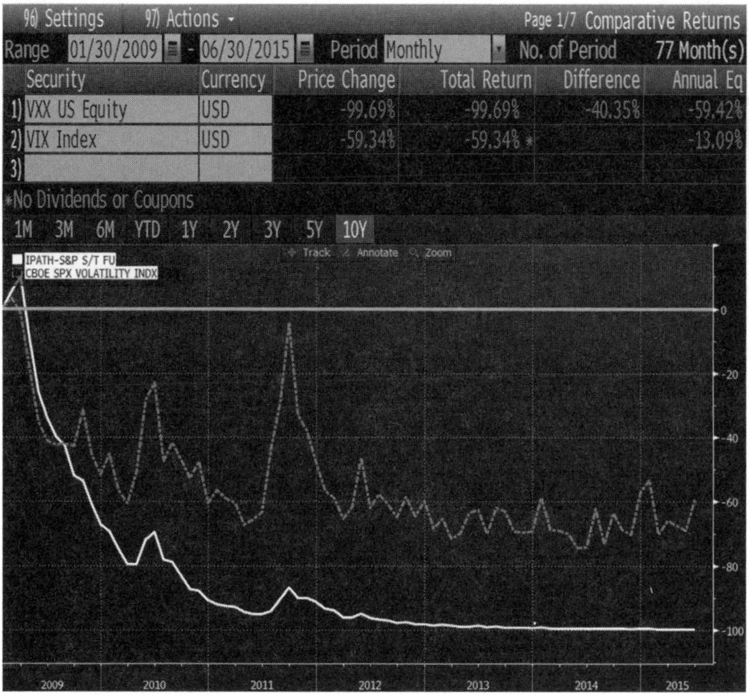

Source: Bloomberg

Moreover, in the past 12 months the VIX was down 36 percent, while VXX fell 66 percent. Or how about in January, when the fear index spiked up 34 percent? VXX was up just half that amount. In short, VXX serves up the worst of both worlds. And not because VXX is a bad product but rather because of the dissonance between spot VIX and VIX futures as well as the cost of rolling.

And how about individual days when VIX spikes; how does VXX behave? If you rank the top five best one-day surges for VIX in 2014, VXX only captured less than half of the actual VIX, as seen in Table 11.3.

According to Larry Seibert, who does like to use VIX products, VXX is not the way to go:

> You don't get enough "vig" in them. They just don't move all that much. For every day that you're wrong, you don't just sit there, you lose value. Even further, if you aren't paying attention you can actually lose a lot of money.

Notice how the better tracker in Table 11.3 was actually the leveraged VelocityShares Daily 2X VIX Short Term ETN (TVIX). It takes leverage to get you even close to VIX's move on a good day (bad day). But then you have the issue of even more losses on days it doesn't work since it is leveraged exposure. Another case of picking your poison.

Speaking of poison, TVIX is one of only a couple of ETFs that gets an NC-17 rating in my system. TVIX has the hat trick being leveraged, suffering from roll costs and coming with credit risk. Put another way, TVIX is a leveraged unsecured debt obligation tracking derivatives on the implied volatility of derivatives on the S&P 500. That should make your head hurt. If it doesn't, you need to get out more.

TABLE 11.3 Largest One-Day % Returns of VIX in 2014 and What VXX and TVIX Did

Date	VIX Index	VXX US Equity	TVIX US Equity
7/17/2014	32.2	9.8	17.0
1/24/2014	31.7	8.8	17.1
7/31/2014	27.2	8.5	16.1
12/10/2014	24.4	10.5	19.6
10/9/2014	24.2	9.0	15.9

Source: Bloomberg

TVIX is also notorious for famously halting creations suddenly, which left a permanent stain on the ETF industry. Remember in the due diligence section when we talked about premiums and discounts and I said that they were natural arbitrage bands? Well, TVIX provided the extremely rare case of an *unnatural* premium that formed because the arbitrage mechanism was cut off. It is a worthy tale to tell. I'll keep it brief.

In February 2012, TVIX shocked the world when they halted creations of the ETN due to "internal limits." This was a complicated situation since it was a leveraged VIX futures product. In short, the fund had grown quickly, with $640 million coming in in the first seven weeks of the year.[4] Credit Suisse (the issuer) had shot through its own internal limits of its ability to hedge the exposure. They bit off more than they wanted to chew. So they decided to stop taking new creations for TVIX. At this point, the price became unhinged from the net asset value (NAV) in a serious way—trading like a closed-end fund from hell.

The premium rose to 15 percent for a week or two and then to 30 percent for a week until it peaked at 89 percent on March 21, 2012, as seen in Figure 11.6. Credit Suisse got hammered in the press and by the ETF industry. So they announced that TVIX would resume limited creations so long as it could find offsetting swaps. Within two days the premium plummeted to 6 percent.

This situation rattled the industry and sparked an investigation from regulators into what happened.[5] This is one case where all the concern and theatrics in the press was totally earned. The TVIX situation was so dramatic that at Bloomberg we quickly added a new field that we put on every ETF's

FIGURE 11.6 TVIX's History of Premiums and Discounts Shows Just How Wild Things Got

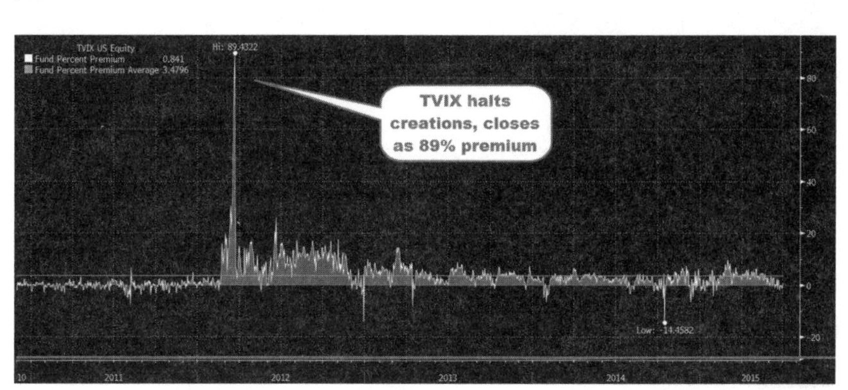

Source: Bloomberg

FIGURE 11.7 The Field We Created Because of the TVIX Situation

TVIX US Equity	98) Report		Page 3/5 Description
1) Profile	2) Performance	3) Holdings	4) Allocations	5) Organizational

Benchmark 6) SPVXSP Index

Top 10 Fund Hlds (MHD)	Net Fund	Net Index	Top 10 Index Hlds (MEMB)	Net Index	Net Fund
No Holdings Reported			No Holdings Reported		

Creation/Redemption Info	No Basket Available	Holdings Statistics	
Total Cash	N.A.	Rebalancing Frequency	Not Applicable
Estimated Cash	N.A.	Replication Strategy	Derivative
Creation Unit Size	25,000	Fund Holdings As Of Date	N.A.
Creation Fee	USD 0.00	Fund Number Of Holdings	N.A.
Create/Redeem Process	Cash	NAV Pricing Methodology	Primary Market Close
Creation Cutoff Time	16:00 est		
Settlement Cycle	T+3		
Open for New Creations	Yes		

Source: Bloomberg

description page called "Open for Creations." You can see in Figure 11.7 that it now says "Yes" for TVIX and 99 percent of all ETFs and ETNs. However, that are about two dozen relatively unknown, low-asset ETNs not open for creations. It is advised to stay far away from these products.

Inverse VIX

You may be wondering if there was a way to actually profit from all the crippling roll costs that plague VXX. Meet the VelocityShares Daily Inverse VIX Short-Term ETN (XIV). XIV shorts short-term VIX futures, which means it benefits from the roll cost because it is selling that exposure, not buying it. In a way buying XIV is like making yourself an insurance provider.

This is why if VIX were to spike, lookout. Not only does that move up in VIX hurt you, but if the crisis is drawn out enough VIX futures will enter into backwardation, where the front-month contract becomes the most expensive as everyone rushes to buy it. This would be a double-whammy for XIV holders.

This is why using XIV has been compared to picking pennies up in front of a steamroller.[6] However, the steamroller has been held back by accommodative Fed policy for the past several years, so it has been more like picking up $100 bills in front of a steamroller to say the least. XIV is up a mindboggling 403 percent since launching in 2010 through July 2015, which is 306 percentage points better than the S&P 500 Index as shown in Figure 11.8.

This kind of unreal performance has investors taking notice. XIV now has over a half a billion in assets while sporting a daily turnover of 116 percent. But even crazier than that is that XIV trades more each day than it has in assets. It has daily turnover of 116 percent. And on volatile days it can trade north of $1 billion worth of shares. I always say the day you know arrived when XIV trades more than Exxon Mobil. Nowadays, $1 billion days are not that uncommon for XIV.

Even though, VXX and XIV account for over half of the assets and volume in this category, there are several other ETFs and ETNs that serve up VIX futures exposure, including some that give exposure to the medium-term futures and/or the entire curve. And just as with oil futures or natural gas futures, the more you go away from the front month, the more you give up sensitivity for the sake of limiting roll costs. Regardless of what you do here,

FIGURE 11.8 XIV Destroying Everyone Since Inception

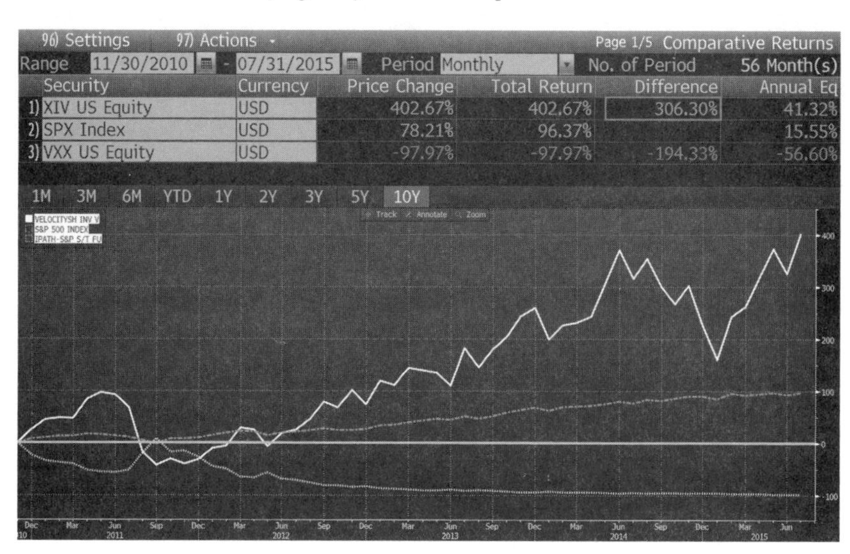

Source: Bloomberg

this is one area of ETF Land that needs to be used with the greatest of care and thought.

Notes

1. McLaughlin, Tim, and Jennifer Ablan, "Blackrock's Fink Jolts ETF Business with 'Blow Up' Warning." Reuters, May 31, 2014; www.reuters.com/article/2014/05/31/us-funds-etf-fink-analysis-idUSKBN0EB0HI20140531.
2. Justice, Paul, "Warning: Leveraged and Inverse ETFs Kill Portfolios." Morningstar, January 22, 2009; news.morningstar.com/articlenet/article.aspx?id=271892.
3. Mackintosh, Phil, and Victor Lin, "ETF Strategy: Longer Term Plays on Leveraged ETFs." Credit Suisse, April 12, 2010.
4. Dieterich, Chris, "How TVIX, a Stock Market Hedge, Came Unglued." *MarketWatch,* March 28, 2012; www.marketwatch.com/story/how-tvix-a-stock-market-hedge-came-unglued-2012-03-28.
5. Condon, Chris, "Credit Suisse Asked by Regulator for Details of ETN Crash," March 29, 2012; www.bloomberg.com/news/articles/2012-03-29/credit-suisse-asked-by-massachusetts-for-details-of-etn-crash.
6. Conway, Brendan, "'Short Volatility' Trade Looking Ever Riskier." *Barron's,* September 18, 2013; blogs.barrons.com/focusonfunds/2013/09/18/short-volatility-trade-looking-ever-riskier/.

CHAPTER 12

Actively Managed ETFs

Actively managed ETF was thought of as an oxymoron for a long time. After all, aren't exchange-traded funds (ETFs) low-cost passive investments that track indexes? Well, this is part of the wonder of the ETF structure—you can fit almost anything into it, and that includes active management.

But let's not kid ourselves. As much as we in the ETF nerd bubble like to think active is dying, the truth is that it isn't. And it could come roaring back during the next prolonged down or sideways market. Although it will be tough to turnaround the longer-term trend towards passive investing over the next 30 years. Either way institutions still love active management. This is why U.S. asset managers have over $40 trillion under management.

With that said, actively managed ETFs have by and large struggled to find investors. There are 121 of them with only $20 billion in assets, which is less than 1 percent of the total assets. They were once hailed as the next big thing, but they just haven't taken off despite offering all the advantages of the ETF structure, such as being more tax efficient and transparent.[1]

Actively managed ETFs offer some great talent. You have ex-hedge fund managers, endowment chiefs, PhDs, authors, and bond kings. There are also plenty of cases of outperformance as well. But even the ones with three-year track records that beat their benchmarks don't see much new cash come in. The only hands-down success has been with Pimco, whose brand name in fixed income is so strong it overcame other headwinds.

There are a couple of reasons that actively managed ETFs haven't done better.

First, ETFs don't carry loads or distribution fees, which is essentially the equivalent of taking an investor's money and using some of it as a kickback to a broker to sell it to them. This is a big reason mutual funds got so big. Some of these ETFs simply don't get the distribution they were used to on the mutual fund side. This is why I say that an active manager moving from the mutual fund world to the ETF world is like going from the country club to the jungle.

Another reason active ETFs struggle is that passive is simply winning over investors in general, as evidenced by outsized flows into index-based ETFs and mutual funds that we showed in Chapter 2. Much of these flows are coming at the expense of actively managed products.

Another reason is cost. Active ETFs, while cheaper than mutual funds are still very expensive relative to the average ETF. The average fee of an active ETF is 0.81 percent, albeit the asset-weighted average fee is 0.61 percent. This is twice as much as the 0.30 percent average asset-weighted fee for passive ETFs. Again, without Vanguard or Schwab, there isn't much pressure to cut fees. Vanguard does have active mutual funds, so it is not out of the question that they offer an active ETF. If any category could use some Vanguard Effect, it is this one.

"There are some areas of the market where active is superior to passive. It's just not superior when you factor in the costs. But they'll get there."

Josh Brown, Ritholtz Wealth Management

A final reason that active ETFs are slow to grow is the incredible rise of smart-beta ETFs. The money that is looking for some kind of tilt or chance to outperform has generally gone into smart-beta ETFs, which have over $400 billion in assets. Smart beta is essentially active management packaged into a passive, low-cost ETF. It has stolen the thunder—and assets—of active ETFs as shown in Figure 12.1.

"I think there is lots of room for active ETFs. But smart beta has sucked the oxygen out of that room for the time being. But they'll grow. It's a crowded supermarket, getting visible shelf space is tough."

Rob Arnott, Research Affiliates

Now, certain active ETFs have been successful in terms of asset gathering. I've studied these and found that those that do well typically have at least two of these three things: brand name, low fee, and outperformance. If an active

FIGURE 12.1 Active ETFs Assets versus Smart Beta and Passive

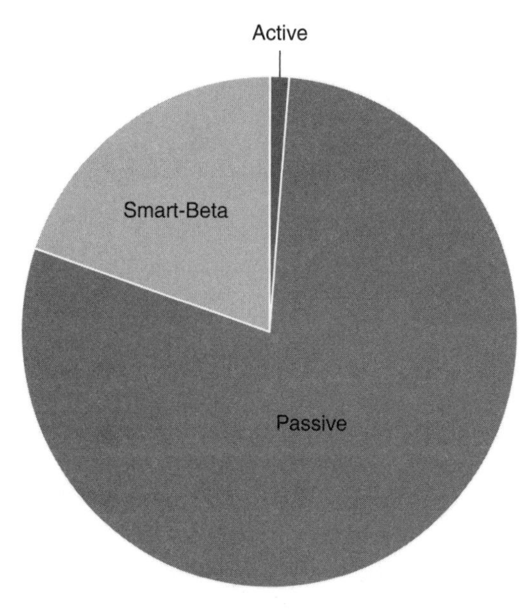

Source: Bloomberg

ETF has only one or none of those things, it will be nearly impossible to gain the assets and volume necessary to attract investors.

In terms of due diligence, active ETFs should be analyzed the same as any ETF: by looking at exposure, cost, liquidity, and risk. But in the case of active, you also want to look at the people who run them and their general management process.

Let's look at a few examples.

Fixed Income

I'm starting with fixed income because that is where all the money is. There are 40 actively managed fixed income ETFs with $13 billion of the assets, or 65 percent of the total. And half of that is just Pimco.

Pimco

The largest actively managed ETF is the PIMCO Enhanced Short Maturity Active Exchange-Traded Fund (MINT), which has $4 billion in assets. MINT is one of the most popular ETFs to run to when the going gets tough as it can be used as a place to park cash, which we covered in Chapter 9.

The other big fish in this pond is the famous Pimco Total Return Active ETF (BOND), which used to be run by Bill Gross and is now run by Scott Mather. BOND holds a wide array of bonds from all over the world. Bill Gross was the first mega-mutual fund manager with a household name to come over into the ETF industry with an actively managed ETF. And he did it in spectacular fashion, with high highs and low lows. BOND at one point had over $5 billion in assets—a record number for an active ETF. BOND showed that active management could be successful in the ETF world but more importantly that having some star power can help immensely.

After a great first year out of the gate, BOND was on the wrong side of a shift towards shorter-duration bonds in2013. When Gross left in 2014, BOND had come down to $3.5 billion assets. It then lost another $1 billion after he left. After that turmoil, since Mather took over, BOND has stabilized and now has $2.5 billion. It also has been performing decently, even beating the Barclays Aggregate Bond Index, and perhaps even more deliciously (considering their ugly divorce), he's beaten Gross, as seen in Figure 12.2.

FIGURE 12.2 BOND's Performance Since Gross's Departure

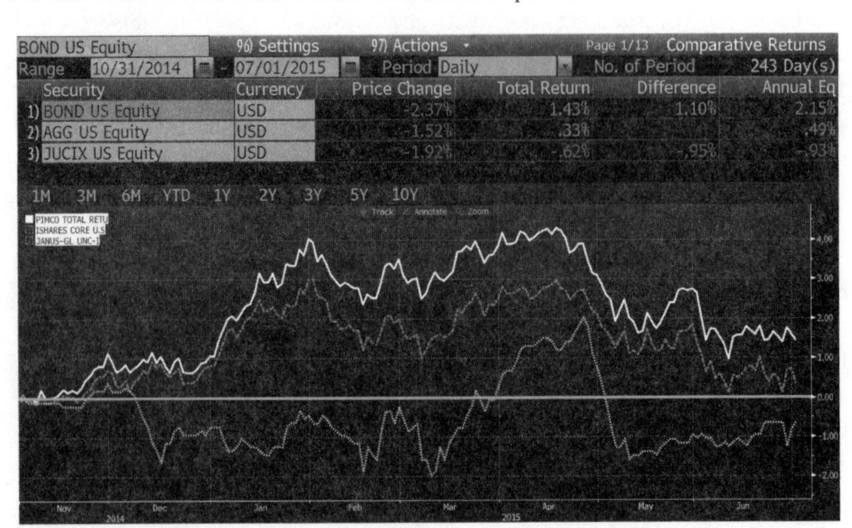

Source: Bloomberg

DoubleLine

Another popular option is the SPDR DoubleLine Total Return Tactical ETF (TOTL), which came into the picture within six months of Bill Gross leaving. So for those ETF investors who are looking for the rock star factor, Gundlach should do the trick.

TOTL is run by Jeffrey Gundlach and basically gives him freedom to invest in a broad range of fixed income securities. The fund will invest mostly U.S. investment-grade debt, but can invest as much as 25 percent in high-yield debt and up to 25 percent in emerging markets.

Like BOND, Gundlach's ETF costs 0.55 percent, which is less than the retail class and more than the institutional class of the mutual fund. While cheaper than a retail mutual fund, TOTL is still six times more expensive than popular aggregate bond ETFs such as the iShares Core U.S. Aggregate Bond ETF (AGG) and Vanguard Total Bond Market ETF (BND). Both charge 0.08 percent in annual fees.

Peritus

Tim Gramatovich, along with co-PM Ron Heller, runs an intriguing actively managed high-yield bond ETF called the AdvisorShares Peritus High Yield ETF (HYLD). It has had quite a dramatic life. Here's a case where active management can cut both ways. The AdvisorShares Peritus High Yield ETF (HYLD) ruled 2013 thanks to great active bets that paid off. It doubled the performance of JNK and HYG, returning 12 percent versus 6 percent for them. But then in 2014, it had overweighed energy and it went down 11 percent versus a gain of 2 percent for HYG and JNK, as shown in Figure 12.3.

One could only have expected these kinds of swings by comparing the standard deviation of HYLD versus JNK and HYG. It is double. HYLD also has more of the junky junk bonds. That's also why it yields 9 percent—nearly double JNK and HYG's yield.

Equity

There are 46 actively managed equity ETFs. It is an eclectic group with many different strategies.

FIGURE 12.3 HYLD's Dramatic Rise and Fall Compared to the Bellwether JNK and HYG

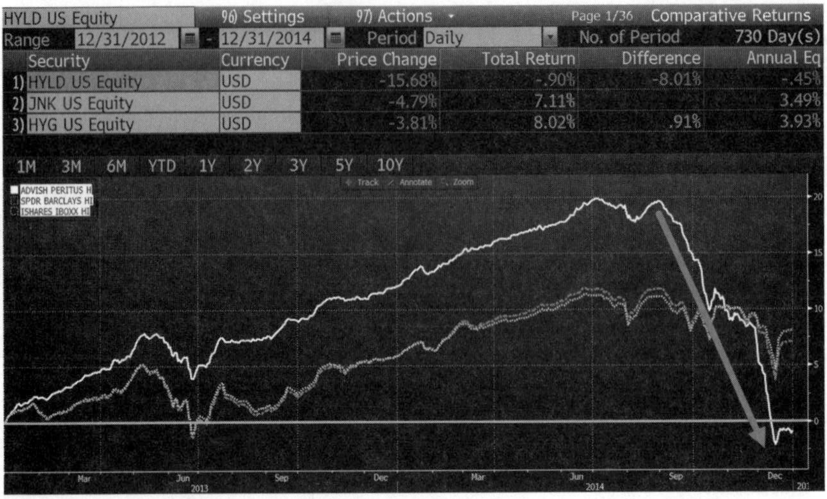
HYLD US Equity
96) Settings
97) Actions
Page 1/36 Comparative Returns
Range 12/31/2012 - 12/31/2014
Period Daily
No. of Period 730 Day(s)
Security
Currency
Price Change
Total Return
Difference
Annual Eq
1) HYLD US Equity USD -15.68% -.90% -8.01% -.45%
2) JNK US Equity USD -4.79% 7.11% 3.49%
3) HYG US Equity USD -3.81% 8.02% .91% 3.93%
1M 3M 6M YTD 1Y 2Y 3Y 5Y 10Y
Track Annotate Zoom
ADVISH PERITUS H
SPDR BARCLAYS HI
ISHARES IBOXX HI
20
15
10
5
0
Mar
Jun
2013
Sep
Dec
Mar
Jun
2014
Sep
Dec

Source: Bloomberg

First Trust

The largest actively managed equity ETF invests in energy companies, believe it or not. The First Trust North American Energy Infrastructure ETF (EMLP), which has \$1.2 billion in assets, invests in energy infrastructure companies located in the United States and Canada. It holds up to but no more than 25 percent in master limited partnerships (MLPs), so as to not break the rule that an open-end fund is not allowed to hold any more than 25 percent of its portfolio in MLPs.

This means EMLP avoids that massive tax that affects most MLP ETFs. On the flips side, it also means it is only partially an MLP ETF. In short, you sacrifice some yield in order to get better tax treatment and broader exposure to the energy sector.

PowerShares

Another popular actively managed ETF is the PowerShares S&P 500 Downside Hedged Portfolio (PHDG), which is run by Peter Hubbard. PHDG moves allocations around between Standard & Poor's (S&P) 500 stocks, VIX futures, and cash. The goal of this ETF is to outsource your use of VIX futures and cash for downside protection. Many managers don't want to mess around with VIX futures; PowerShares will do it for you. It moves some money to VIX futures based on signals from the market.

It is up 21 percent since its inception in December 2012 versus 57 percent for the S&P 500. Given the VIX exposure, you'd expect less upside, but did it protect during a storm? Well, not really. In January 2014, the market was down 3.5 percent while PHDG was down 3.3 percent—not the protection you would hope to see. In January 2015 it was a little better; while the market was down 3 percent, PHDG was only down 1.6 percent.

Despite the mixed results and forgone upside, investors dig PHDG, as it has $724 million in assets. It is also very cheap for an actively managed ETF, charging just 0.40 percent in annual fees, or half the average.

Columbia

Some people have said that the reason actively managed ETFs don't have money is that investors like to see a track record of outperformance. Well, Columbia has some ETFs that do have three-year track records and good ones at that. The Columbia Select Large Cap Value (GVT) is up 67 percent versus 58 percent for S&P 500 Value Index and shown in Figure 12.4. And the Columbia Select Large Cap Growth ETF (RPX) is beating the S&P 500 Growth Index 71 percent versus 67 percent, albeit its other growth ETF the Columbia Large Cap Growth ETF (RPX) lost slightly with a 65 percent return.

FIGURE 12.4 GVT's Past Three Years versus the S&P 500 Value Index

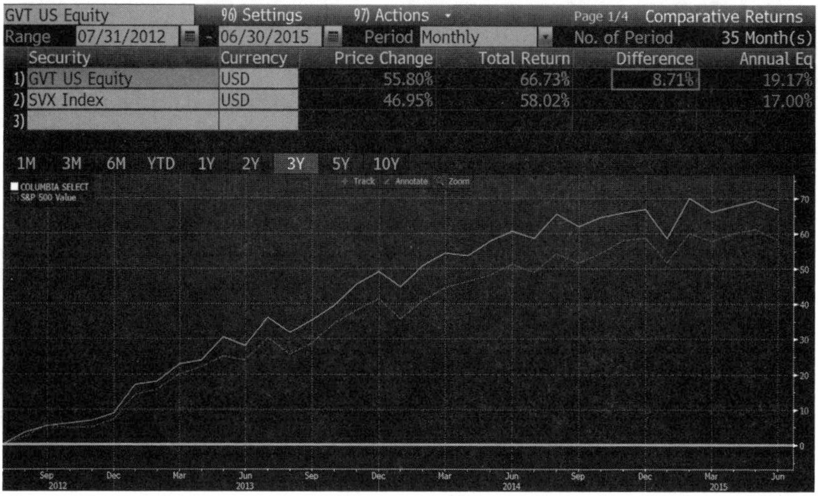
GVT US Equity
96) Settings
97) Actions
Page 1/4 Comparative Returns
Range 07/31/2012 - 06/30/2015
Period Monthly
No. of Period 35 Month(s)
Security Currency Price Change Total Return Difference Annual Eq
1) GVT US Equity USD 55.80% 66.73% 8.71% 19.17%
2) SVX Index USD 46.95% 58.02% 17.00%
3)
1M 3M 6M YTD 1Y 2Y 3Y 5Y 10Y
COLUMBIA SELECT
S&P 500 Value
Track Annotate Zoom
70
60
50
40
30
20
10
0
Sep 2012
Dec
Mar
Jun 2013
Sep
Dec
Mar
Jun 2014
Sep
Dec
Mar 2015
Jun

Source: Bloomberg

Yet those three ETFs combined took in a total of $8 million in the past two years. GVT had the outperformance but doesn't have the brand name or distribution or low fees to turn that into asset growth. This goes back to how hard it is to make it in this ETF jungle.

Cambria

One of the up-and-coming stars of the ETF world (and Twitter) lives in this space, and that is Meb Faber. He has three actively managed ETFs with a total of $306 million. Meb is well known in the investment community and has written numerous books.[2] He also invests a lot of his own money into each ETF.

His most popular ETF is the Cambria Shareholder Yield ETF (SYLD), which picks stocks based on the concept that equity "yield" doesn't come from just dividends, but also shares buybacks and paying off debt. It chooses 100 companies that do this well and then equal weights them. The portfolio is an even mix of sectors and cap sizes and has a low expense ratio for an actively managed ETF of 0.59 percent. It has outperformed the S&P 500 since it came out in 2013, with a return of 37 percent versus 33 percent. There is also an international version called the Cambria Foreign Shareholder Value (FYLD).

Morgan Creek

Mark Yusko—who has been quoted throughout this book—used to run the endowment at University of North Carolina and Notre Dame has an ETF called AdvisorShares Morgan Creek Capital Management Global Tactical ETF (GTAA). GTAA is essentially a global macro hedge fund strategy with freedom to invest in whatever it wants.

The ETF was designed to follow an endowment-like strategy but be available for anyone. It invests in other ETFs representing all major world asset classes, including equities, bonds, real estate, commodities, and currencies. It can also hold cash. It charges a 1.24 percent annual fee, making it one of the most expensive ETFs.

TrimTabs

One of the larger the actively managed equity ETFs is the AdvisorShares TrimTabs Float Shrink ETF (TTFS). TTFS is the brainchild of Charles Biderman with Ted Theodore as PM. It focuses on companies that shrink their equity float—the total number of shares publicly available for trading. It looks for companies that grow their free cash flow and reduce leverage on the balance sheets.

To its credit, TTFS has outperformed two key benchmarks since its inception in October 2011. It returned 91 percent versus 85 percent for the passively managed PowerShares Buyback Achievers Portfolio (PKW) and 89 percent for the S&P 500 Buyback Index. On the downside, TTFS—along with many of these ETFs—charges 0.99 percent, which is tough for some investors to swallow who are used to cheapness in the ETF space.

Ranger

One unique active ETF worth a mention is the AdvisorShares Ranger Equity Bear ETF (HDGE). Instead of picking good companies that it thinks will outperform, it picks companies it thinks will underperform. Run by an ex-hedge fund manager, HDGE utilizes forensic accounting in identifying operational or earnings discrepancies that are masked in reporting/filings.

In a way, HDGE is like an inverse ETF but minus the complications that arise with daily resetting of leveraged ETFs. It has a -85 percent correlation to the S&P 500 Index. While there haven't been many bad runs in the stock market in the past seven years, when there is one, HDGE shines. A prime example is the summer of 2011 when the European debt crisis rattled U.S. stocks. The market was down 10 percent that summer while the ProShares Short S&P 500 ETF (SH) was up 8 percent. HDGE beat them with a 20 percent return, as shown in Figure 12.5. The downside is the cost of borrowing shares

FIGURE 12.5 HDGE Can Do Better Than Inverse ETFs During Long Market Declines

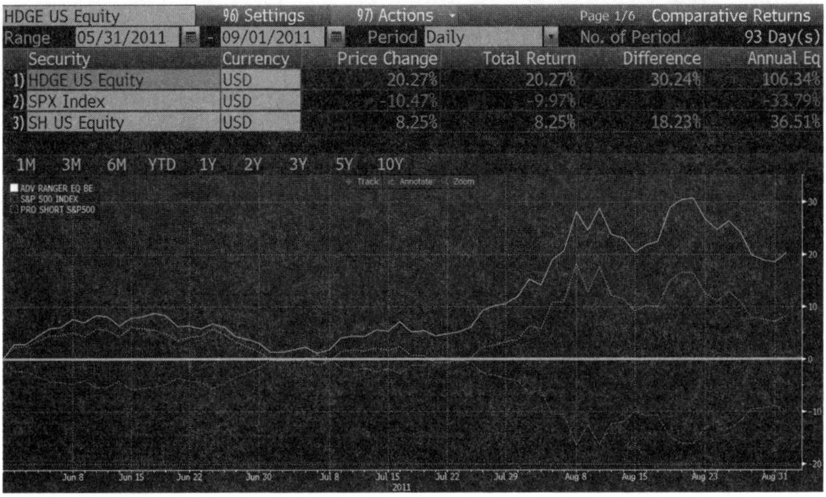
HDGE US Equity
96) Settings
97) Actions
Page 1/6 Comparative Returns
Range 05/31/2011 - 09/01/2011
Period Daily
No. of Period 93 Day(s)
Security
Currency
Price Change
Total Return
Difference
Annual Eq
1) HDGE US Equity USD 20.27% 20.27% 30.24% 106.34%
2) SPX Index USD -10.47% -9.97% -33.79%
3) SH US Equity USD 8.25% 8.25% 18.23% 36.51%
1M 3M 6M YTD 1Y 2Y 3Y 5Y 10Y
30
20
10
0
-10
-20
Jun 8
Jun 15
Jun 22
Jun 30
Jul 8
Jul 15
2011
Jul 22
Jul 29
Aug 8
Aug 15
Aug 23
Aug 31

Source: Bloomberg

to short. It adds to its already expensive management fee of 1.5 percent up to 3.29 percent. However, you'd have to pay those costs if you shorted stocks, too.

Ark

A former global thematic portfolio manager at Alliance Bernstein, Catherine Wood manages three Ark ETFs, which focus on the theme of disruptive innovation. The Ark Genomic Revolution Multi-Sector ETF (ARKG) seeks out any company in any sector relevant to the genomics revolution. The case for using active for a theme like this is that these are areas that are changing so quickly and a rules-based index may not be able to capture the trend as quickly. Another one is the Ark Web x.0 ETF (ARKW), which shifted its technology infrastructure from hardware and software to the cloud, enabling mobile and local services.

These ETFs look like sector ETFs, but because they are truly active, they are not bound by one sector. They are thematic ETFs run actively. For example, ARKW has had consumer discretionary and health care stocks in addition to tech. The funds are pretty concentrated with fewer than 50 names weighted by conviction. All of them charge 0.95 percent in annual fees.

Alpha Architect

Wes Gray is a PhD and former full-time professor at Drexel who now runs two Buffett-esque value ETFs that look for the cheapest stocks that have the highest quality. "We buy the stuff everyone else hates," he told me. The ValueShares US Quantitative Value ETF (QVAL) equal weights about 40 mid- and large-cap stocks picked from a quantitative value system. With such a concentrated number of bets, each stock has much more voice than the typical value ETF, which can easily hold more than 100 stocks and have a high correlation to the S&P 500 Index. There is also an international version of this called the ValueShares International Quantitative Value ETF (IVAL). Both charge 0.79 percent in annual fees. As I write this, they just rolled out momentum ETFs as well. And like Cambria, the management team at Alpha Architect also invest much of their own money in the funds.

Notes

1. Ludwig, Olly, "Actively Managed ETFs Seek Bigger Footprint." ETF.com, May 9, 2014; www.etf.com/sections/features/22063-actively-managed-etfs-seek-bigger-footprint.html.
2. Faber, Meb, "Shareholder Yield: A Better Approach to Yield Investing." Self-published, 2015; www.shareholderyield.com/.

CONCLUSION

Five Takeaways

We learned a lot, didn't we? As I said in the beginning, ETFs are a beast to cover because they track everything under the sun and there are 1,800 of them. If you are still reading, you may have information overload. So, let's attempt to wrap things up with five key takeaways from the book.

1. *ETFs are a "benefit-rich" vehicle.* I think it is safe to say the financial world has never seen one product be so many things to so many different investors. We counted over a dozen advantages in Chapter 1. Many people only use them for two or three of those. A pension may use an ETF for its liquidity, freedom and precision, a hedge fund may like the anonymity and ability to short, while an asset manager may like it for its transparency and low cost. And advisors and retail investors may appreciate them for their use in asset allocation and their tax efficiency. As institutions discover some of these other benefits they didn't know about we could see adoption ramp up even more.
2. *ETFs trade more than you think but own less than you think.* U.S. ETFs traded over $18 trillion worth of shares in the 12 months ending June 2015, but they have only $2.1 trillion in assets. That means they own less than 5 percent of the stock market and less than 1 percent of the bond and commodities markets. This is why ETFs are far from being able to increase correlations in the market on their own or become the "tail wagging the dog."

   With that said, all that trading does legitimately strengthen Bogle's argument against ETFs, which is that they inspire investors to trade too much. ETFs as a group see their assets turnover 870 percent per year.

That is almost triple what stocks turn over. While many investors do hold them long-term, clearly they are seeing a lot of trading activity. And the more trading there is, the more Wall Street, not investors, profit.

3. *Implied liquidity is the key to opening up the full ETF toolbox.* Most institutions only use the top 50 most traded ETFs. We all acknowledge that volume is a great thing, but we also have learned that investors may be selling themselves short by using trading volume as their only criterion. The most traded ETFs tend to be the first-to-market ones launched in the 1990s. That is like using an iPhone 1 despite all the newer models that have hit the market since then.

   Because of the creation/redemption process, the liquidity in the ETF holdings can be sourced to trade the ETF. This is how they are different than stocks. When you understand and utilize implied liquidity, you unlock over 1,500 more ETFs to choose from. The most advanced ETF users—ETF strategists—for the most part only use implied liquidity. And they are putting in sizable trades, too. Other institutions may learn to follow their lead.

4. *ETF due diligence is just as important as active manager due diligence.* Many institutions and consultants will put so much time and effort into vetting active managers, but when it comes to ETFs there is no process whatsoever despite return dispersion amongst ETFs that is as great—or greater—as with active managers. (Mostly because they pick the most traded one and are done with it). Having no due diligence process can lead to using inferior and costlier products not to mention performance you aren't happy with. As we saw throughout the book, many ETFs with very similar sounding names had both big and small difference when it comes to return and cost—just like active managers.

   Beyond performance dispersion, there are also hidden complexities that I described in my rating system, such as underlying liquidity, hidden taxes, derivative usage, and complicated strategies. So why wouldn't you apply a vigorous due diligence process to ETFs as well? Not only does ETF due diligence help you find the right product for you, but it also diffuses a legitimate fear among institutions that ETFs are a threat to their role as fund manager. If you read this book, you can see that selecting and managing the ETFs is no easier than selecting and managing the managers. This is why I think we will see an increase in ETF due diligence as an actual job at both the advisor and institutional level.

5. *ETFs are the tech sector of the financial world.* One thing we have definitely learned is that innovation in the ETF industry is at a fever pitch. There are 1,800 ETFs on the market now and another 1,300 ETFs in registration

with the Securities and Exchange Commission awaiting approval.[1] You can also bet that the products will continue to get more complex as well. More and more we see some of the brightest minds in finance come over into the ETF space with product offerings. Many institutions will have to keep up with all this or risk being left behind by competitors who know how to use and exploit these new ETF gadgets. *Education is going to be the most important thing going forward.*

Continuing Your Education

Speaking of education, if you read this far in the book, clearly you have the potential to be an ETF geek. And, as such, you need to know what ETF geeks read and listen to, and who to follow on Twitter.

Web Sites

www.etf.com—ETF.com is as cutting edge as it gets when it comes to ETF content. When I'm in serious research mode, I will check out what ETF.com says about an ETF I'm looking at. They also have many ETF strategists contributing articles now as well. They also have great webinars and the best conferences. I'd also recommend subscribing to their magazine called *The ETF Report.*

www.etftrends.com—A one-stop shop of easy-to-digest pieces on any and every ETF out there. While most of the articles are riffing off of other articles, they give it some extra information and provide embedded links to other useful sites. It has an easy-to-find and comprehensive education center as well.

www.morningstar.com—Morningstar has an ETF section on their web site that is quite good. They also have smart analysts who know what they are talking about. Mostly, I like to read the articles and watch their analyst videos.

www.barrons.com/focusonfunds—This is Barron's intraday blog. It is a great read with news and analysis on ETFs, mutual funds, and hedge funds.

Podcasts

The ETF Store Show—The ETF equivalent of NPR's *Car Talk.* It's hosted by an amiable group of investment advisors and is aimed at individual investors. The show is constantly comparing ETFs with mutual funds, breaking down industry jargon, and trumpeting the importance of asset allocation. This show features multiple hosts and guests and callers. This show is an oasis of simplicity in a jargon-filled complicated financial desert. The website gives access to all the podcasts.

ETF Gurus—This is the podcast of Dave Nadig, director of ETFs at Factset Research Systems. Each week he has a different ETF guru (aka Nerd) on to discuss recent trends, flows, and so on. Pretty much no one has the same mix of ETF knowledge and communication skills like Dave.

ETF Expert Radio Podcast—This is the podcast of Gary Gordon, a money manager who uses ETFs. The podcast is simply him talking every week for about 10 minutes about what is going on in the market and in the world and how he's positioning himself with ETFs. He will mention a wide variety of ETFs, too, like a painter who uses a lot of colors. This podcast is a hidden gem.

The ETF Report—Shameless plug for a podcast I appear on a lot that is hosted and produced by Catherine Cowdery of Bloomberg Radio. These are little nuggets of information, as the podcast is no more than 2 to 3 minutes long. It is typically on trends, flows, and new launches. And while I'm in self-promotional mode, check out my *ETF Friday* segment on Bloomberg Television on Friday mornings.

ETF of the Week—This is a segment on Chuck Jaffe's *MoneyLife* show at MarketWatch every Thursday. Chuck interviews Tom Lydon, editor and founder of *ETF Trends,* about one ETF that is looking interesting. This is a novel show in that it is 10 minutes of these two guys just kicking the tires on one ETF and the macro-economic issues around it. It also has some really funny intro and sound effects.

Twitter

Twitter is a growing networking and communication tool, not to mention a lot of fun. I am on Twitter at @EricBalchunas and have found it to be a great place for sharing information.

Below are some of my favorite ETF gurus to follow on Twitter. I purposely picked actual people rather than companies. I am also just picking just ETF-focused people. There are plenty of additional financial people I like following, but I want just focus on those who tweet mostly ETF-related content. And finally I'm only choosing people who tweet regularly. There are more

ETF gurus out there, but these are the ones that tweet pretty consistently if not heavily. And if I missed anyone, I'm truly sorry!

@DaveNadig—He doesn't tweet a lot, but when he does it is always a must-read article. This guy is an analyst's analyst. He's a true master when it comes to ETFs. One step ahead of the rest of us. I'd also throw in @Matt_Hougan, although he doesn't tweet that much.

@ETFGodfather—The man, the myth, the legend. This guy has been covering ETFs for a while and may be the only person to have written about literally every ETF. He also loves to tweet about college football—especially his love of TCU and contempt for the Southeast Conference (SEC).

@TomLydon—Tom runs *ETF Trends* and is a mover and shaker in the industry. He tweets mostly *ETF Trends* articles out but since there are about a dozen of those a days it is always fresh.

@ChrisDieterich—Chris Dieterich writes about ETFs for the Focus on Funds section on Barron's and does an amazing job. His insights and volume of production is really great.

@VicRek—Victor Reklaitis is the ETF reporter at MarketWatch. Not only does he know his stuff and post consistently interesting ETF stories, but he is a fellow Lithuanian. We are currently forming a group called "Lithuanians in ETFs" which may also be turned into a semi-pro basketball team at some point.

@MebFaber—He runs a few ETFs and is a big fan of value investing and international issues. Great for those types of issues.

@ETFExpert—This is Gary Gordon, president of Pacific Park Financial. I recommended his podcast above. He will use ETFs to illustrate what the markets are up to.

@AriWeinberg—Ari has been covering ETFs for a long time and his experience shows in his articles. He contributes to *Pension & Investments* and the *Wall Street Journal.*

@mjohnsto—Michael Johnston is another long-time industry veteran. He is currently senior analyst for ETF Reference.

@ChristianMagoon—Christian has been involved in the ETF business for nearly 20 years and is a super-nice guy. He currently runs one ETF that holds closed-end funds. He mostly shares other articles he likes.

@DeborahFuhr—Deborah Fuhr has been covering ETFs since the 1990s and runs ETFGI, an independent research and consulting firm. While most of the analysts here focus on the United States, Debbie knows the entire world and how it is evolving with ETFs.

@RonRowland—Ron doesn't tweet a lot, but when he does, it is always interesting. He keeps a hawk eye on ETFs that do shady things when they delist. He also has something he puts out called "The ETF Deathwatch" where he writes about and lists all of the ETFs that are in danger of closing due to low assets.

@RandomRoger—This is Roger Nusbaum, a money manager who also runs an ETF. Again, his long-term experience in ETFs makes his tweets and the articles he chooses to share or write very good reading.

@Rick_Ferri—Rick is a money manager and a disciple of index investing and John Bogle. You can't help but agree with most everything he puts out there.

@ToddSPCAPIQ—Todd is S&P Capital IQ's Director of Mutual Fund & ETF Research. He has a lot of experience and is quoted a lot in the media.

@AlphaArchitect—This is Wes Gray, who tweets about studies and research as well as some mind-blowing blog posts.

Note

1. Bell, Heather, "ETFs in Registration." ETF.com, July 28, 2015; www.etf.com/etf-watch-tables/etfs-registration.

About the Author

Eric Balchunas is a Senior ETF Analyst and Funds Product Specialist at Bloomberg. In these roles, he writes ETF research available on the Bloomberg terminal as well as helps in designing and promoting new ETF functionality.

He also appears in a weekly on-air segment for Bloomberg TV and Radio called "ETF Friday," in which he discusses different ETFs and the way investors can utilize them. Both of these segments have been running for nearly five years, making them the one of the first-ever regularly scheduled national media shows about ETFs. Eric has also written hundreds of articles on ETFs for Bloomberg.com as well as the occasional *Markets* magazine piece.

In addition, he is responsible for training clients and conducting seminars on how to use the Bloomberg terminal to find and analyze ETFs. He also puts out the Bloomberg ETF newsletter and is a regular speaker at Bloomberg events as well as ETF industry events.

Prior to joining the ETF team, Eric was a Public Relations Associate with Bloomberg. Before joining Bloomberg in 2000, Eric worked as a reporter for *Institutional Investor*'s newsletter division, where he covered derivatives and the mutual fund industry. Eric holds a bachelor's degree in journalism and environmental economics from Rutgers University.

He lives with his wife and two sons in Philadelphia.

Index

C

D

E

U

V